Japan's Financial Markets

£ 3.580.-

D1104378

James Horne

JAPAN'S FINANCIAL MARKETS

Conflict and consensus in policymaking

GEORGE ALLEN & UNWIN   Sydney   London   Boston
in association with
The Australia–Japan Research Centre   Australian National University

© James Horne 1985

This book is copyright under the Berne Convention. No
reproduction without permission. All rights reserved.

First published in 1985 by
George Allen & Unwin Australia Pty Ltd
8 Napier Street, North Sydney, NSW 2060 Australia

George Allen & Unwin (Publishers) Ltd
Park Lane, Hemel Hempstead, Herts HP2 4TE England

Allen & Unwin Inc.
Fifty Cross Street, Winchester, Mass 01890 USA

National Library of Australia
Cataloguing-in-Publication entry:

Horne, James.
    Japan's financial markets.

    Includes index.
    ISBN 0 86861 724 5.
    ISBN 0 86861 732 6 (pbk).

    1. Finance—Japan.   2. Financial institutions –
    Government policy—Japan.   I. Australia—Japan
    Research Centre.   II. Title.

332'.0952

Library of Congress Catalog Card Number: 84-72417

Set in 10/11 pt Plantin Linotron 202
by Graphicraft Typesetters Limited Hong Kong.

Printed in Hong Kong

Contents

Tables

Figures

Abbreviations

ADB	Asian Development Bank
ADF	Asian Development Fund
ASEAN	Association of Southeast Asian Nations
BOJ	Bank of Japan
CDs	Certificates of Deposit
CFSR	Committee on Financial System Research
DSP	Democratic Socialist Party
EPA	Economic Planning Agency
FEFTCL	Foreign Exchange and Foreign Trade Control Law
FEO	Federation of Economic Organisations
FILP	Fiscal Investment Loan Program
FPRG	Financial Problems Research Group
HRBC	House of Representatives Budget Committee
HRFC	House of Representatives Finance Committee
IBI	International Business Information
IBJ	Industrial Bank of Japan
IBRD	International Bank for Reconstruction and Development
IDA	International Development Association
IDB	Inter-American Development Bank
IFB	International Finance Bureau
IFC	International Finance Corporation
IMF	International Monetary Fund
JCP	Japan Communist Party
JDB	Japan Development Bank
JSP	Japan Socialist Party
LDP	Liberal Democratic Party
LIBOR	London Interbank Offer Rate
MAFF	Ministry of Agriculture, Forestry and Fisheries
MFA	Ministry of Foreign Affairs
MITI	Ministry of International Trade and Industry
MLG	Ministry of Local Government
MOC	Ministry of Construction
MOF	Ministry of Finance

MOL	Ministry of Labor
MOT	Ministry of Transport
MPT	Ministry of Posts and Telecommunications
NLC	New Liberal Club
NTT	Nippon Telephone and Telegraph
OECD	Organisation for Economic Cooperation and Development
OPEC	Organisation of Petroleum Exporting Countries
PARC	Policy Affairs Research Committee (of the LDP)
PTAC	Posts and Telecommunications Advisory Committee
SEC	Securities and Exchange Council
SEL	Securities and Exchange Law
SIR	Savings Interest Rate
TBs	Treasury Bills
TFB	Trust Fund Bureau

Preface

In the last year or so Japan's financial markets have become a focus of international policy attention, as American negotiators have sought a wider international role for the yen and greater access for foreign financial institutions through further deregulation of Japan's financial markets. When the research upon which this book was based began in 1979, financial deregulation in Japan had already commenced, albeit in a piecemeal fashion. It was clear then that Japan's financial markets would one day become more closely integrated into the international financial market. But it was not clear when this would occur, nor was it clear which factors would constrain or encourage the evolution of their international role. The study took as its main theme the nature of regulatory policymaking in Japan's financial markets and had, as an underlying but fundamental objective, the development of an appropriate conceptual framework with which to understand Japanese policymaking more generally.

There is a considerable literature on policymaking in Japan. This study questions some of the established ways of thinking about the Japanese policymaking process and attempts to develop a conceptual framework which can accommodate its complexity and variety. The general literature on policy-making provides an important foundation for this endeavour. While the book is primarily concerned with Japan's financial markets and the policymaking processes that have conditioned their recent development, it is hoped that the study will be of more general interest. The reader is left to make comparisons with experience in other countries. The primary objective of this study is to further understanding of economic policymaking in Japan.

Many people have helped me to complete this study. Peter Drysdale of the Australian National University, Arthur Stockwin of the University of Oxford, Hugh Patrick of Yale University and Alan Rix of Griffith University have provided good advice and support at various stages of research and writing. In Japan, I owe much to over 100 interviewees within the Ministry of Finance, Bank of Japan, the finance industry, business and politics, who gave their time generously and in most cases their opinions frankly. Professor Kaizuka Keimei of Tokyo University and Ushimaru Satoshi of Aoyama Gakuin University gave their time freely during my fourteen-month stay at Tokyo University. Haruhiro Fukui, Trevor Mathews, Nancy Viviani and Frances McCall made useful comments and criticisms on various parts of the manuscript.

I am grateful for financial assistance received from the Australian Government and the Australian National University. In particular, my time at the Australia–Japan Research Centre during 1982–83 as a Visiting Fellow, and later editorial assistance provided by the Centre facilitated the completion of this study. Most of the fieldwork was done during 1980–81 when I was a research scholar at Tokyo University, where the assistance I received made my task much easier.

My thanks also to Muriel Hussin and Venetia Nelson for editorial assistance, and to Bev Hargreaves and Bev Wagner for typing the manuscript.

Finally, I would like to express my warm thanks to Tomoko for her help with the finer points of the Japanese language, and for her support while this manuscript was in preparation.

Introduction

The deregulation and internationalisation of Japan's financial markets has been proceeding slowly but surely since the late 1970s, with the speed of change accelerating in the early 1980s. This process has been occurring in a dynamic environment. First, after 1974 there was a massive increase in the level of public sector borrowing which put enormous pressure on traditional domestic financial arrangements. Second, from the late 1960s Japan's financial institutions and corporations began to increase the level of their participation in the international economy. This produced pressures for change to domestic regulations as well as to regulations which determined the way in which Japanese business operated in the international economy. Third, Japan's status in the world economy changed slowly but perceptibly. By the late 1970s Japan was not only an established net capital exporter but there was also an increased demand by foreign financial institutions and corporations to participate more fully in Japan's financial markets. These developments in the structure of financial flows in Japan, in the needs of participants in Japan's financial markets, and in the needs of international actors have promoted the rapid development of Japan's financial markets by producing conditions requiring regulatory reform.

This book attempts to broaden understanding of an important set of financial markets, the Japanese financial markets. It provides a contemporary account and analysis of the major issues in, and structure of, the policymaking processes in Japan's financial markets in the 1970s and early 1980s.

It also analyses, through a set of case studies, the regulatory policymaking process in the financial markets, in particular the relationship between different parts of the Japanese elite. The relationship between industry, the public service and the Liberal Democratic Party (LDP), the ruling government party, has been the object of some important research work.[1] In some earlier work on the Japanese economy much attention was given to static perceptions like 'Japan Inc.' In other work, such as the important and influential *MITI and the Japanese Miracle*, by Chalmers Johnson, there has been what appears to be an unjustified emphasis on the role of the public service. This book aims not only to contribute a case study on the financial markets but also to highlight the ways in which the dynamic features of the relationships between participants in the policymaking process are representative of changing patterns within Japan and influence Japan's role in the international economy.

The main gap in the literature on the financial markets is in the understanding of how the political parties (in particular the LDP), the public service (in particular the Ministry of Finance (MOF)), financial institutions and other corporate and non-corporate interests interact in the development and implementation of regulatory policy, and the reasons for positions taken. There is a good body of information relating to the institutional economic operation of the Japanese financial system, bond market policy, banking policy and foreign exchange policy.[2] This book should assist predictions about the nature of regulatory change that could be expected in the medium-term future.[3]

The financial markets and the mass of regulations that surround them are of considerable significance to every industrialised economy. The main economic function of financial markets and financial institutions is to match the availability of funds with the demand for funds. In all modern industrialised economies, comprehensive regulatory frameworks have developed around the operation of both markets and institutions. The net effect of these regulations is to constrain the allocative function of the financial system. The intermediation function of the market is subject to constraints imposed by government. The rationales for such regulations include the promotion of efficiency, the maintenance of stability in the financial system, the achievement of macroeconomic stability and the furthering of social objectives.[4]

Beyond these rationales, considerations such as electoral politics, jurisdictional interests by public-service ministries and the influence of established policymaking methods and patterns are also relevant in explaining the character of a regulatory framework, as well as the development of new regulatory policy. To understand the process in which regulations are shaped will help to establish how far these non-economic considerations figure in the formulation of policy, and is at the centre of understanding the complex interrelationship between the polity and the economy of every contemporary industrialised country.

The challenge of providing a convincing explanatory typology of policymaking remains as vigorous today as it was two decades ago.[5] Equally, the number of theories of regulatory activity indicates, in addition to the variety of approaches to the subject, the range of plausible explanations for regulatory behaviour. Prominent among these theories are those which suggest that regulations are devised for the public benefit; that regulations reflect the successful capture of public-service ministries or agencies by private interests; and that regulations are designed to promote the self-interest of public servants. It is one of the arguments of this book that political institutions and processes are vital to any explanatory theory that wishes to capture the essence of regulatory activity. This introduction outlines the central propositions relating to the policymaking framework that are advanced in the following chapters. The core of the book comprises a set of case studies drawn from different parts of the financial markets. These case studies are used as a vehicle to explore the propositions set out below.

POLITICAL CONTROL

The public service has played an important role in managing the shape of economic development in all modern industrial economies. But understanding the role of the public service and its relationship with the political wing of government is less obvious. There has been a suggestion that during the postwar period the public service in western democracies usurped some of the authority of popularly elected governments.[6] The first area of enquiry encompasses the relationship between the public service and the elected government in Japan in the formulation of regulatory financial policy. Of central interest is whether the LDP, which has ruled in Japan since its formation in 1955, is influential in the development and implementation of regulatory policy. In particular, the proposition that its oversight is limited to important electoral issues is examined. Although the LDP, like any other political party holding the reins of government, has effective veto over the development of all new regulations, the lack of time and interest in many issues by parliamentary members is a compelling factor radically limiting the extent of LDP oversight. In technical areas such as finance this is even more likely to be the case. The important role of the LDP's Policy Affairs Research Committee (PARC) and its subcommittees in electorally sensitive areas such as the budget and agriculture has been well documented.[7] The position of the LDP is particularly interesting in the area of financial regulation because it is an area which at first sight would not be regarded as electorally sensitive or likely to attract political interest.

In Japan, as elsewhere, there are a range of controls. Laws, cabinet orders and ministerial ordinances represent the end of the spectrum with the most legal weight. Organisation charts are useful in outlining the main relationships between participants but they fail to help us understand motivations and the role of bargaining and negotiating in the reaching of outcomes. The relationship between government and industry is determined partly by the legal framework, but traditions and established practice, logrolling, bargaining and threat all have their moments.[8] 'Administrative guidance' or the implementation of policy through written or verbal agreement relies not only on immediately relevant laws but more on various methods of suasion.[9] The effectiveness of legal initiatives for control depends much upon the circumstances in which they are used. When Japan had a shortage of foreign exchange, MITI was able to 'persuade' companies to follow its established policies by threatening to curtail access to foreign exchange, which required administrative approval.[10] In the 1970s this was no longer possible. In order to define the relationship between the politicians and the public service it is necessary to compare the frequency and character of political intervention in routine administration of regulations supervised by the MOF with proposals that might be raised by the MOF to alter the regulatory framework.

Clearly, senior LDP Cabinet ministers and officials are deeply involved in the management of macroeconomic policies (including interest rate and tax policies) and interested in the impact of policy options on political realities.[11] This falls far short of suggesting continuous political overview. The lack of time, the lack of immediate interest and the cost of acquiring information by ministers, individual politicians or groups of politicians would form part of an explanation of their behaviour. An alternative proposition which warrants consideration is that the shared values of the LDP and the MOF make LDP oversight redundant and reinforce the role of the MOF in areas of routine policy management. This is one area where Japan is potentially different from other comparable countries. Japan has had over 27 years of continuous government under an LDP administration.

One implication of this alternative proposition is that the more changes in regulations that are effected at the ministry level, such as through the use of ministerial ordinances, notifications and informal discussions, the more effective is the MOF's control of regulatory policy. Another is that the MOF operates in a 'Weberian' style; that is, it follows the implicit guidelines defined by the legal framework or the policy of the government and hence the LDP. These two imply that a low level of political interference could be interpreted as support for a strong, independent MOF or a MOF that operates for the LDP. It has been suggested that in the 1950s and 1960s the public service played a stronger role in the policymaking process than previously, citing among other things the increased use of ordinance power and the growing links between the public service and the LDP caused by the continuity of the LDP hold over political power.[12] Exploring the character of interaction will help define the extent of political control of the policymaking process.

APPROACHES TO REGULATORY POLICYMAKING

The diversity of the literature explaining the presence of regulation illustrates the difficulties successive writers have had in providing theories which were borne out by empirical evidence. Public interest theories in one form or another have had supporters over a long period.[13] In the same way as there are difficulties in defining the national interest, there are problems with defining the public interest. Some public interest theories have held that some markets do not operate efficiently or equitably and that government intervention will improve general welfare. Financial regulations in Japan, it could be argued, were adopted to improve the efficiency of the financial markets and ultimately help to produce a higher total real output. Regulation of interest rates was a key tenet of the policy of government and it could be argued that low nominal interest rates and rationed access to capital produced an environment which facilitated economic expansion at a rate at least equal to that of an unfettered market. There can be little doubt that whatever the impact of financial regulation, it did little to hinder economic expansion during the 1960s. Personal savers consistently received a real return on their savings close to zero but they benefited from regular, significant increases in real wage incomes. Although those that did not save clearly benefited far more than those that did, there was little in the way of a free rider problem with savers. That is, few individuals chose to consume their whole income. The overall savings rate remained extremely high. Intuitively the theory cannot be counted as irrelevant to the experiences of the 1960s.

Although it does injustice to their subtlety and range, the various 'capture' theories of regulation can, for the sake of simplicity, be considered together.[14] Capture theories of regulation suggest that private interest groups can persuade the government to develop policies for their own benefit rather than the benefit of the public. Some groups are able to use their strength effectively through voting blocs or campaign funds to promote sectional interests. Some regulations might be established at first for 'public interest' purposes, but over time the agency or ministry might become concerned about the interests of groups within its jurisdiction rather than broader national interests.[15] One of the more sophisticated versions of this group of theories was presented by 1982 Nobel prize winner in economics, George Stigler. Stigler's economic theory suggests that different types of groups have different incentives to organise and bargain. The larger the group becomes, for example, the greater the problem with free riders. The effectiveness of small groups, such as associations representing highly concentrated industries, in 'buying' favourable regulatory arrangements is one of the predictions of this theory.[16] Empirical evidence does not give much support to these types of theories. In Japan one would expect the MOF to operate on behalf of the banks and securities companies, but as later chapters show, there were many cases of disagreement and conflict between the regulator and regulated, and it was more often the case than not that the view of the MOF prevailed. Furthermore, there have been quite fundamental disagreements within the industry about the shape of future developments.

A third set of theories could be called self-interest theories. Public servants could, for example, follow patterns predicted by capture theories as a means of ensuring their subsequent careers. Acceptance of the practice of movement from the public service into private enterprise requires serious consideration of this possibility. Alternatively, as Niskanen argues, public servants might seek to maximise their own jurisdictions in the same sense that corporations attempt to maximise profit. One might expect internecine fighting between ministries, and an overall growth of regulatory activity, if this theory had a substantial base in fact.[17]

An important subset of the above explanations of regulatory activity has its base in economics. One important difference between Japan and other industrial countries has been the continuing success of the LDP at the polls. Although political cycles can be seen in areas such as taxation, there is little evidence of them extending to a broader range of issues.[18] There certainly have been major changes in regulations in the financial markets, and in areas such as tariffs, foreign exchange and industry-related measures. The role of market forces in the context of the political process is one factor which requires examination.

Public servants and their methods and operations are an important element of the political process. One analyst, G.T. Allison, implies that government behaviour is best understood 'less as deliberate choices and more as *outputs* of large organisations functioning according to standard patterns of behaviour...

At any given time, a government consists of *existing* organisations, each with a *fixed* set of standard operating procedure programs'.[19] Rix argues convincingly that a modified version of this approach is useful in understanding Japan's post-war economic aid program.[20] Both writers owe a major intellectual debt to Simon and his concept of bounded rationality: 'Intendedly rational actions require simplified models that extract the main feature of a problem without capturing all of its complexity.'[21] In short, the proposition that the public service is operating rationally by ignoring radical solutions and working very much within the established framework is a useful starting point. As Lindblom argues, this does not necessarily mean no change but rather small incremental changes. Over time, change of this type could have significant repercussions.[22] Another model put forward by Allison, the bureaucratic paradigm approach, is useful in that it focuses on conflict within the public service and the competitive spirit between agencies or ministries in securing expanded jurisdictions or new programs. This approach has problems, however, as it downgrades the purported national interest objectives of programs, stressing that in reality jurisdictional disputes, logrolling and politics play important roles in determining the outcome.[23]

From these perspectives, we can examine the proposition that jurisdictional and political motivations for policymaking are reinforced by an important set of mechanisms based upon career patterns, functional responsibilities within the public service and retirement patterns. Career patterns, it will be suggested, favour short-term rather than long-term attitudes to policy, the functional responsibilities of the public service restrict the amount of research that can be executed, and retirement patterns provide links between industry and the supervising ministry. These factors reduce the scope for major changes in policy direction. These influences are not exceptional to Japan. It has been suggested that the movement of officers from government agencies to private industry has been an influence on agency decisions in the United States.[24] In Japan the influence of retirement patterns has been inadequately examined.[25] The existence of institutionalised early retirement in Japan and the influential position of the MOF in the Japanese government and in post-retirement positions in the LDP create unusual problems in assessing the character of LDP oversight of the policymaking process.

MODES OF POLICYMAKING

A typology which pays attention to two variables, the level of concentration of control that a single policymaking body has over a jurisdiction and the level of agreement between policymaking bodies on a policy issue, is helpful in explaining the policymaking process. This typology is outlined in Figure 0.1. Assume for the moment that political intervention in the policymaking process is absent.

This model has clear antecedents in the work of Lowi and Wilson and seeks to develop the recent Japanese literature which suggests that consensus, rather

A policymaking typology

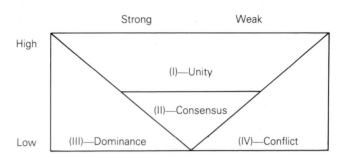

than being a dominant form of decisionmaking, is but one of a range of possibilities.[26] Four types of policymaking processes can be identified.

First, there is a set of policymaking processes which reflects the principle of unity. Shared values between the participants in the policymaking process will result in a process which is confined to sorting out technical problems of policy implementation. Policy which is formed in this way need not be immobilist, or dynamic, but will reflect the aspirations of the participants. These are cases which, by definition, do not infringe on the jurisdiction of antagonistic groups and are labelled '(I)—Unity' in Figure 0.1.[27]

Second, there are those policymaking processes which are based on consensus. A process of consensus seems to imply the fulfilment of at least three conditions. There must be relative equality of influence between participants; relative compatibility of views between participants; and a willingness to resolve disputes among the participants.

Consensus-oriented policymaking processes ((II)—Consensus) involve a certain amount of conflict, but the level of conflict is not sufficient to prevent resolution. One commentator has suggested that this model has widespread applicability.[28] In the area of agricultural policymaking, shared values are enough to overcome problems which may emerge between participants within the policymaking process. The crucial features are that no one group controls the process and that its dominant character is incremental change. The level of agreement between participants is less than in the unity mode. Consensus becomes less likely as the level of agreement between participants falls, and less likely when there is an extreme in the concentration of control.

The third possibility is that set of processes which is based on the principle of dominance. In the extreme, this mode ((III)—Dominance) assumes a sharp difference in the influence of participants, which makes the compatibility of views relatively unimportant. The basis of this difference is in the level of concentration of control over the policymaking arena. For example, two ministries might have interests in policy outcomes but only one has actual influence in forming policy, which permits the dominant participant to ignore the views of the other. The dominant mode can be expected to apply particularly when the level of agreement is low.

Modes (I) and (II) suggest areas in which disputes are resolved, but this does not guarantee change. Support for the status quo can occur either by a party exercising its dominant position or by agreement between parties that the existing policy remains viable. Nevertheless, change is an important element inherent to policymaking in these modes.

All these modes suggest processes through which disputes are resolved positively. The extent of change may only be minimal but at least change will always result from a process where one party, in the third case the dominant party, advances a proposal in support of change. A fourth possibility is somewhat different.

This fourth possibility ((IV)—Conflict) is where the parties in the policy-making process shelve proposals, or the original intent of change is lost in bargaining, because no group is prepared to compromise sufficiently, and no group has overriding authority, or for some reason cannot exert what authority it has to force a policy change. Conflict in this case forces the participant seeking change to abandon its goal. This is the extreme case. As in most typologies there are grey areas between each box. Hard and fast demarcations are constructs of theory. For example, in mode (III) a ministry might have enough control to effect a certain amount of change, but nowhere near the extent required to implement its preferred position in its entirety. Similarly, consensus takes over from conflict and dominance at some level of agreement when the level of concentration of control is neither too high nor too low.

It is the core of the conflict category which includes potentially the most obstructionist area of policymaking. The evidence of chapters 2, 3, 4 and 5 suggests that, in the policymaking processes affecting financial markets at least, the shared values of the unity mode and the relative equality of influence and compatibility of the consensus mode do not prevail throughout the policy-making processes as a whole. It suggests that the focus on 'a bottom-up, group oriented and consensus seeking process'[29] may not be as appropriate or applicable to the explanation of governmental policymaking in Japan as it is to corporate decisionmaking. There are cases, such as in routine policy management, where the consensus model is useful, but this model does not seem adequate in other areas, particularly in the area of regulatory policymaking.[30]

The typology provides a means to view the decisionmaking framework in a dynamic way. Over time, as the relationships within economic and political markets change, the locus of decisionmaking itself could shift, for example, from somewhere in mode (II) to somewhere in mode (IV). That is, it might not be that commentators writing about general policymaking processes of the late 1960s and early 1970s misconstrued the character of the policymaking process with their emphasis on mode (II), but that changes in economic conditions have produced a real change in the level of agreement over basic economic values. In the 1950s and 1960s there was a high level of agreement between participants but from the mid- to late 1960s this began to decline. The case studies explore this issue more fully.

ROLES AND MOTIVATIONS

Up to the mid-1970s, the dominant view of the role of the Japanese public service in economic policymaking was of a successful designer and coordinator of efficient policy which made a substantial contribution to the performance of the Japanese economy in the postwar period.[31] In the late 1970s, this view became the subject of much criticism. Trezise and Ike both indicated substantial reservations, arguing that political realities had constrained the pursuit of efficient policies.[32] George concluded that, in the area of agricultural policy, the pursuit of criteria of economic efficiency was almost completely obliterated by the need to consider political realities.[33] In the area of budgetmaking, Campbell argued that the protection of the MOF's autonomy, elite status and jurisdictional boundaries was taken more seriously than the pursuit of correct fiscal policies, while an even lower priority was, in his view, accorded to the achievement of a desirable policy mix and the elimination of wasteful expenditure and obsolete programs.[34]

A careful study of the MOF—how it has reacted to the prospect of political intervention in the financial policymaking process, and how it has operated in the face of changing market circumstances and demand from within the finance industry—should help to explain more fully the regulatory and policymaking processes in Japan. The possibility of political intervention is implicit in the typology presented above. For the most part, because of the sensitivity of the MOF to the LDP's policy positions, it has not been a key issue. For this reason the relationship between the MOF and the LDP is of special significance, as it suggests that the MOF will not consider a range of policy options which is likely to have political repercussions, such as the introduction of policies with a large impact on a small number of participants.

Financial markets, as with other markets, do not exist in a vacuum. The economy requires different financial services as it develops domestically and in relation to the international economy. But forces operating within existing regulatory systems constrain change. The forces that sustain existing systems of regulation include economic and political groups with vested interests in the established arrangements and inertia. If the need for change is not critical, the public service is unlikely to consider proposals for change seriously, particularly if they have an adverse impact on established groups. It is important to ask whether the main pressure activating discussion of proposals for changes to regulatory policy in the financial markets comes from financial institutions which find the existing market arrangements restrictive. Financial institutions may seek regulatory change because of increased competitive pressure within existing markets, the perception of unsatisfied demand in areas where entry is restricted, or the difficulties resulting from fundamental changes in the pattern of financial flows. In controversial areas, financial institutions can petition for change but they have little power to ensure that change takes place. The level of instability within the existing market arrangements is the most important factor in predicting whether change, in some form, will occur. The greater the instability, the greater the likelihood of some change in regulatory policy. The quest by the MOF for stability in existing market relationships operates as a delaying strategy when some financial institutions are attempting to increase the scope of their activities in quest of profits. In non-controversial areas change will occur after consultation between the regulator and regulated. The rate of policy development will reflect the needs of the market but only with a (sometimes substantial) lag.

The literature on business–government relations in Japan has suggested a range of mechanisms for the transmission of ideas and potentially of influence from the business sector to the public service and the LDP. They include general mechanisms such as contact between the LDP, the public service and peak business organisations (the Federation of Economic Organisations (FEO), the Japanese Committee for Economic Development, the Federation of Japanese Employers Associations, and the Japanese Chamber of Commerce and Industry); common membership of clubs, such as those based on university groups; and intermarriage. The contact between peak organisations and the government operates on specific policies. In addition, links based on business participation in government committees examining the need for regulatory change, and formal and informal discussion between officers of the public service and members of individual corporations and financial institutions provide useful avenues for the exchange of information.[35] It is much more difficult but no less necessary to establish their role in influencing policymaking. There is no certainty that ideas put forward will be accepted. Indeed, there will be countervailing forces emanating from within the affected industry. There is no a priori reason to suggest that different elements of the finance industry will share common goals, or not compete for each other's traditional business. As a corollary, it can be argued that the areas of the finance industry with limited financial horizons (be they the result of traditions, regulations or size), by seeking to protect their own spheres of influence, will oppose freedom to operate in previously restricted areas of activity.

Finally, there is the question of Japan's responsiveness to foreign pressures on policymaking, particularly in relation to the role of foreign participants. In the two decades to 1980, Japan's involvement in the international economic system grew at an astounding rate. Japan-related investment and trade flows became important. In the area of finance, Japanese banks and securities companies rapidly expanded the scope of their international activities. International involvement in Japan, however, grew less evenly and more slowly. This book advances the proposition that the influence of foreign financial and corporate institutions, and of foreign governments, on the policymaking process in the Japanese financial markets is small. Foreign ideas are introduced by domestic participants but frequently face types of resistance outlined earlier. Foreign governments are rarely in a position to demand changes in financial regulations as they too have highly regulated financial markets. The increased flow of financial transactions between the Japanese and other capital markets has arisen partly from changing domestic perceptions about Japan's role in the international economic system. The role of foreign ideas may contribute to this change. Foreign ideas and foreign influence may also create an environment which contributes to the successful amendment of financial regulations by domestic interests favouring increased foreign participation or a less regulated market environment. Greater involvement of foreign participants is hindered by the concern of regulations for market stability and jurisdictional interests, the policy stance taken on the issue by the LDP and the less definable but nevertheless strong antipathy towards significant participation by foreign institutions in Japanese markets. Markets most amenable to foreign penetration satisfy the following two conditions: that a proposed alteration of the status quo in the market would not attract political attention; and that the market is not highly concentrated, or that the barriers of entry to potential domestic entrants have already been broken down.

The growth of Tokyo as an international financial centre in the 1970s was significantly inhibited by domestic regulations. Regulations in some of the markets in which foreign interests participated did undergo some change, but this change was not commensurate with the interest in Tokyo as an international financial centre. During the 1970s there was a great increase in the flow of capital into and out of Japan, but there was little change in the role played by foreign financial institutions in Japan. The early 1980s have certainly produced more change and a serious assessment of the issue of allowing Tokyo to become a fully fledged international financial centre. An important question addressed in this book is whether Japanese regulations developed in response to changing Japanese perceptions of their own needs or because of outside pressures.

THE CASE STUDIES

The case studies cover all the main areas of interest within the financial sector, with the exception of the equities market and the bank loan market. Chapter 1 presents an institutional overview of the Japanese financial system. Chapters 2, 3 and 4 examine case studies which focus on regulatory policy solely administered by the MOF. These case studies explore the role of the LDP and the changing relationship between the public service and the finance industry in the development of the government bond market, the bureau-level policymaking process which was evident in the formation of the Certificate of Deposits (CDs) market, and the conflict within the MOF in regulatory policymaking relating to trading in government bonds. Chapter 5, which examines the postal savings system, analyses the impact of strong LDP interest in the policymaking process, and the impact of inter-ministry disputation on policymaking. Chapters 6 and 7 compare the impact of international and domestic influences on policymaking in the context of the revision of foreign exchange law and the development of the yen bond market. Chapter 8 attempts a different type of analysis, examining the general impact on policymaking of administrative, career and retirement patterns in the MOF.

The nature and breadth of the material analysed in the case studies necessarily introduce issues into policymaking other than those directly concerned with financial regulation. No policy area is completely isolated and the boundaries of policy areas are constantly changing.[36] Thus the problems of fiscal policy and broader foreign economic policy issues were sometimes relevant in the study of the government bond market and the yen bond market respectively.

The case studies reflect the interrelationship between policy and policy-making in different areas. Although the problems in some markets can be dealt with separately from those in others, this is not always the case. The problems of the government bond market were linked with the CDs market, trading in government bonds by banks, and the postal-savings dispute. The MOF, which is the subject of chapter 8, appears as an important participant in every chapter. The yen bond market is linked to the government bond market in many ways. The case study on foreign exchange regulations looks in more general terms at the interface between these financial markets and potential foreign participants.

Consideration of the interactions between policymaking in different areas suggests some generalisations about regulation of the financial sector as a whole. These generalisations may apply to the broader area of economic policymaking processes, but that must be the subject of further research.

1   An institutional overview

The 1970s produced considerable worldwide activity in the area of financial regulations. In the United States, West Germany, England, France and Canada there were important changes in the regulatory framework which determined the way the market operated. In the United States, for example, there was a trend towards deregulation of interest rates, highlighted by the abandonment of regulation Q. In West Germany and England there were some areas in which regulations were strengthened. Throughout the industrialised world there was much discussion of the character of financial regulations which would enable governments to achieve their goals in the 1980s. Japanese authorities were not left out. In the mid-1970s, a long-term review of the 1927 Banking Law began, providing the basis for legislation which passed through the Japanese parliament, the Diet, in April and May 1981. The legal framework is only part of the picture. The institutional overview that follows provides the background for understanding the developments in broad regulatory policy which occurred during the 1970s and early 1980s by outlining the main arms of regulatory policy operating in the Japanese financial markets.

The main functions of the regulators and the regulated involved in the case studies of later chapters are also set out briefly. The diversity of institutions described and the range of their operations underline the potential differences of interest that are focused on in later chapters. The presentation of the institutional structure, while brief, also provides a ready reference point for putting the individual institutions into context.

Finally, the state of the financial system in 1970 is described, and how the fundamental characteristics of the system were moulded by changes in the economic environment of the 1970s is examined. This section draws attention to the major changes in the structure of the flows of funds at a sectoral level (between the household sector, the government sector, the financial sector and the corporate sector) and at an institutional level. These changes formed the basis of demands for regulatory reform in the late 1970s. Financial change involves many areas. In the debate of the 1970s on the need to reform the financial system in Japan the emphasis was on financial deregulation, that is, letting participants in the market make more of the decisions unhindered by the regulators. One important but by no means the only concern was the question of interest rate deregulation, and this is examined also.

25

THE REGULATORY FRAMEWORK

In 1921 the Minister of Finance, Takahashi Korekiyo, recommended the amalgamation of small regional banks to strengthen the foundations of the banking system. In 1924 the MOF outlined its first plans for bank amalgamation. From that time, the government, through the MOF, has played an important regulatory role in the banking sector and the wider financial system. Even in the 1920s, the key feature of the management of the the proposed system was the prevention of excess competition, and the promotion of sound management.[1]

The institutional character of the Japanese financial system derives much of its present form from the rationalisation process that occurred during the 1930s and early 1940s, and the administrative guidance of the MOF during that period.[2] The Banking Law (1927) provided the legislative framework for the banking system during this period, and it remained largely intact until its revision in 1981. The policies of the American Occupation Forces also left their mark.[3] The Securities and Exchange Law (1947) incorporated a rigid division of specialisation into the financial markets; for example, banks were prohibited from operating in most of the securities sector. By the early 1950s the overall legislative framework was firmly in place, and in general the specialised functions of different financial institutions were more pronounced than they had been in prewar Japan.[4]

Whereas the Banking Law and the Securities and Exchange Law provided the legislative framework, the dynamic character of the MOF's regulatory policy came from its use of ministerial ordinances and notifications. Ministerial ordinances were regulations developed within the MOF and did not require the approval of the Diet. Notifications were regulations prepared at the bureau level within the MOF, and were the least rigid part of regulatory policy. Both ministerial ordinances and notifications were used extensively.[5]

Most aspects of the activities of banks and the securities companies were regulated directly by the MOF. In the banking sector, it controlled the rate of expansion of branch banking, the types of financial products which could be offered by the banks to their clients, and almost all interest rates. In the securities sector, it also controlled the rate of expansion of the branch network, the rules for entry by corporations into the bond issue market, the character of the secondary bond market in some areas and the interest rate on bonds in the issue market.[6] Thus the government, through the MOF, had firm control over the shape of financial development.[7]

In the late 1940s and early 1950s the government opted for a major role in the allocation of capital. The establishment of the Japan Development Bank (1951) and the Export–Import Bank of Japan (1950) played an important role in channelling funds into development projects favoured by the government. Even after the volume of funds provided by these institutions had declined sharply they continued to play an important indicative function. Approval of a loan from a government bank was used often as a signal to private sector banks. The government also established a large number of financial corporations, as a means of channelling funds into areas which were not served adequately by existing financial institutions, or which were deemed to justify privileged treatment from a political point of view.[8] These included the People's Finance Corporation (1949), The Housing Loan Corporation (1950), the Medical Care Facilities Finance Corporation (1960) and the Environmental Sanitation Business Finance Corporation (1967).

The role of the government was also reflected in the phenomena of 'overloan' and 'overborrowing'. In the latter half of the 1950s the city banks were unable to satisfy all demands for industrial funds. The shortage of funds was alleviated to some extent by direct loans from the BOJ. This 'overloan' position of the city banks was one of the unusual features of the Japanese financial system during the late 1950s and 1960s.[9] The government recognised that there were problems inherent in this 'overloan' relationship that developed between the city banks and the BOJ,but did little to change it. It was not until the 1970s that the relationship began to change appreciably.[10]

'Overborrowing' described a relationship which developed between city banks and large corporations. It referred to the corporate reliance on borrowings from city banks for the greater part of external financing, and was a phenomenon which resulted directly from government regulations. The failure of government to encourage the development of the bond market, indeed the deliberate restriction of its growth, was quite fundamental to the strength of the banking sector within the financial system.[11]

Funnelling the demand for funds through the banking system was not only a means by which the government could in some ways control the direction of funds, but also a means by which it could control the cost of funds. The Temporary Interest Rate Law (1947) regulated the level of interest rates attached to bank deposits and short-term bank loans.[12] These were linked to the official discount rate, over which the MOF had considerable control.[13] The long-term bank loan rate was linked unofficially to the short-term rate, and the MOF exercised great influence over all the bond-market rates. Interest rates were set at levels which did not permit the clearing of demand and hence the main problem facing borrowers was not the cost of funds but the availability of funds.[14]

The phenomena of overloan and overborrowing reflected the political and social environment of the late 1950s and early 1960s. Prime Minister Ikeda's Income Doubling Plan (1961) illustrated the bullish economic environment, and the political importance attached to economic growth.[15] By the late 1960s the appropriateness of the existing regulatory framework began to be questioned by both government and non-government authorities. In February 1967, the director-general of the Banking Bureau, Sumita Satoshi, made what was perhaps the first important move in this direction when he called for greater attention to be focused upon improving efficiency.[16] Legislation encouraging amalgamations of financial institutions was passed in 1968. Although the legislation did not have an important impact on amalgamations within the major banks sector, it did foreshadow growing concern within the MOF about the structure of the banking industry.

Sumita's concern for improving financial efficiency can be linked to the improvement of Japan's balance of payments position in the late 1960s, and the view that Japanese banks would play an increasingly large role in the world economy. The report of the Committee on Financial System Research (1970) made this explicit.[17] Neither Sumita's concern nor the report resulted in significant regulatory change. The case studies in this book touch on many of the issues that were discussed at that time and offer an explanation of why some were taken up during the 1970s and why most had to wait until the early 1980s before receiving serious consideration.

THE INSTITUTIONAL STRUCTURE

The institutional structure of the Japanese financial system was much the same in 1980 as it was in 1955.[18] The extensive rationalisations of the 1930s and 1940s produced a relatively stable number of institutions within the core of the financial system and regulations effectively barred new entrants.[19] Notwithstanding this, the functions and services offered by banks and securities companies changed significantly, if only gradually, over the 25 years.

The regulated: The banking and securities sectors

The banking sector is organised along the lines of specialised banking. In 1980 there were thirteen city banks, 63 regional banks, three long-term credit banks, seven trust banks, 71 mutual banks, 462 credit associations, 483 credit cooperatives, 64 foreign banks, and a larger number of agricultural co-operatives. The provision of financial services was quite comprehensive and sophisticated. There was very little merger activity between the larger financial institutions in the 1960s or 1970s. Some rationalisation in the area of small financial institutions, such as credit associations and credit co-operatives, did occur but had little effect on the basic structure and functions of the banking sector. The following thumbnail sketches should help to explain the central function of each set of institutions.

City banks

The city banks were by any standards large commercial banks.[20] In 1981 they had an average funds base of 8.8 trillion yen, operated extensive national branching networks which averaged over 200 domestic branches, and had considerable overseas representation and interest.[21]

Among the financial institutions, city banks maintained the closest relationship with the large corporation sector and their deposit bases were inadequate to satisfy the demand thus generated. City banks supplemented their deposits by borrowing from the call market (the interbank market), the bills market, and directly from the BOJ.

From 1979, CDs provided an additional source of funds. Deposits of individuals were the single most important source of funds, but it was not until the late 1970s that loans to individuals amounted to a consistently significant proportion of funds disbursed. Transactions with corporations remain the most important business to the city banks, but their interests diversified beyond the domestic capital-intensive industries of the 1960s. After the 1973 oil shock, the share of funds supplied to small and medium-sized corporations rose slightly. Furthermore, the restraints placed on city banks in the domestic financial markets and the opportunities of the international financial markets encouraged city banks to expand their international activities substantially during the 1970s.

Regional banks

The size of their fund base and national coverage were two factors which distinguished regional banks from city banks. Regional banks were essentially institutions with a prefectural and not a national focus. Each prefecture had at least one regional bank, and some prefectures had two, headquartered within their boundaries. Although the size of the Hokkaido Takushoku Bank (the smallest city bank) and the largest regional banks was quite similar, in 1980 regional banks were on average only one-ninth the size of city banks. Since there were regional banks located in each prefecture a considerable variation in size was to be expected, and in fact the largest regional bank was approximately 33 times the size of the smallest.

When compared with city banks, most of the regional banks had closer ties with small and medium-sized corporations, although it was not at all unusual for them to have important contact with a small number of large corporations. Another feature was the often close relationship between regional banks and local government. Traditionally, the regional banks served as bankers for local government.[22]

Finally, regional banks as a group collected more deposits than they lent directly to clients. Excess funds were channelled through the call market, with the main recipients being city banks. At the end of the 1970s, however, many regional banks were net borrowers from the call market.

The long-term credit banks and the trust banks

The long-term credit banks and the trust banks provide long-term funds for industry. The long-term credit banks raise most of their funds through debenture issues at regulated interest rates. Their existence constituted one major barrier to the development of a negotiable securities market. A less regulated industrial bond market would have permitted many corporations to raise funds there instead of through the long-term credit banks. Even if the development of the corporate bond market were desirable from the viewpoint of national interest, the development would be substantially delayed by the opposition of the long-term credit banks, which formed a powerful interest group. Trust banks were the other group which provided long-term loans to industry. Their main source of funds was trust funds, which were similar to fixed deposits with maturities of two to five years. During the 1970s, both long-term credit banks and trust banks played increasingly active roles in the international financial markets.

Mutual banks

Mutual banks were financial institutions which had several restrictions placed upon their operations, including the requirement that, in principle, they confine their relationships to corporations with capital of less than 800 million yen.[23] They were not permitted to lend more than 20 per cent of their total outstanding loans to local governments or large corporations. This restriction was sometimes a major factor in preventing mutual banks from competing effectively with regional banks. The average funds base of the mutual banks was about one-third the size of the regional banks, at 0.38 trillion yen, and the largest mutual bank was over 30 times the size of the smallest mutual bank.

The postal savings system

The postal savings system was not a financial institution in the normal sense, since it had little authority for using funds. However, it was a very large institution organisationally, and with over 22 000 branches nationwide, it had an enormous potential for collecting deposits. At the end of 1980, it had deposits totalling approximately 68 trillion yen, or more than the entire volume of savings deposits held by the thirteen city banks. Funds deposited in the postal savings system were lent to the MOF, which then determined how the funds were used.

Foreign banks

At the end of June 1980, 64 foreign banks maintained 86 branches in Japan. Another 97 banks maintained representative offices. From the mid-1950s to the early 1970s, the main function of foreign banks was to 'provide a stable source of foreign exchange' through long-term untied loans and through trade financing.[24] These funds increased the ability of Japanese corporations to import both technology and resources otherwise constrained by the lack of foreign exchange. The share of loans and discounts made by foreign banks rose from 1.6 per cent in 1973 to a peak of 3.3 per cent during 1976. At the end of September 1980 it stood at approximately 3 per cent.[25]

As the financial sophistication of Japanese corporations and banks rose, the demand for foreign banks to raise foreign currency funds fell and profitability declined with it. The return on assets fell continually during the second half of the 1970s.[26] Foreign banks were faced with the decline of their established function. Involvement in foreign exchange trading was one option available to the larger banks, in view of the growing volume of foreign exchange transactions. Some foreign bankers saw Tokyo as having a future as an 'international financial centre', based either on the yen or on the dollar.[27] By the end of 1983, progress had been substantial and further developments were being mooted.

The trend of the late 1970s and early 1980s contained evidence that the MOF was prepared in the long term to allow Tokyo to establish a much higher profile in international finance. The deregulation of foreign exchange and capital flows in the late 1970s and early 1980s permitted a significant increase in the volume of two-way financial flows. The opening up of the existing short-terms financial markets to foreign investors, the likely growth in the fledgling TBs market in the mid-1980s, and the establishment of foreign currency, commercial paper and CDs markets will all contribute to the international flavour of the market. The removal of limits on yen swaps by foreign banks and the abandonment of the real demand rule for foreign exchange transactions (which will allow more hedging and speculative activities) should all allow foreign banks to reposition themselves in the changing financial scene. Progress in areas where the foreign banks have made little impact—in the loans and deposit markets—will be much slower. This problem is addressed later in this chapter.

Other small and medium-sized financial institutions

Credit associations, credit cooperatives, agricultural cooperatives and labor credit associations were all small financial institutions which provided limited services within a single homogeneous area. In aggregate terms, these financial institutions were quite important as media for the efficient use of financial resources within well-defined geographic areas. Agricultural cooperatives were linked to a 'central bank' which acted as a clearing house and redistributor of surplus funds. This institution was called the Norin Chukin Bank. It was a government bank similar in size to the large city banks, and in the late 1970s it too became increasingly involved in non-agricultural and international financial transactions.

The securities companies

Set alongside the banking sector were the equities market and the bond markets. Securities companies performed the major role of intermediary in these markets. While there were over 250 securities companies, four companies had a dominating influence. They were Nomura Securities, Yamaichi Securities, Daiwa Securities and Nikko Securities.[28]

Section 63 of the Securities and Exchange Law (SEL) gave the securities companies a virtual monopoly in the underwriting and trading of bonds and equities (except government bonds). However, the government preferred to emphasise financing through the banking sector. Tradition and tax arrangements worked against the development of the equities sector. One market, the short-term *gensaki* market, developed strongly under the guidance of the securities companies. The *gensaki* market was a market where bonds were sold with repurchase agreements (normally with an average maturity of 60 days). The dominant transaction type involved corporations with excess funds buying bonds from the securities companies and reselling them to the securities companies after an agreed period.[29]

In the early 1980s the securities companies began to establish a range of funds aimed at individual investors, and these are proving to be an effective way of gathering funds and are promoting the deregulation of interest rates.[30]

Like the larger financial institutions, the four big securities companies became active operators in the international financial markets, and many of the boundaries which separated banking from securities business within Japan broke down outside Japan during the 1970s. In the 1980s a reverse trend became apparent. Lessons learnt abroad were reintroduced into Japan as the securities companies sought to establish a market for innovative financial products.

The regulators

The MOF and the BOJ were the government authorities which dominated regulatory policymaking. Others such as the Ministry of International Trade and Industry (MITI) and the Ministry of Posts and Telecommunications (MPT) became involved on particular matters.

The Ministry of Finance

The MOF was not only the key ministry supervising the finance industry and controlling the development of regulations; it was also one of the most powerful of the central government ministries in Japan, controlling matters relating to taxation, the budget and customs and excise, not to mention various aspects of the finance industry.[31] For the purposes of this analysis, however, the key role of the MOF was its regulation of interest rates. This was at the core of financial policy. Its desire to maintain a rigidly regulated low interest rate policy did much to determine the range of options of financial development that it could consider.

The case studies outlined in later chapters impinge on the responsibilities of four bureaus: the Banking Bureau, the Securities Bureau, the International Finance Bureau, and the Financial Bureau. On some issues the Minister's Secretariat was asked to coordinate policy planning and resolve intra-ministry conflict, but it was generally unable to exert much influence.[32]

The Banking Bureau and the Securities Bureau were the two bureaus responsible for the development and implementation of policy within the domestic finance industry. It is true that the BOJ played an important role in the overall control and operation of monetary policy. Its guidance to the banking industry on the level of outstanding loans, or its intervention within the financial markets, dictated to a considerable extent the cost and availability of funds within the financial system. But perhaps the most powerful tool, the control of interest rates, fell within the orbit of the Banking Bureau. It controlled the savings interest rate for financial institutions (but not the postal savings rate) and the long-term lending rate, and provided a major input into the determination of the official discount rate. The policy stance of the Banking Bureau on the method of determination of interest rates was a major factor in shaping the speed of regulatory change. The BOJ and the MOF worked closely together on many occasions, but substantial disagreements were not uncommon.

Rivalry between policymaking and implementing bodies was not restricted to that between the BOJ and the MOF. Disagreements between the Banking Bureau and the Securities Bureau were numerous, reflecting their very different jurisdictional interests. The Securities Bureau was concerned primarily with the development and management of direct financing alternatives such as the development of the bonds and equities market. Its day-to-day contacts were with the securities companies, and hence it was often seen as representing their interests. On the other hand, the Banking Bureau was involved in regulating the banking sector and was largely responsible for policy that related to the operation of banks. A close, although at times uneasy, relationship existed between the Banking Bureau and the banking sector. Intra-MOF conflicts are explored in chapters 2, 3 and 6.

The International Finance Bureau (IFB) was responsible for the international conduct of Japanese financial institutions, the conduct of international financial policy, and in general terms the design and implementation of rules and regulations affecting the interaction of Japanese financial markets with international financial markets. Between 1964 when it was established and the late 1970s, it gradually developed its sphere of influence, making important contributions to the formation of international economic policy and decisions relating to international issues.[33] Its growth in status reflected the increasing amount of contact between Japanese financial markets and international financial markets and the growing importance of Japan's role in the international economy.

Finally, the Financial Bureau was responsible for the management and issue of government bonds, and the operation and control of the Fiscal Investment Loan Program (FILP) and the Trust Fund Bureau (TFB). The management of government bonds became an increasingly important issue as the level of outstanding bonds began to affect the interest rate policy of the MOF as a whole.

The Bank of Japan

The BOJ had little statutory authority over the formation of policy that determined the regulatory framework within which financial institutions and securities companies operated. However, it was in many instances far from being a neutral actor. An outline of its main functions indicates the character of its interest.

The BOJ's chief responsibility was the management of monetary policy. There has been some debate over the identification of the main planks of monetary policy during the 1960s. Patrick argued that the central tool of monetary policy was the role of 'window guidance', a form of moral suasion, exerted by the BOJ over the city banks and which played a large role in determining the rate of increase in loan funds made available by city banks to corporations. Suzuki argued that this was only a supplementary technique and that the manipulation of price of funds was the main tool of monetary policy.[34] The official discount rate was certainly used as an indicator of a change in policy, but until the 1973–75 monetary squeeze, it did not appear to have major price effects.

After 1975 the objective of monetary policy shifted from 'chasing around after multiple objectives' to a focus on price stability.[35] A more serious attempt by the BOJ to control the growth in the money stock as an intermediate target, with a greater emphasis on deregulated interest rates, sharpened the differences in outlook of the BOJ and the MOF. The BOJ eschewed the broader pressures placed on the MOF in an attempt to make monetary policy effective in the environment of the 1980s. Its relationship with the MOF was naturally very close, but disputes were also frequent. For example, the BOJ and the MOF disagreed on many occasions on the timing and extent of change in monetary policy. Although the determination of monetary policy was the preserve of the BOJ, actual policy reflected a complex of factors including the state of economic activity, the rate of inflation, the relationship between the Prime Minister and the governor of the BOJ and the political expectations of the period. On balance, the MOF's influence on monetary policy was stronger during periods of easy monetary policy and the BOJ's influence stronger in periods of tight monetary policy.[36] In order to strengthen its position the BOJ began to encourage a greater role for the market in determining interest rates. In concrete terms, it altered the method of determining interest rates in two short-term money markets, the call and the bills market. The aim was to put pressure on the MOF to accept a greater role for demand and supply in the determination of interest rates.

THE FINANCIAL SYSTEM IN THE 1970s

Japan's financial system in 1970 can be described simply by focusing on four major system characteristics, and on the salient features of the flow of funds. The four system characteristics were as follows. First, the Japanese financial system relied upon indirect financing (the use of financial institutions as intermediaries) rather than direct financing (the use of the capital and money markets, and the equities market), and as a result the banking system played a dominant role in financial intermediation. The short-term capital and money markets remained largely underdeveloped from the viewpoint of servicing corporate needs directly. Second, interest rates in the banking sector and the bonds sector were quite inflexible. Interest rates were set at below-market levels and regulated by administrative fiat. This did not mean that competition within the banking sector was restricted, but simply that non-price competition and the use of compensatory deposits were widespread.[37] Third, the city banks were chronically indebted to the BOJ. This allowed the BOJ to use quite effective window guidance as a major tool in the implementation of restrictive monetary policy. Fourth, the Japanese financial system was relatively isolated. There were few ties between the international and domestic financial markets.[38]

In 1970 the flow of funds showed the same relatively stable pattern that it had had over the previous decade. Only the personal sector was in surplus. Most of its financial surplus was held in the form of deposits within the banking and postal savings systems, and only a small portion of funds was held in bonds, equities and insurance. Funds were transferred to the government, the corporate and the overseas sectors. The corporate sector was the main user of funds. It borrowed heavily from the banking sector. The government sector was also slightly in deficit, although the central government was in surplus. Until 1965 the central government maintained a strict policy of balancing the budget, and with the rapid growth in government revenue as a result of large increases in personal income it was frequently in a position where it could both increase public expenditure and offer tax cuts. In 1970 it placed few demands on the financial system. Finally, the foreign sector was relatively unimportant. The inflow of capital into Japan was still severely restricted by regulations and the Tokyo capital market was still closed to foreign borrowers. The outflow of Japanese investment funds was also relatively small.[39]

Shifting deposit shares

Whereas indirect financing continued to dominate the external financing of corporations, the roles of financial institutions within the indirect finance sector did not remain unchanged. The share of private financial institutions in overall provision of funds fell considerably from 72.8 per cent (1970–74 average) to 63.6 per cent (1975–79 average), while the share of government-related financial institutions rose from 17.9 per cent (1970–74 average) to 26.1 per cent (1975–79).[40]

Underlying the increased presence of the government-related financial institutions was the strong performance of the postal savings system. The share of

Table 1.1   Financial assets of the personal sector (per cent)

	1965	1970	1975	1980	1983
Cash & demand deposits	22.1	20.6	18.4	13.3	11.2
All other interest-bearing financial assets, of which	77.9	79.4	81.6	86.7	88.8
Fixed deposits at bank	51.3	48.7	46.9	43.5	39.9
Postal savings	12.8	14.8	17.8	21.8	21.9
Trust accounts	7.1	7.9	7.9	7.5	8.4
Bonds	5.8	8.2	8.9	9.4	9.9
(Govt bonds)	(0.3)	(0.7)	(0.7)	(3.9)	(3.8)
Investment trusts	5.2	2.4	2.3	1.9	2.6
Insurance	17.8	18.0	16.2	16.2	17.4

Note: 1983 figure is for June 1983

Source: Bank of Japan Research & Statistics Department *Special Paper 93*, April 1981; Nihon ginkō, *Chōsa geppō*, February 1984

deposits held by the banks as a group (excluding trusts and insurance, which have remained almost static) fell from 68.8 per cent in 1970 to 54.5 per cent in 1979. The share of city banks fell the most precipitously. On the other hand the share of deposits held by the postal savings system rose from 19.0 per cent in 1970 to 32.6 per cent in 1979. The deposits gathered by the postal savings system fed first into the TFB, and then to the FILP. Loans to government financial institutions were made through the FILP.[41]

The shifts in the flow of funds can also be observed by examining the way the personal sector held its financial assets. Table 1.1 shows the relative decline in cash and demand deposits held by individuals. This affected banks more than the postal savings system, which held mostly fixed deposits. Fixed deposits held in postal savings rose from 14.8 per cent in 1970 to 20.8 per cent in 1979, whereas the share held in banks fell from 48.7 per cent to 42.9 per cent.

The gradual disappearance of 'overloans'

During the 1970s, city banks reduced substantially the level of their indebtedness to the BOJ. From 8.7 per cent as a share of deposits in 1970, their outstanding borrowings fell to 2.1 per cent in 1980. The implications of this change are difficult to assess. Some commentators argued that it was the indebtedness of the city banks which gave the window guidance of the BOJ its bite, when the government wanted to tighten monetary policy. In the past the BOJ adjusted penalty interest rates and access to funds if its guidelines were not met.

The decline in borrowing from the BOJ caused it to look to other measures to supplement its traditional tools. Its policy initiatives in the short-term money markets, which were aimed at improving the responsiveness of interest rate levels in one market to changes in other markets, and its support for a deregulated short-term government bill market, indicated that the BOJ was attempting to develop the role of intervention through the market as a means of implementing monetary policy.

Government and corporate use of funds

Perhaps the main impact on developments in the financial markets in the 1970s was the shift in the use of funds. Some brief remarks are made here to put the discussion of interest rate deregulation in context, but more detailed analysis is left to chapter 2.

The rapidly expanding government bond issues had considerable impact on financial institutions. Banks directly underwrote the majority of the long-term government bonds. During the period of low corporate demand for funds (1974–78) the underwriting of government bonds provided the banks with a useful way to use their surplus funds. When corporate demand for funds increased in 1978, a potential conflict arose between the supplying of funds to

Table 1.2   Funds raised by the corporate sector externally (billion yen)

	1964	1970	1974	1980	1982
Borrowings	3426	9417	13 129	15 399	19 097
from private financial institutions	3056	8546	11 611	13 459	16 817
from government financial institutions	369	871	1517	1939	2280
Securities	923	1347	1414	2218	3570
industrial bonds	152	346	541	563	632
stocks	745	991	843	1441	2045
foreign currency bonds	25	10	29	214	892
Foreign credits etc.	297	431	1447	760	7
Total[a]	4676	11 196	15 991	18 377	22 675

Note: a Totals may not add up because of rounding

Source: BOJ Economic Research Department, Special Papers, various issues

the corporate sector and to the government sector. It was in this environment that the CDs market was created.

During 1977–79 the financial deficit of the corporate sector virtually disappeared, but by the end of 1980 it had re-emerged. The new deficit was different in that it applied to some industries and not others.[42] The corporate sector's external fund-raising methods altered little during the decade (when 1970 and 1980 are compared). Details are set out in Table 1.2. Private financial institutions were the key source of funds, with funds raised in the capital market of secondary importance, and foreign currency bonds for domestic use being only a minor source of funds. With relatively high interest rates overseas, and firm control of interest rates within Japan, one could not confidently predict any rapid growth in overseas financing. Nevertheless, the gradual breakdown of the tradition that shares be issued at par value, and the higher profiles of Japanese corporations abroad, are likely to produce in the longer term a weakening of the relationship between a corporation and its lead bank.

Another feature of the 1970s was the greater tendency for corporations to invest a part of their available funds in negotiable securities. The trend towards comparing financial asset returns with real asset returns increased, bringing with it a growing demand for less regulation of the financial markets.

The deregulation of interest rates

At the beginning of the 1970s there were few deregulated interest rates in Japan, and most political and economic interest groups supported the maintenance of low and regulated interest rates. By the early 1980s, there were still many within the ruling LDP, the MOF and throughout the economy who favoured controlled interest rates, but there was growing diversity of opinion and a strengthening movement towards deregulation in many areas.

At the beginning of the 1970s there were three short-term money markets— the interbank call market, the bond market with repurchase agreement, called the *gensaki* market, and the bills market. The call market and the bills market were subject to considerable BOJ intervention when it was required. Since they both had virtually the same participants, intervention in one market meant potential control of both.

The *gensaki* market was beyond the control of the BOJ; it was controlled by the securities companies over which the BOJ had little control. With the relaxation of the restrictions on participation in the short-term markets at the end of the 1970s, the city banks began to operate in the *gensaki* market and the securities companies in the call market. The formation of a CDs market in 1979 with deregulated interest rates and similar clientele, and a range of BOJ policy changes in the bills and call markets resulted in substantially more interest rate flexibility in the short-term money markets. It also increased the degree of control the BOJ was able to exercise over the short-term money markets indirectly through market forces, by injecting or withdrawing funds.

The obstacles to interest rate deregulation in the bank loan market, the deposit market, the short-term financial market and the capital market differed substantially; each is briefly discussed below.

The bank loan market

Lending rates of banks were customarily set with reference to the short-term prime rate. This was defined as the official discount rate plus 0.5 per cent. There were several occasions when the governor of the BOJ explicitly suggested that the formula should be ignored (when political factors intruded into the deposits market), but by and large the short-term prime rate acted as an indicator of loan rates.[43]

Loan rates were set by bilateral bargaining between the corporation concerned and the bank. Movements in an established rate generally required a change in the official discount rate. In this way the average loan rate moved in close parallel with the official discount rate. Loan rates did not maintain a constant relationship with deposit rates. Competition tended to reduce the bank loan rate in a gradual way after the lowering of the official discount rate.[44] If there was no concomitant fall in the deposit rate, the falling loan rate would reduce the profitability margin.

In as much as the loan rate was affected by the deposit rate and the official discount rate, both of which were subject to varying amounts of political pressure, the true deregulation of this market awaited changes in the setting of these two interest rates.

It should be added that most businesses with high levels of indebtedness favoured strongly the retention of the existing regulated system. The system allowed some differentiation between quality of clients by the use of compensating deposits, and by the establishment of different interest rate levels for different types of borrowers. The main advantage over a deregulated system to these businesses was that interest rates were below their true market levels.

The deposits market

The institutional structure of the deposit market during the 1970s meant that policy makers paid considerable attention to the interest rates attached to savings deposits, and in particular to interest rates on fixed deposits. This was expressed primarily through the postal savings system (discussed at length in chapter 4). Taxation waivers on interest earned from deposits held in both the banking system and the postal savings system were an additional pointer towards the attention accorded the act of saving by depositing.

The savings deposit issue encompassed a complex political problem. The aims of providing low-cost funds to industry and maintaining the real worth of the savings of the depositor were sometimes in conflict. In 1980 officials in the MOF, the BOJ and the MPT readily conceded that there had been no discussion of interest deregulation in this sector and that deregulation was not likely in the medium-term future. This remains the case today. These officials said the political view was that if deposit interest rates were deregulated loan rates would increase substantially.[45] This would have many political ramifications: for example, the increased cost of funds, so the argument goes, would endanger the viability of many small and medium-sized business enterprises which formed an interest group of considerable importance to the LDP. The balance between the two competing aims was managed fairly successfully during the 1970s. Although individuals were demanding greater access to deregulated financial products in the early 1980s, the prospects for substantial deregulation of interest rates in this market appear remote.

The short-term money markets

Substantial deregulation of the short-term money markets occurred during the latter part of the 1970s. A chronology of the main events for 1978–82 is set out in Table 1.3.

The BOJ took the first moves towards deregulating interest rates in the short-term money market in 1977 by creating a new range of short-term financial assets in the interbank market, the call market, and by deregulating interest rates. The establishment of a deregulated CDs market in May 1979 and the widening of the range of permitted participants in the short-term *gensaki* market increased the mobility of interest rates in the short-term markets, and also contributed to increased interest arbitrage between these markets.

In 1982 the BOJ began to operate a 'partial' TBs market, reselling earlier purchases by tender. The deregulation of the short-term markets did not mean that market forces alone determined short-term interest rates. Since the level of BOJ intervention in the bills market (and more recently by sales of TBs) was

Table 1.3   Developments in the short-term money markets, 1978–82

1978

June | Setting call rate in call market becomes more flexible. Resale and interest deregulation of bids in bills market with a maturity of over one month.

October | Establishment of seven-day call notes with deregulated interest rates. City banks permitted to sell bonds in *gensaki* market to twenty billion yen (increased from five billion yen).

November | Interest rate on 3–4 month bills deregulated. New one-month bills market introduced with deregulated interest rates.

1979

February | Non-residents permitted to invest freely in securities, excluding the *gensaki* market.

April | Official setting of the call rate abandoned and interest rates deregulated. New 2–6 day call market products created. City banks framework for operation in *gensaki* market as sellers expanded to 50 billion yen.

May | CDs market established with deregulated interest rates. Banks initially permitted to float CDs to 25 per cent of own capital, increasing gradually to 50 per cent in April 1980. Non-residents permitted to operate in *gensaki* market.

October | Setting bills rate for two-month bills abandoned and interest rates deregulated.

1980

April | Abolition of limits on city banks operating in *gensaki* market as sellers of bonds.

October | Change in bills market with maturity becoming 'simple' months rather than end of months.

November | Regional banks and trust banks permitted to enter the bills market as borrowers as well as their traditional position as lenders. The four big securities companies permitted to enter the market as borrowers.

1981

April | City banks permitted to purchase bonds in *gensaki* market. Call lending by city banks permitted.

May | BOJ begins selling short-term government securities at bills rate.

1982

April | BOJ begins TB sales by tender as a means to improve control over liquidity.

Source: Kin'yū June 1981, p. 18; *Nihon keizai shinbun; Asahi shinbun; Dai 31 Ginkōkyoku nenpō*

very high, it was able to influence short-term interest rates. The nature of the change in the short-term money markets is illustrated in Figure 1.1.

The role of the BOJ changed from influencing the short-term rates by setting rates directly to a more indirect method of market intervention. Participation in the call market, the *gensaki* market and the bills market was limited to a small number of groups which intervened in a consistent way. This permitted close

Figure 1.1   Links between the short-term financial markets

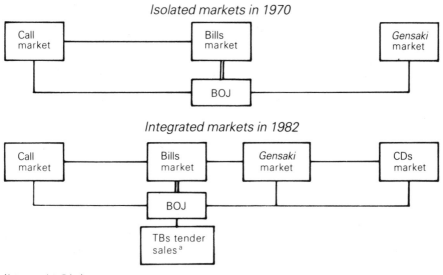

Notes: – interlinked

= strongly interlinked

a A fully fledged TBs market in which the price of government paper is established through supply and demand has yet to be established.

control of market rates by the BOJ through buying and selling in the market. Despite the relatively small size of these short-term markets, the process of integrating and deregulating them was begun, laying the foundation for a more broadly based, perhaps internationally oriented set of deregulated short-term money markets. By the end of 1982 most of the city banks had issued CDs up to the limits imposed by regulations and had begun campaigning for deregulation based on 'self control'. In early 1983 the MOF agreed to increase the framework for issuing by one half, in a stepped expansion over 1983–84. This encountered little resistance as it represented an extension of deregulation only in the wholesale markets, and did not involve any new political problems. An outline of the markets is given in Table 1.4.

The main gap in the short-term markets was the absence of a substantial TBs market. Short-term government securities were issued by the MOF, but with interest rates set at a level below the market rate. As a result, the participation of non-government institutions as purchasers of these securities was very limited. Table 1.5 sets out the details. In the early 1970s the dominant view in the BOJ was against the establishment of a market-determined TBs rate. When the Policy Board of the BOJ met to discuss the issue there was support from the Research Department but little within the powerful Business Department. By the end of the 1970s there was still some resistance to full deregulation, but the body of opinion within the BOJ supported the deregulation option.[46]

Although the MOF attitude on this issue changed little during the 1970s, it might have indirectly facilitated the establishment of such a market during the

Table 1.4   Size and participants in the short-term financial markets

Market size (billion billion yen)

Market	Mar. 1975	Mar. 1979	Mar. 1980	Mar. 1983 (end of month)
Call	2.3	4.5	5.1	5.3
Bills (excl. BOJ operations)	4.8 1.5	4.8 2.9	5.6 1.5	4.5
CDs	— (12.1975)	—	1.3	3.8
Gensaki	1.8	4.9	5.2	4.7

Characteristics   *Main market particular at Dec. 1982 (per cent)*

Market	Maturity length at 3.1981 by percentage	Borrower	Lender
Call	No fixed period (80) 2–7-day transaction (20)	City banks (52) Foreign banks (20) Security co.	Norin Chukin Bank (12) Federation of Credit Associations (12) Trust banks (31) Regional banks (14)
Bills	Maturity within: 1 month (88) 1–2 mths (12) over 2 mths (0)	City banks (92) Foreign banks (8)	Bank of Japan (35) Norin Chukin Bank (24) Federation of Credit Associations (15) Trust banks (13)
CDs	Maturity within: 3–4 mths (75) 4–5 mths (9) 3–6 mths (16)	City banks (48) Foreign banks (8) Regional banks (17) Long-term credit banks (8) Trust banks (9)	Corporations, Non-residents
Gensaki	Maturity within: 1 month (81) 1–2 mths (14) over 2 mths (5)	Security co. (65) City banks (10) Enterprises (5) Norin Chukin Bank (15)	Corporations (58) Non-residents (19) Norin Chukin Bank Regional governments (19)

Note: Percentages of market share refer to average balances during December 1982 for call and bills market and at end of month for CDs and *gensaki* market

Source: Adapted from *Kin'yū* June 1981, p. 21; Bank of Japan *Economic Statistics Monthly* January and August 1983

Table 1.5 Short-term government securities by holder (billion yen; (per cent))

	End Fiscal Year				
	1970	*1975*	*1980*	*1981*	*1982*
Government	691	1720	5161	2536	1923
	(35.6)	(41.7)	(43.5)	(21.9)	(19.6)
[Trust Fund Bureau]	[608]	[1244]	[3653]	[1798]	[1180]
Government-related	150	353	856	723	592
organisations	(7.7)	(8.5)	(7.2)	(6.3)	(6.0)
Bank of Japan	678	1863	5164	8158	7104
	(34.9)	(45.2)	(43.5)	(70.5)	(72.7)
Other	422	187	679	146	148
	(21.7)	(4.5)	(5.7)	(1.3)	(1.5)
Total	1941	4123	11 859	11 565	9767

Note: Note the virtual absence of holdings by financial institutions, corporations and individuals, although from time to time (e.g. 1970) foreign speculators used this market in their operations

Source: Bank of Japan *Economic Statistics Annual 1983* Tokyo, 1984

1980s. From 1985, large volumes of government bonds will be nearing maturity. Trade in these bonds in the secondary market will expose the gap between the issue rate and market rate on TBs, and put increased pressure on the MOF to rethink its strong pro-regulation position. The BOJ's activity in offering TBs by tender could be seen as the first step in preparing the market for an active short-term bonds trade by 1985.

The capital market

There was little change in the method of interest rate determination in the long-term bond market during the 1970s. Interest rates moved with more flexibility, but in general they were still determined by administrative fiat in the MOF.[47]

Some noteworthy changes did occur. The growth of the secondary market for long-term government bonds in the late 1970s and early 1980s put substantial pressure on the MOF to consider more closely the secondary market rate when it determined the interest rate for the issue market. By the early 1980s, the fundamental mechanism for setting the long-term government bond rate remained largely unchanged but there had been an important diversification in the medium-term bond market, where rates were set by tendering.

In the yen bond market (a market open primarily to sovereign foreign issuers and international financial institutions), the issue rate on bonds was often determined with reference to the market rate, but this was not consistently the case. The government intervened in order to maintain balance between the rates in the yen bond market and other domestic bond markets.

For the most part, however, the method of determining interest rates and the structure of the bond markets (the government bond market excluded) changed little. All issue rates were neatly slotted into a hierarchy determined by the MOF.

The arguments against deregulation of interest rates were many, but two stood out. First, any movement towards deregulation of interest rates would involve higher interest rates and the privileged groups that had access under the existing arrangements would be disadvantaged. Second, as a market-determined interest rate system would incorporate the assessment of risk, there would, it was argued, need to be a major re-education of the investing public. This argument was used to oppose deregulation in the corporate bond market.

The corporate bond market was based on the tradition of collateral. Default risk was virtually zero as corporations had to offer liens over land, plant and machinery to issue bonds. The US and British concept of risk being reflected in the yield of the bond was not a major factor in the Japanese system. There was a bond rating system but the reduction in risk meant that the investing public tended to support the highest yielding bonds. However, having risk explicitly incorporated into market terms in the bond market would not have necessitated a re-education of the investing public because Japanese investors were already experienced operators on overseas bond markets and Japanese corporations use international bond markets to issue considerable quantities of bonds.

In fact little change occurred in the bond markets because there were strong factions within the MOF (in particular the Banking Bureau) and the banking community which did not support change. Chapters 2, 3 and 7 examine the problems in more detail.

The discussion of change, and the need for it, was, however, one which became more central in the late 1970s and early 1980s. By the early 1980s the financial system was really in a transitional phase. Rarely did a week go by when newspapers or financial weeklies failed to mention a new plan or proposal for financial innovation. Some of this was merely speculatory but the interest underlined a new consciousness about financial matters. By the early 1980s many groups that had benefited from the highly regulated financial markets of the 1960s and 1970s could no longer see the benefits so clearly. Financial diversity and choice had become, to many, more important than having a close relationship with a particular bank. Banks continued to play the role of central financiers to most business enterprises but their position was less certain than it had been two decades earlier.

Although the city banks supported a whole range of deregulatory initiatives, they were not in favour of total deregulation. They did, for example, view the small lot savings of individuals as properly falling in the area of continuing regulation. The captive market was important to the continuation of the financial system as it was operating. In other words, the debate was not solely cast in terms of free markets but in terms of a notion of efficiency which reflected accepted methods of interaction and constraints. Changes in the administration of bank branching policy, which were implemented soon after the passage of the partially revised Banking Law (1981), showed the extent that the MOF viewed it necessary to adapt the character of regulation; it gave greater emphasis to self-regulation by the banks. That is, the MOF was seeking to shift the locus of decisionmaking on many issues regarding bank performance.[48]

Deregulation is very much a political question, as it might confer substantial costs as well as benefits on existing participants. Arguments for and against deregulation of interest rates, and other forms of regulation which constrain the allocative function of the market, could not be considered outside the context of such things as the existing financial products and financial performance of currently participating institutions. From the postwar period up to the late 1970s, the highly regulated financial system was at least adequate to the task of providing most of the financial services required by participants. There was, for much of this period, widespread support for the system within financial institutions, business corporations, the public service and the political world. The extent to which regulatory change occurs depends very much on the reactions of these groups to changes in the economic environment and on the successful advocacy of their positions in the policymaking process. This problem is one which can be best examined through analysis of the case studies that follow.

2 The government bond market
Conflict among the elite

Economic policymaking in Japan is one area where it has been assumed that the role of the public service was paramount in formulating and directing the evolution of policy. This chapter looks carefully at this assumption. It examines the political, institutional and market elements in the evolution of regulatory policy in the government bond market in Japan. The government bond market is the largest of Japan's bond markets, with outstanding issues at the end of fiscal 1982 of 96.5 trillion yen, or about 60 per cent of all outstanding bonds. The level of government bonds issued in fiscal 1982 was about ten times the level of domestic corporate bonds issued in the same year.[1] The development of the government bond market had a major impact on institutional relationships within the MOF, which managed the market, within the finance industry and between the industry and the public service. It also had an impact on the rate of change of policy in the bond markets more generally.

The events of the 1970s provide good support for the view that the LDP played a more important role in shaping policy outcomes than is often suggested.[2] In this chapter the focus is on three issues. First, the role of the LDP in constraining the activities of the MOF is established. Second, the motivation of the MOF in its pursuit of policy in the government bond market is examined. An assessment is made of the relative strengths of competing bureaus, the impact of interbureau rivalry on the development of the regulatory framework and how the MOF responded to often competing demands from the market place and the LDP. Finally the aims and problems of finance industry participants within the market are examined, together with the limitations they faced and how and why their approach to policy altered during the period under observation. A study of the approach and roles of each of these participants over the 1970s will show why, despite broadly similar general interests relating to economic activity, there was ample scope for important and deep-seated differences in the approach to the question of regulation. At the outset, however, the history and structure of the market are briefly outlined to put the subsequent analysis of policy positions into context.

THE STRUCTURE OF THE MARKET

Throughout the postwar period up to 1964–65, macroeconomic management in Japan relied heavily on the use of monetary policy. Tight monetary policy was used to remedy imbalances in the current account of the balance of payments. A relaxation in policy signified to business the green light to expand economic activity. Contrary to the practice in other industrialised countries, fiscal policy was not used periodically to boost the level of economic activity.[3] Following the implementation of the report of the Dodge Commission in 1949, which recommended a mix of fiscally conservative and monetarily stringent policies designed to reduce the rate of inflation and to keep government expenditure within the limits of revenue, the balanced budget concept became an entrenched pillar of postwar fiscal policy.[4]

The downturn of 1964–65, however, was different from earlier experiences. Even after the government had indicated a more relaxed stance on monetary policy, the economy failed to recover in line with expectations, and the sluggish state of the economy meant that taxes also failed to grow at the rate predicted in the budget of fiscal 1965. The government was faced with the dilemma of cutting back its expenditure (which would have compounded the recession) or funding the expenditure through deficit financing.

We need to consider briefly why the LDP, which had supported the balanced budget concept for a decade, was prepared to adopt a more Keynesian approach to fiscal policy and countenance the issue of government bonds. The answer is fairly straightforward. During the 1950s and the first half of the 1960s, Japan had experienced continued high growth, which in turn fuelled business and political expectations. In November 1964 the first Satō Cabinet was formed amid a weakening economic outlook. The failure of the economy to respond to an easing of monetary policy left the new Prime Minister with few options. There was strong support for the government to finance a fiscally expansive program with bond issues, and there were no voices in opposition.[5] The establishment of a government bond market was seen as giving added flexibility to government policy, but not as a major change in stance. The sparing use of government bonds in the 1960s showed that a less dogmatic version of fiscal conservatism was still functioning in Japan.[6] After a Cabinet reshuffle in June 1965, the MOF began internal discussions on the mechanics of issuing bonds when its minister, Fukuda Takeo, endorsed proposals to boost economic activity through fiscal expansion despite a probable shortfall of revenue. The first issue was made in January 1966.[7]

The issue market

Formally, and in fact, the structure of the government bond market and the relationship between the underwriters and the government changed little over the decade 1965–75.[8]

Even before a decision was made to issue government bonds, the elimination of various methods of issuing bonds illustrated the approach of the MOF to the development of a regulatory framework. In theory, there were at least four options available to the government: direct underwriting of the debt by the BOJ; issuing the debt by public tender; issuing the debt by public flotation; and the formation of an underwriting syndicate along the lines of those underwriting other bond issues. Issuing the debt by public tender and issuing the debt by public flotation were the two options often used in deregulated bond markets, and both implied that the interest rate attached to the bond would be determined in the marketplace. Although these methods were used to issue bonds in London and New York, they were not used at all in the Japanese bond markets in 1965. The emphasis that Japanese governments placed on the minimisation of the interest rate during the early postwar years ruled out the possibility that these two options would be considered. In the wide debate that ensued among businessmen, public servants and politicians, argument centred on the alternatives of underwriting by the BOJ and issue by an underwriting syndicate.[9]

The first alternative, that of direct underwriting by the BOJ, was less popular in both government and industry circles than the alternative of an underwriting syndicate. After it became clear that the government proposed to issue bonds during fiscal 1965, the various interested parties made their positions clear. In mid-August 1965, the governor of the BOJ, Usami Makoto, indicated his opposition to direct underwriting, and instead promoted the alternative of absorption through the market. Usami's comments were followed by those of the Minister of Finance, Fukuda, who stated that he did not envisage a direct BOJ role, preferring the option of having the bonds underwritten by private financial institutions and the TFB.[10] Direct underwriting by the BOJ was prohibited under Article 5 of the Finance Law (1947), unless specifically approved by Diet legislation.[11]

Opposition to direct underwriting was based upon a number of grounds. The BOJ did not want to become further controlled by, or subject to, the demands of the MOF. As the manager of monetary policy, the BOJ saw potential incompatibility between this responsibility and being required to underwrite government debt on demand. For example, if legislation permitted direct underwriting by the BOJ, it would permit the government to finance expenditure programs that the BOJ regarded as financially reckless. The chance of this occurring was only slight, but a change back to the pre-1947 legislation would reopen the possibilities of misuse of this tool. At a more general political level, resistance to direct underwriting reflected the experiences of the late 1930s when underwriting directly facilitated increased military expenditure, and concern was also expressed at the inflationary impact of such a method.[12] Opposition to BOJ underwriting also came from banks and securities companies, which saw the development of a government bond market similar in character to existing bond markets as offering a new area for the potential expansion of their respective businesses.[13] In short, the policy option that the BOJ should underwrite government bond issues was the subject of much opposition.

The final option open to the MOF was the flotation of bonds by an underwriting syndicate, a system which was being used for underwriting regional bonds, government-guaranteed bonds and industrial bonds.[14] Issuing bonds through an underwriting syndicate meant that participating institutions usually underwrote and then held a given proportion of bonds from each issue.

The MOF's support for a market based on the structure of existing bond markets was evident from three reports published in November 1965.[15] These MOF reports endorsed the principle of public underwriting, which, in the Japanese context, meant underwriting by syndicate. The policy produced was consistent with the proposition that established practices tended to dominate approaches to new problems. The fact that deregulated market options were not even seriously considered underlies the sharply constrained set of options which the public service began considering.

The underwriting syndicate which was formed to handle the government bond issues was a broadly based one, including city banks, regional banks, long-term credit banks, mutual banks, the Norin Chukin Bank, credit cooperatives, life insurance companies and the securities companies.[16] The government TFB also underwrote bonds but more irregularly, and it was not a member of the underwriting syndicate. Within the syndicate shares were relatively fixed, although the securities companies did not commit themselves to underwriting a defined proportion but preferred to bargain yearly for their share.

Table 2.1 outlines the shares underwritten by each group for selected years between fiscal 1965 and fiscal 1982. The table shows clearly the dominant role played by the city banks, regional banks, long-term credit banks and the securities companies. In fiscal 1965, they underwrote 82 per cent of the syndicate's share and in fiscal 1982, 77 per cent.

To facilitate negotiations between the floater (the government) and the underwriters (the financial institutions and the securities companies), the underwriting side appointed a managing underwriter which negotiated the quantity and conditions of the flotation. The position of managing underwriter by tradition rotated each year between four of the leading banks. After the formation of Daiichi-Kangyo Bank in 1971, these were Daiichi-Kangyo Bank, Fuji Bank, Mitsui Bank, and Mitsubishi Bank.

In addition to negotiating with the government, the managing underwriter was obliged to listen to and reconcile the opinions offered by the members of the underwriting syndicate. The position of the managing underwriter was potentially circumscribed by the diverse range of interests within the banking and securities community. This limited the range of issues which could be raised by the underwriters as a bloc, and reduced the extent of direct input by the underwriters into the policymaking process. Where the underwriters could not agree on a negotiating position, the MOF was by default put in a strong bargaining position. We shall examine this problem at length when the 1975–82 period is considered, but it is sufficient here to note that this problem of divergent interests was not of central importance during the initial ten years from 1965.

Although in a technical sense the BOJ was the government's agent in bond flotations, in practice the important decisions were made in the MOF. The

Table 2.1 Government bond underwriting (long-term bonds) (100 million yen; (per cent))

Actual shares[a]	1965	1970	Fiscal year 1975	1980	1982
Total floated	2 000	3 557	53 626.5	119 318	108 628
TFB	900 [45.0][b]	307 [8.6]	8 526.5 [15.9]	37 318 [31.9]	35 628 [32.8]
Underwriting Syndicate of which	1 100 (100.0)	3 250 (100.0)	45 100 (100.0)	82 000 (100.0)	73 000 (100.0)
City banks	444 (40.4)	1 408 (43.3)	18 222 (40.4)	25 857 (31.5)	25 180 (34.5)
Regional banks	219 (19.9)	622 (19.1)	8 430 (18.6)	12 124 (14.8)	11 807 (16.2)
Long-term credit banks	108 (9.6)	302 (9.3)	4 386 (9.7)	6 224 (7.6)	6 062 (8.3)
Trust banks	38 (3.5)	117 (3.6)	2 576.5 (5.7)	4 087 (5.0)	3 981 (5.5)
Mutual banks	38 (3.5)	117 (3.6)	1 873.5 (4.2)	3 065 (3.7)	2 985 (4.1)
Norin Chukin Bank	38 (3.5)	117 (3.6)	1 873.5 (4.2)	2 724 (3.3)	2 654 (3.6)
Association of Credit Cooperatives	38 (3.5)	117 (3.6)	2 107.5 (4.7)	3 406 (4.2)	3 316 (4.5)
Life insurance co.	38 (3.5)	117 (3.6)	2 576 (5.7)	3 814 (4.7)	3 713 (5.1)
Non-life insurance co.	—	—			
Securities companies	139 (12.6)	333 (10.2)	3 057 (6.8)	20 700 (25.2)	13 300 (18.2)

Notes: Long-term bonds include only 10-year interest-bearing bonds. Discount and
        medium-term bonds are excluded
   a   The major difference between actual and allotted shares is that the securities
        companies, although allotted a 10-per cent share, would not commit themselves to
        a fixed share. Their shares have fluctuated between 6.8 per cent (fiscal 1975) and
        25.2 per cent (fiscal 1980)
   b   The TFB share is the share relative to the total volume issued

Source: Kin'yū 4.1983, p. 110 and other compiled tables, mimeo

Government Debt Division within the Financial Bureau of the MOF was
responsible for the management of the government bond market. In the early
years of the market's operations, however, the Banking Bureau and the Budget

Bureau had more influence over the setting of the government bond interest rate than did the Financial Bureau. The Banking Bureau effectively controlled all long-term interest rates, and it insisted on a balance being maintained between the government bond rate and other long-term rates. The Budget Bureau's main aim was to minimise the size of the government debt. The position of both the Banking Bureau and the Budget Bureau was well established within the MOF. As a bureau whose functions were underdeveloped, the Financial Bureau began its operations by working well within the scope of these accepted principles. As was the case with other long-term interest rates in the late 1960s, the government bond rate was altered little and infrequently: between January 1965 and September 1973 inclusive, the highest interest rate offered on government bonds was 7.189 per cent and the lowest was 6.717 per cent, and the rate was changed only nine times.

After 1966, negotiations between the managing underwriter and the Financial Bureau fell into a regular pattern. Discussions of the proposed volume of issue in the following financial year were held once a year, and monthly meetings were held to discuss volumes and interest rates for monthly issues. These patterns changed little during the first decade of operations.[17]

The quantity to be floated for the coming fiscal year was formally decided at the yearly meeting of the Conference of Government Bond Issuance, held in November or December of the previous year. During the 1960s and early 1970s, these meetings served largely to acknowledge publicly what had previously been agreed to in lower level discussions. The speeches from the government side outlined the outlook for the coming year, and the need for cooperation on issues of general concern.[18] The concerns of the underwriting side were noted but apparently had little impact on policy. Table 2.2 summarises the issues of primary interest to the underwriting syndicate. (By the late 1970s, the character of these meetings had changed considerably, and they became a forum for strident criticism of government policy).

The comments made each year had a fairly predictable ring. In the early years of issue, underwriters called regularly for cuts in the quantity to be issued during the coming fiscal year, arguing that improved economic performance would obviate the need to expand the use of deficit finance. Further, at several meetings they also called for more flexibility in the determination of flotation conditions.

After the budget passed, meetings of the senior level of the Bond Flotation Council were held to discuss, in general terms, the MOF's proposed issue program for the first and second half of the fiscal year. These and the monthly meetings of director- and general-manager-level representatives of the underwriters with the MOF, could not be termed 'negotiations'. As with the Conference on Government Bond Issuance, opinions were exchanged and positions were noted, but it was not until 1978 that 'demands' were made and confrontation resulted.[19]

The underwriting syndicate had little real say in the determination of plans for the quantity of bonds to be issued in the coming year. Budget negotiations would normally begin in August and September, and when estimates of revenue

Table 2.2   Issues concerning the underwriting syndicate in the government bond market, fiscal 1967–80

	Attitude to total issue quantity	Attitude to issue shares	Attitude to flotation conditions	Attitude to secondary market
1967	Reduce volume if possible	Preference for reduction of syndicate's share		
1968	As above		Improved adjustability	
1969		Preference for reduction of syndicate's share	as above	
1970	Reduce volume if possible		Adjust interest rate	
1971	Reduce volume to the extent that taxes increase			
1972				Improve operation
1973		Preference for reduction of syndicate's share	Float according to market price	As above
1974		As above	As above	As above
1975		As above	Make condition adjustments more flexible	As above
1976	Consider fiscal efficacy of increasing issue		Improve conditions	As above
1977	As above	Increase role of Trust Fund Bureau	As above	Make national bond negotiable
1978		As above	Improve adjustability	Expand secondary market
1979	Reduce volume	As above	As above	
1980	Reduce volume	As above	As above	Improve negotiability and expand market size

Note: Drawn from statements to the Conference on Government Bond Issuance. In some years there were other issues which were of central importance, such as the desire to have government bonds made non-taxable (1967) and the desire to avoid issuance of deficit bonds (1972).

Source: *Kokusai hakkō sankō shiryō*, various issues; newspapers; interviews

and expenditure had been prepared, the difference would become the estimate for the next fiscal year's bond issues. The Financial Bureau, whose job it was to raise the funds, was presented with the estimates, formed largely as an outcome of Budget Bureau discussions. The quantity of government bonds to be floated was a dependent variable in the budgetary process. This process did not change substantially until the late 1970s. The relatively low level of bond issue during the decade 1965–75 was a major contributing factor to the congenial relationship between the MOF and the underwriters during this period.[20]

The secondary market

Between 1977 and 1982, the secondary market for government bonds grew 95-fold, mainly as the result of the relaxation of the restriction on the resale of government bonds. In 1982, the turnover was Y232 trillion (US$892 billion) or 68 per cent of the total turnover in the Japanese capital market. The development of this secondary market had the significant effect of providing an accurate 'market rate' estimator on short- and long-term assets, and continues to be a stimulus towards further deregulation of interest rates.

From the first issue in January 1966, to the late 1970s, there was no effective large-scale secondary market for government bonds: that is, the underwriters were unable to sell freely the scrip they had purchased because there was no framework within which these sales could take place.[21]

Secondary markets had in fact always posed a major problem in Japan. It was generally conceded that the long-term issue interest rates in all long-term bond markets were set below the rates that would have prevailed in an open market.[22] Had a secondary market existed, one would have expected the secondary market interest rate yields to be higher than the issue interest rate, which in turn would have attracted investors away from the issue market into the secondary market. Sales of new bonds would thus have become difficult (unless some form of coercion was used). For this reason, the establishment of a deregulated secondary market would have forced the MOF either to use coercion to sell the government bonds or to allow the general level of long-term bond rates to rise to market or near-market levels. Neither option was immediately palatable but in particular the second option was, in practice, not available.

The LDP was a strong supporter of low regulated interest rates, and it extended this policy from the private business sector to the government sector when the latter became temporarily short of funds. For all concerned (the LDP, the MOF and the underwriters), the least troublesome option was to avoid establishing a secondary market and to use instead an alternative mechanism involving the BOJ.

Up to and including fiscal 1974, the BOJ pursued a policy of repurchasing bonds from the underwriters after they had been held by the underwriters for at least one year. The purchases formed a part of the BOJ's overall effort to ensure that money supply growth was in line with the economy's needs. Purchase operations fluctuated considerably, and were not simply an arrangement to relieve the underwriters of their government bond holdings. Nevertheless, the policy was effective in limiting the growth of the holdings of those members of the underwriting syndicate who did not want to hold the government bonds. It also removed the risk of holding them, in the sense that the repurchase price or 'secondary market price' was approximately the same as the purchase price. The net result of this policy was that the aggregate volume of bonds held by underwriters before 1974 grew very little.[23]

After fiscal 1974, the BOJ altered its repurchase policy. In the five years to the end of fiscal 1979, holdings by private financial institutions grew from 1.9 trillion yen to 23.6 trillion yen. This growth was one factor which led to the significant deterioration in the relationship between the MOF and the underwriters, and the demands for the formation of a secondary market: that is, for the introduction of sales of government bonds at market prices by the city banks and the BOJ.

In the period 1975 to 1982, the most important factor producing change in the structure of the government bond market was the volume of bonds issued. The volume of bonds grew so rapidly that it destabilised the existing practices. After a secondary market for government bonds was established, that market moved at times in a direction opposite to that of other long-term markets. The underwriting of government bonds in the absence of adequate opportunities for resale led to increased pressure from the underwriters on the MOF to change its policy on sale of bonds in the secondary market, and to demands for a wider range of asset types more closely linked with the structure of their liabilities.[24] The growth in the flotation of government bonds is shown in Table 2.3.

In fiscal 1975, the BOJ adjusted down its purchases in line with the reduced requirements of money supply growth. Further, as demand for government expenditure through the FILP increased, the TFB's willingness to hold government bonds also fell. These adjustments marked the beginning of a new relationship between the government and the underwriters. As the volume of government bonds floated increased, the volume held by the underwriting syndicate soared by a disproportionate amount. By the end of 1979, financial institutions held 42 per cent of outstanding bonds in a pie that had grown tenfold in five years. The shares of the main government bodies involved, the BOJ and the TFB, fell significantly and the arrangement whereby the TFB acted as a surrogate secondary market for resale of syndicate holdings broke down completely.

The underwriters apparently had little difficulty in absorbing the increased demands of the public sector during 1975–78. The low demand for bank loans during this period was an important factor permitting this expansion. The expansion did, however, begin to cause the underwriters concern, not with the volume per se, but with the lack of negotiability of their assets. In fiscal 1976, the managing underwriter, Mitsui Bank, focused attention on the resale restrictions which applied to the holdings of the main financial institutions. During the negotiations which lasted from late September 1976 to early 1977, the Financial Bureau revealed a new, more sympathetic attitude to Mitsui Bank's arguments. The agreement reached was an important compromise,

Table 2.3   Flotation of government bonds (100 million yen)

Fiscal Year	Quantity	Market[a]	TFB	Dependence ratio[b] per cent	Interest claim on government expenditure per cent
1965	1 972	1 085	887	5.2	0.3
1966	6 656	6 656	—	14.9 (16.9)	0.9
1967	7 094	6 110	984	13.8 (16.2)	2.1
1968	4 621	4 375	245	7.7 (10.9)	3.2
1969	4 126	3 826	300	5.9 (7.2)	4.0
1970	3 472	3 172	300	4.2 (5.4)	3.5
1971	11 871	9 172	2 700	12.4 (4.5)	3.4
1972	19 500	17 000	2 500	16.3 (17.0)	3.8
1973	17 662	14 722	2 940	12.0 (16.4)	4.6
1974	21 600	17 400	4 200	11.3 (12.6)	4.4
1975	52 805	44 405	8 400	25.3 (9.4)	5.3
1976	71 982	61 844	10 138	29.4 (29.9)	7.5
1977	95 612	85 612	10 000	32.9 (29.7)	8.0
1978	106 740	103 740	3 000	31.3 (32.0)	9.5
1979	134 720	108 079	26 641	34.7 (39.6)	11.3
1980	141 702	102 018	39 684	32.6 (33.5)	12.7
1981	128 999	84 759	44 240	27.5 (26.2)	14.2
1982	140 447	103 447	37 000	29.7 (21.0)	15.8

Notes: a   Market includes purchases by underwriters of 10-year bonds, 5-year discount bonds since fiscal 1976 and through public tendering since fiscal 1978

b   Dependence ratio = quantity of bonds issued ÷ expenditure through general account, expressed as a percentage. Figures in brackets were initial budgetary estimates for each year

Source: From tables provided by Yamaichi Securities, October 1980, mimeo; MOF, private correspondence.

gaining the underwriters a significant concession without weakening the MOF's position.[25]

In permitting sales of government bonds which had been held for a minimum of one year, the MOF was ensuring that a direct link between primary and secondary yields would not be established. As a result, the MOF believed that the concession of allowing sales after a one-year period would not weaken its position in negotiating new issue yields. From the underwriter's viewpoint, being able to sell, even after the one-year lag, was a considerable improvement on the 'no sale' framework; being able to sell at some stage gave them more flexibility in managing their bond portfolios. It was an agreement reflecting a consensus-cum-compromise solution which benefited both parties. Resale after one year meant that these holdings could be reduced if there was a need, or if a favourable opportunity presented itself in the secondary market. In the climate of falling interest rates which existed after 1975, the underwriters were little concerned that a direct link was not established.[26]

The new policy allowed the rapid growth of the secondary market. The market provided a close, if not exact, estimate for the market interest rate for government bonds,[27] and highlighted discrepancies between the interest rate attached to new issues of government bonds and the interest rate in the secondary market. After interest rates began to increase in late 1978 this problem emerged as one of great importance.

During the period 1979–81, further pressure was applied to the MOF by the underwriters about the state of the issue and secondary markets for government bonds. After a bitter struggle over setting the interest rate in the issue market for government bonds in April 1979, the government relaxed its position toward the secondary market as part of a new government bond policy announced in May 1979.[28] This new policy reduced the holding time from one year to seven to nine months. In the face of almost total collapse of the market in early 1981, the period before resale was further reduced to one hundred days. The current secondary market for government bonds is vigorous and deep and provides the main forum for trading in bonds in Japan today.

THE ROLE OF THE LDP

In the establishment phase of the government bond market, the LDP played an important if indirect role in the framing of government policy. The LDP's support for the bond issue option paved the way for its consideration within the MOF, and in a sense the LDP's policy stance on interest rates (its support of low interest rates) effectively ruled out the selection of any deregulated market option. It was likely that these options would have been rejected anyway, given the strength of the Budget Bureau's resolve to minimise the cost of government debt and the Banking Bureau's concern for a rigid hierarchy of interest rates, but the position of the LDP was sufficient to set the tenor of the discussion, which was marked by broad agreement on key objectives.

The role of the LDP in the 1970s was instrumental in defining the shape of the government bond market, and by virtue of this was also the catalyst in forcing the public service to consider new options to accommodate the LDP. The quantity of bonds issued was largely an outcome of the LDP's intransigent position on taxation, a position which increased in significance in the second half of the 1970s.

Until 1975, there was little need for great concern with the revenue side of the budget. Revenue had kept pace with expenditure and, in addition, had provided funds for a regular cut in taxes. From 1965 to 1974 the controlled issue of government bonds gave no cause for alarm. There was continuing political interest in the relative scale of government debt and in fiscal 1970 the MOF was able to reduce the level of government bonds to less than 5 per cent of government expenditure, in line with the recommendation of the report of the Fiscal System Council of 1967.[29] The formation and implementation of debt management policy had been carried out smoothly within the existing financial framework, drawing on previously established methods and relationships.

There was no need for LDP involvement in a market which was creating few problems for the MOF and the participating members of the finance industry. The market provided a short-term stopgap for revenue shortfalls. The conservatism of the 1960s remained largely in charge.

The tight monetary policy which extended from mid-1973 into early 1975 was accompanied by a weakening demand for investment funds. In contrast with previous periods of tight monetary policy, which were aimed at the reduction of pressure on the foreign exchange account, the central objective of the 1973–75 tight monetary policy was to reduce the level of inflation. The first quarter of 1975 saw a 2 per cent fall in GNP. The original budget plan for fiscal 1975 emphasised the continued importance the government was attaching to price stability, and it also envisaged a slight cutback in the level of national bonds it planned to float. But as the economy continued to deteriorate the plan was abandoned. The slowness of the recovery led to a stimulatory package in June (also related to upper house elections), and by October the entire original allocation of national bonds for fiscal 1975 had already been issued.[30]

The level of bond flotation in fiscal 1975 and thereafter was quite different from the earlier period. In fiscal 1975, over 5 trillion yen was issued. Within three years (that is, fiscal 1978) this had more than doubled to 10.67 trillion yen. The dependence ratio (the volume of national bonds to general account expenditure) also rose rapidly, from 11.3 per cent in fiscal 1974 to 31.3 per cent in fiscal 1978.

The fall in economic activity in 1974–75 cut into the high rate of growth of government revenues, which had been a generally accepted fact of economic life. Tax revenues actually decreased. After the major reduction in tax rates in 1974, the failure of revenues to grow at the expected rate in 1975, and the decision to reduce taxes slightly, led to a substantial widening of the gap between revenue and expenditure. That gap was filled by issuing national bonds.

Between 1954 and 1974, personal income tax rates were reduced eleven times and increased only once.[31] Tax reductions had become a feature of the postwar political and economic environment. In every year preceding a House of Representatives election from 1958 to 1972, there was a reduction in tax. In addition to reflecting fiscal conservatism, reducing taxation rates was seen by the LDP as having important political advantages. Unfortunately, the tax cuts contributed to the size of the gap which developed between government revenue and expenditure;[32] the fall in the rate of growth of taxes in 1975 was the central factor in restraining the growth of revenues. On the expenditure side, an institutionalised budgetary decision-making process saw the growth of the budget continue relatively unabated. The LDP faced a choice between increasing taxes and bond flotation.

Increasing the tax rate was not regarded as a feasible proposition politically. The LDP held 271 out of 491 seats in the House of Representatives, which gave it only a bare majority in terms of control of the Diet's committees, and between late 1974 and 1976 it had to contend with the turmoil of Prime Minister Tanaka's resignation and later the Lockheed scandal. The point to be stressed is that the policy response of cutting taxes in 1974, and later permitting budgetary expenditures to run ahead of revenues, was based upon established practices and constant and distorting political imperatives.

The LDP responded to the 1974–75 slump in economic activity in much the same way as it had done to earlier recessions. The idea that a tax reduction would necessarily boost economic activity and not create a Keynesian style 'liquidity trap' where 'additions to income are saved and money is not borrowed despite lower interest rates'[33] was firmly entrenched in both the business world and the LDP. Both consumer and investor responses in the period after the 1973–74 crisis were, however, very different. They reflected considerable uncertainty about the future of the Japanese economy, and the policy adopted by the LDP was not flexible enough to deal with this change.

The shift in 1975 to a policy of raising large volumes of government bonds reflected the important role played by the LDP in determining sensitive fiscal policy decisions. The LDP had to balance the demands of interest groups and appropriate policy action. Political necessity came first.[34]

The MOF for its part was bound by the parameters set by the LDP. It was unable to lift taxes or cut expenditures. Instead, its responsibility was that of implementing the policy of the LDP, which it tried to do within the established framework of the government bond market.

During the period 1975–80, the LDP and hence the government had four possible options. Two options—of mixing increased or decreased expenditure with increased taxes—posed major problems because of political resistance to increasing taxes. With the economy in a depressed state there were calls for cuts in taxes and increased expenditure. The use of this option or the option of keeping taxes steady in an environment of increasing expenditure reflected the pressures on the LDP, and perhaps the belief that following these paths would boost economic growth and eventually lead to a cutback in bond issues. The issue of bonds was endorsed partly by default and partly because it made short-term economic sense.

The LDP did become concerned with the level of government bond issue when the MOF was required to use an alternative issuing method in 1975. Before 1975, all but one issue of national bonds had been executed under the Finance Law, which allowed the provision of supplementary funds to public corporations that were financed through the budgetary framework. These bonds, known as construction bonds, were issued without the need for special accompanying legislation. With the rapid growth of the gap between government revenue and expenditure, the construction bond framework became inadequate.[35] From late 1975, the government was forced to start issuing deficit bonds to finance the shortfall in revenue to cover everyday recurring public expenditure. Issuing deficit bonds required annual legislation specifying the quantity of bonds to be floated. In terms of accountability and an opportunity for the Diet to intercede, the issuing of deficit bonds offered a forum to debate the problems of national bond policy. Moreover, as the opposition controlled the House of Representatives Budget Committee from 1976 to 1980, the Diet provided a potential forum for the discussion of government bond policy.[36]

However, the existence of this forum had little impact on government bond policies.

The debates in the House of Representatives' Finance Committee (HRFC) on government bond market policy from 1975 to 1980 were lengthy but had little impact on policymaking. The 'debates', if they can be called that, were sessions when the Opposition asked a range of questions and senior public servants or the Minister of Finance provided vague answers. Invited guests, such as the heads of the Federation of Bankers' Associations and the Bond Underwriters' Association or the governor of the BOJ, added informed comment and sometimes trenchant criticism of government policy, but with little apparent effect on policy.[37]

The role of the public service in these debates was to provide information, but it was under little pressure to listen. As in other policy fora, LDP backbench members had no opportunity to participate in debates, as the government attempted to push through its policy proposals in minimum time. Of course the LDP had internal committees which discussed policy, but in the area of government bond policy they made little contribution to the development of policy.

In the HRFC debate of 1975, the Minister of Finance, Ōhira Masayoshi, said that the need to issue deficit bonds was regrettable, but necessary to avoid a deeper recession. Ōhira refused to acknowledge the fact that increasing the level of issue would require an increase in taxes at some stage, and public service officials all refused to be drawn on the issue.[38] The statements of Ōhira and the public servants added little to the debate or policy, and in subsequent years the debates became more perfunctory in the sense that the basic premises of the government's policy were not challenged.

Indeed, in 1977, against its initial intention, the LDP agreed to an opposition amendment to reduce taxes by 300 billion yen. In an interview with one well-known Democratic Socialist Party parliamentarian the tax cut was recounted with great pride, and it was made abundantly clear that tax increases were not acceptable.[39] The parliamentary opposition had nothing to gain politically from endorsing electorally unpopular moves, even if they made good economic sense. Even though the 1977 'forced' tax cut was small, it showed that the option of increasing taxes was largely theoretical.

The LDP leadership was prepared finally to consider the enormous shortfall of central government revenue as a serious economic problem. At the beginning of the campaign for the 1979 House of Representatives election, Prime Minister Ōhira argued publicly that tax increases would be necessary if further increase in the government's deficit was to be avoided. The hostile reaction from within his own party, and his subsequent retraction, indicate the difficulty the LDP leadership and the MOF faced in attempting to re-establish a closer parity between government revenues and expenditure. By the end of 1979, it was clear that any further increase in the level of long-term government bond issues could result in substantial instability creeping into interest rates in the bond markets. The backbench LDP members, however, were considering their own electoral positions. Although the state of the bond markets affected the general level of interest rates, the linkages were unimportant in political terms. A policy of increased taxes, whatever the explanation given, was bound in the short term to have a negative impact on electoral popularity. The postponement of the policy of increasing taxes, the small reduction in taxes which the opposition forced on the government and the inability to cut back expenditure levels, all aggravated the problem and widened the gap between revenue and expenditures. The LDP's fear of tax increases and their electoral repercussions played an important role in shaping these variables, and hence indirectly played an important part in structuring the character of the government bond problem.

Again in 1980 the Prime Minister, Suzuki Zenkō, made the reduction in flotation of government bonds one of the central tenets of his government's administration. In his effort to bridge the revenue–expenditure gap he was no more successful than Fukuda and Ōhira before him, despite cutting back the growth in expenditure to historically low levels. Sluggish economic growth in fiscal 1982 again set the scene for an expansion in the level of debt flotation after it had been contained in 1981. The LDP's blanket refusal to increase taxes played an important role in forcing the pace of regulatory change in the government bond market, including the decision to allow banks to sell government long-term securities from April 1983.[40]

Seen in the above terms, the MOF did not control policy outcomes, but in some senses acted as an implementor of policy. Efforts to float alternative revenue-related policies by the MOF were thwarted by the prevailing political climate. The LDP, by acting as a force preventing the re-establishment of an equilibrium between revenue and expenditure, defined the range of available policy options in the government bond market.

THE ROLE OF THE MOF

Whereas the role of the LDP was directly relevant in determining the scale of issue in the government bond market, and indirectly relevant elsewhere, the MOF was the forum for discussions which determined the character of the market, the regulations and the management practices in use.

There were several MOF bureaus intimately involved in the government bond market area. The Financial Bureau was responsible for ensuring that the funds necessary for budgetary expenditures were available. It was also responsible, through the Government Debt Division, for the implementation of the government's bond market operation and policy. The Banking Bureau, with its responsibility for long-term interest rates, exercised considerable influence over the setting of bond market interest rates. The Taxation Bureau and the Budget Bureau were involved indirectly. They were responsible for formulating estimates of government revenue and expenditure which, until the late 1970s, determined the extent of the Financial Bureau's flotation activities. In recent years, the Minister's Secretariat has apparently become more involved in coordinating disputes between the relevant bureaus but it is not clear that its role has developed beyond that of a mediator.[41]

The Financial Bureau

The role of the Financial Bureau grew with the increasingly large flotations of government bonds, and the growing difficulties experienced with the implementation of the existing system of interest rate determination.

Officials of the Financial Bureau readily concede that issue interest rate yields during 1978–80 were below the market level.[42] In an effort to overcome some of the problems involved in marketing bonds which yielded below the market rate, they attempted to diversify their sources of funds and methods of funding. But within these areas also, their endeavours did not overcome the difficulties of operating within a strongly regulated market. Two examples will help to explain the problems of adapting the existing system to new demands and requirements.

Between 1975 and 1978, bank holdings of long-term government bonds grew rapidly. In that period, the ratio of new government bond underwriting to new deposits of the city banks grew alarmingly, from 24 per cent in fiscal 1975 to 90 per cent in fiscal 1979. Government policy was effectively forcing banks into maintaining an inappropriately high ratio of long-term assets to short-term liabilities. From the standpoint of sound banking, this was not a welcome trend.

In response to this problem, in 1978 the Financial Bureau began to consider the available options at the short end of the market. But its options were constrained by the activities of financial institutions already tapping various segments of the market. It could not issue bonds with a two-year maturity, as this was a major source of deposit funds for city banks and regional banks. Five-year debentures were already being issued by the long-term credit banks, which made even four-year bonds a difficult proposition. The result was the introduction of a three-year maturity tender issue system in mid-1978.

Since the introduction of the public tendering system, a greater and more consistent role of the market in forming interest rates might have been expected. That was not always the case. For example, for the five issues of three-year government bonds between July 1979 and April 1980 the Financial Bureau chose on the whole not to accept the judgment of the market. Whereas the average ratio of quantity subscribed to quantity offered by the Financial Bureau was 1.5, the average ratio of quantity accepted by the Financial Bureau to the quantity initially offered was 0.8. The market response to issue offers is not in question, as it generally exceeded substantially the quantity on offer by the MOF.[43] The central issue is how far the MOF was prepared to accept the judgment of the market.

In fiscal 1979, the MOF's original aim was to raise 2.7 trillion yen by medium-term tender issues. The failure to do this (it actually raised 1.93 trillion yen) was largely attributable, according to one interviewee, to the resistance to paying going market prices. The Financial Bureau official estimated that double the quantity of bonds could have been floated had the MOF been prepared to accept rates up to 0.7 percentage points higher.[44] The use of terms like 'poor market conditions' reflected more the attitudes of the Ministry than the actualities of the market. The term 'poor market conditions' merely indicated that the MOF was not prepared to pay the going market interest rates at the time.

There is also evidence that, on occasions, parts of the MOF attempted to exert direct influence on the participants in the market. According to a securities company source, the Securities Bureau offered 'advice' from time to time on the quantities and interest rate yields that should be bid by the securities companies. One such instance was in late 1979 when the MOF announced the fourth issue of two-year government bonds by tender. Securities companies would have preferred to avoid the issue, as market interest rates were climbing rapidly. The minimal difference between the average bid and the highest bid (0.017 percentage points) is one indication of the pressured character of the bidding. Another indication of this was the lower level of the interest rate. Compared with the third issue of two-year bonds in September 1979, the December issue yield was 0.089 percentage points higher. In the same period, short-term interest rates had risen by over 1 percentage point and NTT interest rate yields (a representative long-term bond rate) by approximately 0.5 percentage points. One could have expected a rise between these two limits.

The Financial Bureau had very little direct influence on the bids of the underwriters. The extent to which securities companies and banks follow the 'request' of their supervisory bureau reflects, according to another source, the degree of perceived obligation to that bureau and not the character of the relationship with the Financial Bureau. The operation of this forced bidding was some consolation to the Financial Bureau when the 'acceptable range' of interest rates, defined by the Banking Bureau, was not at one with market realities; but as a long-term alternative to deregulated interest rates it was far from satisfactory.

The level of flotation by tender of two-, three- and four-year bonds gradually expanded during fiscal 1981 and 1982 and the projected flotation level for fiscal 1983 was 5322 billion yen, an increase of over 85 per cent above the original prediction for fiscal 1982. To succeed in its objective to float this high volume, the government will have to pay close attention to interest yields. Tenderers have an accurate means of evaluating the medium- and short-term markets with the high volume of government bonds of those maturities available in the secondary market.

The inversion of the interest rate in the issue market for government bonds and the interest rate of 'AA' corporate bonds in early 1983 illustrated the gradual growth in the role of the market. This is making easier the job of the Financial Bureau. Within the Financial Bureau the Government Bonds Problem Research Group (*Kokusai mondai kenkyūkai*) has become something of a focus for analysing the problems of the government bond market, and this too should contribute to the growth in the overall function of the Bureau.[45]

The banking bureau

Responsibility for private sector long-term interest rates and banking sector deposit rates (besides having some influence in setting the official discount rate) fell within the domain of the Banking Bureau. Control of these interest rates gave the Banking Bureau considerable practical influence over the entire regulated sector of interest rates. Being responsible for the banking industry as a whole, the Bureau always strove to maintain what it considered to be an appropriate balance between the sectors for which it was responsible. Within this framework, the Bureau maintained a policy of ensuring balance between public sector and private sector interest rates. Sometimes this was at the expense of distorting the relationship between issue market rates and secondary market rates.

If government bonds were floated at the market interest rate, recent experience would suggest that, at the present relationship between volumes issued in the public and private sectors, an inversion of interest rates would occur within the primary issue rates: that is, government bonds would bear an interest rate above some other long-term bonds. In order to maintain sales of these bonds, interest rates in the private and semi-public sector would be forced to rise; and this would run against the important low interest rate philosophy of the LDP. Whereas it might have been the best policy from the viewpoint of the Financial Bureau, it would have been the first step in breaking down the regulated character of the long-term bond market. This would end the power base of the MOF and be resisted by the LDP. As Table 2.4 shows, the gap between the long-term government bond market and other bond markets fell significantly between the beginning of the 1970s and the beginning of the 1980s.

Over the decade of the 1970s, the role of each individual bureau did change. Policy developed piecemeal, and only then when the integrity of the market was itself under threat. The structure of the MOF and the character of interaction between bureaus contributed to the shape of the policymaking process. Each bureau had its jurisdiction, which was jealously guarded and was amenable to change only under extreme pressure. In the 1950s and 1960s, the banking industry and the Banking Bureau were at the centre of the financial system. During the late 1970s, the changes in financial flows, and in particular the demands of the public sector, had created major internal inconsistencies within that system, seen to good effect in the operation of the government bond market. The government tapped that market until it became destabilised, to the point where the secondary rate for government bonds frequently exceeded the secondary rate for other types of bonds.

When the gap between the issue market and the secondary market was small, the Banking Bureau had little difficulty in reducing the long-term bond rate. In July 1980 a substantial reduction was achieved with the aid of LDP backbench pressure. However, the fall in the long-term bond rate meant a fall in the government bond rate. By the end of the 1970s, the Banking Bureau was constrained in its manipulation of the former by movement of the secondary market yield in the latter. In November 1980, when the Banking Bureau tried to reduce both the long-term bond rate and the government bond rate it was hampered by the trend in the secondary market for government bonds. Only a small reduction was achieved, despite considerable purchases by the MOF in the market.[46] Not only was the volume of bonds issued hampering the Banking

Table 2.4:   Margins between issue yields on government bonds and other bonds, 1972–82

	July 1972	Dec. 1975	Dec. 1980	Dec. 1981	Dec. 1982
Long-term government bonds (10-year) Actual yield	6.717	8.227	8.227	8.367	7.969
Government-guaranteed bonds (10 years)	+0.151	+0.164	+0.056	+0.008	+0.010
Regional government bonds (10 years)	+0.304	+0.412	+0.102	+0.008	+0.010
Industrial bonds (AA, 10 years)	+0.451	+0.667	+0.182[a]	+0.042[a]	+0.053[a]
Bank debentures[b] (5-year)	+0.383	+0.073	−0.327	−0.367	+0.031
Reference: Secondary market yield[c]	—	—	8.931	8.150	8.290

Notes: a   12-year bonds
b   These are bonds issued in the long-term credit banks and are included to show a representative trend among medium-term bonds. The interest in the primary market in each of these markets was determined by the MOF
c   Interest rate yield for long-term bonds on sale in the secondary bond market. I have included only dates from 1980–82 because in 1975 the secondary market was non-existent. The yields are for the month before, simple average, so they do not reflect exactly the circumstances at bargaining time

Source: Nihon kōgyō ginkō Shōken binran 1979–80 and Kin'yū, 4.1983, p. 107

Bureau's ability to handle the long-term government bond rate flexibly, but the link between the long-term government bond rate and private long-term bond rates also affected the MOF's ability to handle flexibly overall long-term interest rate policy.

Whereas the strength of the Banking Bureau was reduced, the power of the Financial Bureau (through the Government Debt Division) to make small independent adjustments to the long-term government bond rate (within a range of ± 0.3 per cent) gradually emerged in 1980–81. When the required changes fell outside this range, the influence of the Financial Bureau fell sharply, as consideration of the interest rate structure became the central concern. The trend, however, is indisputable: the role of market forces and the Financial Bureau is growing.

Rather than alter the fundamentals of the system to permit greater allocative efficiency, the Banking Bureau maintained the central features of the earlier system, including the regulation of interest rates. But in doing this it had to make other concessions. The long-term market, constrained by the low interest rate, could not satisfy the public sector's demand for funds. Hence, while in the period under examination regulated interest rates still existed in the long-term markets, the maintenance of those rates led to some changes in other short-term markets.

A threshold effect had begun to operate. Up to a certain level, the government was able to issue its debt through the bond markets within the regulated interest rate framework. Beyond that level, the power of the MOF to control the market operators declined. The period can best be seen as one of transition from a completely regulated system to a deregulated system. That point has yet to be reached, and hence the remarkable inconsistencies involved in the transition are still very much in evidence.

The different interests of each bureau meant that some were inclined to support the deregulated market options more than others. To the Financial Bureau the deregulated market option meant that it would be able to fulfil its quota with a minimum of fuss. The greater the level of regulation the harder it was to achieve its goals. During the 1970s the Banking Bureau and the Budget Bureau made concessions on the issue of regulation, and the extent of these concessions was one measure of how far the existing regulatory framework for the government bond market had become unworkable and traditional interest rate relationships upset. The problems with the existing set of arrangements were also seen in the relationship between the MOF and the underwriting syndicate. It was after all the underwriters which had to bear the cost of supporting the existing regulations.

Negotiations with the underwriters

Negotiations between the MOF and the underwriters held during the two years from August 1978 and summarised in Table 2.5 provide evidence of a radical change in the character of the relationship between the underwriters and the floater.

By early 1979, the interest rate climate had changed from declining to increasing. In the short-term money markets, rates had begun to increase, although not to the same extent as long-term yields in the secondary government bond market. In January 1979, '6.1 per cent bonds' (known as *rokuichi*) first appeared on the secondary market, and the yield gap stood at nearly 0.6 percentage points (very large for the time). During the monthly negotiation between the MOF and the syndicate, the MOF did not agree to the underwriters' request for higher interest rates, but as a compromise was forced to cut the proposed issue volume back by approximately 80 per cent to 100 billion yen, the smallest monthly issue since September 1976.

As the gap between the issue and the secondary market interest rate widened, the February negotiations for the March issue intensified. The MOF gave no indication that it would change its position. The managing underwriter responded provocatively, stating that unless the MOF increased the interest rate it would not underwrite.[47] On this occasion a compromise was again reached,

Table 2.5 Controversial negotiations between the MOF and the underwriting syndicate, 1978–81

Negotiation date	Issue month	Gap between primary & secondary rate[a] (A)	Yield trend[b]	Relation with NTT[c]	Impact on interest rate (B)	A/B in per cent	Impact on quantity (Q)
8.78	9.78	0.463	Up	Normal	No change	—	No impact on Q
1.79	2.79	0.716	Up	Normal	No change	—	Q reduced
2.79	3.79	0.853	Up	Normal	Up 0.402	47	Q reduced
3.79 into 4.79	4.79	1.161	Up	Inverse	Up 0.704	61	Q increased
6.79	7.79	1.717	Up	Normal-Inverse	No change	—	No change
7.79	8.79	1.291	Down	Inverse	Up 0.502	39	
11.79	12.79	1.564	Up	Inverse	No change		
2.80	3.80	1.474	Up	Inverse	Up 0.302	20	
3.80	4.80	1.474	Up	Normal	Up 0.798	54	Q reduced
6.80	7.80	-0.637	Down	Normal	Down 0.342	54	
11.80	12.80	0.055	Up	Inverse	Down 0.319	Not calculable	Q reduced
4.81	5.81	-0.242	Up	Normal	Down 0.359	148	Q reduced

Notes: a Calculated with the weekly price closest (after) the 20th of the month. The exceptions were Issue month 4.79 taken on 30 March 1979 and 4.80 taken on 4 April 1980

b Up or Down recorded according to relationship with yield of the previous month

c Normal: NTT > government bond yield

Source: Raw weekly interest rate data from Yamaichi Securities; information for 'Impact on quantity' from interviews

involving a small increase in the interest rate yield and a small reduction in the volume of bonds to be issued.

In March, disagreement between the two parties led to a complete breakdown in negotiations.[48] The abandonment of the monthly meeting between the underwriters and the Financial Bureau underlined the extraordinary character of the environment. Indeed, newspaper articles of early April 1979 referred to the negotiations as a write-off.[49] Had this been the case, it would have been the first occasion since 1966 that a monthly issue had not occurred.

The deadlock was broken by the intervention of the Prime Minister in the debate on whether the official discount rate should be raised. The Prime Minister dropped his opposition to an increase in the official discount rate, thus providing room for an increase in all long-term interest rates.[50] Although the MOF had initially argued that general economic conditions did not justify a change in the government bond rate, its position was based more on the problem that an independent rise in the long-term government bond rate would pose for the overall structure of long-term bond rates. For example, the March increase of 0.4 percentage points had lifted the primary yield on government bonds above the yield on five-year interest-bearing debentures for the first time. A further independent adjustment would make these debentures impossible to sell. A rise in the yield on government bonds would necessitate other rates rising if the existing structure of interest rates were to be maintained. The problem in essence was that the volume issued in the long-term government bond market was beginning to affect the performance of government bonds in the secondary market. The trend therefore was atypical in the overall market, but the regulated structure of the primary long-term markets made it difficult to accommodate. The Banking Bureau, in particular, was an important influence on restricting the negotiating hand of the Financial Bureau, as it attempted to maintain the existing structure of interest rates, and to satisfy LDP groups which were opposed to a rise.[51] An agreement was finally reached on 16 April 1979 when the MOF secured an increased volume of issue as a trade-off for the higher rate of return.[52]

The stand taken by the underwriters in the period January–April 1979 was their first concerted attempt to have their view considered more fully. It can be argued that, up to this point, the cost to the syndicate of the existing arrangements was low, but that negotiations in 1979 and 1980 took place in a completely different market situation involving considerable cost to the syndicate. The result was that a very different attitude towards the MOF was adopted by the underwriters.

The underwriting side had problems, including in particular the uncertainty of some members as to how far the MOF's bond flotation program should be questioned. The conflict between the rates on interest-bearing bank debentures (issued by the long-term credit banks) and government bonds has already been mentioned. A further source of conflict arose from the fact that financial institutions with surplus funds were more prepared to go along with the government position than were the city banks, which had to finance their purchases at least partly from short-term fund sources. During the negotiations of March–April 1979, for example, some groups within the syndicate were prepared to underwrite 500 billion yen without any change in rates. Needless to say, the city banks were strongly opposed, forming the vanguard of the opposition to the acceptance of such a compromise.[53]

The period February–April 1980 had many similarities with the conflict of early 1979. The trouble began with a sudden increase in the gap between the issue market and the secondary market in February 1980. On 15 February the gap was 0.992 percentage points for the longest maturity bonds. The gap on 6.1 per cent bonds stood at almost 2 percentage points. In its submission to the Financial Bureau, the managing underwriter argued that, notwithstanding the traditional link between the official discount rate and the long-term bond rate, and the fact that the official discount rate was traditionally not adjusted during February when the budget was before the House of Representatives, the link between the long- and short-term interest rates should be broken. Although initially it had made no offer to alter conditions, the Financial Bureau reconsidered when the official discount rate was increased on 28 February, and finally offered a small 0.2 percentage point increase in yields. A flat refusal to accept this offer led to a second offer of 0.302 percentage points, which was still small when compared with the size of the gap. The MOF believed that the gap was not a true reflection of the market, and argued that the secondary market yields would soon fall.

Acceptance of the second offer by the underwriting syndicate did not reflect agreement with the MOF's reasoning, but underscored the internal divisions within the syndicate. When the market again failed to recover, the process began again. The dispute was resolved without any break in the link between short- and long-term interest rates, and the MOF had again kept the issue market interest rate well below the secondary market rate.

By 20 March 1980 the gap between the new issue yield (8.090 per cent) and the secondary market yield (approximately 9.5 per cent) was about 1.5 percentage points. At first the managing underwriter said the syndicate would refuse to underwrite without an increase of at least 1 percentage point. The negotiations that followed were protracted and bitter, often resulting in all-night sessions on both the government side and the underwriting side. There were three formal offers from the Financial Bureau:

First Offer: made after a ministry-wide conference on 1 April 1980. Terms 8.7 per cent, (99.5) Yield 8.793 (a rise of 0.703 percentage points). This was refused immediately.

Second Offer: a 'final' offer made on the night of 1 April 1980. Terms 8.7 per cent, (99.25) Yield 8.841 (a rise of 0.751 percentage points). The managing underwriter spent the night of 1st April assembling the syndicate's reaction. The reply termed the offer 'totally unacceptable'.

Third Offer: made following a ministry-wide conference on 5 April 1980. Terms 8.7, per cent (99.00) Yield 8.888 (a rise of 0.798 percentage points). Wavering among the smaller members of the syndicate that began during discussion of the second offer intensified. The big city banks remained strongly opposed to the compromise, even though it was accepted.[54]

The MOF conceded little on the surface. Its offer rose from 8.793 per cent to 8.888 per cent, and the syndicate was unable to negotiate the minimum rise of 1 percentage point for which it had first argued. The agreement did, however, reflect some important changes in the character of negotiations. The syndicate had forced the MOF to reconsider its offer twice. It had extracted the largest rise and highest yield that had ever been offered. Moreover, it was not prepared to let the matter rest with the compromise settlement. Appearing as invited guests before the HRFC on 7 April 1980, two prominent members of the finance industry, representing the banking community and the securities' companies, argued that there was an urgent need for 'realistic sales conditions' to be offered in the remainder of fiscal 1980, a clear reference to the dissatisfaction with the terms negotiated in April 1980.[55]

In comparing the relationship between the MOF and the underwriting syndicate at the beginning of the 1970s (for example during the 1973–75 tight money period) and in the 1978–80 interest rate swing period, the conclusion is inescapable that the relationship deteriorated sharply. Analysis of the controversial negotiating sessions during 1978–80 shows that a big gap between the issue market yield and the secondary market yield was not a sufficient condition to ensure a change in the government bond interest rate. A key consideration at all times was the state of other bond markets and long-term interest rates.[56]

However, by early 1979 the MOF's interest rate policy was having some effect on the government's bond flotation program. Although the MOF had been able to hold issue yields increasingly below secondary market yields, the gap between the issue yields of government bonds and other bonds gradually fell. Table 2.5 shows this clearly. Rather than fundamentally changing the method of interest rate determination to increase the volume of funds available, it switched some of its effort to new areas. It had introduced five-year maturity discount bonds in 1977. In 1978, three-year government bonds were issued by public tender, and this was expanded to two-, three- and four-year bond types in 1979.[57] In 1983, a small issue of non-marketable fifteen-year bonds marked the first development in the opposite direction. This diversification program can be seen as a direct result of the failure of the MOF to meet its needs in the ten-year government bond market.

The early 1980s saw the relationship between the MOF and the underwriters deteriorate to its logical conclusion. In July and August 1981, in July 1982, and again in February 1983, the negotiations between the MOF and the underwriters broke down and no bonds were issued. The failure of the MOF to give enough consideration to market interest rates finally began to affect directly the ability of the MOF to collect funds.

The MOF was able to call the shots despite the internal differences between bureaus in the 1970s. Policymaking—how to manage the market and how to proceed with the development of the market—was very much in the hands of the MOF, and its actions reflected its strong desire to maintain the existing regulated structure of interest rates. The LDP's attitude to tax and the budget framework itself did a lot to set the parameters for bond issues, whilst the underwriting syndicate operated as the major pressure group petitioning for a less regulated market. The differences which emerged in the interests of individual bureaus in the MOF resulted in a shift in the internal distribution of decisionmaking authority. But it was the force of the volume of bond issues, through the development of the secondary market and the concentration of bond purchases falling on the city banks (which by the end of the 1970s were able to participate more directly through their power to withdraw from underwriting), that contributed most to making the MOF address the central issues. Political insecurity on the tax issue overshadowed even these developments and it was this attitude which set the general framework for action.[58]

THE ROLE OF THE UNDERWRITING SYNDICATE

As with the MOF, the underwriting syndicate did not have a single, unified set of interests on which to base its negotiating stance. The diverse interests represented in the syndicate undoubtedly worked to assist the MOF in limiting and shaping the extent and direction of policy change.

Within the banking sector, groups reacted differently to the prospect of change. The small and medium-sized banks (the regional banks, mutual banks and credit associations) and, in a different manner, the long-term credit banks were on balance supporters of the structural divisions that were established in the 1950s. In sharp contrast, the city banks (especially the six largest) sought to break down traditional restrictions within the financial sector. These variations in opinion were present in debates over the efficacy of campaigning for change in the management of government debt policy, and by implication financial policy.

Attitudes of syndicate members on the level of government bonds to be issued were unanimous. All members would like to have seen a reduction in the volume of government debt. Given that a reduction could not be expected to occur quickly (because of difficulty in reducing the rate of expenditure growth, continuing resistance to increased taxation and the looming problem of redeeming bonds issued over the past ten years), debate focused on more practical questions. On these questions, opinion was often far from united. The attitude of long-term credit banks on the question of interest rates in the issue market was one such case.

Long-term credit banks were better able to hold government bonds than other banks (particularly commercial banks) because of the longer maturity of their major source of funds. In contrast to city banks, which obtained 86 per cent of their funds from deposits (over 54 per cent being of one-year maturity) and 13 per cent from the volatile short-term financial markets, the long-term credit banks obtained approximately 83 per cent of their funds from bank debentures with a maturity of five years (at the end of 1980).

With their emphasis on long-term loans and long-term fund sources, the long-term credit banks saw more benefit than cost in retention of the stability of interest rates of the 1960s. The main concern of the long-term credit banks with increased flexibility of the long-term government bond rate was the impact an increase would have on sales and profitability of their bank debentures.

If the secondary market government bond yields were to begin to diverge from other long-term rates (in an upward direction), a market-determined primary market rate would result in upward pressure on other long-term bond rates (including the medium-term bank debentures) if their saleability were to be maintained. On the other hand, a controlled bond sector enabled some parity to be kept between rates in the loan sector (which were based, in the case of city and regional banks, on the cost of deposits and short-term money). 'Controlled rates' generally meant that interest rates were being held below the deregulated market level. The long-term credit banks would fear a loss of advantage if their major funds supply source was decontrolled (and interest rates increased) when other sectors, most notably the deposit sector of other banks, remained controlled (and hence below the market interest rate). Hence long-term credit banks were often opposed to city banks in the extent of adjustment sought through negotiation with the Financial Bureau. This was sometimes expressed in the form of how far banks should underwrite government debt if a gap between the issue market and the secondary market interest yield existed.

The four big securities companies maintained a very market-oriented approach to the questions of sale of bonds and interest yield. The percentage of an offer that the securities companies underwrote varied greatly from month to month, and hence year to year, according to the perceived saleability (the relationship between primary yields and secondary yields). In the late 1970s they made a concerted attempt to lift their underwriting share in a defensive bid to maintain their monopoly over the sale of government bonds and dealing in the secondary market for government bonds.[59] They were vigorous proponents of market yields. As their business was an intermediary function (they sold what they underwrote), they received no benefit from controlled interest rates. When the gap between primary and secondary markets interest rates was small, they were prepared to underwrite large quantities; when it was not, they simply declined to underwrite beyond a minimum amount. Although their freedom was limited by considerations such as maintaining their reliability as underwriters (which was linked to the sale of bonds by banks), the securities companies were able, to some extent, to shield themselves from poor primary yields.

Underwriters did not rely solely on representation to the MOF. In late 1978, the managing underwriter (Fuji Bank) made informal approaches to LDP members of the HRFC. These approaches were not directed at gaining support for short-term changes in conditions, but rather at explaining the long-term requirements of the market. The underwriting side set out to convince members of the LDP of the growing need to consider market balance in setting interest rates. Only by doing this could smooth digestion of government bonds in the future be assured. In discussions with members of the banking community, the comment was often made that approaching members of the Diet on the problem of conditions of issue was not considered 'proper'. City banks had eschewed LDP favours on banking matters because they felt it would result in bad publicity and was anyway unnecessary. However, in this case it was felt necessary to make representations at the political level in order to make parliamentarians more aware of the complexities of the long-term government bond market of the late 1970s. In particular, if the existing interest rate conditions continued to prevail, city banks would be placed in a situation where they would have to withdraw or scale down their involvement in the underwriting syndicate. Ultimately this would limit the government's ability to float bonds.[60]

Despite a common outlook on the interest rates issue held by the city banks and the securities companies, there remained areas of sharp disagreement. The issue of immediate saleability of bonds underwritten by banks was one of these areas. If banks became able to sell their underwritten shares when they pleased (instead of after the three-month lag which existed from 1981), securities companies would see this as likely to lead to a breakdown of one of the traditional barriers which divided the securities and banking industries in postwar Japan. This difference of view meant that such issues could not be raised by the underwriting syndicate, but had to be raised by individual members, normally with their supervisory bureaus. This procedure ultimately meant that several bureaus became involved and the policymaking process considerably lengthened and complicated.

The cohesion of the underwriting syndicate was continuously subject to these types of pressures, which in turn hampered the operation of the managing underwriter in its liaison with the MOF. The managing underwriter could only push so far, knowing that some of its own members (the long-term credit banks and regional banks in particular) had more sympathy with the government position than with its own. The limited framework within which the managing underwriter operated meant that, in attempting to form positions on questions relating to regulations, there were frequently discussions impinging on issues outside the immediate objectives. With each bureau in the MOF thinking of its own charges and its own jurisdictional reponsibilities, rather than broader national interests, the process of developing new policy was extremely difficult. Internal syndicate problems, therefore, also contributed to slowing down the rate of regulatory change.

The development and operation of the government bond market between 1965 and 1982 illustrate many of the complexities of the Japanese financial system. They provide glimpses of the impact that the LDP can have on policymaking, as well as the problems involved in altering an established set of financial markets to meet a new set of financial needs.

The analysis in this chapter underlines the fact that at different times during the period under examination, different images were best used to capture the character of the policymaking process. Whereas 'consensus' was quite adequate to describe the period from 1965 to 1974, thereafter it became increasingly inappropriate. It was the dominance of the MOF which ensured the continued operation of the existing system into the early 1980s, and even that was inadequate to handle the conflict which arose sporadically after 1981.

The LDP's role in the policymaking process was small in the area of policy implementation, but vital at two other points. In 1965 it was the momentum of support from the LDP which enabled the market to be established in the first instance. Later, in 1974, it was the refusal of the LDP to increase taxes or to countenance a significant redistribution of expenditure that led to the establishment of a policy of large-scale flotation of government bonds. Electoral considerations and the political taboo against increasing taxes were important elements in the formation of LDP policy. The result was that the MOF was forced to maintain an overall policy in which several elements became increasingly contradictory. The main problem was in the maintenance of a framework of regulation of interest rates in the face of large-scale bond issues. The attempt to maintain this framework led to a significant deterioration of relations between the MOF and the participants in the finance industry. The LDP also played an implicit role in retarding the rate of policy change through its support for low and regulated interest rates. Had the LDP maintained a more flexible stance on this issue, the options of the MOF would have been more numerous.

The MOF established its regulatory policy on the basis of existing and tried methods. It sought to accommodate the various interests within the industry, its own requirements and those of the LDP. It was not in the business of pursuing efficiency in an unconstrained sense.

The MOF fought strenuously to protect the existing interest rate system, and hence its own jurisdiction. It was fighting essentially a rearguard action, reacting to pressures from the market. It was not a policy innovator in its own right but more a reactor with a basic desire to preserve the status quo. The MOF was forced to alter its policy in several areas, which led to the establishment of a large secondary market for government bonds and several short-term markets. In general, the MOF ignored calls for change from groups of financial institutions unless it perceived that the problem faced by them was acute. Differences of opinion emerged within the MOF in the late 1970s on interest rate policy and on policy aimed at developing a new regulatory framework. Each bureau sought to protect the interest of market participants within its jurisdiction. In those circumstances, the MOF looked for the least controversial means of implementing change. Many of the problems that emerged in the late 1970s and early 1980s in the way the market operated developed because the market was in the process of moving from a completely regulated to a deregulated framework. This transitional system was the root cause of the contradictions and problems which emerged in the late 1970s and early 1980s.

3 The establishment of the CDs market

Management of conflict at the bureau level

In the late 1970s, the Japanese city banks' share of total deposits fell to a postwar low. This was at a time when an ever-growing volume of government bonds was being issued by the MOF, thus placing increased demands on these banks' funds position. Further, it was a time when the availability of surplus funds in the corporate sector was large, relative to a decade earlier. It was in this climate that the Certificates of Deposits (CDs) market was established. By the end of 1982 there were renewed calls for the abolition of the remaining restrictions in the market.

The first CDs market was established in the United States in 1961. CDs were first issued by the First City National Bank in an attempt to stem the decline in share of deposits that it and other commercial banks were experiencing as a result of competition from other sectors of the United States finance industry. In later years CDs markets were established in most major financial centres. By 1978, the CDs market in New York had grown to US$156 billion or 16.1 per cent of all deposits. The CDs market in London was also of considerable importance. The character of CDs varies from market to market but they are generally a short- or medium-term negotiable security issued by financial institutions. They are generally directed at the wholesale or large unit market. In the US, for example, the minimum unit size is US$100 000.[1]

In Japan, the larger city banks showed some interest from the early 1960s in using CDs to boost their funds position, but it was not until early 1979 that permission to establish a CDs market was given by the MOF.

The process of establishing the CDs market in Japan sheds light on several important aspects of policymaking. It illustrates the difficulty in changing the regulatory framework to permit the use of new financial products by participants when some, if not the majority, argue that no good will come from the change. This chapter seeks to establish why CDs were successfully introduced despite widespread opposition from within sections of the finance industry. It evaluates the importance of the role of the Banking Bureau of the MOF in confining the arena of policymaking and how much this contributed to the successful introduction of CDs. The typology outlined in the introduction suggests that the higher the level of concentration of control the more chance that a particular policy could be successfully implemented. Other means that were used to contain the level of conflict are also examined, most notably the role played by the director-general of the Banking Bureau in making regulatory change possible. Finally, the CDs case contrasts the attitude of authorities to activities of domestic financial institutions within Japan and abroad. Intra-industry conflicts, resistances within the public service and intervention by the polity are prominent in delaying regulatory change in Japan, but these factors tend to be less important overseas. A contrast is drawn between the discussion of the CDs question within the policymaking arena in the late 1960s, and the granting of permission by the MOF for CDs to be floated abroad in 1972.

DOMESTIC AND INTERNATIONAL CONSTRAINTS: A COMPARISON

CDs and the 1967–70 inquiry by the CFSR

The CDs question first became a matter for serious discussion in Japan during the 1967–70 meetings of the Committee on Financial System Research (CFSR). It had new terms of reference which reflected the feeling that the Japanese economy was at the crossroads. As early as February 1967, the director-general of the Banking Bureau, Sumita Satoshi, had said publicly for the first time that some change in the structure of the financial system might be necessary to accommodate the developing economy.[2] The CFSR was charged to report on the role of finance in the economy, and to comment on the efficiency of the existing institutional framework. Its terms of reference were, therefore, quite broad. The investigation represented a continuation of the work undertaken by the CFSR in its study of the problems of small and medium-sized financial institutions during 1966–67.[3] The investigation fell short of a review of the legislative framework, but it did examine thoroughly the needs of both the suppliers and users of finance.[4] It was in this context that the CDs issue arose.

In the final report of the CFSR, which was presented to the Minister of Finance, Fukuda Takeo, on 2 July 1970, the committee stated that 'considering such matters as the present state of the financial market and the low level of excess industrial capital, the committee feels that it is not appropriate to introduce CDs'.[5] Its conclusion was based on the expected impact that a CDs market with deregulated interest rates would have on the rest of the financial system, and the low level of support that the campaign to introduce them attracted. Set out below are the positions adopted by committee members on the CDs question. The following section details the reasons for the positions held.

Of all the comments on the CDs question, only the one made by the president of Fuji Bank, Iwasa Yoshizane, supported immediate introduction. He argued that introduction of CDs would provide a financial service for coping with the increased financial surpluses of corporations, and would help to promote interest rate deregulation. Few discussions of the financial system by other financial institutions included comments on the CDs problem, but those that did were critical. For example, Hirano Shigetarō, chairman of the Regional

Banks Association, and Minato Morishige, president of Nikko Securities, representing the securities companies, both stated that introduction would increase the cost of funds and that there was simply no demand for the product.[6]

Just as damaging to the position of the city banks as the opposition from other financial institutions was the failure of city banks as a group to agree over a statement on the issue. Meetings of the City Banks Discussion Group in mid-1968 failed to produce a unified position. While the large city banks supported introduction, the small city banks remained opposed. In the existing environment they were competitive but felt the more deregulated the financial markets became the harder their position would be.[7]

Table 3.1   Surplus capital held by corporations (per cent)

		1969[a]	1978[b]
1	The existence of surplus capital		
	Frequently	6.8	16.6
	Occasionally	17.4	36.3
	Rarely	25.4	16.1
	None	24.7	29.9
	Unclear	25.7	1.1
2	Approach to the use of excess capital[c]		
	Good return	24.9	39.6
	Good negotiability	33.2	42.3
	To smooth relationship with banks	30.2	23.2
	Attribute of safety	13.6	34.4
	Lighten the interest rate burden		31.7
	Other	5.3	0.4
	Unclear	37.7	3.5
3	Method of use of excess capital[d]		
	Demand deposit	30.3	36.3
	Fixed deposit	25.9	34.6
	Bonds	34.1	47.1
	Gensaki	(22.8)	(41.1)
	Other	(11.3)	(6.0)
	Trusts	6.1	4.4
	Shares	2.9	9.1
	Speed up loan repayments	36.3	39.5
	Other	7.5	3.7
	Unclear	26.6	2.7

Notes: a   Refers to the four years from April 1965
          b   Refers to the three years from January 1975 to March 1978
          c   Companies asked to select one or two reasons
          d   Companies asked to select up to three replies each

          In both [c] and [d], percentages were devised by dividing the number of replies by the number of companies. Replies from companies totalled 794 in 1969 and 1396 in 1978

Source: Kin'yū seido kenkyūkai hen *Futsū ginkō no arikata to ginkō seido no kaisei—kin'yū seido chōsakai no tōshin* Tokyo: Kin'yū zaisei, 1979, p. 235

The MOF too did not support immediate change. On the basis of a survey it commissioned, there was little apparent need for a new service. Table 3.1 shows that the number of corporations with surplus funds was quite small. Furthermore, although there had been a substantial shift in deposit shares, it had been away from the larger financial institutions towards the smaller mutual banks, credit associations and the postal savings system. For example, although the share of city bank deposits, in a relatively broad definition of total deposits, had fallen between 1960 and 1968 from 48.8 per cent to 39.6 per cent, its share of 'all bank' deposits only fell from 62.9 per cent to 58.2 per cent.[8] The MOF argued that the lack of need, the possible impact of introduction on interest rates and the legal problems of introducing CDs similar to those used in the United States, were sufficient reasons to shelve the proposal quietly.

According to one of the members of the secretariat based in the Banking Bureau, which provided research support for the CFSR, much of the discussion that occurred in the CFSR meeting of 1967–70 was exploratory, rather than intended as a basis for immediate policy change. Reading between the lines of the report's statement on the CDs question, it could be said that although it was brief and strongly negative, it did put the question of change in the financial markets on the agenda. The report was, in effect, conveying the message that introduction was unlikely unless there was a significant change in the structure of the underlying financial demands by corporations or a redistribution of market shares between the banks sufficient to make the existing system unworkable.[9]

It is not known precisely how many committee members opposed introduction, but according to a member of the committee's secretariat it was overwhelming.[10] The opposition of the majority of the financial institutions and the MOF was enough to prevent any change to the regulatory framework.[11]

Permission to float CDs abroad

Although in 1970 the CFSR felt that immediate introduction of a CDs market into Japan was premature, in 1972 the city banks' applications to float CDs on the London and New York capital markets met little opposition from the MOF.

In the late 1960s, the activities of Japanese banks abroad began to expand at a rapid rate, following in the wake of the increased activity of Japanese corporations in overseas markets in the latter half of the 1960s. Until the early 1970s, Japanese banks relied heavily on the Eurodollar market as their prime source of dollar funds. This dependence was not without its problems. The market offered essentially short-term funds at a time when demand for funds by both Japanese and non-Japanese borrowers was for maturities which were gradually lengthening.[12] This placed Japanese banks in a disadvantageous position relative to other international banks because the latter could, for example, freely operate in the London US$-based CDs market which had been operational since May 1966. Sourcing funds through the Eurodollar market also produced mismatching of maturities of assets and liabilities. A principle of sound banking is to balance maturity lengths of assets and liabilities. The existing arrangements forced banks to borrow money for short periods whereas the demand for funds was for longer periods.

The MOF had several reservations about permitting overseas flotation of CDs by Japanese banking institutions.[13] The first was that increased borrowing abroad by Japanese banks would increase the level of foreign exchange reserves, and hence increase pressures on the yen. Japan revalued the yen in late 1971, and was extremely wary about doing anything that might lead to a further revaluation. It handled this problem of the linkage between international borrowing and foreign exchange reserves by permitting the funds raised by issuing CDs to be used only for financing activities of corporations in the international marketplace.

Second, there was the added concern that strong issuing activity by Japanese banks would destabilise the London market (towards which applications had been directed). Although the market was quite large (with outstanding issues in August 1972 standing at US$5.7 billion), around 90 per cent of the volume was in short-term maturities of less than one year. The demand of Japanese banks would be concentrated at the long-term end of the market. The possibility of destabilising the London market was all but eliminated by the MOF's imposition of limits on the quantity of CDs it permitted each bank to issue. This restriction was eliminated in December 1972 when it became clear that the issues in the September–November quarter had little, if any, impact on the market.[14]

Third, there was the concern expressed by securities companies and long-term credit banks to the MOF that the granting of permission to city banks to issue CDs abroad would give those banks a lever to promote domestic flotation. The character of this 'lever' was unclear, and the MOF did not believe that what happened overseas would affect the domestic financial system. It is certainly difficult to understand what the groups opposing introduction had in mind, except the fear that expanded overseas operations of the city banks would gradually reduce their own competitiveness domestically. This argument was not accepted by the MOF and when a group of the largest city banks (including the specialised foreign exchange bank, the Bank of Tokyo) asked for permission to float CDs in London in May 1972, the MOF indicated, after an internal investigation, that it supported the request.[15]

It is worth noting here that on this occasion, and later in 1975, the MOF took an active interest in promoting Japanese banking abroad, an interest which tried to accommodate the demands of Japanese banking, subject to the demands of foreign economic policy, and a consideration of the impact on the domestic market.[16] As Japanese banks became more practised in the art of international banking, so the restrictions on their activities were lifted.[17]

The difference between the resistance to establishing a domestic CDs market and allowing city banks to use international CDs markets was straightforward. In the domestic case, there was an established regulatory framework which ordered relations between competing financial institutions on the one hand, and between competing non-financial corporations on the other. An alteration of the regulatory framework required a consideration of the impact of the change not only on these groups but also on the MOF and its component bureaus. Significant opposition among both groups was sufficient to ensure the continuation of the status quo. In the foreign case, however, Japanese financial institutions were competing with financial institutions from other countries. The maintenance of regulations by the MOF which inhibited the ability of Japanese banks to compete overseas was hardly in the best interests of Japan or the institutions concerned. Provided that dropping of the regulations did not have an unacceptable impact on the domestic financial system, the MOF was amenable to change. Coalitions which had to be built to facilitate change in domestic regulations could be dispensed with on these occasions. The MOF could operate largely by exercising its own administrative authority. It was unnecessary to consult groups such as the CFSR.

THE CDs POLICYMAKING PROCESS 1977–79

The discussion fora

Despite the debate over the need to improve the general efficiency of the financial system in the late 1960s, the market instabilities of 1971–75 (the shift to floating exchange rates, the period of high inflation, the oil crisis and then the depressed level of investment activity) focused attention on other issues. By the second half of the 1970s, the MOF, and in particular the Banking Bureau, once again began addressing these issues. In 1975 the CFSR was given a brief by the Minister of Finance to 'present its opinions on what types of improvements in the existing laws relating to banks and other related legislation were necessary in view of the developments in the economic and financial environment.'[18] The investigation was to cover the whole banking system.[19] One part of this massive project was to re-examine the CDs problem.

In August 1977, some two years after the CFSR had begun its general deliberations but before any actual debate on the CDs and other measures which would expand the range of financial services provided by banks, another research body was formed within the Banking Bureau called the Financial Problems Research Group (FPRG). Among the first group of issues the FPRG was asked to examine was that of CDs.[20]

There were several differences between the FPRG and the CFSR. Unlike the CFSR, the FPRG did not have any legal standing. It was formed by the director-general of the Banking Bureau, Tokuda Hiromi, as a private study group intended to provide an informal forum for the discussion of policy options, uninhibited by the trappings of bodies such as the CFSR. In addition, members of the FPRG were younger and, because of the committee's lack of legal standing, more able to participate freely in argument.[21] Finally the size and membership of the FPRG was different from the CFSR. Whereas the CFSR was a quite large committee made up of very senior businessmen, financial industry representatives and others, the FPRG was numerically small and made up

Table 3.2   Membership of the CFSR and FPRG in 1978

1   Members of the CFSR

Permanent Members

Sasaki Tadashi[a]	chairman, CFSR; chairman, Committee for Economic Development
Inagawa Miyao	president, Osaka Securities
Okawa Ichiro	professor, Tokyo University
Kondō Michitaka[a]	president, *Kabushikigaisha Hakuhōdō*
Saheki Isamu	chairman, Osaka Chamber of Commerce
Sakisaka Masao	president, *Sōgō kenkyu kaihatsu kiko*
Suzuki Haruo	director, Federation of Economic Organizations president, *Shōwa denkō*
Takahara Sumiko	economic consultant
Takeuchi Akio[a]	professor, Law Faculty, Tokyo University
Tachi Ryūichirō[a]	professor, Economics Faculty, Tokyo University
Tanabe Bun'ichirō	president, Mitsubishi Trading
Tsuruta Takuhiko	general editor, *Nihon keizai shinbun*
Nishizaki Tetsurō[a]	head, Economic Communication Bureau, *Kyōdō tsūshin*
Maekawa Haruo[a]	deputy governor, BOJ
Matsuzawa Takuji[a]	chairman, Federation of Bankers' Associations president, Fuji Bank
Mizuno Shōichi	professor, Nagoya University
Morimoto Osamu	president, Norin Chukin Bank
Yamauchi Takahiro	president, Securities Dealers Association of Japan
Watanabe Yoshifude[a]	president, Small Business Financial Corporation

Temporary Members

Ohara Tetsugorō	chairman, Federation of Credit Associations
Katō Kan	professor, Keio University
Sakaya Takashi[a]	chairman, Better Living Information Centre
Shiino Kōkichi	chairman, Association of Trust Banks
Suzuki Susumu	chairman, Federation of Credit Unions
Sumita Satoshi[a]	president, Import–Export Bank
Soyama Katsumi	director, Nippon Electric Co. Ltd
Takaragi Fumihiko	trade union representative
Takita Minoru	trade union representative
Nakamura Kii	deputy chairman, National Housewives Association
Hayasaka Jun'ichirō	chairman, Federation of Mutual Banks
Masamune Isao	chairman, Industrial Bank of Japan
Yokoyama Sōichi	chairman, Federation of Regional Bankers Associations

2   Members of the FPRG

Itō Mitsuharu	chairman and professor, Chiba University
Iida Tsuneo	professor, Nagoya University
Ikeuchi Masato	economics manager, *Nihon keizai shinbun*
Ishi Hiromitsu	professor, Hitotsubashi University
Ibara Tetsuo	assistant professor, Keio University
Onizuka Yūsuke	assistant professor, Osaka University
Kaizuka Keimei	professor, Tokyo University
Koga Kensuke	general manager, Planning, Nippon Steel
Mr Sugiura	general manager, Finance, Mitsui Trading Co.
Nishino Mari	assistant professor, Meiji University
Hayashi Toshihiko	assistant professor, Kobe Shoka University
Yamamura Yoshiharu	editorial staff, *Mainichi shinbun*

Notes: a   Members of the subcommittee of the CFSR

Source: *Kin'yū zaisei jijō* — 18 September 1978; Kongo ni okeru wa ga kuni no kin'yū kikan no arikata—kin'yū mondai kenkyūkai no hōkoku naiyō, Tokyo, 1978

mainly of academics with several journalists and finance specialists from industry. Membership of each committee in 1978 is listed in Table 3.2. Although the FPRG did not contain the diversity of opinion among its members that the CFSR did, its diversity was supplemented, in the same way as the debate in the CFSR, by submissions from invited parties. For example, in the discussions of the CDs question, fourteen individuals made individual or joint submissions to the FPRG.[22]

When the FPRG met in April 1978 to organise its recommendations on the CDs issue, it produced a strong recommendation in favour of introduction. Perhaps this was not surprising given the composition of the group, which was free from the traditionally conservative elements found in the CFSR. Whereas the reports of the CFSR represented the view of the Banking Bureau, the status of the report of the FPRG was less defined. The first report of the FPRG, which was published in June 1978, created much controversy because it appeared to be heavily influenced by the policy stance of the Banking Bureau. This might be interpreted as a very practical and effective way to present feasible policy programs within the context of the existing system. A report based on economic theory would clearly have played little role in the development of new policy. Some critics were less charitable, arguing that the report read like a Banking Bureau document, something which was expected of CFSR reports but not of a semi-academic report. For example, one argued that the report should have explained why the introduction of a CDs market was preferable to the establishment of a TBs market.[23] Reasonable as this comment was in the context of normalising the character of the short-term money markets, it might not have been wholly valid. Support for the introduction of CDs was based on the imbalance in growth of deposits that had developed relative to the use of funds. The main difference between a TBs market and a CDs market from the standpoint of the banks was that only the latter could provide a source of funds.

The fact that the FPRG was given terms of reference similar to those of the CFSR indicated that the Banking Bureau could have had ulterior motives in establishing the FPRG. Indeed, in the context of the CDs debate, the importance of the FPRG debate was not in the greater understanding it promoted on policy issues, but in its use as a testing board for policy proposals. In this sense it was much more than an academic body merely advising the director-general of the Banking Bureau. It was, during Tokuda's period as director-general, one means of publishing policy proposals that had the support of the Banking Bureau.[24]

Private sector arguments for and against CDs

As the FPRG was concluding its discussion of the CDs problem, the CFSR was preparing to begin. Over the three months from 19 April to 21 July 1978, a subcommittee of the CFSR spent eight sessions looking at a similar range of questions discussed earlier in the FPRG.[25] Outlined below are the arguments for and against the introduction of CDs put forward by the various participants

Table 3.3   Invited contributions to the debate on CDs in the CFSR

Name and interest group affiliation	Summary of opinion	Stance
Itakura Jōji, City banks	Need for new short-term market to satisfy corporate needs. CDs market will not have major impact on finance order.	For
Ujiie Eiichi, Regional banks	No specific comment. Stress on maintaining existing character of banking relationships, which implies opposition.	Against
Shijima Tsukasa, Mutual banks	Proposed content of plan not clear. Opinions of concerned interest groups should be heeded.	Unclear/Against
Tamura Fumio, Credit associations	Plan not presented so opinion cannot be stated. But problems exist.	Unclear/Against
Sugiura Binsuke, Long-term credit banks	Competition with financial bonds would adversely affect long-term credit banks. Would only redistribute deposit shares and increase costs.	Against
Akama Yoshihiro, Trust banks	Will have an adverse impact on financial order. Consensus needs to be established.	Against
Kashiwagi Yūsuke, Bank of Tokyo	Need for new market to satisfy investors needs. Should be a wholesale market.	For
Kitaura Kōichirō, Securities companies	Problems relating to bank power groups in establishing a free market. Proposals for interest deregulation and not increasing bank fund-raising capabilities should be studied.	Against
Kawai Ryōichi, Large-scale manufacturing	CDs a good way of improving efficiency of using surplus funds. Stresses importance of negotiability in secondary market.	For
Sasaki Hideichi, Main body of industry	Diversification beyond the *gensaki* market would be welcomed	For
Ueno Kintarō, Small & medium-sized industry	No specific mention. Favours keeping interest rates down. Capital position of small firms weak.	Against
Okada Takuya, Transport industry	Favours introduction and wants good secondary market negotiability.	For

Notes: These views were presented at the 41st, 42nd and 44th meetings of the subcommittee of CFSR on 10 May, 2 June and 22 June 1978. Foreign banks also presented an opinion on the CDs debate in discussion on the role of foreign banks at the 54th and 55th meetings held on 15 November 1978 and 22 November 1978. They strongly favoured introduction. Their views are not considered here because, by the time of their submission, the decision to establish CDs had been taken and most of the details had already been finalised

Source: Kin'yū seido kenkyūkai hen *Futsū ginkō no arikata to ginkō seido no kaisei* pp. 191–208

in the policymaking process. The views of a range of participants in the CFSR hearings is given in Table 3.3.

The banks favouring introduction were a small though economically powerful minority. The large city banks (Daiichi Kangyo Bank, Fuji Bank, Mitsubishi Bank, Mitsui Bank, Sumitomo Bank and Sanwa Bank), the one specialist foreign exchange bank (the Bank of Tokyo), and the foreign banks were the only financial institutions to support strongly the introduction of CDs. Even some of the middle- and lower-ranking city banks lacked enthusiasm (without being overtly opposed).

In a joint submission to the FPRG by the general managers of research at Mitsui Bank, Sumitomo Bank and Sanwa Bank, the city banks put a case for introducing CDs containing demand and supply side components. Client demand, they argued, was growing for short-term readily negotiable assets which also had deregulated interest rates. The introduction of a CDs market could, in their view, satisfy both these requirements. At the centre of the city banks arguments, however, were supply side problems that they were experiencing.

During the 1970s, the growth rate of the city banks' traditional sources of personal deposits had been lower than most other financial institutions and a great deal lower than the postal savings system. As a result, the share of deposits held by city banks declined sharply, falling from 39.6 per cent in 1968 to 32.8 per cent in 1977. With increasing demands being placed upon city banks by way of underwriting government bonds, these banks were being put in a position of having to allocate a larger proportion of their growth in funds to financing the public debt. A recovery in industrial demand for funds, and a continued expansion in personal financial activities, was bound to result in conflict developing between the demands of the public sector and the needs of the private sector. Satisfying the public sector's demands would reduce the funds available for private sector use.[26] In the five half-year periods to the end of September 1977, the proportion of growth in deposits allocated to government bonds had grown from 17 per cent to 28, 32, 36 and finally to 52 per cent.

The argument of the city banks amounted to a statement that the falling rate of growth of city banks' savings deposits was putting increasing pressure on the balance of the financial system. During the high growth period, the minimal requirements of the public sector, and relatively stable share of savings deposits collected by the post office meant that the existing financial system was relatively stable and workable. The shifting preferences of individuals towards the postal savings system away from the banking system, and the demands of government in the bond market, introduced an element of instability into the financial system. Were the supply side trends to continue, the city banks would not have been able to fulfil their obligations to both sectors.

The two submissions from large-sized business also favoured the introduction of CDs. A director of Marubeni Corporation, Kojima Masaoki, said that CDs would fulfil a need of business. He did, however, add a cautionary note that excess competition between banks might occur, and this would force up interest rates. As a trading company, this would increase Marubeni's costs. A director of

Asahi Chemical Industry Co. Ltd, Takada Tetsuo, went much further, saying that to improve use of surplus funds by corporations, there was a need for a range of new short-term financial markets including a TBs market, a bankers acceptance market, a commercial paper market and a CDs market. Introduction of these facilities would allow a more flexible use of funds and improve the ability of corporations to maximise the return on funds. The reduction in indebtedness of large firms after 1975 meant that an increasing number of firms was looking for short-term assets offering a market rate of return on funds. In 1977 there was only the *gensaki* market to meet these needs.[27]

Opposing introduction were the representatives of the long-term credit banks, the regional banks, the trust banks and the securities companies. Their arguments had changed little in the decade since the CFSR inquiry of the late 1960s.

Jinnouchi Satoichirō, a director of the Industrial Bank of Japan (IBJ), represented the long-term credit banks at the FPRG inquiry. He focused on the question of the legality of issuing CDs, and the potential threat that CDs would pose to the viability of the financial bonds issued by the long-term credit banks.[28] The legal problem was simply whether, under the Securities and Exchange Law (1948), the banks were permitted to issue contracts which had all the characteristics of bonds. As was explained in chapter 2, banks were not permitted to buy and sell bonds, with the exception of government bonds and the financial bonds issued by the long-term credit banks. Valid as this argument was, the central reason for opposing introduction lay elsewhere. If CDs of the type issued in London (that is, with maturities of up to three years) were available in Japan, the long-term credit banks' major source of funds, their financial bonds, would be subject to increased competition. In addition to this, they feared that it would result in higher financial bond interest rates and hence higher costs relative to the costs of financial institutions with normal deposit sources of funds. This argument was very much dependent on the character of the CDs market that was to be introduced. If it had had deregulated interest rates, if it had offered an equivalent unit size to the US market (US$100 000), if it had been negotiable and with a maturity range similar to that of the London market, then the very core of the regulated interest rate framework and existing financial structure would have been challenged.[29]

The regional banks also opposed introduction. They were, by and large, institutions with a regional outlook and sound deposit base. They argued that introduction of CDs would adversely affect this deposit base, by encouraging local government organisations to use their periodic surpluses in the CDs market rather than deposit them for a lower return in the regional bank. This would not only cause a deterioration of their existing deposit position but force a reassessment of the cost of loans to local government. They argued that the existing business relationship with local government was based on a 'package' rather than the return on, or cost of, component parts. Removing part of that package would require the reassessment of the remainder. The regional banks therefore argued that they could only lose by the introduction of CDs. The argument must, however, be put into perspective. The largest monthly deposit average in 1978 from local government was 9.4 per cent of deposits in November 1978. At the end of 1978, outstanding loans of regional banks to local government and public corporations stood at 12.4 per cent. These figures amount to a significant but not major proportion of business. As in the case of the long-term credit banks, the effect of CDs would be largely dependent upon the characteristics that were ultimately approved. It was clear, however, that the competitive position of the regional banks could not reasonably be expected to improve vis-a-vis the city banks.[30]

The securities companies were also strongly opposed to the establishment of a CDs market. At the forty-third subcommittee meeting of the CFSR on 10 May 1978, the president of Nomura Securities, Kitaura Kōichirō, put the view of the securities industry.[31] He opposed bank participation in the traditional securities area (which would have been the case had American-style CDs been intro-duced), but his opposition went deeper than this. Even if CDs were non-negotiable and had regulated interest rates, CDs would challenge the monopoly of the securities companies in the *gensaki* market. The position of the securities companies was canvassed in more detail in an internal document of the Bond Underwriters Association of 20 July 1978 (the day before the Banking Bureau presented a summary of findings from the discussions held in the subcommittee).[32] The document made it clear that, although the principle of deregulation was generally supported by the securities companies, the possibil-ity that banks would be permitted to operate in the market was sufficient reason not to support its establishment publicly.

If a CDs market was to be established, the securities companies favoured a market where the banks would be able to issue CDs, but not trade in them in a secondary market. This type of market had the advantages of expanding securities companies' business and helping to expand the short-term financial markets. It was felt that the control of the secondary market by the securities companies would give the securities companies considerable say in the flotation market. (The undertones of this argument should be noted, as it was the securities companies which later were to argue the problem of bank power over corporate activity.) After assessing the benefits and costs of the establishment of a CDs market, however, the securities companies concluded that the threat to the *gensaki* market was of overriding importance. The securities companies preferred the monopoly they had in the restricted market to the competition they could potentially face in a less restricted one. When they made public their opposition, the report continued, two points had to be stressed. They were that the benefits to big depositors that could accrue from CDs and the development of the short-term money markets, would be obstructed by bank power. If the intention was to deregulate interest rates, then the government should begin with the establishment of a freely operating TBs market.[33]

In the context of these arguments, the securities companies faced the problem of how to convince the MOF that there was a threat to the freedom of the market from the 'power' of city banks, and that a TBs market was really the place to start.

The first point was difficult to argue. Already the four large securities companies had a virtual monopoly over the *gensaki* market. It could as easily be argued that the four large securities companies were acting in collusion in the formation of prices in this market. Moreover, the securities companies retained a monopoly over business in the major bond markets, which in purely legal terms was by no means their 'right' (see chapter 4).

The second point had much merit and was supported throughout the financial community, but it went against MOF's long-held policies of minimising the cost of government funds. The opposition of the MOF to a freely operating TBs market was well known, and indeed the BOJ had developed an alternative strategy, based on the development of the CDs market, as a second-best alternative. In 1978 the BOJ began moves to deregulate interest rates in the call and bills market, and to introduce a wider range of financial assets (see chapter 1). These moves were a part of its plan to develop a more unified system of short-term money markets which were more responsive to market forces, and which allowed it to intervene through the market in pursuit of its monetary policy goals.[34] The BOJ's strategy recognised the fact that it did not expect the MOF to change its policy on the TBs market. There was no reason to expect the securities companies to be more successful. Nevertheless, it was on the basis of these arguments that the securities companies opposed the introduction of CDs.

Compared with the position it took in the CFSR inquiry of the late 1960s, the view of industry had shifted appreciably by 1978 in favour of the introduction of CDs. Table 3.1 shows that in the period between the two CFSR inquiries, the number of corporations which had excess capital, either frequently or occasionally, had grown from 24.2 per cent to 52.9 per cent. If the approaches to the use of excess capital are examined, it can be seen that the importance of rate of return on investment and negotiability of investment had both grown: the development of these preferences would suggest increased support for an unregulated market over the traditionally used fixed deposit market. Working on the assumption, which no one disputed, that rates in the deposit market were low, returns could be expected to be higher in an unregulated market. Whereas placing funds in fixed deposits accounts made them less than fully negotiable, a CDs market of the US type would offer complete negotiability. Three out of the four industry representatives who spoke before the CFSR subcommittee favoured introduction.[35]

The fourth representative, Ueno Kintarō, who represented small and medium-sized industry, made no specific comment on the CDs issue but implicitly argued against introduction. In his view, small corporations only had a limited number of fund sources and the main one was banks. If the short- and medium-term deposit markets were deregulated, he argued, the general level of the cost of funds would increase.[36]

Table 3.4 shows the range of views expressed on the CDs question in the 1978 debate, along with the views expressed in earlier fora. The table shows the stability of views held within the financial sector. Outside the financial sector, opinions shifted in favour of introduction. In the business world, support for introduction had grown substantially, although reservations remained in some

Table 3.4   Attitudes to CDs in three prominent fora

	1970 Committee on Financial System Research Report	1978 Financial Problem Research Group Report[a]	1978 Subcommittee on Financial System Research
Financial Institution			
City banks[b]	Positive	Positive	Positive
Foreign banks[c]	Unrepresented	Unrepresented	Positive
Regional banks	Negative	Unrepresented	Negative
Trust banks	Negative	Negative	Negative
Long-term credit banks	Not clear	Negative	Negative
Mutual banks	Negative	Unrepresented	Negative
Credit associations	Unrepresented	Unrepresented	Negative
Securities companies	Negative	Negative	Negative
Others			
Ministry of Finance[d]	Negative	Positive	Positive
Bank of Japan	Not clear	Unrepresented	Positive
LDP Committee[e]	Not clear	Unrepresented	Positive
Large-sized industry	Not clear	Positive	Positive
Medium/small– sized industry	Unrepresented	Negative	Negative

Notes: a   The Financial Problem Research Group only canvassed a cross-section of opinion
   b   The attitude of city banks really only refers to the largest city banks. The smaller ones were carried along with the tide of opinion
   c   Foreign banks were not asked for an opinion in the early inquiry
   d   This refers to the dominant opinion in the Ministry of Finance
   e   This refers to the view when finally presented to the LDP

Source: Kin'yū seido kenkyūkai hen *Kin'yū seido chōsakai shiryō* vol. 4, pp. 342–48;
   Kin'yū mondai kenkyūkai hen *Kongo ni okeru wa ga kuni no kin'yū kikan no arikata* Tokyo 1978, pp. 260–69;
   Kin'yū seido kenkyūkai hen *Futsū ginkō no arikata to ginkō seido no kaisei* pp. 191–208

areas. This shift in opinion is one factor which would have contributed to changing the MOF's position, but it was hardly a sufficient reason.

Explanation of the MOF's position

Four explanations of why the MOF began to advocate the introduction of CDs need careful examination.

The first explanation was the desire of the MOF to improve the effectiveness of monetary policy. Introduction of a deregulated CDs market would certainly have given the short-term money markets more diversity and created a basis for the implementation of monetary policy by intervention through the money markets. If this had been the MOF's main concern, however, the logical place to start would have been the TBs market. This would have provided a larger and more powerful means of improving the effectiveness of monetary policy. Further, when the MOF released its initial plans for the CDs market, it favoured a regulated interest rate.[37] Had this been the case, the introduction of CDs would have contributed nothing to the BOJ's ability to manage monetary policy through the money markets.

A second explanation was that introduction of CDs would diversify the range of assets available to corporations with surplus funds. This would certainly have been one effect of introducing CDs, but the fact that corporations already had access to the *gensaki* market, and that there was some industry opposition, suggest that this was not the MOF's main reason. Rather, it was a supporting reason, and important in as much as it elicited the backing of industry interest groups on which the MOF could rely.

A third possible explanation was one based on foreign economic policy considerations. For most of the 1970s, the activities of foreign banks in Japan had been sharply limited because they had little or no direct access to yen deposits. Most of their funds came from swap quotas (the extent to which they could bring funds into Japan from abroad and convert these funds into yen) and some access to the call market. The problem of foreign banks received considerable attention when the European Community Commissioner Tugendhat visited Japan in May 1978, and complained of unfair treatment for foreign banks.[38] Whether or not the foreign banks were unfairly treated is not the point at issue here. The main point is whether the introduction of CDs can be attributed to foreign pressure in any way. Foreign banks played only a marginal role in the Japanese financial system, and, while it could be argued that foreign pressure might add weight to the arguments in favour of introduction, it was inconceivable that they constituted a central force.

Had the authorities wanted, they could have: increased the swap limits available to the foreign banks; permitted them greater access to the call market; or allowed the larger foreign banks to borrow from the Central Bank itself. All these measures could have been implemented with minimal fuss. The dispute which occurred over the CDs issue was one which created major controversy within the industry and to suggest it was waged for the foreign banking community vastly overstates the importance of that sector. The role of the foreign banks had been purposefully limited, and the penetration of the foreign banks into the Japanese finance industry had not altered markedly during the 1970s.[39]

The fourth and most convincing explanation was that the MOF's central objective was to maintain the stability of the financial system. An important element of this was the buoyancy of the city banks. In the decade 1965–74, the profit margin on city bank loans averaged 0.82 per cent and, between the first half of 1972 and the first half of 1974, had risen from 1.20 per cent to 1.63 per cent.[40]

In the decade to 1974, the profit margin never fell below 0.5 per cent, and rarely below 0.8 per cent. Although it remained relatively constant from the second half of fiscal 1974 to the second half of fiscal 1976, thereafter it fell sharply and continually until 1979. For the first half of fiscal 1978 it stood at 0.11 per cent.

The profit margin of city banks was affected by three factors:

1 the long monetary ease period which had reduced the gap between the cost of funds and the return on funds because of the relative downward inflexibility of deposit rates;
2 the large volume of bonds which city banks were required to underwrite and the relatively low return on government securities;
3 the relatively slow rate of growth of deposits which meant that the proportion of funds being used to buy government securities grew, in turn depressing the rate of return.

The management of the postal savings system was causing two problems. The relative downward inflexibility of deposit interest rates (see chapter 5) meant that the ratio of the interest rate on fixed deposits to the official discount rate fell, with a resultant fall in the profitability of banks. The MOF was in a weak position to do anything about this because it did not have the authority to set postal savings interest rates. The second problem was that the share of individual savings being attracted by the private financial institutions was decreasing relative to the share being attracted into the postal savings system. This reflected the slightly better deposit interest rates on long-term deposits and the character of the taxation system. Both these problems are given more detailed consideration in chapter 5 but it should be noted that political considerations meant that the MOF had little leverage for reversing the trend.

The slow rate of growth of deposits of city banks was not so much a problem in the mid-1970s when demand for investment funds was low. Recovery in investment activity meant, however, that the more profitable sector of loans to industry would be squeezed by public sector demand for funds. When the private sector demand for funds was relatively low (fiscal 1975–77), there was an incentive to take in the government debt that was being issued. As the private sector's demand for funds improved, there was a need to give consideration to the funds position of the city banks which underwrote large quantities of government bonds, and were the most affected by the shift in consumer preference towards the postal savings system. Other banks were also affected but it was the city banks, with their less than adequate deposit bases, which were affected most.

It has been explained that the decline in profitability of city banks, in as far as it was directly related to deposit interest rates and the return on government bonds, was determined by policy. The MOF could do little about the deposits interest rate and deposits shift problem, and it had shown that it was not prepared to alter radically the method of operation of the government bond market. If a CDs market were introduced, it would give the city banks an opportunity to compete for funds in another area. In particular, it would compete for funds held in the *gensaki* market (which was the main source of funds for the securities companies), and for the deposits of local governments (which were at the time monopolised by regional banks). Assuming a cake of fixed size, a larger share going to the city banks would potentially improve the position of city banks within the general financial system. Since it was the city banks which were most affected by regulations, it was possible to argue that it made good sense in economic terms (as the city banks were the most efficient) and in an equity sense, to restore partially the balance that had been upset in the second half of the 1970s.

The above argument assumes that the MOF was concerned with maintaining a balance within the financial system, rather than necessarily maintaining the status quo. That is, the MOF sought not only to maintain the relativities between financial institutions but also to provide access to funds for those that required them. It suggests that the MOF was aware of existing problems and sought a method to intervene given a set of restrictions on what it could do. It is this explanation which offers the most complete understanding of why the MOF altered its 1970 position against introduction to a strong positive one.[41]

In the summary of the discussion on the CDs problem presented to the subcommittee of the CFSR on 21 July 1978, five reasons were given why introduction of CDs should be supported:

1 CDs were required in order to respond to the needs of enterprises;
2 they were seen as a step in the interest deregulation process;
3 they were expected to improve the efficiency of capital-raising methods of banks;
4 they would contribute to the functioning of the short-term capital market;
5 they would assist in the normalisation of an unbalanced capital structure (referring to the perpetual deficit state of city banks).[42]

There was no doubt that introduction would have these effects. Effects are, however, not reasons. In the brief analysis above it was argued that points 3 and 5 formed the basis of the MOF's support for the introduction of CDs. The other reasons contributed to building the coalition of interests which was necessary in the light of continuing opposition from parts of the financial sector. The management of this conflict provides further evidence to support this contention, as well as contributing to an understanding of policymaking and conflict management.

MANAGEMENT OF CONFLICT BY THE BANKING BUREAU

Despite the recommendation in favour of issuing CDs made by the subcommittee on 21 July 1978, the general session of the CFSR on 7 September produced continued opposition. Although a majority expressed support for the introduction of CDs, the opposition of the securities companies, long-term credit banks and regional banks remained.[43] Given this continuing public opposition, it is interesting to consider how the Banking Bureau was able to contain the conflict and what factors were important in the policymaking process.

Tactics of the Banking Bureau

The position of the Banking Bureau on the CDs issue was relatively clear with the release of the FPRG report in mid-1978.[44] The statement of the subcommittee of the CFSR to the general committee, in early September 1978, confirmed the intentions of the Banking Bureau. But the high level of opposition to introduction that was expressed in the general session of the CFSR made it clear that successful resolution would require careful negotiation and ultimately would determine the character of the CDs market. Table 3.5 shows the options which were aired during the discussion process, and the outcomes which resulted.

One key issue was that related to negotiability. Securities companies had potentially the most to lose from the introduction of CDs. The fixed deposit market, with interest rates regulated and negotiability limited, was a fairly unattractive avenue for corporations with surplus funds to invest. The only other option was the *gensaki* market. The securities companies felt that if CDs with comparable characteristics to those issued on the United States market were introduced in Japan, their own strong grip on surplus corporate finance would be weakened greatly. The Banking Bureau had two choices on the negotiability issue.

It could have attempted to introduce a CD with a negotiable 'securities' character. In discussions between the Banking Bureau and the Ministry of Justice in August 1978, it became clear that introducing a CD with a negotiable securities character would require an amendment to the Securities and Exchange Law.[45] This would not only delay introduction but would also widen the participation in the policymaking process. During the initial stages of planning, the Banking Bureau had controlled the debate and organised the discussions that were held in official and private MOF fora. This was a powerful argument for adopting the alternative, a CD with a 'deposit' character.

Although restrictions on the negotiability of the CDs (implied by the 'deposit' characteristic) would reduce its attractiveness to buyers, this option at least ensured that the Banking Bureau retained control over the policymaking process. By adopting this option in its initial plan, the Banking Bureau signalled its intention to minimise the input into the policymaking process from the Securities Bureau. In this way, the opposition of the securities companies could not be channelled directly into the policymaking process. Although the Securities Bureau made representations to the Banking Bureau, several of those interviewed made the point that the Banking Bureau used these occasions to convey information to the securities companies rather than to listen to the opinions which were being advocated.[46] More than anything else, the Banking Bureau's decision to reject the negotiable 'securities' type CD limited the access of non-banking interests to the policymaking process.

Table 3.5   The CDs issue: options and outcomes

Characteristics	Options		Result	Reason
Legal character	1	Deposit	1	Legal problems for
	2	Security		banks with the
				alternative method
Negotiability	1	Endorsement	1	Legal problem with the
		required		no endorsement
	2	No endorsement		alternative
Management of	1	Security co.	2	Reflection of Banking
secondary trading	2	Issuer		Bureau stance
Interest rate	1	Completely free	1	Strong pressure from
	2	Upper limit set		within market and BOJ
		by two-year		for first option
		fixed deposit		
	3	An upper limit		
Period	1	90 day – 1 year	2	Consideration of position
	2	90 day – 6 months		of trust banks and
	3	30 day – 1 year		long-term credit banks
		or 6 months		at long end and
				securities companies
				(*gensaki* market) at short
				end
Flotation unit	1	100 million yen	3	Consideration of position
	2	300 million yen		of long-term credit
	3	500 million yen		banks
Volume	1	Unlimited	2	Concession to regional
	2	Fixed limit		banks' interests, but
		according to		general agreement from
		financial institution		financial world
Participants	1	All financial	2	Minimisation of valid
		institutions		reasons for opposition
	2	A wider definition		
Flotation method	1	At issuers'	1	
		discretion		
	2	Like bonds with		
		a fixed period		
Buying & selling	1	No restriction	1	
	2	Restricted to		
		corporations		
	3	Partial		
		restriction		

Source: Interviews; *kin'yū zaisei jijō* 27 November 1978; *Nihon keizai shinbun* 12 November
1978

The role of the CDs Discussion Group

After the continued opposition expressed at the general session of the CFSR on 7 September 1978, the Banking Bureau in conjunction with the chairman of the CFSR, Sasaki Tadashi, decided to form a small committee, called the CDs Discussion Group, to minimise the level of opposition to the CDs proposal. The Discussion Group was formed not to ponder on whether or not a CDs market should be established, but to consider what character it should have. Groups which were opposed to the introduction of CDs realised that the deliberations of the Discussion Group would result in a firm proposal for the introduction of CDs and that they could do nothing to prevent it.[47] The identity of those involved in the selection of the Discussion Group strongly influenced the outcome. The chairman of the CFSR and senior officers of the Banking Bureau decided the membership.[48] The Discussion Group had six members headed by Sumita Satoshi, a former Banking Bureau director-general and MOF administrative vice-minister. Others were the deputy governor (now governor) of the BOJ, Maekawa Haruo; a legal specialist, Takeuchi Akio of Tokyo University; an economist, Tachi Ryūichirō also of Tokyo University; the editor of the *Nihon keizai shinbun*, Tsuruta Takuhiko; and the head of the Economic Communication Bureau of *Kyōdō tsūshin*, Nishizaki Tetsurō.

The membership of the Discussion Group was not neutral in the sense of lying between two extremes. There were no strong opponents of CDs, nor for that matter of slow deregulation. Sumita was perhaps the strongest Banking Bureau 'representative' in the group. His support for greater efficiency in the late 1960s and early 1970s was sufficient reason to suggest his continued support for gradual change. Maekawa represented the BOJ and therefore was a strong proponent of introduction and interest rate deregulation. The others were supporters of deregulation first and foremost, and therefore of CDs in as much as they contributed to this end.[49]

There were several possible explanations for the Group's formation. One person interviewed suggested that it was a means of giving the chairman of the Federation of Regional Bankers (and former MOF administrative vice-minister), Yoshikuni Jirō, a way of accepting the outcome without great loss of face. A more subtle explanation was that Yoshikuni represented a very powerful interest group, the regional banks, which simply could not be ignored. Both these explanations provide part of the answer.[50]

From the Banking Bureau's viewpoint, a Discussion Group was necessary to defuse the remaining opposition and to legitimise the outcome. The director-general of the Banking Bureau, Tokuda Hiromi, was well aware of the need to formulate a policy based on as wide a support group as was possible. The cost to the MOF of forming the Discussion Group was small. Although it meant that the Banking Bureau would lose direct control over formulating a plan, it still retained effective veto rights as the conditions for introduction were implemented through administrative means.

Confirmation of the negotiation role of the Discussion Group emerges on examining the way in which its business was conducted. The Banking Bureau's initial position on what characteristics were appropriate for the CDs market included the following:

Period:	less than one year, probably six months
Flotation Unit:	formally 100 million yen, but in practice 1000 million yen minimum
Interest rate:	controlled at the upper limit, at a level determined by the rate on two year fixed deposits.[51]

These characteristics were included in the document which formed the basis of the Discussion Group's deliberations. It was called the 'proposal of the Head of the Discussion Group' but was, in effect, a proposal developed in the Banking Bureau.[52] The Discussion Group experienced great problems with this proposal on the questions of flotation unit size, the nature of negotiability and interest rates.

The importance of unit size related to the question of who was expected to purchase the certificate, and this issue was of major interest to the long-term credit banks. If the unit was 100 million yen then there was the prospect of some shift of individual clientele from the long-term credit bank's financial bonds to CDs. The position of the long-term credit banks became the key in establishing the level at 500 million yen, which virtually excluded participation by individuals. This level caused no great problem for the MOF which had always seen the market primarily as wholesale rather than retail. In this respect, the proposal differed considerably from the rules obtaining in New York, which set a minimum limit of US$100 000, or about one-twentieth of the proposed Japanese level.[53] It was not a decision welcomed by the very large city banks but, because the question would be administrative rather than legal once introduction was achieved, it was an area which could again be subject to negotiation.

The negotiability question was a second area of dispute. The Banking Bureau proposed that the certificates should be endorsed by the issuing bank before any resale could occur. Although the Discussion Group questioned the need for endorsement, the failure to include this restriction would have created delaying legal problems, and opened the policymaking process up to other influences. Reluctantly, it agreed with the MOF's position. It was the question of interest rates that became the key problem and the last to be resolved.[54]

On this issue, the position of the BOJ was important. It regarded the introduction of deregulated interest rates in the CDs market as a useful contribution to improving the effectiveness of monetary policy by intervention in the money markets. Although various studies on interest rate deregulation had been made by the Research Department, and recommendations put to the Executive Board of the BOJ during the governorship of Sasaki Tadashi, they had all been rejected. The dominance of the regulated interest rate philosophy was shaken during the great inflation of 1972–73, and gradually the view of the economists who support deregulation came to prevail over the administrators, who preferred regulatory guidance. At the same time, the objective of monetary policy switched from concentrating on external balance (the problem of the balance of payments) to internal balance (control of the level of inflation). The dominant view in the BOJ favoured the introduction of CDs providing interest rates were completely deregulated. Without deregulated interest rates CDs meant little to the BOJ.[55] Interest rates established in the market were the cornerstone of its plan to develop the short-term capital markets. In the Discussion Group, the BOJ's representatives were at the forefront of opposition to regulated interest rates.

As for the MOF, one explanation of its initial position was that it had included regulated rates because of the opposition shown to deregulated interest rates in the submission of many of the banking groups, which argued that deregulated rates would cause an increase in overall interest rates. This position was maintained by two former Banking Bureau officials interviewed. If this was true, as it seems, the MOF interpreted opinion badly. As it became clear that the time period would be restricted, all but the securities companies favoured completely deregulated rates. If CDs were going to be introduced, the long-term credit banks argued, then they ought to be competitive with *gensaki* transactions. Finally, the Banking Bureau changed its position, and permitted the establishment of a CDs market with deregulated interest rates.[56]

A DIGRESSION: INDIVIDUALS IN THE POLICYMAKING PROCESS—THE CASE OF TOKUDA HIROMI

Up to this point, the roles of individuals in the policymaking process have not been analysed. Given, however, the view encountered in many interviews with bankers and public servants that the role of Tokuda Hiromi, the director-general of the Banking Bureau, was crucial in the process which led to the introduction of CDs, some discussion of this key figure in the MOF seems necessary.

Tokuda Hiromi became director-general of the Banking Bureau in mid-1977 after a career in the MOF which had included many years working within the Banking Bureau. Included among these was his period as advisor to the CFSR in the late 1960s and early 1970s, and his role in the 1970 CFSR report. He was thus involved intimately in major CFSR inquiries of the 1960s and 1970s.

On becoming director-general, one of his first and perhaps most controversial actions was to establish the FPRG which was designed to assist the exploration of policy options. It was also of potential use as a means of assessing the reaction of industry and the LDP to a range of policy proposals which might not otherwise be able to be stated in such a forthright manner. The establishment of the FPRG was not universally popular as it largely overlapped with the existing functions of the CFSR. Initial distrust of the FPRG was compounded by the publicity given to its first report, which was published at a time when the same types of issues were being discussed by the CFSR. Much of the hostility could probably have been avoided but Tokuda's willingness to talk about policy options made him somewhat atypical among his MOF contemporaries.

The establishment of the FPRG was significant in that it introduced less institutionalised opinion into the policymaking process through participants who were mainly younger academics from a range of universities and not representatives of interest groups. How much the group contributed to the development of policy is another question; had the group become an established part of the policy process and met regularly and frankly it might have contributed significantly. The fact that it was a private body of the director-general meant that it could easily fall into disuse after Tokuda ended his assignment. This, in fact, happened when Tokuda was replaced by Yonesato Hiroshi in 1979.[57]

The use of the FPRG did not imply that Tokuda wished to become involved in all matters of detail. The comment of Komiya and Yamamoto that the function of the director-general was to keep the bureau operating smoothly, and to leave the detail to his subordinates, was appropriate in the CDs case.[58] The day-to-day support work at various stages of the CFSR investigation was done by middle-ranking public servants such as Noda Minoru, Nakahira Yukinori and Seki Kaname. Tokuda was involved intimately in the key stages of the policymaking process, such as in the decision to proceed with the development of a detailed plan and in the appointment of the Discussion Group. This is what one would expect of any senior executive. The decision to go ahead with CDs was based on the view, held not only by Tokuda but widely within the Banking Bureau, that the costs to the city banks of the existing framework of regulations which controlled their activities had become too high. Other directors-general might have refrained from introducing CDs because of the opposition from within the banking industry, but they would have had to take some action.

Tokuda's approach both limited and aggravated conflict. He limited conflict by deciding to form the CDs Discussion Group after public opposition to the introduction continued beyond the point where it would normally have petered out. He was not prepared to alter his position but he was prepared to examine the alternatives within the option to introduce CDs. His decision to restrict the character of CDs to 'deposit' type enabled him to introduce CDs with minimum fuss but also created considerable conflict within the MOF. The relationship between the Banking Bureau and the Securities Bureau deteriorated during the two years Tokuda was director-general. There had always been animosity between the two bureaus, and during 1977–79 it again became very noticeable.[59] Whether Tokuda or the director-general of the Securities Bureau, Yamauchi Hiroshi, was to blame, or whether the imbalance of financial relations between competing institutions made conflict inevitable given the nature of the institutional processes, is difficult to assess. A case can be made for each of three possibilities. Tokuda was not a reckless man, but a moderate reformer. He argued on the one hand that the banking system was not the sole province of one group of financial institutions and attempted to maintain this philosophy in practice. On the other hand, he was not encouraging rapid reform. He viewed the financial system as a part of the support structure of society and believed that the MOF had an important role to play in managing the evolution of the system. If he was different from his MOF contemporaries it was in his belief that some change was necessary. In the CDs case, he removed immobilist influences where he could, and used the strength of the Banking Bureau to its fullest. The fact that CDs were a new asset type reduced from the outset the likelihood of LDP intervention. The LDP showed no interest in the CDs policymaking process at all. The matter was made a Banking Bureau problem with the decision to introduce 'deposit' type CDs, so that outside opposition had to be channelled through the Banking Bureau.[60]

When the record of Tokuda Hiromi's two years at the helm of the Banking Bureau is compared with that of other directors-general, the similarities rather than the difference appear important. For example, Tokuda took a strong interest in issues of economic efficiency. He encouraged merger activity between financial institutions with almost no success; he attempted to introduce the sale of government bonds at bank windows, again with no success; he examined the issue of appropriate disclosure provisions for Japanese banks, but the matter was unresolved when he retired. The only major change in regulation achieved was on the CDs issue. Tokuda's track record showed that the power of the director-general was indeed limited. Tokuda was the consummate senior public servant in the way that he briefed politicians and the senior members of the finance industry, and made himself regularly available to the press.[61] These factors made him prominent in everyday affairs but they did not change his fundamental role as director-general. Like all directors-general he was important in as much as he was a senior player in the policymaking process, but he still operated within the constraints set by established methods, and with the assistance and guidance of other members of the Banking Bureau.

The policymaking process on the CDs issue showed clearly that the central aim of the Banking Bureau was not to encourage the development of the short-term money markets but to respond to the deterioration of the balance and stability of the financial system. The explanation of that process offered here concentrates on highlighting the narrowness of the policymaking process, and the ability of the Banking Bureau to exclude other parts of the MOF from it, by opting for a compromise solution at the outset on issues which could have broadened participation. The technical character of the issue, the lack of established interest groups and the restrictions on the shape of the market, were all factors likely to ensure minimal political interest in the issue. The Banking Bureau showed how strong an individual bureau could be when the policymaking process was defined narrowly. Its concern that financial institutions be able to meet the demands placed on them overrode pressure from individual financial institutions that their own existing jurisdictions should take priority in determining new policy. Groups opposed to change had an impact on the character of CDs but not on the fundamental decision taken by the Banking Bureau to proceed with the policy proposal. The following chapter presents a case study in which the interests of two bureaus of the MOF were inextricably interlocked, and the impact that this had on the policymaking process.

4 The issue of trading in government bonds

Intra-ministry policymaking

A recurrent theme in the contemporary history of the Japanese finance industry was that of disputes between financial institutions concerning which group was responsible for a particular area of business. Jurisdictions were, in most cases, defined by law, although new areas of business and areas which were administered differently from the stipulation of law provided many exceptions. Chapter 3 examined an example involving a new area of business. This chapter examines the issue of trading in government bonds where administrative guidance rather than the law determined which groups conducted the business.

The issue of trading in government bonds by banks involved two separate elements. One was 'dealing' in securities, which involved banks being able to buy and sell government securities in the same way as the securities companies operated in all other bond markets. The term 'dealing' included not only the direct sale of bonds underwritten by banks as members of the government bond underwriting syndicate but also trade in the secondary market. As noted in chapter 2, banks were not allowed to operate freely in this area. The second element was buying and selling of government bonds at banks by individual customers. The difference between the two was that the latter would involve small-scale transactions and individual investors, whereas the former was the arena of large-scale transactions and institutional investors.[1] Table 4.1 outlines the management of the bond market between 1965 and 1982, a period in which the regulatory framework changed little. Banks had a legal right to operate in both the abovementioned areas but were prevented from doing so by administrative guidance emanating from the MOF. In March 1982 a three-man government committee suggested that banks be permitted to sell government bonds to the public, but that the dealing issue be left open for the present. On 30 March 1982 this became MOF policy, and since April 1983 banks have been conducting over the counter sales of government bonds.[2] The debate on the issue during the previous seventeen years provides the basis for examining the importance of intra-ministry negotiations in determining policy outcomes.

According to our model outlined in the introduction, the development of new policy initiatives might be hindered at many levels by immobilist forces within the policymaking system. Three of these influences are examined in this chapter. First, the proposition raised in the previous chapter that conflict

Table 4.1   Management of business in the bond market, 1965–82

Type of Business[a]	Management Role[b]	
	Banks[c]	Securities Companies[d]
Issue market for bonds		
Underwriting bonds		
1 government, regional &	A	A
govt-guaranteed bonds		
2 industrial bonds	C	A
and shares		
Selling, subscribing		
and managing sales of bonds		
1	B	A
2	C	A
Secondary market for bonds		
Buying & selling bonds		
1	B	A
2	C	A
Acting as intermediary,		
agent or representative		
1	B[e]	A
2	C	A

Notes: a For a complete coverage of bond market-related business see full table in source
cited below
  b A: Permitted; B: Possible but not permitted under administrative guidance; C:
Prohibited
  c Under section 65, SEL
  d Under section 2.28, SEL
  e Trust banks permitted to undertake this business

Source: Kin'yū mondai kenkyūkai *Kongo ni okeru wa ga kuni no kin'yū kikan no arikata* 1978,
pp. 224–25

between participants in the industry leads to non-acceptance of new policy options is re-examined. In chapters 2 and 3 we noted the fragmented interests of different banking groups. The impact of this fragmentation on the development of policy in the issue of trading in government bonds is examined, and contrasted with the relationship between securities companies. Second, the proposition that politicians were little interested in matters which did not affect their electoral prospects is revisited. Whereas the debate in PARC was minimal on the issues of CDs, in this case it was more substantial. The reasons for this involvement are analysed and its impact on the formation of policy assessed. Third, and of central importance, the proposition that regulatory change can be impeded by the presence of several bureaus with competing interests in a policymaking process is discussed and, in doing so, a contrast is drawn between the policymaking process that dominated formation of policy in this case with the case presented in chapter 3.

FACTORS HINDERING POLICY CHANGE

Under the influence of the Occupation forces, the Securities Exchange Law passed in May 1948 introduced at least one novel feature into the Japanese financial system. The law drew a clear distinction between securities business and banking business. Had it been left at that the problem which is the subject of this chapter would not have arisen. In November 1948, however, article 65(2) was added to the law, making it legal for the banks to underwrite and sell government securities. As government bonds were not issued until fiscal 1965, the application of the law to practice was not raised until that time.[3]

The establishment of policy

The first tentative delineation of government policy on the involvement of banks in the buying and selling of government bonds was in 1965, at the time when the MOF was forming its policy towards the operation of the government bond market as a whole. In a preliminary statement in September 1965, the Financial Bureau argued that all members of the underwriting syndicate for government bonds (which at the time was itself only a proposed syndicate) should be permitted to sell government bonds, but that any subsequent trade in the secondary market should be transacted through the securities companies. This was an even-handed proposal working within the shape of the existing financial system. The Financial Bureau proposed that the banks be permitted to sell their holdings but stopped short of suggesting they should be allowed to operate in the way suggested by the Securities and Exchange Council (SEC). It was sufficiently realistic to note that the securities companies might complain if the banks were given any right of resale and even that opposition from within the deposit section of banks might necessitate seeking a different outcome. Deposit sections of banks saw their jurisdictions being infringed by the development of securities business within banks.[4]

By the end of 1965, a MOF policy began to emerge which favoured giving the securities companies a central role in the handling of secondary market trading. The banking community was persuaded by the MOF to forego its legal right in the area of sale of government bonds at banks, and with it the more disputed right to deal in government bonds. The reasons why the banks did not actively pursue their rights were threefold. First, there was opposition from within the banks to the expansion of business into the areas of securities trading. Second, there was informal agreement by the BOJ that it would buy a large proportion of government bonds held by banks for over a year. Third, banks were responding to requests of the MOF which was attempting to re-establish stability in the securities industry. In 1964 Yamaichi Securities was on the verge of bankruptcy and was only saved by emergency loans from the BOJ. The MOF hoped that the development of the government bond market would help securities companies re-establish their profitability. The policy which was established conformed with the rest of the regulatory framework in operation and at the time did not create major opposition within the banking community. The policy imposed no new major costs on either the banks or the securities companies.[5]

In subsequent years, most notably in 1976, 1977–78 and 1979–81, the debate for policy change was begun and reactivated with increasing acrimony. On each occasion after the establishment of policy, alteration of that policy was prevented by a different set of circumstances.

1976: Disunity amongst the banks

Although trading in government bonds by banks became a topical subject on at least one occasion during the decade to 1976, the support for a change in the status quo was limited to the largest of the city banks.[6] Their interest was insufficient to provoke a change in existing policy. At the end of 1976 trading in government bonds at banks (which would later have resulted in dealing) was offered to the banks as part of a package. The Financial Bureau was preparing the way for the introduction of five-year discount government bonds, a line of business which would be handled by the securities companies. Five-year discount bonds were regarded as one method of increasing individuals' participation in the government bond market and thus expanding the quantity of bonds which the market could absorb. But the banks, particularly the long-term credit banks, were vociferously opposed to the move, arguing that it would divert funds away from the traditionally strong fixed deposit and bank debenture area. Anticipating opposition, the Banking Bureau was able to offer the banks the quid pro quo of access to the selling of government bonds business. The Securities Bureau was not in a position to oppose the move: the securities companies were being offered a new area of business (the discount bond market), their existing business was strong, and in law the banks had the right to buy and sell government-related bonds. The agreement to forego involvement in selling government bonds originated at a time when the securities industry was in a depressed state, something which could not be said about the industry in 1976.[7]

Despite being presented with this ideal opportunity, the banking community could not reach an agreement within its own ranks. The problem of competition with the banks' established deposit business, and the concern in many banks that diversification would benefit only the largest city banks, proved too much. The head of the Federation of Bankers' Associations in 1976 turned down the offer of the director-general of the Banking Bureau, and was forced to watch the introduction of five-year discount bonds without any commensurate change to the framework of banking business.[8] In this case it was not a problem of overcoming differences of opinion with the MOF, or political interference (which did not occur), but simply lack of agreement within the banking community itself. The inability of the banks to formulate a united position underlined one important contrast between the banks and securities sectors. In banking, interests differed significantly, whereas in securities, although there were different views within the industry, the four large securities companies dominated so completely that they could dictate policy.

From the outset, the interest of large city banks in selling government bonds was not in their sale to individuals, which would only be marginally profitable, but in the area of dealing. Smaller banks were concerned that the entry of larger banks into the area of buying and selling government bonds would reduce further their own ability to compete. Their interest was, as observed in earlier case studies, in preservation of the existing status quo. Long-term credit banks also adopted a negative position towards the involvement of other banks in securities activity. Such involvement would have further eroded their specialised function within the banking sector.

At the organisational level banks were represented first by their functional groups. For example, the peak association of regional banks was the Federation of Regional Bankers' Associations. As the general level these functional associations were grouped to form the Federation of Bankers' Associations. Unity was feasible at the less aggregated level of functional groups but was often difficult at the level of the Federation of Bankers' Associations. Although the large city banks were an order of magnitude larger than many regional banks, they were not significantly larger than the long-term credit banks or the trust banks, and often had conflicting interests.[9] The organisation and interests of the securities companies offered a stark contrast.

The Securities Dealers' Association of Japan was the peak body of the securities community but, unlike the Federation of Bankers' Associations, it was dominated by the 'big four'—Nomura, Yamaichi, Daiwa and Nikko Securities. The underlying assumption of the organisation was that the large companies got their way on crucial matters but were prepared to support small companies in matters not so important to themselves. Furthermore, the close relationship between the large securities and the small ones made the actual business environment of the securities sector more oligopolistic than competitive.[10]

1977–78: Intra-MOF disputation

In 1977, the question of limitations on the sale of government bonds after they had initially been underwritten by banks became a focus of attention by city banks. In the same year, the MOF permitted the banks to sell their holdings of government bonds through the market (i.e. via securities companies) after they had been held for a period of one year. The stipulation that the sale process should use securities companies and the realisation of the size of the potential market made the banks reconsider the position they had formulated in 1976.

In a detailed statement of their position, in December 1977, the city banks called for permission to be granted to the banks which underwrote government bonds to trade on the same grounds as the securities companies.[11] The statement said that approval to conduct this business could be given by the Banking Bureau since it came under the Banking Law, and was approved under the Securities and Exchange Law. City banks strongly supported both the sale of government bonds to individuals, and dealing. Anticipating opposition from securities companies on the latter problem, the banks suggested that step-by-step introduction would prevent any disturbance to the market. They argued, however, that after an introductory period there should not be any restrictions imposed upon the banks; rather the quantity and timing of sales should be left to the discretion of individual banks.

The more organised and unified sense of group action can be attributed to a growing feeling of the importance of the government bond sector. While acknowledging that some adverse impact on savings deposit business could occur, the new emerging consensus focused on the importance of dealing in government bonds, in other words, in large transactions, and being able to offer a wider service to individual customers.

During 1977, however, the circumstances which had favoured the granting of bank access to the trade in the secondary government bond market all but disappeared. In late 1976 the securities companies obtained a monopoly on the underwriting and sale of medium-term discount bonds (the first issue occurring in January 1977), and this had become an accomplished fact.[12] The involvement of banks in the government bonds business in new areas, as far as they were concerned, was a problem which stood by itself. In early December 1977, the Bond Underwriters Association made representations to the MOF opposing any change to the existing status quo and more than anything else was sceptical of the ability of banks to improve the market's absorptive capacity.[13]

The negotiations within the MOF were at the level of director-general, with Tokuda Hiromi representing the Banking Bureau and Yamauchi Hiroshi respresenting the Securities Bureau. In late December 1977, the Minister of Finance, Murayama Tatsuo, announced that the problem was being examined within the MOF. By the end of January 1978, plans to widen the scope of banking business, argued by the Banking Bureau, were shelved. The main factors working against policy changes were the strong stance taken by the Securities Bureau, the strong underwriting performance of the securities companies in fiscal 1977 and the failure of other bureaus within the MOF to back up the stance taken by the Banking Bureau. Most important was the fact that the Securities Bureau became less accommodating; in 1976 it had no room to bargain as securities business was expanded simultaneously and it was only proposed that banks be given what was already theirs in law. In 1977–78 the Securities Bureau did not feel so inhibited, and presented a case similar to that argued by the securities companies. The Banking Bureau tried to reopen the case but its bargaining position was much weaker than in 1976. It did not have sole control over policy in the area, so it could not take a unilateral stance as it did in the CDs case in 1978–79.[14]

Besides the Banking Bureau and the Securities Bureau, the Financial Bureau had an interest in the outcome of the debate on policy relating to trading in government bonds by banks. The Financial Bureau was caught between two conflicting positions. On the one hand, it realised that allowing banks into the market would even up the level of sales to individuals and lead, overall, to a greater placement of bonds in the individual sector. During the 1970s the securities companies did not achieve a consistent level of sales of government bonds and were even criticised by the Minister of Finance for only supporting the market when profitability appeared assured. On the other hand, the Financial Bureau recognised the importance of the securities companies to the underwriting syndicate and did not want to risk offending them by siding with the Banking Bureau. Finally, the Financial Bureau adopted a policy of non-intervention. Both the policy of the Financial Bureau and the outcome itself are impossible to understand in purely economic terms. The policy did not allow choice nor did it permit bonds to be sold in the widest possible market. Had the banks been able to buy and sell bonds, negotiability would have improved as the number of transaction outlets increased. There would probably have been some shift from competing deposits to government bonds.

In the end, the decision not to proceed signified that the Securities Bureau and the Banking Bureau could not agree on the need for change or the terms of change. The surrounding economic environment was such that there did not appear to be any reason for change other than that it would benefit the banks. In late 1977 and early 1978 the bond markets reflected the easy monetary policy that had existed since 1975. Whereas twelve months earlier banks were being offered the right to buy and sell government bonds, in late 1977 the administrative framework of competing jurisdictions prevented its realisation. Economic conditions did not change, only bargaining ones. The 1977–78 decision highlighted the importance of intra-MOF bargaining to regulatory policy.

PUBLIC SERVICE DOMINANCE AND INTRA-MINISTRY CONFLICT

The fourth time when the issue of the trading in government bonds by banks was actively discussed within the MOF was during 1979–81. Discussions were drawn out, complicated and acrimonious, but did show to good effect the character of the policymaking process.

On 20 June 1979 the CFSR, which had earlier recommended that CDs be introduced, made an unequivocal recommendation that banks be allowed to operate in an unrestricted way in the sale of government bonds. The contribution to wider asset choice and the improvement of absorption of government bonds by individuals were sufficient reasons, it argued, for overturning the status quo.[15] A week later the SEC, which had conducted considerable research into the future options for the securities industry, issued a similarly comprehensive report, with far more equivocal conclusions on the role of banks in the trading of government bonds. It felt that many legal problems remained, and that questions concerning supervision and regulation of banking activity needed to be more thoroughly investigated before any change should be contemplated.[16] The differences between the two reports served to emphasise an important characteristic ascribed to formal research bodies in chapter 2, namely that the reports represented quite faithfully the views of their supervisory bureaus, the Banking Bureau and the Securities Bureau respectively.[17]

Five months later both views were once again presented to the MOF, this time by the respective industry organisations. In November 1979, representatives of the two major securities industry organisations made a submission to the Minister of Finance, asking that when a decision was taken on the question of the extent of bank business, the SEC report be given due consideration.[18] The submission was made in the context of the legislative redrafting of the Bank Law that had been under way since 1975 and for which the 1979 report of the CFSR was to form the basis for legislative amendments. The city banks also made a submission two weeks later, but directed it at the director-general of the Banking Bureau, Yonesato Hiroshi. The submission entreated the MOF to convert the major thrusts of the CFSR report into clear principles of action.[19] First the reports of the two MOF committees, and later the submissions of the securities companies and city banks, made the probability of conflict on the issue of legislative reform high.

The impact of political lobbying

In the summer of 1980, following the release of the CFSR's report on legislative reform to the Banking Law, the MOF began a detailed examination of the problem of trading in government bonds by banks. Realising that there was a strong feeling in favour of reform within the MOF, the securities companies took the fairly unusual step of beginning a low-key political campaign aimed at ensuring the retention of the status quo.[20] Senior executives of the major securities companies were assigned politicians to lobby, with the emphasis on LDP politicians who were members of both the House of Representative's Finance Committee and the PARC's Finance Committee. Both these committees had many new members following the July 1980 election which made the task of the securities companies even more difficult. The lobbying was designed to ensure that if negotiations with the MOF went badly, the contingency plan of taking the debate to the political level would remain.[21]

Associated with this campaign were several pamphlets prepared by the securities companies, outlining why the banks should not be permitted to buy and sell government bonds. The main points of their argument were that:

1 the holdings of individuals were high by world standards, and bank operations could not be expected to result in a greatly expanded volume of sales;
2 the secondary market was the second largest in the world, and relatively stable, so that little improvement could be expected;
3 banks would not be able to function satisfactorily as intermediaries, given that they had been consistenly big sellers of government bonds;
4 bank involvement would disturb the establishment of a fair market price;
5 the division between banking and securities business ought to be maintained.[22]

In logical terms the case was not strong.

First, although individual holdings were substantial (something which could be attributed to lucrative tax concessions), the central question was whether bank involvement would stabilise the fluctuations and increase the overall level of purchases by individuals. The securities companies failed to address this question completely. Their comparisons with the United States on level of bonds purchased by individuals were misleading because the savings rate of Japanese far exceeded that of Americans, and the range and preference of assets were also quite different.[23]

Second, greater competition would normally be expected to improve the stability of the market rather than hinder it. Under the existing system the four big securities companies could have asserted oligopolistic control. Increasing the diversity of participants would reduce the likelihood of this occurring.[24]

Third, banks were consistent sellers in the government bond market because they were required to underwrite bonds and were not permitted, like the securities companies, to buy and sell at will, or to balance their portfolios. The obvious retort to the position of the securities companies was that under existing administrative guidance no other position was possible.

Fourth, the argument of unfair competition was often used but little evidence was ever produced. Before the introduction of CDs a similar argument was used, yet there is no evidence that the envisaged distortion in the market occurred. There was indeed no reason to assume, given the dominant position of Nomura Securities, and the virtual oligopoly of the four major securities companies, that a fair price had existed over the years.

The final argument, that the divisions between banking and securities ought to be maintained, is the most difficult to assess. It is indisputable that the financial system performed effectively over most of the postwar period, based on a system of specialised financial institutions. The fact that one system worked well for so long was no reason, however, that it should remain appropriate indefinitely. The reason why banks showed an increased interest in this area of business was related to the increasing involvement of banks in securities work in the international arena in the 1970s, and the growth of secondary market activities in Japan towards the end of the 1970s. There were no economic arguments why the developments that blurred the distinction between banking and securities business in the international arena should not be contemplated in Japan.[25]

If the outcome was determined simply on the merits of their case, one would not have expected the securities companies to enjoy much success. Having watched the Securities Bureau being overriden on the CDs issue, the securities companies began from the outset to activate a campaign based on the political level as well as within the public service.

The canvassing of politicians that the securities companies conducted throughout 1980 illustrated another important difference between securities companies and the banks, particularly the big banks. In general, the securities companies paid more attention to political connections.[26] Close relationships existed between small banks (particularly mutual and regional banks) and politicians, but the big city banks based their strength not on political contacts but on sound economic expansion and their relationship with the regulatory body in charge of the behaviour of banks, the Banking Bureau.[27] It came as no surprise that the banking community did not attempt to agitate on a political level until the important decisions had all but been made.

Traditionally the views of the banking community (and in particular the city banks) were organised by the bank whose president was, at the time, chairman of the Federation of Bankers' Associations. In fiscal 1980, Mitsubishi Bank handled the secretariat functions of the Federation. Normally it would have maintained close and cordial ties with the Banking Bureau, but in fiscal 1980 the relationship between Mitsubishi Bank and the Banking Bureau at one level, and between the president of Mitsubishi Bank, Yamada Hajime, and the director-general of the Banking Bureau, Yonesato Hiroshi, was less than cordial, reflecting the position that Mitsubishi Bank was taking on the issue yields of government bonds. It appears likely that the MOF took the unusual step of discussing its proposals with some of the major city banks in confidence, but not with Mitsubishi Bank.[28] No better evidence exists than the range of disagreement over the Banking Law that existed when the Banking Bureau presented its draft. Under normal circumstances the draft would have been discussed in detail with the banks before public release, thus avoiding the acrimonious debate that followed. For a document which was several years in preparation, the differences between the industry and the MOF were numerous. It was not a document which furthered or even fully defended the interests of the banking community. Hence, although it was apparent that a policy position had been established within the MOF, it was clear that the Banking Bureau did not have the support of the banking community for its proposed amendments.[29] Only at this stage did the banks begin a politically based campaign.

After intense negotiations in the latter part of 1980 between the Banking Bureau, the Securities Bureau, and to a lesser extent the Financial Bureau, a proposal emerged which had the backing of the MOF. The plan was clearly a compromise solution, but perhaps most importantly it did not bring the banks any closer to realising their immediate aim for trading in government bonds. The securities companies did not achieve all they wanted in this first plan but they were successful in their aim of delaying any change.[30]

On 12 December 1980, the MOF's plan for the revision of the Banking Law came before the PARC's Financial Problems Research Committee. When the problem of sale of government bonds by banks arose, the committee decided in that meeting to leave the resolution of the problem to the MOF.[31] The reason that the LDP attempted to eschew involvement in the dispute was simply that it had no direct interest in what was an industry matter and it could not possibly benefit from involvement. Both the banks and the securities companies made substantial contributions to the LDP's electoral campaigns and any involvement was bound to be interpreted as favouring one side over the other.[32] The dispute was seen as essentially jurisdictional and hence one which should be left to the MOF. It was a dispute which the LDP as a whole did not want to touch. To some extent, however, the LDP was drawn into the dispute against its will. Debate shifted from the LDP back to the MOF and in December the MOF unveiled a plan based on three principles:

1   even if approval were given under the Banking Law, actual approval would
    not be immediately forthcoming;
2   banks would be required to obtain approval for any operation related to
    securities business under the Securities Law;
3   business would be restricted to public bonds.[33]

This plan drew a strong reaction from city bankers, and in particular from
Yamada, who called the proposed law a big step backwards when compared
with the existing law.[34]

On 10 January 1981, a position paper by the Federation of Bankers'
Associations focused on the main point of contention with the MOF's plan. In
the long run, reclassification of the banks' securities business from 'attached
business' to 'other business' was seen as a change which could substantially
restrict the ability of banks to move into the securities business and also bring
that business under the control of Securities and Exchange Law. 'Attached
business' of banks were those activities that banks were allowed to undertake
outside their main banking business and in which they were supervised by the
Banking Bureau. 'Other business' covered those areas which required approval
and supervision by other government authorities or MOF bureaus. For the first
time, the banks said that if the classification was changed they would have to
reconsider carefully their position towards underwriting government bonds.
The mere mention of this possibility, part bluff though it probably was, showed
the intensity of their reactions. During December 1980 and January 1981 the
dispute raged between the Banking Bureau and the banks, rather than the more
usual intra-industry or intra-MOF disputation.[35]

The role of the LDP

Although negotiations between the Banking Bureau and Mitsubishi Bank
continued through January and into February 1981, no resolution was achieved.
When the matter came up before the joint meeting of the PARC's Financial
Problems Research Group and Finance Subcommittee (bodies headed by Satō
Ichirō and Koizumi Jun'ichirō respectively) on 23 February 1981, Mitsubishi
Bank's Yamada Hajime made a strong request that the whole law be re-
examined carefully.[36] Although the Minister of Finance, Watanabe Michio,
stood firmly behind the plan proposed by his ministry, a comment by the head
of the PARC, Abe Shintarō, that there were reservations within the LDP
towards the legislation, would have given Yamada some cause for hope.[37] But
Watanabe stood his ground and refused to make any major concessions. All
appeared to be proceeding smoothly when, in early March, Watanabe briefed
Prime Minister Suzuki on the major issues of the law as a preliminary to Cabinet
approval. But that was not the case: it was not until 20 April 1981 that the draft
Banking Law reached the Cabinet. In the interim period of six weeks one
of the longest discussions on a single piece of legislation on financial matters
took place within the LDP. At a meeting of the Joint Committee, on 9 March

1981, opposition to the revision in its existing form was sufficient to force a clause-by-clause consideration of the legislation.[38]

It is difficult to analyse the meetings of the Joint Committee on the Banking Law. On the question of membership any member of the LDP could participate. The Financial Problems Research Group had approximately 100 members, of whom 30 or 40 generally attended meetings. Weight cannot be attached to membership alone, as members often showed their faces, spoke for several minutes to fulfil outstanding obligations, then departed. Lack of formal voting procedures within the Committee gave the Head of the Committee an important policy role in forming the precise character of the LDP position. When broad agreement was absent at the committee stage, the head of PARC, the Prime Minister and other senior party officials were consulted.[39]

General comments can be made about the handling of the Banking Law in the LDP.

First, as a party, the LDP's role was consistent from the outset: that the MOF was the proper place for the policy decision to be made. In the Financial Problems Research Group in December 1980, and the Joint Committee meetings between February and April 1981, the dominant view was that resolution of the dispute and development of new policy should be left to the MOF. Watanabe Michio was an uncompromising minister from the outset, a fact which underscored the low level of political input in the decision.

The political concern within the LDP was conveyed through the remarks of the chairman of the PARC, Abe Shintarō, on draft revisions to the Bank Law. The bulk of this concern related to the role of the MOF under the proposed law. The draft law envisaged an expanded role for administrative guidance within the MOF, which was not welcomed by the LDP backbench. In response to the LDP opposition to some clauses, several important revisions were made in the area of disclosure and the extent that banks could loan funds to a single client. The intent of the legislation was to make controls on banking operations more explicit but these changes were interpreted, by members of the Joint Committee, as an attempt by the MOF to increase the extent of its control. They had little to do with the trading in government bonds by banks, but they did show that what the LDP did not like was readily amended.[40]

Second, although the complaints of the Federation of Bankers' Associations were heard at the Joint Committee, there was little evidence of widespread support for the bankers' position.[41] Former bankers such as Karasawa Shunjirō and Koyama Asanori strongly supported the case of the banks. Their persistence created much discussion and delay but had little impact on the final policy. The supporters of the securities companies were less vocal within the LDP, and their support group was also small but had done the groundwork to create opposition to change if the debate within the MOF proceeded badly. The securities companies were apparently satisfied with the result to the extent that they believed further overt lobbying would be counterproductive.

One noteworthy criticism of the MOF made by the LDP was the fact that it allowed the problem to get out of control. One can speculate on what would have occurred had the negotiated agreement between the Securities Bureau and

Banking Bureau been very different and based, for example, on the immediate introduction of dealing by banks within an appropriate framework (as occurred in the CDs case). This would have produced a campaign by the securities companies to reverse the decision. The securities companies would have attempted to activate support within the LDP to reverse the decision, but it was not likely that they would have been able to canvass sufficient political support. An understanding of the decision to draw back from making any immediate changes to the status quo involves understanding the compromise that was reached between the Banking Bureau and the Securities Bureau in early December 1980. The reasons why the Banking Bureau was content with merely defining more clearly in the Banking Law the role of the banks in the securities business holds the key to understanding this policy decision.

Bargaining within the MOF

After the long and sometimes bitter debate on the role of banks in trading in government bonds during the second half of the 1970s, the 1980s brought the prospect of a policy change. Opposition to any change in regulations was still strong within the securities companies and Securities Bureau, but the unstable state of the government bond market, and the fact that the Banking Bureau was expected shortly to finalise the new Banking Law, were expected to lead to an early change in MOF policy. Resolution of the problem required an agreement to be reached between the Banking Bureau and the Securities Bureau, and any plan had to keep in focus the needs of the Financial Bureau, which was experiencing increasing difficulty fulfilling its fund-raising obligations.

The Banking Bureau's bargaining position had improved in the sense that the unreliability of securities companies as purchasers of government bonds had become more apparent. In addition, the volume of bonds had grown to an extent which put pressure on government to try any available method to improve digestion in the market.[42] Offsetting these pressures was the desire of the Banking Bureau to incorporate an explicit reference to the issue in the new Banking Law, which indirectly strengthened the position of the securities companies and the Securities Bureau.

The position of the Securities Bureau was complex. It had to consider not only the position of the securities companies, but also the increasing pressures for change within the bond markets. The initial agreement, reached in early December 1980, showed that the Securities Bureau was also considering its broader jurisdiction. Allowing banks to operate appeared inevitable at some stage, be it in one, two or five years. In particular, in 1985 the MOF's financial authorities would have to cope with large quantities of bonds due for redemption. There was little prospect of redemption, or of reissuing outstanding debt as it matured, if the market retained its existing structure. Negotiating with the Banking Bureau while the latter was under some pressure by way of the Banking Law gave it the best chance to achieve a satisfactory result on both grounds.

The essence of the initial agreement was that legal approval for trading in public bonds by banks would be given in the Banking Law but that banks would only be given authorisation at the discretion of the Securities Bureau. The active supervisory role over the securities business of banks would result from a change in designation of their securities business from 'attached' to 'other'. The Banking Bureau supported this plan because it offered the prospect of bank operations in the securities area at some stage, which it felt was a step ahead of the current position, and because it was promised the Securities Bureau's support in placating the securities companies, which were opposed to any concession on the issue. On the other hand, the Securities Bureau was ensured control across the whole securities area and was not required to make any immediate concessions. From the perspective of the MOF as a whole, it was seen as a skilful means of diffusing an increasingly troublesome problem.[43] In normal circumstances the call by the LDP for the MOF to sort out the problem itself indicated that the MOF plan would be implemented with little further comment.

Nonetheless, although the plan had apparently been in the making since August, and despite MOF claims that there had been adequate communication with the industry, both the securities companies and the banks were far from satisfied. There was little evidence of consensus outside the MOF. For example, on 5 December 1980 in the HRFC, the president of Nomura Securities, Kitaura, strongly voiced his opposition. This was, however, overshadowed in the following months by the quarrelling that occurred between Yamada Hajime of the Federation of Bankers' Associations and the MOF. The banks worded their position in the strongest and sharpest language, but made little inroad into the 'three principles' solution. They did, however, succeed in having many other changes made to the Banking Law, and received a guarantee that in all new areas of securities activities their position would be on an equal footing with the securities companies. They would, however, continue to be excluded from all non-government bond transactions within Japan. They also secured changes in the classification of business which meant that what they underwrote through established syndicates would not be subject to the SEL, although all other transactions would.[44]

The general view on the result of the bargaining process was that the securities companies had outshone the banks in political terms, and that this had a major impact on the outcome.[45] We have concluded differently, arguing that while the LDP was involved in the latter stages of the political process, bargaining between the Securities Bureau and the Banking Bureau largely shaped the outcome. The guidelines which were established protected the existing non-government bonds business of securities companies and delayed any change to the government bond sector, until the need became more pressing. In return, the Banking Bureau secured the rights of banks and facilitated, although with much more trouble than was initially envisaged, the passage of the revised Banking Law. The rapid acceptance of the views of the three-man committee, set up to recommend on a range of controversial issues, backs up this judgment. After the passage of the Banking Law, it was clear that it was only a matter of time before the pressures of the market dictated the need to diversify the avenues for absorption of government bonds as much as possible. In 1983 banks were permitted to sell government bonds directly to the public and from June 1984 were to be permitted to trade in government bonds, both areas from which they had been excluded by internal MOF administrative guidance.

BUREAU-LEVEL VERSUS INTRA-MINISTRY-LEVEL POLICYMAKING: A CONTRAST

In the case of both CDs and the trading in government securities by banks, it has been shown that regulatory constraints slowed down and influenced the extent of change in policy. Throughout the banking and securities industry, the public service in the first instance and the political environment more generally had a major impact on the character of the financial market which developed. Both cases illustrate that interest groups opposed to change had effective access to the policymaking process, even if their opposition was not always successful. In both cases, the demands for change came first and foremost from the city banks. These banks were the most constrained by the system of regulations that existed within Japan and thus had the most to gain from a breakdown of the established specialised banking system. In related cases of floating CDs and performing securities operations abroad, the city banks had shown that the skills needed to move into new areas of business were readily learnt. The international market provided the initial avenue to 'escape' from the constraints imposed by regulations in the domestic market and that it was explored enthusiastically is shown by the fact that during the 1970s overseas business expanded more rapidly than domestic business.

Overseas markets, however, could not be used as a means of delaying change indefinitely. By the latter half of the 1970s, the MOF and parts of business also recognised the need for a more diverse range of domestic assets, and in turn began the process of investigating the available options. In a regulated environment, the demands of one group are unlikely to be enough to produce regulatory change, unless the impact of that group is dominating. In Japan, there was a range of participants with varying degrees of influence but none within the industry with what could be called overriding influence. A coalition of interests was required before change would be considered. The main issues pertaining to each policymaking process are set out in Table 4.2.

In both cases the LDP was not interested in becoming involved in the policymaking process. It regarded both as industry issues, most appropriately resolved within the industry in conjunction with the MOF. This view reflected the predominant lack of interest in financial issues among LDP parliamentarians, which stemmed from the complexity of the subject, the competing interests of groups which were all LDP supporters and the existence of an ever-present time constraint. Despite the similarities between the CDs example and the problem considered in this chapter, the role of the LDP was different. In the CDs case, the LDP played no role and this can be attributed to the fact

**Table 4.2   Changing the structure of financial markets: the cases of CDs and
the trading in government bonds by banks**

	CDs	Trading in government bonds by banks (1980–81)
Contribution to solving existing industry problem	Improve banks' ability to raise funds, and diversify the options for industry's use of funds.	Improve the sale of government bonds. Impact on bank business positive and securities companies negative.
Nature of change	New financial product	Widening the range of intermediaries that could participate in existing markets.
Policymaking process	Limited to one bureau, the Banking Bureau.	Two key bureaus involved and the interests of a third important.
Attitude of interested parties to issue	Banking Bureau and some banks in favour. Securities Bureau, securities companies and some banks opposed.	Banks and securities companies held diametrically opposed views. Banking Bureau and Securities Bureau formulated compromise solution not agreed to by industry.
Extent of political involvement	Virtually none.	Some lobbying by securities companies before decision and by banking sector after the MOF had formulated its position. LDP, for the most part, not interested, although LDP fora used for intense debates.

that CDs were an asset which diversified the range of existing services into a new area. No sectoral group lost substantial business from their introduction, although several may have lost marginally.

The issue of trading in government bonds was of a different magnitude, and the costs of change would have been concentrated among fewer industry participants. The four largest securities companies stood to be most affected. Even in this case, however, the role of the LDP was to direct the MOF to settle the issue itself. Here the main problem of LDP involvement was that it would be forced to choose between the interest groups which supported it as a political party both financially and through services rendered. The LDP's decision to entrust the matter to the MOF was based as much on the fact that it did not

Figure 4.1 – Bureau-level policymaking

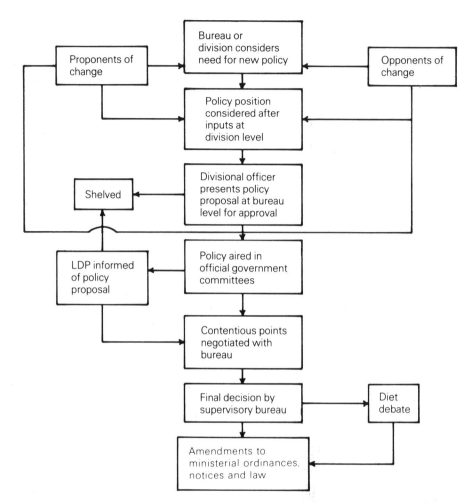

want to be involved as on the fact that it approved of the course that the MOF proposed (first and foremost to satisfy intra-MOF conflict), and was not based on the expected reactions of individual sectors. Each sector was consulted but the agreement satisfied neither of the two main interest groups. It was an agreement between the regulators of the banking and securities industries, and a response to growing financial problems within the existing set of regulations. It established a framework for change in the mid-1980s.

The main factor influencing the character of the policymaking process was the degree of control invested in each bureau. Figures 4.1 and 4.2 are structural representations of the policymaking process in the case of CDs and the trading

Figure 4.2   Intra-ministry policymaking

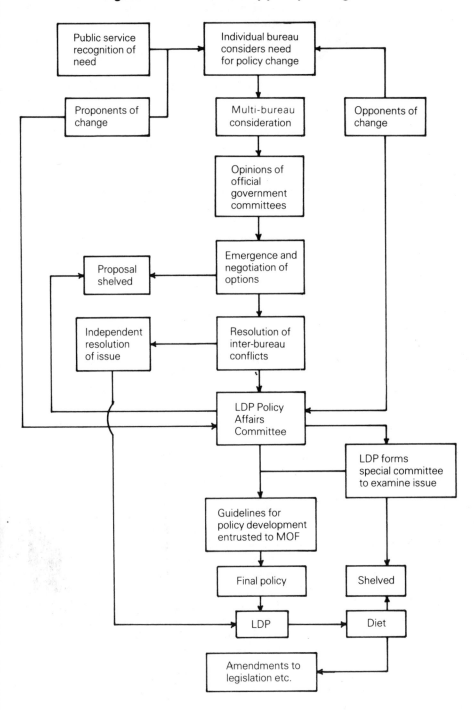

in government bonds respectively. Figure 4.1 represents the simplest and 'narrowest' form of policymaking. Here an individual bureau was considered to have sufficient authority to determine, within the confines of general ministry policy, the rate of change of regulatory policy. The bureau determines the need for change, and the problems involved in altering established methods and restrictions.

Interest groups fed into the policymaking process, and official committees were used to determine the opinion of a broad cross-section of economic interests. However, these groups gave opinions rather than dictated policy.

In the CDs case the Banking Bureau argued that the needs of the city banks, and the requirements of industry, were sufficient to warrant introduction of CDs. Having decided its basic policy position, it proceeded to deal with outstanding opposition, a matter which involved complicated negotiations. Although the Banking Bureau controlled the policymaking process, it still required a broad endorsement of its policy proposals. As was argued in chapter 2, this endorsement process necessitated some concessions, but these did not compromise the Banking Bureau's basic aims. The LDP's approval was *pro forma*, and the decision soon became authoritative. In terms of the typology outlined in the introduction, this decision fell very much within mode (III), the dominance mode of policymaking.

Of course it is possible to conceive of a line of action which would have met with LDP disapproval, although the likelihood of this occurring was very low. Officers of the MOF had contact with the LDP from relatively junior points in their careers, and were unlikely to misread what was acceptable or otherwise. In short, one would expect the LDP's role to be small in an industry matter with a narrowly defined policy jurisdiction. If the LDP had a strong interest in the policy area, the outcome, no matter how narrow the policymaking process, would be subject to interested LDP oversight and the LDP's position would play a positive role in determining the eventual outcome. Such a case is examined in chapter 5.

A 'wider' policymaking process is one which involves several bureaus. It allows a greater range of groups to affect the development of new policy. A structural representation of this process appears in Figure 4.2. In this case, as in the example discussed in this chapter, opinions might differ from the outset. Whereas one bureau might argue the need for a new policy, and be backed up in this by an official government committee, another bureau might argue against regulatory change and have a similarly 'wide base community support' from another official government committee. The distribution of jurisdictional control and the aims of each bureau are the key factors in predicting the outcome in this type of policymaking process. Again, the role of the public service is central, but here the policymaking outcome is contingent on a larger number of possibilities. Disagreement within the finance industry can be expressed within the MOF and this, along with different aims among the competing bureaus within the MOF, means that the formation of new policy is far less likely than in the narrower policymaking process. As Figure 4.2 shows, the proposal can be shelved before it becomes bureau policy, after it becomes bureau policy but before it becomes ministry policy, and, in theory, after it becomes ministry policy but before it becomes government policy. The final stage is unlikely since the MOF would normally canvass thoroughly the LDP's view before it put forward policy proposals. There were cases where the MOF was disputing policy with other ministries which ended up in the LDP policymaking forum but, at the intra-ministry level, the LDP played a limited role in issues in which it did not have close electoral interest.

In 1979–81 the compromise policy defended the status quo very adequately in the short term, although at the same time it offered prospects for change in the long term. It also enabled other unrelated parts of the Banking Bureau's policy program, in the Banking Law and other related laws, to be passed unhindered by intra-ministry infighting. There was little doubt that the MOF was fully aware of the intense opposition of securities companies to change, and of the pressure they were exerting on parts of the LDP. This might have affected the shape of the compromise, but it was not of overriding importance. The Banking Bureau drew back from pushing further because of the influence it might have had on the passage of the Banking Law. The public service again had played a vital role, but was revealing more awareness of political considerations even on this relatively non-political industry issue.

Over the seventeen-year period, the policymaking arena was predominantly in the conflict mode—mode (IV) (see Figure 0.1). On the last occasion, however, we noted a vertical move through the grey area between conflict and consensus into consensus—mode (II). The consensus was not within the industry but much more within the public service. In the next chapter a very different case is explored: one in which the LDP had a strong political interest, and where two government ministries had an interest in the policymaking arena.

5 The postal savings system
Inter-ministry conflict

Since its establishment in 1875 the postal savings system has functioned predominantly as a gatherer of funds. From 1951 funds derived from postal savings were channelled into the MOF's Trust Fund Bureau and used as a major source of funds for the Fiscal Investment Loan Program.[1] The structure of this loan fund program is outlined in Figure 5.1. It was the main source of funds for many public national and regional projects, government-related institutions (including a whole range of financial institutions), education, welfare and housing. In fiscal 1981 approximately 32 per cent of its funds (or 7.7 trillion yen) was derived from the postal savings system, a vital and growing source of funds available at relatively low cost to the public sector.

The existence of a public savings sector, controlled by the Ministry of Posts and Telecommunications (MPT) and managed by the post office, played a large part in harnessing funds for public sector activities. It also imposed, through powers based upon separate legislation and effective bipartisan political backing, constraints on the MOF's attempts to define independently the parameters of financial policy.[2] Because of the quantity of funds it attracted, it was a potential policymaking trouble spot. This chapter explores the proposition that in policymaking areas where the LDP had an interest it was able to exercise considerable influence on the resulting policy. The roles of the Prime Minister and committees within the LDP policymaking structure are examined separately. In contrast to the relatively insignificant role of the LDP in the cases of the CDs market and the trade in government bonds, discussed in chapters 3 and 4, the LDP's interest was significant on the issue of postal savings.

Furthermore, this issue raises again the question of the impact of divided jurisdictions. The savings system in Japan was divided into two parts, bank savings and postal savings. The individual systems were linked by legal requirements, discussions between the supervising ministries and political direction. Despite the checks and balances within the overall savings system, there were several attempts during the 1970s to alter the framework of regulations governing it. The positions and objectives of the parties involved in the policymaking process are examined, including the intervention of LDP in the issue of postal savings and how that affected the resolution of inter-ministry

Figure 5.1 The structure of the Fiscal Investment Loan Program

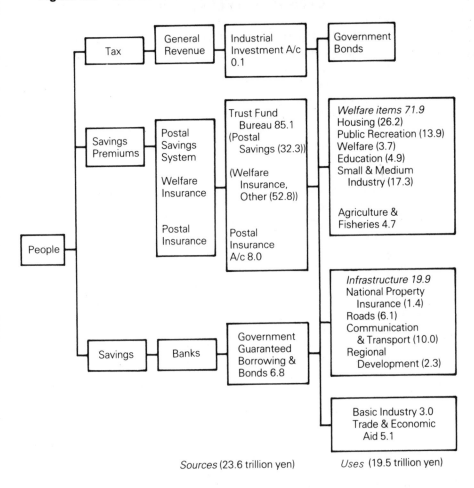

Sources (23.6 trillion yen)   *Uses* (19.5 trillion yen)

Notes: In fiscal 1981 revenue raised amounted to 23.6 trillion yen and expenditure through FILP was 19.5 trillion yen. Figures given are percentages of total revenue or expenditure. The funds are dispersed through public enterprises (JNR, NTT); finance corporations (Peoples Financial Corporation, Small Business Financial Corporation, JDB etc.); public corporations (Japan Housing Corporation, Japan Highway Corporation); local governments; schools; and a range of special companies such as Electric Power Development Co.

Source: Nenkin shikin kenkyūkai *Kongo no nenkin shikin un' yō no arikata* Tokyo, 1982.

policy disputes in 'routine' interest rate decisionmaking and in the broader field of regulatory policymaking.

The reason for looking at the postal savings system is not to take sides on what are very topical and controversial issues within Japan today. The purpose here is to show how arguments are presented, and the way in which the structure of arguments indicates the support base and the underlying rationale for supporting or opposing a move to develop new regulations.

POLITICAL INVOLVEMENT IN DETERMINING THE POSTAL SAVINGS INTEREST RATE

Since the end of World War II, the Postal Savings Law (1947) has formed the basis for the operations of the postal savings system, and for making decisions relating to postal savings interest rates.[3] The law established a decisionmaking framework quite independent of the decisionmaking framework which covered savings deposits held by private financial institutions. Regulations relating to those deposits were managed by the Banking Bureau of the MOF. Postal savings matters were managed by the Postal Savings Bureau within the MPT, in conjunction with the Posts and Telecommunications Advisory Committee (PTAC).[4]

The Postal Savings Law made two important statements about interest rates. Article 12.2 stated that the Minister of Posts and Telecommunications should not only take into account the interest rates offered on deposits by other financial institutions but also give consideration to the role of postal savings as a simple and safe means for small savings aimed at securing the economic well-being of the saver.[5] This explicit reference to a social objective was ultimately the source of much conflict between the MPT and the MOF. During the 1960s when inflation rates were relatively modest, and the rate of growth of incomes was high, there was little conflict. The 1970s were a different story. The rate of real income growth fell appreciably and the rate of increase in the consumer price index rose.[6]

The MOF approached the interest rate on savings deposits in a manner quite different from the MPT. Deposit rates were considered as the cost of loan funds. As a means of stimulating economic activity, or simply as a means of reducing the cost of loan funds to corporations, the MOF attempted to minimise the level of interest rates on deposits. It gave little consideration to the social objective so explicit in the Postal Savings Law.

During the 1960s, differences in principle had little impact on actual policymaking. With a high rate of real income growth, a wage earner's real standard of living rose rapidly, and more than compensated for the increase in consumer prices. During these years, the MPT and the PTAC did not adopt a policy of resistance to downward pressure on postal savings rates, but at the same time the savings deposit rate was inflexible when compared with other interest rates.[7] After 1970, the potential conflict built into the decisionmaking mechanism began to be displayed.

The decisionmaking process which incorporates both the postal savings system and the bank savings system is shown in Figure 5.2. During the 1970s and early 1980s the two mechanisms were formally quite distinct, with the MOF being responsible for decisions about bank savings and the MPT responsible for decisions about postal savings. Furthermore, in theory, the key relationship in the decisionmaking process was that between the MPT and the PTAC. In practice, the important stage of the policymaking process changed from case to case, depending greatly upon the attitudes of the MPT's Postal Savings Bureau and the MOF's Banking Bureau, and the political sensitivity to a change in the

Figure 5.2   The Savings Interest Rate (SIR) decision making process

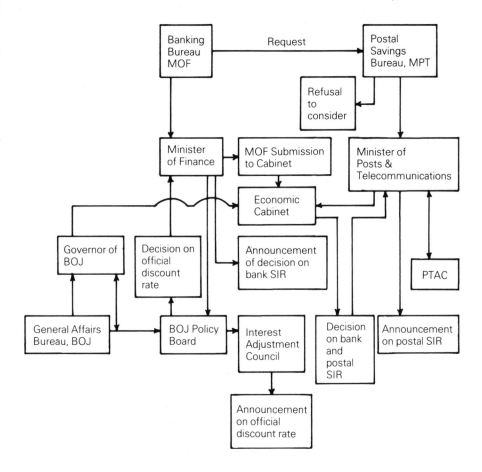

interest rate.

The process normally began with the MOF asking the MPT to consider a proposal it had prepared. Discussions took place between assistant directors or at the level of director. Negotiations between the two ministries were only difficult when the MOF was considering a reduction in the interest rate. A proposal to increase the interest rate level helped the MPT to promote savings per se, and to promote also the welfare of the small saver.[8] As with other areas of policymaking both within and between ministries, if difficulties arose, they were handled by more senior officers. For example, when a proposal called for a reduction in the postal savings rate in the 1970s, discussions which began at the level of assistant director and director usually went to the level of director-general in order to be resolved. Non-resolution of conflict at this level meant that the issue was either shelved or taken by the MOF to Cabinet.[9]

Between 1970 and 1980 there were many occasions when the MOF and the MPT argued strongly about the appropriate level of the postal savings rate. The MOF claimed that the approach of the MPT frustrated its implementation of monetary policy. Put another way, the MOF did not always succeed in persuading the MPT to lower postal savings rates when it wanted to reduce the official discount rate. As a result, the lowering of bank savings rates was sometimes delayed and this led, on occasions, to a fall in the profitability of financial institutions. Two examples help to clarify the respective roles of the MOF and MPT, and how the LDP and Prime Minister participated in this policymaking process. They both involve circumstances when the MOF asked the MPT to reduce the postal savings interest rate.

1971–72: The problem of a high CPI

Between October 1970 and July 1971, four small reductions in the official discount rate occurred. For the most part, while the MITI and the Economic Planning Agency (EPA) were prominent in promoting a bullish atmosphere, the MOF and the BOJ were restrained in their promotion of economic expansion.[10]

None of the four reductions in the official discount rate to July 1971 were accompanied by a reduction in savings deposit interest rates. Although banks would have welcomed a fall in deposit rates, the MPT opposed it, and as a result the gap between bank savings deposit rates and loan rates became smaller. Although there was considerable discussion of the merits of a further reduction in the official discount rate in September and October 1971, this option was ruled out by continuing opposition from the MPT.[11]

In December 1971, when it appeared that a yen revaluation was likely, the MOF and the MPT recommended negotiations on savings rates. The BOJ had earlier announced that it would not countenance a further fall in the official discount rate without a fall in deposit rates. Increased pressure for a reduction in all interest rates from the business community, the MITI, the EPA, and some sectors of the LDP, followed the official announcement of the revaluation on 19 December 1971. They argued that a policy counterweight to the economic effects of the revaluation was necessary. The outcome was a reduction in the official discount rate by half a percentage point, but all savings rates remained unchanged. There was substantial political resistance to a reduction in savings rates from within PARC's Communications Subcommittee (which was responsible for the LDP's policies relating to the MPT). It argued that there was a need to maintain a basic relationship between the level of interest on postal savings deposits and the inflation rate; to ensure sufficient funds for public investment projects (which relied to a large extent on the growth of postal savings); and finally not to insist on parallel changes in the postal and bank savings rates because the products were quite different and aimed at different sectors. The fact that Prime Minister Sato did not intervene when the matter went to Cabinet amounted to an acceptance of the position of the Communications Subcommittee. The petitioning of the Prime Minister by the Minister of Finance, Mizuta Mikio, had no effect.[12]

This was the first occasion when the MPT, with backing from the LDP parliamentarians who supported the postal savings system, came into serious conflict with the MOF. In the words of the Minister of Posts and Telecommunications, Hirose Masao, up to this time the Postal Savings Bureau had thought and acted like the 'Savings Division' of the Banking Bureau.[13] Hirose's stance was effective only because he had the backing of the Communications Subcommittee and, finally, the implicit support of the Prime Minister in Cabinet. The Cabinet decision was of little concern to ministries like MITI as it was the official discount rate, and not the savings rate, which set the trends for loan rates. When that was lowered they had achieved their aim. Only the MOF remained discontented. On this occasion the sagging growth rate, relatively high inflation and concern over a political backlash were factors that supported the MPT case.

Whether as an impact of the revaluation, or of some other factor, the rate of growth of economic activity did slow down significantly in the first quarter of 1972, and resulted in the BOJ asking the MOF to recommence negotiations with the MPT over the savings rate. The BOJ wanted to reduce the official discount rate, but would not do so without a fall in the savings rate. Initial negotiations produced no result and the matter went to Cabinet in late May 1972.[14] Although opposed by the Minister of Posts and Telecommunications, the rest of the Cabinet urged a reduction in the savings interest rate, and hence all the Minister could do was accept the Cabinet decision or resign. He succeeded in delaying the reduction by arguing that he was reluctant to approve a fall without the approval of the PTAC, which under the Act he was bound to consult. Hirose and the MPT saw some need to reduce savings interest rates, but not to the extent demanded by the MOF.[15] A compromise agreement was reached after some debate and included the acceptance of an MPT proposal to introduce a small loans scheme within the framework of the postal savings system.[16]

The protracted period of negotiation before the savings interest rates were lowered was subsequently used by groups opposed to the maintenance of separate savings deposit rate decisionmaking mechanisms to show the disastrous consequences that could result for monetary policy. They argued that the delays caused by the negotiating process ultimately delayed the transition from easy to tight monetary policy, which occurred in 1973. This argument was little more than a thinly disguised attempt to make the MPT the scapegoat for the major error in monetary policy of 1972–73 which resulted in a period of very rapid inflation in Japan.

In April 1972 a reduction in the official discount rate may have been the appropriate policy. By July it may have been appropriate to tighten monetary policy slightly.[17] The economy was already showing signs of overheating. The pursuit of a flexible approach to monetary policy was shackled by the governor of the BOJ, Sasaki Tadashi, who virtually committed himself to a reduction in the official discount rate in early May 1972, and then had to wait nearly two months before he was assured that the savings rates would also be lowered. Given the state of the economy at the time, a more cautious approach would have been to adopt a wait-and-see stance in May. The inflexible determination of Sasaki to see a project through, combined with the dominance in the BOJ of the Business Department (which favoured a continuation of expansionist policy), prevented an early reversal of policy.[18]

Moreover, the political environment did not lend itself to a flexible approach to monetary policy. The election of Tanaka Kakuei to the position of Prime Minister in early July soon made fiscal policy even more expansionist adding to already expansionist monetary policies. While Minister for International Trade and Industry, Tanaka gained a reputation for supporting expansionist fiscal policies by advocating an ambitious plan for redeveloping Japan. When he became Prime Minister there was no reason to suggest that he had changed his position. The combination of these two factors, and not the delay tactics of the MPT and its minister, was responsible for the ineffective handling of price inflation in 1972–73.

1977: The role of the Prime Minister

A second case illustrated the pivotal significance of the Prime Minister in determining reductions in the postal savings rate, and the problem of balancing concern over the state of economic activity against the political significance of the postal savings rate.

In early 1977 the BOJ and the MOF were giving preliminary consideration to reducing the official discount rate, not on the grounds that it would boost economic activity, but as a measure which would reduce the cost structure of business.[19] However, before any reduction in the official discount rate would be contemplated, the governor of the BOJ, Morinaga Teiichiro, insisted that prior agreement be reached on an accompanying fall in the savings rate.[20] Prime Minister Fukuda was confronted by two problems.

On the one hand, a House of Councillors election was scheduled for July 1977, and any reduction in the postal savings interest rate without good reason would give the opposition parties a useful campaign advantage.[21] On the other hand, the LDP did not have a majority on the House of Representatives Budget Committee (HRBC).[22] If a reduction occurred, there was always the prospect that the opposition might attempt to amend the Budget due before the House of Representatives in February 1977.[23] Although there was some support within the LDP for a reduction, no immediate reduction occurred. In mid-February the Prime Minister began exploring ways to circumvent this dilemma. By floating the suggestion that a small independent reduction in the official discount rate (of 0.25 percentage points) should be feasible, he was trying to find a way to satisfy both business interests and those of the electorate. By the end of February internal pressure within the LDP, and from the business community, for a reduction in the interest rate had grown considerably stronger. In a meeting between the chairman of PARC's Financial Research Study Group,

Uchida Tsuneo, and the chairman of the Federation of Economic Organisations, Dokō Toshio, there was general agreement that a fall in the official discount rate would reduce the increasing sense of economic instability, increase the annual growth rate to 6 per cent and reduce the burden of holding excess stock.[24]

In early March the BOJ became more concerned with the deteriorating state of the economy and its position on the interest rate question changed appreciably. It was prepared to accept a delayed fall in the savings rate, as long as an agreement was reached before the official discount rate was lowered.[25] On 11 March Fukuda partly resolved this dilemma by securing an almost simultaneous fall in the official discount rate and the interest rate on demand deposits. The all-important fixed deposit rate was left untouched.

The decision to lower the official discount rate had no sooner been made when there were demands for further falls. Kōmoto Toshio, chairman of PARC, argued that another reduction of the official discount rate was necessary to prevent international criticism being levelled at Japan. Although international considerations were discussed, most politicians were more concerned about the state of the domestic economy. On 15 April, only one month after the previous reduction, Fukuda stated his support for an early general reduction in interest rates.[26] On this occasion prime ministerial intervention on the savings rate issue was unnecessary, with the majority of the PTAC regarding the fall as inevitable given the substantial reduction of deposit rates in the private sector.[27] There was a need to retain the balance in interest rates. Whatever the electoral costs, the health of the economy finally became the predominant concern. The Prime Minister had not supported the reduction in the savings rate until the economic downturn itself looked like becoming an electoral problem.[28]

In this case, had the dual savings decisionmaking framework not existed, savings rates would have been reduced early in 1977. This would not have had much impact on monetary policy but would have redistributed interest income away from individuals with deposits in postal and bank savings to those groups, mainly in corporations, with outstanding loans. It was a moot point whether the MOF was more qualified to make decisions on these distributional issues than the MPT.

These examples show the persistent concern of the MPT, the PTAC, the PARC's Communications Subcommittee and the Minister of Post and Telecommunications for the real level of return on postal savings accounts, particularly the long-term fixed deposit accounts. The Postal Savings Bureau of the MPT which established the basic policy parameters hinged its policy on two factors: the relationship between the consumer price index and the interest rate on postal savings, and the movement of interest rates in other markets.[29] The former was more important than the latter, as the MOF rarely proceeded with a reduction in the savings rate of private financial institutions unless it had an implicit guarantee that the interest rate on postal savings deposits would also be lowered.

Because of the duality of the savings system there was, in theory, a chance that the MPT could frustrate the implementation of appropriate monetary policy. In practice, however, the MPT operated in a constrained environment. The Cabinet was able at will to call for a change in MPT policy, although in actual fact it rarely did. The postal savings system evolved on the basis that it provided a substantial source of loan funds for government projects and reasonable protection for the savings of the small individual. The banking system, under the MOF's direction, functioned to provide funds for corporate needs. As borrowers, individuals had little access to the banking system until the late 1970s, and as lenders, they had little selection between assets. The postal savings system had little to offer individuals who sought to borrow funds, but its services complemented and supplemented those offered by private banks to lenders as well as placing a high priority on 'real rate of return' when considering the apropriateness of any downward change in interest rates.

The experiences of the 1970s provide the basis for understanding the role of the MOF, MPT and LDP on the savings interest rate question. When interest rates were rising there were generally few problems between the MOF, the MPT and the LDP. There were, in addition, periods when there was no expectation within the MOF that long-term deposit rates should change. Problems did arise, however, in periods after monetary policy changed from tight to easy and was becoming progressively easier. The LDP was far from neutral in dealing with the MPT and the MOF on the savings interest rate issue. By its actions it was taking the best from both worlds: it supported strongly the minimisation of loan rates but at the same time backed the MPT in maintaining postal rates above the level they would have been had the MOF had complete control. On the occasions when political pressure prevented the MOF from negotiating a reduction in all savings rates, it was the banks which suffered reduced profitability. This was the main effect of the dual savings system.

CHANGING THE STRUCTURE OF THE POLICYMAKING MECHANISM

The MOF attempted on three occasions, in 1972, 1977 and 1980–81, to take control of the entire savings deposit market arguing for a variety of reasons that policymaking on the savings deposit interest rates should be handled by a single decisionmaking authority. In 1972, when attempting to settle the dispute between the MPT and the MOF over whether or not the savings rate should be reduced and whether a new postal savings system loan program should be introduced, the chairman of PARC, Kosaka Zentarō, suggested that a compromise be made. His plan was that, in return for the loan program, the MPT should relinquish to the MOF control of the postal savings interest rate. Hirose, the Minister for Posts and Telecommunications at the time, flatly rejected the trade-off, and, with the aid of solid parliamentary backing, successfully withstood pressures from Kosaka and the MOF to change the system. A second demand for unification in 1975 met the same fate.[30]

In 1980 the circumstances were somewhat different. Originally the postal savings system was designed to collect the savings of individuals on relatively low incomes. Up to the end of the 1960s it fulfilled this function with few complaints from private sector financial institutions. A limit was imposed on the level of funds that could be deposited. In the early 1970s this limit stood at one million yen. In 1972 the limit was raised to 1.5 million yen, before being doubled in 1973 to three million yen. The share of postal savings in total deposits grew steadily from approximately 20 per cent in 1972 to approximately 30 per cent in 1980. During 1980 the level of deposits exceeded 60 trillion yen (or approximately US$240 billion). The persistent growth in the share of postal savings deposits in total deposits produced strong demands from private financial institutions and the MOF for reform of the postal savings system. A meeting was held at the end of December 1980 between the Minister of Finance, Watanabe Michio, and the Minister of Posts and Telecommunications, Yamanouchi Ichirō, and their respective advisors from the MOF and the MPT. At that meeting, Yamanouchi acceded to the MOFs demands that, in return for a new pension scheme, the MPT would permit the role of the postal savings system and the method of determining interest rates to be the subject of an inquiry under the auspices of the Prime Minister. In what was seen at the time as a major strategic error, Yamanouchi acceded to a plan apparently devised by the Cabinet Secretary, Miyazawa Kiichi.[31] But although the inquiry which submitted its report in autumn 1981 favoured a unified system, at the end of 1982 no final decision had been made on the future control of postal savings interest rates, once again illustrating the strength of the MPT, or put another way, the indecisiveness of the LDP.

The above incidents illustrated both the strengths of the postal savings lobby in resisting the demands of the MOF and the persistence of the MOF in trying to change the status quo. They indicated clearly the plurality of views in the public service and the LDP, and the presence of unresolved conflicts which are inadequately handled by descriptions of policymaking focusing on consensus. In cases of a low level of agreement, dominance and conflict modes of policymaking offer greater insight into the character of the policymaking process.

The arguments of the MOF

The MOF used several arguments to justify its position that the function of the PTAC, and hence the interest rate decisionmaking functions of the Postal Savings Bureau within the MPT, should be handled by the Interest Rate Adjustment Committee, and hence the Banking Bureau.

One was the impact of delays in the adjustment of the postal savings interest rate on the distribution of funds between the two parts of the savings system. There were six occasions during the 1970s when the interest rate on postal savings deposits did not fall simultaneously with the rate in the banking sector. Delays also occurred on two other occasions. Table 5.1 estimates the significance of the shifts resulting from the delays for which data is available. It compares the share of increase in deposits that occurred during the quarter

Table 5.1 Impact of delays in adjustment of postal savings rate on deposit
shares (per cent)

Date of interest rate change	Delay (days)	Period examined	Post office (a)	Post office (b)	Private banks (a)	Private banks (b)
1 Aug 1972	15	July–Sept	19.6	19.0	80.4	81.0
4 Nov 1975	0	Oct–Dec	22.8	16.7	77.2	83.3
21 May 1977	15	April–June	26.4	36.1	73.6	63.9
29 Sept 1977	3	July–Sept	26.4	31.0	73.6	69.0
25 April 1978	8	April–June	27.4	28.8	72.6	71.2

Notes: (a) Overall share
         (b) Share of increase

Source: Yūseishō 'Yūbin chokin nippō shiryō' mimeo, 1981; Nihon ginkō chōsakyoku 'Shikin
         junkan kanjō ōyōhyō'

surrounding the fall with the share of total deposits. The results are inconclusive. The table shows that on one occasion no difference is detectable, and that on the next occasion the growth in postal savings was actually smaller. The three observations since 1975 provide evidence to support the argument, but they do not constitute proof. During this period the share of postal savings in the growth of savings as a whole was consistently larger than its existing share. It appears therefore that eliminating these delays would only have had a limited impact on stabilising deposit shares of the public and private sector.

The core of the MOF complaint was that the existence of the dual mechanism delayed the timing and frequency of reductions in the savings rate, and ultimately that the existence of this check reduced the flexibility with which it could operate the official discount rate. Although the formulation of monetary policy, including setting the official discount rate, was the legal responsibility of the BOJ's Policy Board, in practice the MOF exerted considerable influence over the official discount rate decisionmaking process, particularly when interest rates were declining.[32] There were several instances when the timing of official discount rates decisions was 'delayed' by the intransigence of the MPT, but this is very different from arguing that the MPT's stubborn defence of its position adversely affected the operations of monetary policy.

The main tools of monetary policy were the use of window guidance and the official discount rate. Window guidance was the control exercised by the BOJ over 'the future loan plans and the prospective fund position of banks'.[33] In periods of easy monetary policy this tool became largely ineffective, and on several occasions it was abandoned by the BOJ. Similarly, the official discount rate in the 1970s was more effective as a deterrent against monetary expansion than as a major tool for regenerating economic activity. In 1971–72 and in 1975–78, fiscal policy shouldered the burden of encouraging an expansion in economic activity. There is little evidence to suggest that delays in reducing the official discount rate did more than marginally slow down the reduction in the cost of funds to enterprises and, periodically, substantially affect the profitability of banks. Until the late 1970s, postal savings deposits were regarded as long-term assets and hence not immediately affecting the impact of short-term monetary policy.[34] Aside from the 1972–73 incident analysed earlier, monetary policy during the 1970s was remarkably effective.[35]

The two reasons presented above were at the centre of the MOF's official position. Unofficially, however, the MOF's main reason for wanting to take control of the entire savings deposit interest rate framework was more related to bank profitability than to monetary policy. Had a clear relationship been established between the official discount rate and the savings deposit rates, the gap between loan interest rates and savings deposit rates would have remained more stable. As it was, margins shrank in periods of easy monetary policy and increased in periods of tight monetary policy. By the end of the 1970s, the margin between the loan rate and the yield on one-year bank deposits was slightly lower than at the beginning of the 1970s, but of the same order of magnitude. In contrast the margin between the return on funds and the cost of funds had fallen, during the same period, to about 20 per cent of the level achieved at the beginning of the decade. In focusing on the postal savings system the MOF was ignoring the impact of perhaps the main cause of the decline in bank profitability, the impact of purchases of large volumes of government bonds. Particularly after 1978, when the private demand for funds recovered, the return on government bonds was substantially less than comparative free market rates. Correcting this problem would have had a more immediate impact on bank profitability than the simultaneous movement of savings rates, unless the existing general relationship between savings rates and loan rates had been changed.

The position of the BOJ

Although the governor of the BOJ (1980–84), Maekawa Haruo, recognised that there was no necessary connection between the savings deposits interest rate and the official discount rate, both he and his predecessor, Morinaga Teiichirō, frequently stated that they would not countenance a fall in the official discount rate without a fall in the postal savings rate.[36] The most often quoted reason was the level of bank profitability. Although public evidence supports the view that on occasions the BOJ did not welcome the dogged stance of the MPT, it appears that, in some instances, the stance of the MPT coincided with that of the BOJ. For example, at the end of 1976 and in February 1977 Morinaga talked to the Minister for Posts & Telecommunications, Komiyama Jūshirō, about the need to reduce the postal savings rate, and on both occasions it was agreed that no need existed. On 4 January 1977, Morinaga was reported to have told the Prime Minister, Fukuda, and the Minister of Finance, Bō Hideo, that he was prepared to accept a reduction in the official discount rate if savings rates fell concurrently. He was fully aware of the political resistance to reducing the postal savings rate and hence knew that all savings rates would remain unchanged. In fact he felt that a reduction in the official discount rate was premature and was using the postal savings rate as a means to bolster his bargaining position. It provided an effective argument and buffer in Cabinet to counter the attempts by the MITI, the EPA and the MOF to lower the official discount rate faster than it, the BOJ, desired.[37]

When the issue of unifying the savings deposits interest rate system once again became topical in 1980–81, the BOJ gave strong support to the MOF's position. Two possible explanations of this are consistent with the argument outlined above.

From the late 1970s, the BOJ played a more central role in the official discount rate decisionmaking process. The increased political importance of minimising the rate of inflation, the less than unanimous support for the MOF's low interest rate policy, and the strong leadership of both Governor Morinaga and Governor Maekawa all contributed to this more central role. In view of this, the BOJ argued that dealing with the MOF directly, and not being subject to possible deals struck bilaterally between the MOF and the MPT, would maximise its effectiveness in the policymaking process.

A more convincing and in no way contradictory scenario can be related to the BOJ's policy of promoting deregulated interest rates. The BOJ's preferred option regarding savings deposits interest rates was gradual deregulation similar to the abandonment of regulation Q in the United States. But it was politically realistic enough not to place much hope in this outcome eventuating in the short term. In a regulated market where the savings deposits interest rate was unified there would be two possibilities. The first was that the MOF bid for control over savings interest rates would be successful. The second and more likely outcome was that, out of the dispute between the MOF and the MPT, the Inner Cabinet and Cabinet (or Prime Minister) would decide that although one decision-making authority was preferable, political considerations required that the regulatory agency be identified more with the interest of individual savers than was the MOF. The BOJ would then be the obvious candidate to take over the whole savings deposits interest rate framework. Such an outcome would also further strengthen the independent function of the BOJ in future official discount rate decisions.

Further, towards the end of the 1970s, the BOJ began looking at the stock of postal savings deposits more in terms of 'cashlike' deposits. The reasons for this are none too clear as the overwhelming majority of deposits were of a long-term nature. The best explanation is that the relative size of the postal savings system had grown so much that relatively small shifts in preferences of individuals could have a significant impact on monetary policy. This would have been an added reason for supporting the MOF's position.

The position of the MPT

The most bitter clashes between the MOF and the MPT (1971–72, 1975, 1977) occurred when the level of consumer price inflation exceeded the level of interest paid on postal savings of two-year maturity. The question then becomes not whether the position adopted by the MPT was reasonable, for under the law maintenance of the real value of savings was an important obligation, but more whether there was any need for postal savings to respond to the wishes of the MOF. If the products being offered by the two sectors were the same, there would certainly be a powerful argument for amalgamating the decisionmaking mechanisms, under one decisionmaking authority, be it the MPT, the MOF or the BOJ. If the products were different, then arguably different criteria might be appropriate. Under the existing arrangements, the Postal Savings Law stated that consideration should be given to the direction of private financial institution interest rates, and hence ensured that interest rates moved at approximately the same time. The advantage of the existing system from the MPT's standpoint was that it accommodated the difference between products, while at the same time recognising the need for broad parity between savings rates. It meant that decisions on the savings rate generally would incorporate consideration of the needs of individuals holding postal savings, as well as the desire of the MOF to minimise the cost of funds.

In the Finance Committee of the House of Representatives in May 1981, the director-general of the MPT's Postal Savings Bureau, Arase Kōichirō, argued that there were two reasons why the MPT-based system should be maintained. First, post office deposits were predominantly deposits of individuals, whereas bank deposits included a larger proportion of business deposits. Second, protection of the individual saver was rarely considered outside the MPT, whereas the business sector had many political avenues through which it could advocate its positions.[38]

The first reason can be dealt with quickly. The deposits held in the postal savings system might be almost entirely deposits of individuals, but a greater quantity of deposits of individuals was held by banks.[39] The key argument is the second one. The MPT and the PTAC functioned as a means of ensuring that the interest of one diverse and, in a political sense, weak group in the community, individual savers, was not subjugated at will by the interests of big businesses and the financial community, or the specific interests of the MOF. In the 1960s and 1970s, the MOF did not go out of its way to protect these interests.

A third difference between the two sectors was the average length that time

Table 5.2   **Investment character of postal savings: average length of deposit in savings institutions, fiscal 1979 (months)**

Type of Deposit	Postal Savings	Banks
Demand deposits	6.1	0.2
Fixed period and quantity character deposits	39.8	9.9

Note: Length of deposit = average outstanding balance ÷ monthly average payment level

Source: Yūseishō 'Kin'yū no bunya ni okeru kangyō no arikata nado ni tsuite February 1981, p. 47; Nichigin Keizai tōkei geppō

deposits were held. As Table 5.2 indicates, deposits held in the postal savings system have a strong investment character. In fiscal 1979, the postal savings system's 'fixed deposit-type savings' were held for approximately four times the period of a similar deposit type in the private financial sector. Amalgamation of the two decisionmaking systems would have resulted in these differences being ignored. Had the MOF controlled the whole savings interest rate framework, its consistent failure to cater for the needs of individuals indicates that it would probably have materially affected the welfare of the individual household sector.

POLITICS IN INTER-MINISTRY REGULATORY DECISIONMAKING

The political basis of support for the extensive postal savings system, and hence for the MPT in its confrontations with the MOF, was multifaceted.

First, in 1979 nine members of the Japan Socialist Party (JSP), six in the House of Representatives and three in the House of Councillors, were former officers of *Zentsūshin rōren*, the union of the postal workers. In 1980 it had a membership of 188 000 making it the thirteenth largest union in Japan; it was closely related to the General Council of Japanese Trade Unions. Along with members of the national railways union (*Kokutetsu rōdō kumiai*), the communications union (*Zenden tsūshin rōren*), and the teachers union, the postal workers union accounted for most of the 'union representatives' in the JSP. A list of the parliamentary members is given in Table 5.3.[40]

Second, there was a small but steady stream of members from the Postal Workers Union in the House of Representatives and House of Councillors in the LDP, including Hirose Masao, who became Minister for Posts and Telecommunications. At the end of 1980, Satō Megumu, the former postmaster of Murayama post office, was a member for the fourth electoral division of Osaka. Nishimura Shōji and Osada Yūji, both former administrative vice-ministers of the MPT, were members of the Upper House. Both were elected from the National Electorate and had been elected three times. These two groups could be thought of as direct representatives of the interests of the post office, providing a parliamentary political base for the MPT whose interests were much the same. But when these numbers are compared with the number of former MOF public servants elected to the Diet (totalling 30–40 at any one time), then there must be another explanation of the strength of the political base supporting the postal savings system.

Third, and more generally, there was the influence of the post office in putting together a winning electoral coalition of interests. In 1980 there were over 20 000 post offices in Japan, and a majority of these were categorised as 'special post offices'. These special post offices differed from normal post offices in that their management received a commission on sales. Although the branch heads of the special post offices were appointed by the MPT, the lack of any formal selection processes meant that there was some room for political affiliation to influence selection. The fact that the position of postmaster was

Table 5.3   JSP members with backgrounds in the post office or postal workers union, 1979

House of Representatives
Ōide Shun, Kanagawa 1,
Takebe Bun, Tottori
Tanabe Makoto, Gunma 1
Nakamura Shigeru, Nagano 2
Noguchi Kōichi, Shiga
Morinaka Moriyoshi, Kumamoto 1

House of Councillors	
Ōmori Akira	National Electorate
Sakakura Tōgo	Regional Electorate, Mie Prefecture
Murata Hidezō	Regional Electorate, Fukushima Prefecture

Source: Yamaguchi and Sugimori *Rōkumi giin ga shakaitō o sashita* Tokyo: Nisshin hōdō, 1980

held in respect by the local people meant that the role of the post office network in the electoral support system for politicians could be important. On average there would be about 400 post offices in each electorate. The support of postmasters in the electorate (through the local postmasters association) could be of considerable importance, if it was used effectively. At 200 votes per postmaster, opposition from this group would have important implications for conservative politicians in marginal seats. Clearly there are many different organisations which play political roles of this type. Curtis mentions the role of the prefectural Dental Association in Satō Bunsei's electoral strategy in the second electoral division of Ōita.[41] Passin mentions other types of organisational support used by the LDP in the House of Councillors election of 1974.[42] George gives the example of over 50 recommendations adorning the walls of one politician with an agricultural base.[43] These examples all point out the differences between passive organisational support and active support. For the post office to have electoral significance it clearly must be able to influence votes or contribute to building successful electoral coalitions.

The postal savings issue was politically significant to politicians of all political parties because of the financial implications to most Japanese of a fall in the postal savings rate. At any one time, about 300 LDP parliamentarians were said to be members of the internal LDP 'postal savings lobby'. One LDP parliamentarian interviewed confided his support for the MOF proposal to unify the savings interest rate decisionmaking mechanism but stated that the number of votes which the network of small post offices in his electorate was capable of returning outweighed any consideration of this policy option. He argued that alienation of this network of at least neutral interests would have made his political survival much more difficult.[44] The high 'membership' of the postal savings lobby within the LDP backbench made the job of the Cabinet very difficult, even if it wanted to move, and provided a politically based barrier which the MOF had to overcome before it could achieve its goals in this area. It was similar to the problem faced by the LDP if it wanted to reform the agricultural system. According to George, Diet membership of agriculturally based groups supporting particular causes reached 170.[45] Both groups had strong political support which brought the LDP very much into the policymaking process when the groups considered that a problem was worthy of their interest. There was the case of the introduction in 1972 of a small-scale 'loan scheme' by the MPT, despite the opposition of the MAFF and the MOF. On that occasion approximately 290 LDP parliamentarians belonged to a group formed specifically to support that cause.[46] The case of the establishment of the MPT pension plan also illustrates how the LDP could be drawn into and influence the policymaking process. Opposition parties were not altogether without influence, particularly during the period 1976–80. Rarely were they as important as the LDP's own backbench but nevertheless they were significant in that they helped to create an atmosphere which favoured the maintenance of the existing savings deposits interest rates. In cases such as 1977 they clearly played an important role.

The MPT pension plan and the LDP

In 1980 the MPT and the MOF held discussions on the MPT proposal to introduce its own pension plan. The MOF opposed the plan outright, arguing that this area should be left to the private life assurance companies which came within its orbit of influence. Its argument was based on jurisdictional rather than ideological grounds. In the case of the MPT pension scheme, the Banking Bureau was antagonistic because it was responsible for the life assurance companies which managed the existing pension funds, whereas it would have had no power over the operation of the postal savings pension plan.[47] This was similar to its position on the postal savings system. It was not upset with the fact that the postal savings system existed per se, but more with the fact that it did not control it. At various times during the 1960s and 1970s, the MOF supported the growth of the postal savings system on the grounds of the fiscal role played by the FILP and the contribution to that fund from the postal savings system. This support came from the Financial Bureau which administered the FILP, with the implicit concurrence of the Banking Bureau during the 1960s and early 1970s since the FILP (and hence the postal savings system) provided the main component of funds to underwrite the lending activities of the government-controlled financial institutions.[48]

Negotiations over the pension fund continued for several months at the interministry level but no agreement emerged. The MPT then took the matter to the LDP, where it was examined by the Communications Subcommittee of PARC which was positively disposed towards the plan because it had obvious electoral advantages, and it would make a substantial contribution to government finances. The intervention of PARC was caused by two factors. First, the MOF and the MPT were incapable of reaching any compromise agreement. The MOF would not budge from its position of total opposition and the MPT was determined to introduce the plan. In one sense the LDP's intervention could be seen in terms of mediation, but in practice it acted as an adjudicator. The second point was that the LDP was interested in the outcome and not prepared to see the matter shelved because of the lack of an agreement between the MOF and the MPT. The introduction of a scaled-down version of the MPT plan was a direct outcome of LDP involvement.[49]

There were limits on how far the LDP would support the diversification of the postal savings framework. The very low limits imposed on the loan scheme showed that there was little support for the public sector to be involved in lending directly to individuals. The fund-gathering function of the system remains its central attraction. The support for the postal savings system was unlikely to change rapidly. Although the Japanese government instituted committees to look at the shape and size of the public service, the results were only modest. The ideological commitment to smaller government existed in principle, but it was not matched by administrative reforms. In an environment where general revenue from tax sources was substantially less than general expenditure, the postal savings framework provided one source of loan funds which made it possible to avoid tax increases. The whole central government loans framework was of great political significance, and for this reason the LDP's continued support was assured.

In contrast to the lack of an LDP role when CDs were introduced, and a reluctant role in the formation of policy on the trading in government securities by banks, in this case the LDP was involved in everyday policy (in the determination of interest rates on postal savings) and in the formulation of regulatory policy (on the pension plan). In the former case, the LDP slowed down the pace at which the MOF could adjust savings rates it controlled because of their interdependence with postal savings rates. In the latter case, LDP involvement assisted the MPT in developing the regulatory framework. The dual regulatory system came under close scrutiny during 1980, illustrating not only the strengths of the MPT but also its potential weaknesses.

The Prime Minister's Committee on the postal savings system

On 7 January 1981 a committee was established, under the auspices of the Prime Minister, Suzuki Zenkō, to examine the future of the postal savings system. The central matter under consideration was whether the dual savings interest rate mechanism should continue to be used. From the outset the MPT was on the defensive. The establishment of the committee was with the agreement of the Minister of Posts and Telecommunications, Yamanouchi Ichirō, who had capitulated under pressure from Miyazawa Kiichi, head of the Cabinet Secretariat, and Watanabe Michio, Minister of Finance.

The PARC Communication Subcommittee was upset and astounded by the capitulation, as was the MPT. Both were aware that the committee would be stacked in favour of the option supported by the MOF, a single unified policymaking mechanism. What was surprising about the report was that it made little attempt to disguise its strong and unequivocal support for the position of the MOF.[50]

The Committee on the Postal Savings System recommended strongly that a unified system should be established, and in doing so it almost completely accepted the arguments of the MOF and the private financial institutions. But although it prefaced its argument with the statement that deregulated interest rates were most desirable, it rejected a rapid move to this state on three grounds. First, the market strength of the postal savings system was such that even if there were deregulated savings rates the MPT could exercise price leadership because of its size. Second, if interest rates were going to be deregulated there was considerable need for improved efficiency in the existing financial system to allow weaker institutions to improve their competitiveness. Finally, if interest rates were liberalised it would result in an increase in costs.[51] Each argument provided interesting insights into the approach of the committee (and the MOF).

The first argument holds good if one assumes that the MPT was able to conceal subsidiary elements or permit the postal savings system to run at a loss. One way of avoiding this problem would be to hive off the postal savings system, making it an independent government authority which was required to balance its books and police the limits on individual deposits. In order to allow individuals a market return on funds, it could be required to invest a given proportion of funds (even 100 per cent) in government securities issued at the market rate instead of being given a fixed return from the TFB. The report did not consider this option, probably because adopting it would have required abandoning the existing system of regulated interest rates, something which the committee stopped short of advocating.

By making criticisms of the postal savings sector and not considering the state of the financial system as a whole, the report left itself open to criticism.[52] For example, the report said that the postal savings system offered savings accounts with higher returns than the private sector, citing this as a reason for the deficit accumulated by the post office. However, it made no mention of the fact that if deposit rates were deregulated, returns to savers would be even higher or that if the FILP paid market rates on deposits from the postal savings system, the deficit would not have existed.[53] In short, the report eschewed consideration of the basic question of equity which needed addressing, that of whether the individual household sector should be asked to continue to bear the burdens of low interest rates as it would in a system managed by the MOF. The problem was implicitly recognised by the criticism within the report of the MOF's actions in propping up inefficient financial institutions,[54] but the report completely avoided offering a more general statement of the political problems of financial adjustment in the area of small and medium-sized financial institutions. As with these institutions, the existing arrangements prevented the MPT maximising the return on funds within the postal savings system. What the report did was to single out the postal savings system, arguing that because it was so big something had to be done to curb its power. A more complete report would have included a statement of political and institutional adjustments necessary to improve the efficiency of financial intermediation throughout the financial sector, including a point-by-point analysis of the impact of political interference which was the basis of the maintenance of the small and medium-size financial institutions, and the popularity of the postal savings system.

The final argument to justify its position of advocating the maintenance of regulated interest rates was a familiar MOF stance, adopted on TBs and government bonds, and had its basis in the philosophy that the MOF was better able to manage the price of funds than the market. Although it had support in industries with high outstanding debts, it ignored the interests of the surplus sectors of the economy. In economic terms, it amounted to one sector subsidising another sector. In political terms, the existing regulatory framework ensured the continued existence of many small financial institutions which would otherwise collapse or merge and would affect one of the traditional support groups of the LDP. A deregulated interest rate system would also have diminished the role of the Banking Bureau within the banking system.

To summarise, the arguments outlined in the report to support the continuation of existing interest rate regulations made it clear that the committee wanted to ignore the interrelationships between the postal savings system and the broader financial system. The arguments presented to support unification of the two savings interest rate decisionmaking mechanisms were identical to those the MOF presented earlier. In a financial system with a great amount of implicit and explicit political and administrative interference, these arguments left something to be desired.

The establishment of the Committee on Postal Savings showed the MOF had substantial backing in the Cabinet and in the senior echelons of the LDP, and that it was there that the MPT was most vulnerable. Events in the week after the report was delivered, however, showed the strength of the MPT. Yamanouchi, who had agreed to respect the finding of the report when the committee was established, said immediately after its release on 20 August 1981, that it was insupportable. On the same evening the PARC's Communications Subcommittee, chaired by Mori Hideyoshi, expressed its opposition, and Miyazawa Kiichi said that, given internal opposition within the LDP, he doubted the report would be implemented. Shiokawa Masajūrō, the Minister of Transport, said that about 330 parliamentary members of the LDP were opposed to the main recommendation of unification of the two decisionmaking mechanisms. Even the Prime Minister was having second thoughts. Backbench opposition was sufficient to delay any changes in the regulatory framework, and hence protect the position of the MPT. The weakness of the MPT in the inner Cabinet and Cabinet was overridden by strong backbench support.[55]

The green card system

Of perhaps equivalent interest in political terms was the regulatory issue known as the green card system. In March 1980 the Diet passed legislation designed to tackle the problems of tax avoidance on savings deposits.[56] Amendments to the Income Tax Law and Special Taxation Measures Law were designed to provide the legal basis for a checking system, called the green card system, which would facilitate monitoring the level of deposits held by individuals in tax-free savings accounts.

Under the Postal Savings Law, an individual was permitted to hold a given amount of savings deposits in the postal savings system. The quantity allowed by law was increased gradually over the past 100 years, and in 1980 it stood at three million yen. All deposits within the postal savings system attracted tax-free interest payments. The problem with the system was not that a limit on individual deposits did not exist, but that the system was not effectively policed in the postal savings sector. In the banking sector, the MOF audited bank accounts and kept strict account of holdings of individuals. When individuals wanted to hold savings in tax-free accounts (which they could up to the same level as in the postal savings system), they had to apply specifically to the Tax Office. Auditing controls in the banks were far stricter than in the post office.

There is considerable difficulty in determining the extent to which a particular individual deposited funds in the postal savings system. For demand deposits there was little problem as these were covered by accounts, and only amounted to a small percentage of overall deposits held within the system. Most funds were deposited in fixed quantity 'accounts'. These were not accounts in the true sense, but scrips issued with face value varying from 1000 yen up to 500 000 yen. Between 1975 and 1979 the number of outstanding scrips rose by about 80 million to 237 million. The average size of each incremental certificate was about 257 000 yen.[57] According to many accounts, tax avoidance occurred by registering funds in the names of family members and even under pseudonyms. There were good reasons for a shift to the use of the postal savings system: first, the marginal rate of tax on bank deposits exceeding the tax-free level of three million yen rose significantly during the 1970s; second, the utilisation rate of the tax-free framework of banks was higher than that of the post office; and third, a switch in consumer preferences occurred towards longer, higher yielding deposit forms which would have encouraged a movement of funds to the postal savings system's fixed quantity deposits. The existence of hidden caches of funds within the postal savings system was not disputed by politicians and public servants who were interviewed.[58] It is necessary to establish here why auditing procedures in both systems were not equally rigorous.

In the debate on the Diet legislation, the Federation of Bankers' Associations endorsed the proposals, stating that they would eliminate the difference in procedures which were operating, and thus make it almost impossible for an individual or organisation to deposit more than a legally laid down maximum quantity of funds within the postal savings system.

The MPT was more equivocal as its attractiveness and ability to grow would have been constrained by the implementation of a tighter set of rules. Even after the legal framework was established, the MPT argued that it did not envisage any major changes in its operations.[59] By September 1980, however, the MOF and the MPT came to an arrangement which pointed to closer inspection of postal savings accounts by the post office, although it still left many details to be clarified.

Although the positions of the MOF and the MPT grew closer, the LDP's opinion became increasingly critical. By early 1981, the LDP had had sufficient time to assess the public's reaction to the proposed system which it had supported less than a year earlier. The chairman of PARC, Abe Shintarō, expressed doubts about the system. His comments reflected a political concern: 'All those I have talked to since the passage of the legislation have been opposed. If it encourages the flight of financial assets overseas, what will become of the Japanese economy?'[60] The opposition of all those he had spoken to was the driving force behind Abe's public position. He went on to raise the possibility of re-examining the proposal agreed to in 1980. Between September 1980 and May 1981, the green card question (and many other issues related to the administration of the postal savings system) was discussed exhaustively in the House of Representatives and House of Councillors Finance and Budget Committees.[61] The opinion held by the LDP changed gradually. In 1982 it decided to postpone the introduction of the system indefinitely.

There are two reasons for the volte-face in the LDP stance over the green card issue.

Abe's comment that the green card system would encourage a shift from saving to speculation, and the flight of financial assets abroad, was explicit recognition that the new system would uncover tax avoidance. The fear within the LDP that eliminating this avenue of tax avoidance would affect its political support base was perhaps one reason for the lengthy debate within the LDP on the privacy issue. In essence, the issue was whether the taxation office should have access to details of the quantity of funds held by individuals in tax-free accounts. No one could object to adequate checking arrangements designed to ensure that individuals were unable to abuse the existing system. But there was legitimate concern over the desirability of government having access to detailed accounts of individuals. The government had an obligation to minimise the level of tax evasion, but it had little right to the other details of the financial status of individuals that it would gain from an on-line computer system holding lists of financial assets within the non-tax framework. A noteworthy aspect of the renewed debate in the Diet was that the Japan Communist Party was the only political party to object to the original legislation on these grounds. This suggests that the public backlash against the legislation and its electoral implications were of more importance to LDP thinking than concern for individuals' rights to privacy. Some have extended the argument of tax evasion further, suggesting that it was tax-free caches of politicians which were being hidden by the existing system.[62]

A second reason of relatively little direct significance was that some members of the LDP objected to the new system as it represented a trend towards increased and not reduced regulation. The objection was rather naive, as all government taxation measures are regulatory. Blanket objections to adjusting and amending such legislation leads to the conclusion that restrictions should be opposed per se because the end product would involve regulation. Furthermore, it is noteworthy that the objection was not voiced before the legislation was passed originally. Whereas the banking community was essentially interested in ensuring that the system was implemented with equal vigour in both the private and public sector, at least one large group within the LDP, the Posts and Telecommunications Business Discussion Group, expressed its intention of making substantial revisions to the system before it became operational in 1984.[63] This was despite one MOF comment which expressed opposition to any revision: 'Delaying the legislation amounts to overlooking hidden income.'[64] The position of this group within the LDP was clearly at odds with the MOF, and again intervention by the LDP promised to upset the MOF's plans.[65]

A common thread running through the attempts by the MOF to unify the postal savings and bank savings interest rate mechanisms, to introduce the green card system and to prevent the introduction of an MPT-based pension plan was the interest within the LDP in the policy outcomes. About 80 per cent of LDP parliamentarians supported the MPT position (explicitly or implicitly). The method of support was through the formal institutions of PARC, or by establishing groups in support of a particular cause. Support for these post office-based groups overrode the normal importance of the finance committees in the Diet, and the Finance Subcommittee in PARC. The reason for this widespread support was based on the importance of the postal savings system to most Japanese and an electoral sensitivity to downward changes in the postal savings interest rate. The importance of the postmasters' organisation and postal workers' union was sufficient to organise a small number of successful election campaigns, but in a broader sense the potential opposition from alienating the regional post offices was sufficient to guarantee support on many issues in much the same way as many proposals on agricultural policy receive strong LDP backing.

The issues raised in this chapter represent a range of issues, such as subsidised housing interest rates and the role of public financial institutions, which link the political arena directly to the financial arena. The support for the postal savings system illustrated this set of linkages. Through these linkages the individual household sector was not as unrepresented as might first appear in models of decisionmaking which stress only the interests of the business sector, the LDP and the public service. In fact, the decisionmaking process was so much more complex than this that these 'tripod'-type theories represent a major distortion of reality. On the other hand whether individuals benfited from this intervention is a different question, to which there is no simple answer.

Unlike other areas of financial policy examined in earlier chapters, the LDP's role in the formulation of regulatory policy was, during the 1970s, quite significant. There were strong reasons for an LDP interest in the postal savings system, including its electoral significance and importance in financing government expenditure. The management of the postal savings system gives credence to the proposition that the LDP's interest in policymaking was significant in matters with electoral ramifications.

Bargaining at the ministry level failed to produce results because the MPT and the MOF had different objectives and jurisdictional interests. When resolution could not be achieved because of incompatible proposals, the lack of complete jurisdictional authority meant that matters were periodically referred to the Cabinet and Prime Minister. Even in more routine matters, such as the level of interest rates, the Prime Minister's role was of central importance. Where the deadlock was over a matter of regulatory policy, the role of PARC was noteworthy. In both areas, however, the limitations of public service authority were well apparent. In short, politics still played an important role in some areas of economic policymaking.

6   The new foreign exchange law
Inter-ministry conflict in a non-political environment

Regulatory policy in financial markets in Japan goes beyond purely domestic considerations to include the set of financial interactions between Japan and the international financial markets. In Japan this set of interactions was subject to vigorous scrutiny by the MOF and to a lesser extent MITI. The main concern of this chapter is with the capital flow aspects of these interactions during the 1970s and early 1980s, and the regulatory framework which moulded them.

During the 1970s the adjustments to regulatory policy were transmitted primarily through ministerial ordinances and notifications. In 1978 the Foreign Exchange and Foreign Trade Control Law (FEFTCL), which had been the main source of legislative control over the direction of capital flows and foreign exchange usage generally, became the subject of administrative review which continued into 1980.[1] An examination of each period illustrates well the difference between adjusting the existing regulations and the revision of the legal framework in terms of interaction between ministries. An analysis of this issue in general also permits comparison between inter-ministry disputes in which the LDP was involved, such as the postal savings issue, and disputes where it had little interest, exemplified by this case study.

Studying the regulation of capital flows allows consideration of the proposition that international influence on regulatory policymaking is small. There are problems involved in this type of analysis because of the general nature of foreign pressures and the specific nature of Japanese reactions. In this chapter the evidence is presented at a general level, while a detailed case study of the yen bond market which appears in the next chapter certainly supports the broad thrust of this proposition.

REGULATION OF CAPITAL FLOWS BY ADMINISTRATIVE MANAGEMENT, 1973–79

Historical environment

The decade of the 1970s encompassed years of profound change in the international financial system beginning with the collapse of the Bretton Woods

Agreement, which had provided the central tenets of the fixed exchange rate system.

After a period of protracted bargaining, the world's major industrial countries moved to a flexible exchange rate system in early 1973. In late 1973 the direction of capital flows changed dramatically as a result of the successful attempt by the Organisation of Petroleum Exporting Countries to increase oil prices. This price increase placed many new demands upon the existing international financial system. Private banking institutions and public bodies such as the International Monetary Fund (IMF) sought ways and means to accommodate these new demands. The Eurodollar markets increased in both size and sophistication, although not without incidents such as the Herstatt bank failure in 1974. Negotiations from 1973 to 1975 finally produced the Jamaica Agreement. Although in many respects confirming an acceptance of the status quo, the agreement illustrated some international preparedness to make concessions and to return to a system using an agreed set of rules. Considerable uncertainty remained (particularly in developing countries) over the ability of the international financial system to cope with the demands placed upon it. One of those uncertainties was the extent to which national governments would permit their financial markets to become a part of the broad international financial market. The Japanese monetary authorities were one group of actors which experienced many of these anxieties and uncertainties.[2]

Even though there was a rapid growth in the volume of international financial transactions (trade-related transactions as a consequence of the oil price increases and other capital transactions), most national governments remained very wary about these flows. The main concern was the impact of outside flows on domestic monetary policy, the critical object of which had become inflation control. Although before their introduction flexible exchange rates were thought sufficient to reduce this problem, experience in the 1970s showed that speculative capital flows and capital flows resulting from changes in willingness of investors to hold assets in particular currencies increased tension among policymakers. Since free inflow and ouflow of capital could easily disturb the effective management of domestic monetary policy, many governments continued to maintain varying degrees of control over capital flows in an attempt to minimise their effect.

A foreign exchange management policy might have other objectives than the control of changes in domestic monetary aggregates. For example, it might attempt to regulate the inflow (or outflow) of funds for investment purposes, on grounds related to foreign ownership and not to the growth in the money supply. Permitting certain types of industries to purchase foreign exchange for importing purposes may reflect the government's intention of promoting certain types of industry over others. Banning the use of foreign exchange for investment abroad (in securities or real estate) could reflect the government's desire to maximise the 'productive' return from the available level of foreign exchange at a given time in a country's development.

Apart from several partial amendments of limited significance, the FEFTCL (1949) and the Foreign Investment Law (1950) provided the legislative framework which controlled foreign exchange transactions until the end of 1980. The legislation prohibited in principle all foreign exchange transactions, but as the government determined, exemptions were made to permit certain transactions. In the early postwar years, Japan suffered from a critical shortage of foreign exchange. The regulatory framework devised by the government was a reaction to this shortage, and allowed the government to establish a set of priorities for the use of foreign exchange and for the inward and outward flow of capital (which on occasions overlapped). In short, the regulatory framework explicitly defined the nature of Japan's involvement in the international financial market. The operation of the law, and the cabinet orders, ministerial ordinances and notices which set out the details in practice, reflected the belief of government that it, and not the market, was the best judge of how to maximise the benefits that could be derived from available foreign exchange.[3]

On the inflow side, impact loans and portfolio investment in a range of securities were unrestricted, but there were strict limits on the size of acquisitions by individual foreigners and foreigners as a group.[4] Along with restrictions on direct investment (where, incidentally, the scope for foreign involvement was allowed to increase with a series of liberalisation measures beginning in 1967), the measures relating to portfolio investment defined priorities with respect to foreign ownership and management of enterprises.[5] During the 1960s, Japanese firms were permitted to raise funds abroad for domestic use only after each case was approved by the MOF. Again, the restrictions on tapping international markets reflected considerations other than foreign exchange management.

Long-term outflows were dominated by direct investment abroad and export credits, with every project in excess of US$1 million requiring approval from the BOJ. Investments in portfolio investment and loans raised from Japanese sources were restricted. Foreigners' use of the open capital market to raise funds publicly was virtually prohibited before 1970. On the short-term side, the use of foreign exchange by individuals for travel purposes was strictly controlled, as was the remittance of monies abroad.

Taken in its entirety, the policy pursued by the MOF encouraged foreign capital inflows subject to an investment policy constraint, and restricted outflows subject to a needs constraint. The needs constraint recognised the role of export credits in securing export sales, and the need for some investment in sales networks, manufacturing and resource development. Outflows for investment purposes were small, totalling US$3.58 billion between 1951 and the end of fiscal 1970.[6]

Economic and political responses

The development of regulatory policy on capital flows in the period 1973–79 can be seen in terms of economic and political responses. Economic responses were related to the resolution of problems with the current account of the balance of payments, the fulfilment of domestic monetary and financial objectives, and the satisfaction of economic demands as the business horizons of Japanese corporations changed. Political responses were related to the needs of domestic and foreign interest groups, to the maintenance of the MOF's sphere of influence and to the changing position of Japan in international economic and political affairs. The analysis below will attempt to identify which elements of capital flow policy were most responsive to economic and political factors. Then the question is addressed as to whether the general level of regulation in the area of capital flow policy changed during the 1970s. If it did change, an explanation of the main factors contributing to the change is required.

Tables 6.1 and 6.2 outline the state of the balance of payments during the 1970s, and the level of short- and long-term assets and liabilities respectively. Read in conjunction with Appendix 1 which outlines the broad shifts in regulatory policy relating to capital transactions, these tables provide a guide for establishing the impact of policy measures on the balance of payments.

In a period of current account deficit, one option for a government wanting to minimise further deterioration in reserves was to adopt a policy which reduced the level of capital outflow and encouraged the level of capital inflow. Similarly, in a period of current account surplus, the converse should be true. This study looks at the character of regulatory policy on direct investment, indirect investment, the issue of bonds abroad by Japanese corporations and banks, and short-term capital flows.

Direct investment

A range of factors contributed to the rapid increase of Japanese investment abroad during 1971–73. An official MOF publication suggested six possibilities. These were the strengthening performance of Japanese corporations after a sustained period of economic growth; the need to assure increased stability of supply of natural resources in the face of increased nationalism and demand; shortages in Japan's workforce; land price and environment problems in Japan; enticements by foreign governments; and problems with import restrictions facing Japan's exports. This catalogue avoids mentioning what are perhaps the two key factors: the changing regulatory framework and the rapid growth in Japan's current account surplus. From 1969 until 1972, the controls on capital export were reduced greatly. Automatic approval was given to investments up to US$0.2 million in 1969, expanding to US$1 million in 1970, before the quantity controls were abandoned in 1972.[7]

The rapid growth of overall Japanese investment abroad during 1969–73 petered out very quickly in 1974. One explanation was that corporate planners were badly shaken by the oil crisis of 1973, and as a result, foreign investment plans were curtailed in a similar way to domestic investment. Direct investment abroad by Japanese grew by 4 per cent in 1974 and then declined. Regulations did not play an important role in curtailing outward direct capital investment flows, although the decision in November 1973 to prohibit medium- and long-term lending by Japanese banks abroad and to amend the government foreign currency loan system would have made foreign investment more

Table 6.1   Japan's balance of payments, 1970–80 (US$ million)

	Current account	Trade account	Exports	Imports	Services	Unrequited transfers	Long-term capital	Basic balance	Short-term capital	Error & ommissions	Overall balance	Balance of monetary movements	Gold & foreign exchange reserves	Other
1970	1970	3963	18969	15006	-1785ª	-208	-1591	379	724	271	1374	1374	903	593
1971	5797	7787	23566	15779	1738	-252	1082	4715	2435	527	7677	7677	10836	3031
1972	6624	8971	28032	19061	-1883	-464	-4487	2137	1966	638	4741	4741	3130	1771
1973	-136	3688	36264	32576	-3510	-314	-9750	-9886	2407	-2595	-10074	-10074	-6119	-3955
1974	-4693	1436	54480	53044	-5842	-287	-3881	-8574	1778	-43	-6839	-6839	1272	-8111
1975	-682	5028	54734	49706	-5354	-356	-272	-954	-1138	-584	-2676	-2676	-703	-1973
1976	3680	9887	66026	56139	-5867	-340	-984	2696	-111	117	2924	2924	3789	-865
1977	10918	17311	79333	62022	-6004	-389	-3184	7734	-648	657	7743	7743	6244	1499
1978	16534	24596	95634	71038	-7387	-675	-12389	4145	1538	267	5950	5950	10171	-4221
1979	-8754	1845	101232	99387	-9472	-1127	-12618	-21372	2377	2333	-16662	-16662	-12692	-3970
1980	-10746	2125	126736	124611	-11343	-1528	2394	-8352	3071	-3115	-8396	-8396	4905	-13301

Note: a—means excess of foreign exchange outflow over inflow

Source: BOJ *Balance of Payments Monthly* March 1981

Table 6.2   Japan's gross foreign assets and liabilities (US$ million)

	1973	1975	1977	1979	Share of total 1973 %	Share of total 1979 %
ASSETS (OUTFLOWS)						
Long-term	24 733	32 357	42 085	83 663	52.0	16.8
Private sector	18 806	24 522	31 177	62 141	39.5	45.9
Direct investments	4 546	8 322	11 958	17 227	9.6	12.7
Export credits	6 191	6 832	8 791	10 468	13.0	7.7
Loans	3 969	4 984	4 322	14 938	8.3	11.0
Portfolio investments	3 898	4 104	5 595	19 003	8.2	14.0
Other	202	280	511	505	0.4	0.4
Government sector	5 927	7 835	10 908	21 522	12.5	15.9
Export credits	270	330	330	575	0.6	0.4
Loans	3 874	5 497	8 022	16 574	8.1	12.2
Other	1 783	2 008	2 556	4 373	3.7	3.2
Short-term	22 818	25 977	37 975	51 702	48.0	38.2
Private sector	10 567	13 162	14 764	31 087	22.2	23.0
Monetary movement	10 003	12 947	14 457	29 946	21.0	22.1
Other	564	215	307	1 141	1.1	0.8
Government sector	12 251	12 815	23 211	20 614	25.8	15.2
Monetary movement	12 246	12 815	23 212	20 614	25.8	15.2
Other	5	—	1	—	0.0	—
Total assets	47 551	58 334	80 060	135 365	100.0	100.0
LIABILITIES (INFLOWS)						
Long-term	10 061	13 603	19 575	36 355	29.1	34.1
Private sector	9 025	11 886	16 048	27 970	26.1	26.2
Direct investment	1 602	2 084	2 229	3 422	4.6	3.2
Import credits	130	98	80	38	0.3	0.0
Loans	1 694	1 702	1 758	1 815	4.9	1.7
Portfolio investments	4 940	6 044	11 908	22 606	14.3	21.2
Other	659	1 958	73	89	1.9	0.1
Government sector	1 036	1 717	3 527	8 385	3.0	7.9
Loans	493	414	341	268	1.4	0.3
Portfolio investments	204	214	2 186	8 117	0.6	7.6
Other	339	1 089	1 000		1.0	—
Short-term	24 474	37 713	38 505	70 233	70.9	65.9
Private sector	23 369	36 395	36 075	64 408	67.7	60.4
Monetary movement	13 468	26 418	26 865	50 208	38.9	47.1
Other	9 901	9 977	9 210	14 200	28.7	13.3
Government sector	1 105	1 318	2 430	5 825	3.1	5.5
Monetary movement	708	712	1 505	3 852	2.0	3.6
Other	397	606	925	1 973	1.1	1.9
Total Liabilities	34 535	51 316	58 080	106 588	100.0	100.0

Source: Ōkurashō *Zaisei kin'yū tōkei geppō* Nos. 278, 290, 302, 314, 326

difficult and costly in some cases. Offsetting these reductions, however, was the easing of regulations on loans raised for use abroad, with the number issued for this purpose rising from three in 1973 to thirteen in 1974, and the volume rising by approximately US$140 million. See Table 6.3.[8]

Table 6.3   Foreign currency bond issues by Japanese corporations (US$ million)

	For domestic use				For external use			
Fiscal	No.	Total value	Value per loan	% of total	No.	Total value	Value per loan	% of total
1969[a]					13	270		
1970[a]					7	120		
1971[a]					5	122		
1972					1	31		
1973					3	39		
1974	2	69	34.3	27.7	13	179	13.8	72.3
1975	37	848	22.9	60.5	20	525	27.6	39.5
1976	44	1087	24.7	64.4	25	602	24.1	35.6
1977	44	1109	25.2	60.5	20	559	28.1	33.5
1978	72	1977	27.5	72.5	23	749	32.5	27.5
1979	123	3311	26.9	82.9	15	686	45.7	17.2

Notes: a   Total of external plus domestic. Corporations were not permitted to issue for domestic use from February 1971 to November 1974

Source: Ōkurashō Kokusai kin'yūkyoku nenpō Dai 4 kai

During the second half of the 1970s, the level of direct investment rose again, with the 1979–80 average being 35 per cent up on 1973–74, and 7.3 times the 1970–71 level. The change in the regulatory framework in the early 1970s and the strengthening of the current account at that time facilitated the first massive surge in outward investment, whereas the need to keep industry competitive and the opportunities for overseas investment sustained the outward investment flows in the late 1970s. Japan had a strong interest in maintaining these investment levels abroad. Fears related to resource security prompted Japanese investments in resource-related projects, and rising domestic wage rates and infrastructure costs caused some industries to re-establish overseas, particularly in the ASEAN countries. These types of projects were largely unaffected by regulatory controls.[9] Some forms of direct investment, such as in real estate, were not treated so liberally, and, although small in dollar terms, were severely affected by regulations.[10] The differentiation between types of investment flows showed that policymakers felt the need for government control still remained in the allocation of foreign exchange resources.

Direct investment into Japan grew little during the 1970s. In the five-year period 1971–75 aggregate direct investment inflow averaged US$53 million, whereas during 1976–80 it averaged US$131 million. It was more erratic than direct outward investment flows, reflecting exchange rate conditions and the difficulties foreign corporations perceived or actually experienced in establishing investment projects in Japan. It is fair to say that investment projects by foreigners in Japan were not encouraged.[11] At the beginning of the 1970s, a range of regulations controlled direct investment inflows and outflows, representing the interests of foreigners and residents respectively. At the end of the 1970s, foreign exchange-related controls which had previously affected both sets of interests had all but disappeared, and all that remained was the residue of control on foreign investment into Japan for other than foreign exchange reasons.

Indirect investment

Indirect investment outflows were treated more ruthlessly by policymakers than direct investment outflows. Regulatory changes in 1971 encouraged indirect investment outflows, resulting in a record outflow in 1973 of US$6564 million. In November and December 1973 regulations on investments in securities and stocks abroad, and the outflow of loan capital, were tightened significantly, and precipitated a fall in outflow in 1974 to US$2051 million.[12] In the same period indirect investment inflows were also affected by regulations. In 1971, for example, corporations were refused permission to issue bonds abroad, because the funds would have added to the balance of payments surplus, and put increased upward pressure on the yen. In December 1973 this regulation was reversed and in November 1973 restrictions on foreign purchases of domestic securities were abolished, signalling the movement to a policy position encouraging indirect capital inflow.

Our explanation of indirect capital inflows in the 1973–75 period contains two parts. There were straight economic considerations.[13] Tight monetary conditions in Japan meant domestic interest rates were relatively high in international terms, and the uncertain foreign exchange markets reduced the economic incentives for investing abroad. The crucial explanatory factor was, however, the changes in regulations. Even if there had been incentives, regulatory measures would have prevented investors taking advantage of them. In January 1974 the purchase of all foreign securities (such as TBs of the US government) with maturities of less than one year was prohibited. At the same time the MOF introduced a form of administrative guidance: it asked domestic investors to exercise self-control on all portfolio investment, meaning that there could be no net increase in the level of outward portfolio investment. The yen bond market was also closed from December 1973 and not reopened until July 1975. The regulations delineated clearly the character of policy favoured by the MOF during the current account deficit and surplus during the early 1970s. Regulations did not discriminate between domestic interest groups and foreign interest groups. In the deficit period of 1973–76, for example, the MOF prevented by regulation both domestic interest-oriented outflows and the foreign interest-based groups from raising funds in Japan.

During the current account deficit period of 1979–80, a different pattern emerged. The outflow of capital related to domestic interests was not regulated, whereas the yen bond market was regulated severely, although not closed. In this case, policymakers exercised the choice they had of determining how available funds should be allocated. The MOF permitted residents to send funds abroad, but did not permit a significant level of participation by foreign interests wanting to borrow funds in Tokyo's capital markets. Again this difference can be explained not in terms of foreign exchange usage but in terms of other domestic problems. The domestic bond markets were themselves highly regulated and the MOF was worried that issues at market prices in the yen bond market would influence adversely the trend of interest rates in other long-term bond markets. The decline in yen bond issues during this period was certainly not related to a lack of willingness by foreign issuers to pay market prices.[14]

Issue of bonds abroad and impact loans

Controls on foreign bond issues by domestic corporations and impact loans were related to the state of the current account as well as the impact on monetary policy.

A ban on foreign currency bond issues by domestic corporations was maintained until late 1974 when the domestic monetary squeeze was considered to have served its purpose. Although controls on long-term impact loans were relaxed during 1974, the volume of these loans which had begun decreasing in 1970 fell steadily to the end of 1974. The reduced importance of long-term impact loans reflected the growth in alternative methods of financing, such as issuing bonds abroad.

The increased use of foreign bond markets indicated the increased sophistication of Japanese corporations in assembling capital funds. Once this pattern was firmly established it was not amenable to sudden policy changes.[15] During the balance of payments surplus of 1976–78, the MOF was aware of the problem that cutting Japanese corporate exposure to international financial markets would create, recognising the time it took for corporations to establish their creditworthiness in international markets. When Japan had a current account deficit in 1979–80, the volume of corporate bonds issued abroad for use in Japan rose significantly. Whereas long-term capital inflows were once controlled, changes in corporate horizons, combined with the massive use of the domestic long-term bond market by government, led to a gradual breakdown in controls. It is unlikely that current account surpluses of the future will lead to controls on long-term capital inflows.

Domestic banks were given permission to operate in the area of long-term impact loans in March 1980, but still their participation was controlled. Administrative guidance was used to limit the extent to which domestic banks became involved in this area as the authorities feared that their close ties with local corporations would further reduce the number of opportunities for foreign banks. After an adjustment period, one could expect a larger capital inflow in this area, to service not established corporations, but those without names on the international market. Both these areas became less subject to government regulation during the 1970s.[16]

Short-term capital flows

Throughout the 1970s, the MOF imposed controls on short-term outflows and inflows. On the inflow side, regulations controlled purchases of bonds with 'short' maturities (on some occasions the regulations affected only the purchase of government securities and on other occasions the purchase of bonds with a maturity of less than five years and one month). On the outflow side it controlled the flow of funds for remittance, travel and the purchase of short-term foreign government securities. The 1970–72 surplus period saw a wide range of controls being used on capital inflows. In 1977–78 the range of controls was similar. In both cases, controls on short-term impact loans and investment in short-term securities were used. Short-term controls were used to reduce speculation in yen, to prevent the embarrassment of large buildups of foreign exchange reserves, and to reduce the likelihood of speculative disturbances on the money supply.

The level of controls varied in intensity. The level of control used during the 1979–80 balance of payments deficit was considerably less than during the 1973–75 period. In the later period, few controls were placed on short-term outflows. This reflected, in part, the increased short-term capital inflow into Japan which occurred despite the balance of payments deficit problems caused by the second oil shock. Development of international investor interest in Japanese securities stemmed from the need for international fund managers to balance their portfolios with yen holdings and the interest of Arab investors in holding a slightly more diversified portfolio of assets, and reflected the continuing strong performance of the Japanese economy. As long as international investors retained their confidence in the Japanese economy, the inflow would continue, providing Japan with a valuable source of foreign capital without the problems associated with direct foreign investment. Although the inflow was modest before 1980, it is important to note that the second oil shock in 1979, unlike the 1973–74 shock, had no major impact on it, or at least it did not cause a reversal of the trend.

During the 1970s, non-residents were able to hold yen as 'free yen deposits'. To neutralise this source of inflow during periods of speculation against the yen, or in periods of strong current account surplus, two reserve deposit mechanisms were used.[17] Table 6.4 shows how the rate of change of free yen deposits was subject to considerable control during current account surpluses. The system was abolished with the introduction of the revised FEFTCL in 1980, but in its place a system was introduced whereby interest payments on deposits of non-residents could be set at zero. In short, the government showed no inclination to alter its position of maintaining adequate measures to control speculative capital inflow, although it did change the form of the controls.

Between 1970 and 1980, the administration of the FEFTCL changed considerably, and for the most part towards reduced levels of regulation. Several patterns became increasingly clear. First, authorities began to treat long- and short-term flows very differently. Whereas controls on the former were on the whole relaxed considerably, the armoury of controls on short-term flows was always kept in readiness. Second, in the case of short-term controls, foreign interests were most affected as they tended to include those involved in speculation. Where domestic interests also speculated, such as in the case of the

Table 6.4   The use of reserve deposit mechanisms (per cent)

Reserve deposit on increase in foreign exchange holding[a]		Reserve deposit on overall holdings	
1 June 1972	25	1 June 1977	0.25
1 July 1972	50		
10 December 1973	10		
12 September 1974	0		
22 November 1977	50		
18 March 1978	100		
17 January 1979	50		
9 February 1979	0		

Note: a   The maximum legal reserve deposit on increases in holdings was 100 per cent

Source: Ōhashi Muneo (ed.) Kokusai kin'yū p. 163

Table 6.5   The impact of foreign exchange control on interest groups

State of balance of payments on current account	Interest group	Period and Impact			
		1970–72		1976–78	
Surplus					
Impact loans (supplied by foreign banks)	foreign	affected		affected	
Bonds issued by Japanese corporations	domestic	affected		partly affected	
		1973–75		1979–80	
Deficit					
Direct investment abroad	domestic	unaffected		unaffected	
securities	domestic	strongly affected		unaffected	
Yen bonds	foreign	strongly affected		affected	

Notes: Strongly affected: Regulations prohibiting certain types of capital flows
Affected: Direct regulation substantially affecting flow of funds
Partly affected: Regulation subject to preservation of corporate bond ratings abroad
Unaffected: No visible regulatory control having a substantial effect on capital flows

trading companies, then they also were affected. Third, in the case of regulatory policy on long-term capital flows, controls on foreign interests were more persistent than those on domestic participants. The main reasons for this development were not related to foreign exchange policy per se, but to other problems within the domestic markets. Until those problems were resolved no significant change in policy could be expected. The conclusions are summarised in Table 6.5.

The highly restrictive character of the FEFTCL and the Foreign Investment Law gave the MOF (and in the case of trade items, MITI) considerable administrative discretion which, in the implementation of the law, it used extensively. The wide discretion available to the MOF allowed it to alter regulations to suit its perception of the needs of the market.

Regulatory policy developed in response to both economic and political factors, but perhaps the most significant were factors originating from domestic market interests. By the end of the 1970s, all the remaining major impediments to long-term capital flows were related to the strength of specific interest groups. In contrast, the consistent approach to monetary policy was the key factor in explaining policy towards short-term capital flows. Even here, however, institutional rigidities, such as the role of banks in foreign exchange flows, played an important part in shaping the system. The main conclusion to be drawn is that the involvement of foreign interests in Japan was far more indirect and probably less important in determining policy outcomes, than the involvement of Japanese interests abroad. Further, the effect of balance of payments on long-term capital flows gradually declined.

THE REFORM OF THE LEGAL FRAMEWORK

The FEFTCL (1949) and the Foreign Investment Law (1951) provided the framework for the administration of foreign exchange policy, and through it, a policy controlling the movement of capital flows by administrative fiat. As noted, there was substantial liberalisation of controls in many areas of policy in the late 1960s and early 1970s before the sudden change in economic conditions that resulted from the oil crisis saw many dramatic, if temporary, reversals in policy. But the relationship between Japan and the international environment was far from static. Japanese corporations and investors were becoming involved increasingly in the international economy. Changing demands of business and financial institutions, the altered position of Japan in the world economy and a changing structure of international capital flows all imposed new pressures on the conduct of foreign exchange policy and the management of capital flows.

The initiative for legislative reform

In early 1977 the International Finance Bureau of the MOF (IFB) began looking at ways to simplify the regulations controlling the use and flow of foreign exchange.[18] It made clear that this did not mean it would forsake control over areas such as impact loans or yen bonds which would affect the order of domestic capital markets. Instead, the purpose of simplification was to reduce what may be called the information and processing costs of a transaction. These improvements, argued the IFB, would improve the image of Japan in the international marketplace. In an article written after the major simplifications were introduced in May and June 1977, the head of the IFB, Fujioka Masao (now governor of the Asian Development Bank), argued that the measures that had been introduced went far towards answering international criticism directed at Japan's trading and capital control arrangements. Fujioka argued that while there was some merit in the idea of changing from a system based on prohibition in principle to one based on freedom in principle, there were several important problems. First, since there was a range of areas where controls were desirable, shifting to free-in-principle with a long list of exceptions would not create a good impression internationally.[19] Second, there had been precedents, in 1958–59 and 1963–64, when a reform of the foreign exchange law had been debated and no result had emerged, not auguring well for another attempt. Third, although there was some support for the idea of law reform, preparations would take time, and there was no guarantee of a swift passage in the Diet. It is clear that Fujioka thought more could be achieved working within the existing legal framework than recasting the framework. The simplifications implemented in May and June were seen by him as wholly adequate answers to foreign critics.[20]

Japan's current account surplus on the balance of payments was not, as it turned out, the main issue that caused its policymakers to consider revision of the FEFTCL. There was little international criticism of Japan's current account or overall balance of payments position at the IMF General Meeting in Washington in late September 1977.[21] According to the governor of the BOJ, Morinaga Teiichirō, the chairman of the United States Federal Reserve Board, Arthur Burns, appreciated the policy stance taken by Japan. He accepted, however, that the US government and Congress did not much like Japanese policy. The central problem in Burn's view was the United States–Japan trade imbalance. The rapid growth in that imbalance can be seen in Table 6.6. Burns had warned Morinaga of the depth of feeling in the US Congress on the trade issue. In early October, Morinaga conveyed these remarks to Prime Minister Fukuda who apparently felt some significant action was necessary.[22] Typical of American political opinion was the belief that the Japanese did not really understand the meaning of the word 'internationalisation'.[23]

The view of the MOF at the end of October was generally unsympathetic, and

Table 6.6   Japan–United States trade balance, 1975–78 (US$ million)

Year	Imports from United States	Exports to United States	Surplus of exports over imports
1975	11 608	11 149	− 459
1976	11 809	15 690	3 881
1977	12 396	19 717	7 321
1978	14 790	24 915	10 125

Note: — means surplus of imports over exports

Source: IMF Balance of Payments Statistics

rather similar to Fujioka's view presented in July. MOF officials were reported as saying that, in the long term, legislative reform might be possible but, in the short term, proposals for further liberalisation were more important.[24]

The flow of events between October and December cannot be exactly determined. It appears that the Prime Minister was most concerned with the problem of United States–Japan trade relations and saw the existing FEFTCL as part of the public relations problem.[25] The Ministry of Foreign Affairs (MFA) was similarly concerned. Discussions were held at the Prime Minister's office between Fukuda's staff and senior officials of the MOF and MFA. Among Fukuda's advisers—leaving the bureaucracy aside—were former officers of the MOF, including Hosomi, Sumita, Kashiwagi, Inamura and Murai.[26] This group, backed by the MFA, succeeded in overcoming current MOF opinion, resulting in the announcement by Fukuda on 11 January 1978 of the initiative to reform the FEFTCL. The announcement, then, was in large part a direct response to US criticism and was very much a political decision responding to the needs of trade diplomacy between Japan and the United States. The chain of decisionmaking was unusual, as it ignored the mainstream opinion of the MOF. It was not, however, as if the initiative came out of nowhere. There was substantial difference between existing law and actual practice; there was a balance of payments surplus and the exchange rate was revaluing steadily; former MOF officers were urging action and last of all the law invited international criticism in its existing form.

In the days after the announcement, MOF officials were quoted as saying the project would take at least two years, yet Fukuda wanted a draft law to put before the Diet within a year of the announcement. Fukuda, himself a veteran senior public servant from the MOF, is likely to have been well aware of the difficulties of redrafting what had grown into a very complex area of law. The difference in the estimates of how long a review of the law would take indicated something of how the Prime Minister and the MOF viewed the reform proposal. At his press conference on 12 January 1978, Fukuda stressed the need to match the law with the reality of foreign exchange control.[27]

Fukuda was not concerned with the detail of reform but with the public relations benefits which would flow from having a legislative framework which mirrored more closely the actual set of regulations in use.[28] The initiative for legislative reform stemmed from a consideration of the problems in the United States–Japan trade relationship and the predominantly political response to this problem. The emphasis of the legislative reform would be placed on foreign economic policy goals rather than a new approach to controlling foreign exchange movement.[29] Fukuda was not promising any change to the substance of the law.

Inter-ministry conflict in the development of the legislation

Whereas the Prime Minister played an important role in setting up the legislative review process, it was the public service that dominated the formulation of the new legislation. This analysis attempts to provide an understanding of how the public service operated in the policymaking process, and the role of interest groups and advisory bodies on the outcome of that process. In particular, the interaction of the MOF and MITI is examined to see whether the policymaking processes, involving inter-ministry bargaining, were subject to the significant levels of conflict seen in the previous chapter.

The MOF and MITI were the two ministries most deeply involved in administration of the foreign exchange and trade control system (and issues relating to foreign investment). As a consequence, those ministries became the centre of reform activity. The process of reform began in earnest in April 1978, following the decision of the inner Cabinet meeting on economic policy measures on 25 March 1978, which directed the MOF and MITI 'to start working on the full-scale revision of the Foreign Exchange and Foreign Trade Control Law concerning Foreign Investment, with a view to presenting an amendment bill to the coming ordinary session of the Diet.'[30]

Within the IFB of the MOF, the Office for the Preparation of Revising Laws was established. Its counterpart in the International Trade Administration Bureau of MITI was the Office for Examining the Trade Finance System. Both offices were small, and the bulk of the work was executed by a total of less than ten officers. When problems arose, other divisions of each respective bureau made contributions, but the bulk of the revision was managed at the director, councillor and assistant director level within each office.[31]

The first step was to define the scope of the problem. Discussions were held between the two offices, and then, in a process that lasted about a month, a joint group from the two offices conducted intensive discussions with interested groups. Trading companies, banks, manufacturing companies and industry organisations such as the FEO participated in formal discussions. Outside these formal sessions, both ministries met informally with the interest groups they supervised. For example, the MOF group met frequently with representatives from the foreign exchange banks.[32] The importance of these discussions became apparent later in the legislative process when disagreement between the MOF and MITI arose, based on the differences between the interests of the groups each ministry was supervising.

Before the establishment in August 1978 of the Advisory Committee on the Legal System of Foreign Exchange and Foreign Trade (Advisory Committee), the working groups of MOF and MITI had formed reasonably firm positions on the content of revision. MITI had taken the position that the emphasis of reform should be on controls relating to capital flows. It argued that for all intents and purposes trade flows were liberalised.[33] In an interview after the passage of the new law, a middle-ranking MITI official argued that foreign governments could not control their own corporations. For this reason, there was a need for Japan to retain regulations that gave the government power to prevent disruptive trade flows. These sentiments were reflected in MITI's negotiating stance.[34] Underlying this position was not only the relationship between MITI and MOF. A contributing factor, according to MITI officials, was that attempting to relax controls would have run into opposition from the LDP and from other

Figure 6.1   Interaction in the foreign exchange market

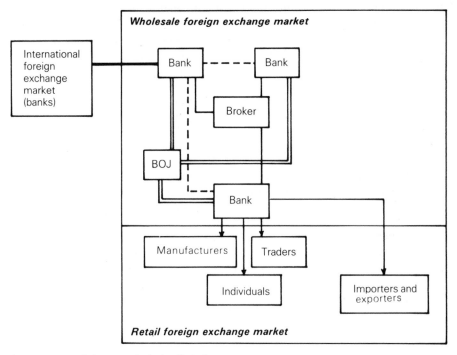

Source: Ōhashi Muneo (ed.) *Kokusai kin'yū* 1981 edn. p. 75

ministries.[35] This position was criticised by the MOF which argued that, if it were to be done at all, the whole law should be written in a clearer, more straightforward manner. Since the purpose of the legislative revision was to recast the vocabulary contained in the law to reflect contemporary practice, to leave whole chapters unchanged reduced the value of even this modest proposal and would result in a law lacking a unified approach to foreign exchange and trade regulation.[36]

The MOF also had areas that it wanted left alone. One such area was the method by which foreign exchange entered and left Japan. Figure 6.1 shows the basic structure of the postwar system. The main feature was that all transactions with the international foreign exchange market were carried out by banks which held foreign exchange licences.[37] Users and holders of foreign currency among the non-banking sector were required to buy and sell foreign exchange requirements through their banks. Although the regulations on how much foreign currency non-banking groups were permitted to hold had changed over the years, the principle was retained. The MOF argued that retention of this information-creating system enabled it to retain control over speculative capital flows. Among the domestic groups which felt penalised by the system were the trading companies.

In fiscal 1976 the ten largest trading companies handled 52 per cent of Japan's exports and 53 per cent of Japan's imports. Some attempt had been made to permit them to balance their demand with supply, by allowing offsetting with small transactions.

However, for all transactions exceeding one million yen (approximately US$4000), the accompanying exchange transactions had to be routed through a bank. It was not so much a question of the rate they received, for that differed little from the market rate for buying or selling. The trading companies had two complaints. One was the commission which they paid to banks, and the accompanying increase in paper work reporting of each transaction involved. The other and more important complaint was that the system did not permit the companies to take positions in the foreign exchange market.[38]

From the standpoint of the MOF, there were two principles involved. The MOF argued that requiring all transactions to be funnelled through one set of institutions, with which it had constant contact, allowed it to monitor the flow of foreign exchange and isolate speculative elements fairly easily. The MOF had been able to observe the German system of foreign exchange control in operation. The German system permitted large manufacturers to participate directly in the foreign exchange market.[39] The MOF argued that it wanted a more complete control over potential speculative foreign exchange flows than the West German system allowed. In later debate on the issue, it cited illegal dealings of corporations, typified by the Nisshō Iwai case, that had been detected through the existing system.[40] A less centralised system would have allowed these illegal dealings to pass undetected. The other principle of the MOF also related to speculation. If it permitted corporations to decide how far they should cover themselves against currency fluctuations, they would have been given the right to engage in activity (potentially speculative) from which banks had been barred. The MOF had required banks to balance spot purchases and sales, to balance forward purchases and sales, and to balance spot and forward transactions.[41]

The prime aim was, in short, one of limiting speculation. However, what the MOF failed to answer adequately was why trading companies should not be permitted to operate in the foreign exchange market if they fulfilled the same conditions required of banks. As well as looking at it in terms of currency stability and the desire to maintain control over short-term capital flows, it is also useful to look at the issue in terms of protection of vested interests.

Under the existing administrative arrangements, the foreign exchange system was administered at no cost to the government by banks with foreign exchange licences. The *quid pro quo* for operating this system was the return from commissions earned from foreign exchange transactions. At a time when profits of banks domestically had slumped to all-time low levels (especially among the city banks), profits from foreign exchange transactions partly compensated for substantial losses being incurred in their government bond business and restrictions on more competitive operations, such as between banking groups. Making an exception of trading companies would have led to other exceptions and a substantial redistribution in profits away from foreign exchange banks. The MOF's public stance was that control of capital movements was the key element involved in maintaining existing policy. An explanation based on protecting the interests of banks for which it was responsible is more persuasive. Had the MOF also been responsible for the trading companies, the result might easily have been different. As it was, MITI was more responsible than any other ministry for the activities of trading companies, although it must be added that the 'political' power base of trading companies was weak, partly reflecting intense independence, and partly the fact that there was no ministry which could be said to represent their interests strongly.[42]

Alternatively, it could be argued that the interests of the MOF and the foreign exchange banks merely coincided. Even if a system could be devised which resulted in retention of the existing level of safeguards against speculative capital flows, the introduction of such a system would not be without cost to the MOF. The MOF would be required to deal with a wider range of corporations which would place further strains on already overstretched resources. From its own viewpoint there seemed little merit in considering any change.

A third interpretation is that the position of both parties could be seen in terms of jurisdictional control rather than interest representation. In the same way that MOF had argued that MITI's reluctance to examine the level of regulation on trade matters was related to vested interests, the charge was levelled at the MOF by MITI. On the issue of the foreign exchange system, MITI argued that foreign exchange transactions were linked with trade transactions and hence were a MITI responsibility. As such, the question of retention of the foreign exchange control system was within its responsibility. The MOF rejected this line of argument completely. It held that finance was separate from trade, which in turn made it responsible for the shape of the foreign exchange control system.[43]

Given the plausibility of this argument, that jurisdiction can have a major impact on the shape of policy, then one can also argue as Krasner and others have in their work on the concept of national interest, that in Japan non-singularity of the concept is plausible. This chapter and the previous one have illustrated this clearly. Yet there were significant internal redistributive implications derived from adopting one view of 'national interest' over another. The implications for macroeconomic management would depend upon how the more 'liberal' system would have been implemented had it been adopted.[44]

This debate over jurisdiction adds to the 'interest-related' debate presented in an earlier section. Both illustrate ways in which control measures could result or be retained for other than economic reasons. The debate over the foreign exchange system gives good reason to suggest that non-economic reasons played a major part in the formation of the MOF's position on the matter, as indeed they did in MITI's position on trade-related items.

The role of the Advisory Committee

The development of the new FEFTCL also involved discussion in the Advisory Committee. The Advisory Committee had twenty members who are listed in Table 6.7. In terms of its composition, it was unexceptional, resembling the CFSR discussed in chapter 3. All members were elderly, respected members of the community, with most having strong interest group affiliations. Apart from strong industry and banking group representation, 30 per cent of the members were former public servants working with banks or corporations.

The role of the Committee was to fulfil customary expectations that some public debate had occurred. The format allowed little room for positive contributions. Since only six meetings were to be held, and since of these one was introductory, one was for presentation of conclusions and three were for presentation of the issues, only one meeting was left for free discussion.[45] More than make a positive contribution, the Committee system was designed to

Table 6.7   Advisory Committee on the Legal System of Foreign Exchange and Foreign Trade, 1978

Nagano Shigeo (Committee chairman)	President, Japan Chamber of Commerce
Uchida Tadao	Professor, Tokyo University
Kawasaki Kunio	President, Tōyō bōseki
	Deputy President Kansai keidanren
Kōno Mitsuo	Editorial Board, *Yomiuri shinbun*
Kojima Kiyoshi	Professor, Hitotsubashi University
Komatsu Yūgorō[a]	Advisor, Industry Research Institute
Sumita Satoshi[a]	President, Import–Export Bank of Japan
Taguchi Renzō	President, Ishikawajima harima jūkōgyō
Tsukuda Masahiro	President, Nikkei fudōsan
Tsunoda Ryōsaku	President, National Federation of Small and Medium-sized Traders
Hirose Yoshio	Member, NHK News Commentary Team
Maekawa Haruo[a]	Deputy Governor, Bank of Japan
Matsuo Taiichirō[a]	President, Marubeni Trading Co.; Deputy President, Japan Traders' Association
Matsuzawa Takuji	President, Fuji Bank; President, Federation of Bankers' Associations
Mizukami Tatsuzō	President, Japan Traders' Association
Mizuno Sōhei	President, Arabia sekiyu
Yamauchi Takahiro	President, Daiwa Securities; President, Securities Dealers' Association of Japan
Yokoyama Sōichi	President, Bank of Tokyo; Chairman, International Finance Committee of Keidanren
Yoshikuni Ichirō[a]	President, Regional Promotion and Facilities Corporation
Watanabe Makoto[a]	Advisor, Long-term Credit Bank of Japan

Notes: a   Members with public service backgrounds

Source: *Ōkurashō kenkyū* 1979, p. 213

'approve' the detailed plans developed by the public service. It is not correct to say the Committee was always a rubber stamp. Concerted opposition from within the Committee could force the bureaucracy to shelve carefully prepared proposals. On this occasion, however, the agreement by the two supervising ministries on the general issues to be reported in the proceedings of the Committee's activities reduced the scope for effective dissent. According to interviews with officials of both the MOF and MITI, disagreements with their drafts did occur at the initial presentations, but no dissenter's suggestions were incorporated in the draft of action.[46] For example, on the question of settlement method, the disagreements were noted in the following way:

> A part of members advocated that the regulations on the settlement method should be extensively liberalised in consideration of our recent foreign exchange position. But the majority opinion contested that if certain types of settlement method were allowed without restrictions, they might ... make the proper overview of our external transactions difficult.[47]

The MOF and MITI were more concerned with protecting their own interests and the interests of those which they represented directly. In the case of both the CFSR and the Advisory Committee, the main interests that were represented were functional ones: financial institutions as a group in the former and the subset with foreign exchange responsibilities in the latter. The views of academics and journalists were given little consideration. In interest group terms, the Advisory Committee was an extension of interests represented in the two working groups within the MOF and MITI. Views of other members were treated with little respect, and in the event those men did not make an issue of it.

Underlining this close relationship between a ministry and particular industry groups was the practice of prior consultation given by the public service to certain members of the Committee. A careful prior briefing of banking interests by MOF, for example, had the advantage of reducing the range of touchy issues beforehand. This method took the counterproductive 'surprise' elements out of more formal presentations when they occurred.[48] However, it did not mean that the public service was 'captured' by industry, but more that it fulfilled a range of roles, including servicing the needs of industry seen from its vantage point, managing the stability of foreign exchange flows, protecting its own administrative jurisdiction and listening to the views of industry. The roles of both the CFSR, which was managed entirely by the MOF, and the Advisory Committee, managed jointly by the MOF and MITI, were similar in that their recommendations were formulated by their public service support staff. The ministries thus were responsible for the document which provided the guidelines on which they based later legislative changes. Rather than serving to prepare new policies based on requirements of their leading participants, the advisory bodies served to legitimise the work of public servants. Before the first committee meeting of the Advisory Committee on the Legal System of Foreign Exchange and Foreign Trade, the general trust of the planned legal revision had been agreed upon, but details such as the debate on revision of trade-related provisions and the role of foreign exchange banks had yet to be decided. Although it has been argued that these bodies issue reports which are 'joint ministry–council products' and function 'to set the basic goals for different sectors of the economy' there is little evidence to support such a strong conclusion in the financial sector.[49]

The impact of political uncertainty

The initial rush to resolve problems within a short period of time was directly related to the fact that Fukuda played an important part in setting the whole revision process in motion. Although discussion between the MOF and MITI proceeded smoothly in the early stages, the final months of negotiations before the Committee's sixth meeting indicated that major problems remained. Much of the trouble was linked to the role of the foreign exchange banks, but the fact that MITI was able to delay the process of presenting a draft bill to Cabinet was a reflection of the political climate.

Not long after the initial meeting of the Advisory Council, the Prime Minister's political future was somewhat uncertain. It was widely expected that Fukuda would retain his position of Party President of the LDP in internal party elections, scheduled for November 1978. But, as a report in the *Asahi shinbun* of 17 September 1978 noted, the Prime Minister's position would be less secure should the Party Secretary, Ōhira Masayoshi, have the backing of the Tanaka faction.[50] Without prime ministerial insistence on a rapid conclusion to the reform process, the disputes between the MOF and MITI were sufficient to abort the entire proposal of reform. The subsequent defeat of Fukuda left the reform process rudderless, as each ministry waited to appraise the new Prime Minister's stance on the FEFTCL.[51] Fukuda's role, it will be remembered, was catalytic, forcing the MOF and MITI to consider a legislative revision which, to them, did not have a high priority.

Even when Ōhira announced his support for the reform process some of the urgency was gone, as the balance of payments and the foreign exchange rate had begun to weaken. Problems with the United States–Japan relationship nevertheless remained, and the public relations value of unveiling a revised foreign exchange law at the Tokyo Summit in June 1979 remained considerable. On balance, the change of Prime Minister probably reduced the momentum of the reform program and, had the explicit support of Ōhira not been forthcoming, there is every chance the reform would have suffered the fate of its 1963–64 forerunner.

An agreement was reached and a law drafted, but there was a wide discrepancy between the outcome desired by each party and the end product. In each of the eight substantive areas raised in the Proceedings of the Advisory Committee (reproduced in full in Appendix 2), there were important disagreements. Article 1 of the new FEFTCL set out new principles relating to deregulation of foreign exchange and capital flows, but the law in its entirety left the uneasy feeling that very little had changed.

Figure 6.2   Inter-ministry policymaking and regulatory reform

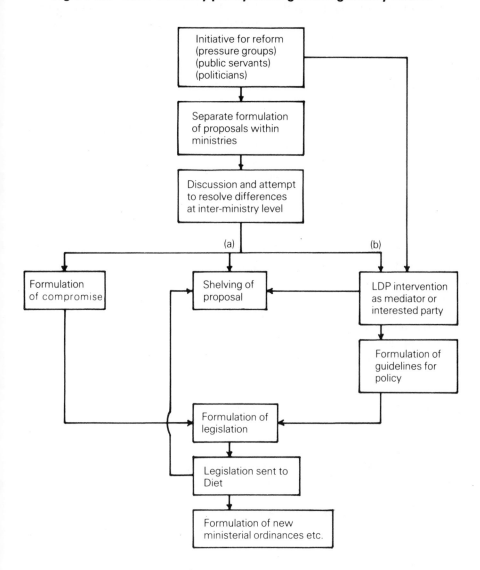

Inter-ministry conflict: a comparison

The role played by the LDP was the central difference between the character of the policymaking process during the reform of the FEFTCL and during attempts to alter the regulatory framework of the postal savings system.

In the first case resolution was effected primarily through prime ministerial involvement. Attempts to reform the same piece of legislation in the late 1950s and the early 1960s were shelved completely because of the inability of the two negotiating ministries, the MOF and MITI, to settle their differences. Conflict led to the abandonment of the attempts at reform. In 1978–79, prime ministerial involvement did not reflect an interest in the issues, but in the public relations value of the revision. Most government and opposition parliamentarians knew little and cared even less about the legislation. Alternative (a) in Figure 6.2 provides a schematic representation of the policymaking process. In this case, shared responsibility for regulations made it difficult to alter the established regulatory framework without agreement between the two ministries. Even in 1978–79 political involvement had little effect on the disagreements between the MOF and MITI.

In contrast, the postal savings system was the centre of much public and political debate. The LDP was intimately involved in proposals to alter regulations which shaped the function of the postal savings system. Alternative (b) in Figure 6.2 effectively describes that policymaking process. The main difference between the two relates to the role of the LDP. In both cases shared and diffuse location of responsibility for policy meant that a stalemate could result, in the absence of political intervention. In the case of the postal savings system, political intervention was common, sometimes operating to slow down the rate of regulatory change and sometimes to speed it up. The result was that intimate involvement of politicians on the side of one ministry, the MPT, sharply weakened the power of the MOF in this area. Both cases studied nonetheless shared difficulties inherent in areas where the level of concentration of control was low. A plurality of perspectives meant that conflict was bound to arise and difficult to solve in the absence of political intervention.

DEREGULATION OR ADMINISTRATIVE GUIDANCE: AN EVALUATION OF THE NEW FEFTCL

The new law, rather more than the old law, embodied the potential for free capital flows.[52] But within the law were emergency regulations and many 'prior notice' and screening procedures which in practice would allow the government to intervene if it was required. Thus, whereas capital transactions under the old law were permitted by government discretion, the new law gave the government authority to intervene if intervention was considered necessary. One issue which will require careful assessment is that relating to the level of discretion entrusted in the ministries responsible, and the level of discretion readily available for use. The distinction between being 'entrusted' and 'using' requires further elaboration.

Clearly, simply having a power is of little significance if exercising that power is constrained in a way that prevents its use when it is most required. Some estimation of whether the new law constrained use of entrusted discretion is also required. Administrative guidance posed another problem. The setting of informal limits on the management and execution of transactions in different categories, or informal price leadership in areas of so-called free interest rates, was an effective means of reducing the size of (and hence the potential problem with) a given 'liberalised' capital flow. Table 6.8 outlines the important capital flow-related measures of the foreign exchange system which became operative on 1 December 1980. Some concrete examples will facilitate the explanation of the problems mentioned above.

At the end of November 1980, there was some speculation that liberalising holdings of foreign currency deposits would open up a new high interest-bearing asset medium to residents. The new FEFTCL removed the limit of three million yen on foreign currency deposits. The argument was that if a holder of foreign currency took out a contract for a covered, fixed time-length deposit (say six months), it would be the same as having a yen deposit at international interest rates. There was an underlying presumption that these interest rates were higher than Japanese interest rates.

In the case of corporate deposits, where large quantities of foreign currency were concerned, the argument had some validity in times when an interest rate differential existed after adjusting for commission. This presumed that large domestic banks offered foreign currency rates. Interest arbitrage would then occur and the rates would equalise. There are, however, several important qualifications.

First, individuals with small quantities to deposit would not necessarily be offered market rates. In early 1980, interest rates being offered in this category were below current Japanese deposit interest rates. Since manufacturers did not operate under the three million yen restriction in the first place, the implications of this 'liberalisation' in terms of freeing domestic savings interest rates from their controlled state were minimal.

Second, should the buildup of foreign currency deposits be disturbing to government, a framework such as that which existed for impact loans could readily be 'arranged' between the MOF and the banking community.[53] The coincidence of a surplus on the current account of the balance of payments and an easy monetary policy might be one such instance. Holders of yen currency could change it into foreign currency, bring it back to Japan, deposit it and reap the rewards. The problem with this sort of argument was that it presumed, unjustifiably, unlimited access to foreign currency.

The Japanese foreign exchange system was 'liberalised', but the notification system that existed could pick up this speculative behaviour and enable the government to act appropriately. If foreigners attempted to take advantage of arbitrage opportunities, the MOF was able, through the new legislation, to prohibit interest rate payment on deposits.[54] In short, the extent that the level of foreign currency deposits held by residents increased was partly determined by whether the government saw these deposits hindering the implementation of its policy objectives.

The flotation of securities by non-residents in Japan and residents abroad was shifted from a licensing arrangement to a requirement of prior notification of intention, which could be supplemented by controls when the MOF deemed it appropriate. The two major areas of concern were yen bonds floated by foreign governments and international institutions within Japan, and bonds floated by

Table 6.8 Capital flows in the aftermath of the new Foreign Exchange and Foreign Trade Control Law

Transaction	Legal impact of new law	Flows of funds	Comments
1 Impact loans	Need for prior approval abolished	Outstanding loans increased from US$9.3 billion (November 1980) to US$27.7 billion (March 1983)	Domestic banks, particularly local banks, have been participating fully
2 Residents' foreign currency deposits	Ceiling on holdings abolished	Outstanding deposits increased from US$2.3 billion (November 1980) to US$3.7 billion (December 1980) to US$7.2 billion (March 1983)	Clear benefits to residents in that abolishing of ceilings improved choice
3 Intercorporate borrowing from abroad	From prior approval to prior notice; auditing undertaken in the case of direct investment	Flow increased from US$74 million in 1980 to US$780 million in 1981	Greater potential for shifting funds in stable international and domestic environment
4 Intercorporate lending abroad	Prior approval (automatic in certain cases) to prior approval with auditing	Short-term lending increased from virtually zero to US$824 million in 1981 and long-term rose from US$1799 million to US$3473 million in 1981	
5 Yen bonds floated	From prior approval to prior notice with auditing—little procedural change	1980 ¥2806bn 1981 ¥4756bn 1982 ¥6436bn	Volume increase reflects strong foreign demand and surplus domestic funds. Level of issue controlled
6 Flotation of bonds abroad	From prior approval to prior notification with auditing	(US$m) 3452 (US$m) 4659 (US$m) 5868	Continuation of internationalisation of corporate borrowing. Partly regulated

7 Foreign investment in domestic securities	Prior approval to prior notification; where designated security is used, notification unnecessary	11947	15075	7553	Interest rate differentials key to determining level of activity. Little interference
8 Foreign direct investment in Japan	Prior approval to prior notification with auditing	278	189	439	Remains very low but MITI involved in some public relations posturing to increase flow
9 Direct investment abroad	Prior approval to prior notification with auditing	2385	4894	4517	High profile in resource projects and manufacturing in local markets to protect market share. Minimal interference
10 Lending by foreign exchange banks abroad	Prior approval to prior notification; major banks not required to notify but a system of overall supervision continues to operate				Framework of overall lending set by MOF. Country risk of increasing importance
1 Yen lending		¥194bn 6704	¥463bn 12688		
2 Foreign currency					

Source: *Kin'yū zaisei jijō* 15 March 1982, MOF, mimeographed summary of new FEFTCL; BOJ *Economics Statistics Annual 1982*; newspapers

Japanese corporations abroad. The new FEFTCL had no immediate impact on the yen bond market. The government continued to regulate the level of issues according to the state of the domestic bond market, the state of the foreign exchange market and the state of the balance of payments. When a conflict in objectives arose, the outcome was determined by negotiations within the MOF. The old law provided the framework for regulating yen bond issues in that all transactions were prohibited unless an exception was granted. In practice exceptions were granted, and the market was operated by the MOF through administrative guidance. Under the new law, the position was much the same. Under Article 23.1 the issuing of yen bonds was subject to prior notice and screening. Effectively, the MOF continued to operate the market by administrative guidance as it had done previously under the old FEFTCL although, as its general objectives changed, so did the character of its policy. The development of this market is examined in detail in the next chapter.

A similar conclusion applied to the flotation of bonds abroad by Japanese corporations. It was not in the interests of Japanese corporations, or in the long-term interests of the Japanese nation, to restrict unduly the flotation of corporate bonds abroad. In tight monetary periods, the MOF had an interest in being able to restrict capital inflow, reserving the right to restrict access to potential external capital sources. It could be said that such a control was required for effective macroeconomic management, but equally it was also the basis for preserving MOF control over the domestic banking sector and the foreign exchange system.

During the 1970s Japanese corporations used international financial markets at an increasing rate. Financial institutions also became more involved internationally, supporting not only Japanese corporations but also multinational and foreign national corporations. The trend was towards internationalisation, in much the same way that the banks of the United States and Europe to greater and less degrees internationalised. The extent that Japanese banks alter their *modus operandi* towards a return-on-asset basis (instead of a growth-of-loans basis) would be likely to promote this trend. At first the authorities argued that only a small number of corporations had a sufficiently strong financial basis to borrow internationally. Gradually the restrictions were relaxed, and a fairly large number of corporations were permitted freedom from the confines of the regulated market. The larger banks also continued to upgrade their international operations. The Japanese economy was continuing to become more integrated into the international economy and more slowly, but nevertheless perceptibly, Japan was increasing its role in international political affairs. Although the MOF, MITI, MAFF, MPT and other central government ministries can be expected to support smaller economic units which have political backing, many sectors of the economy will become more sensitive to the international environment. But even small financial units could become more involved if the internationalisation of Japan's financial markets continues. The relaxation of financial regulations which inhibit these trends can therefore be seen as furthering the national interest. Country risk has clearly become a central issue in international finance in the 1980s. The establishment of the Japan Center for

International Finance in 1983 again illustrates the important role of the MOF in organising a collective tool to manage the problem which at the same time will allow the authorities to monitor closely developments in the marketplace.

Another category of capital flows was impact loans. Under the FEFTCL these were grouped with other measures for borrowing overseas funds by residents. In principle, an impact loan has the same effect on the money supply and the capital account of the balance of payments as raising funds by bond issuance. Under the new law there was no discrimination between the two. It is unlikely that discrimination which occurred between the two during the current account surplus period of 1977–78 will recur. In 1980, domestic banks were given permission to raise funds abroad and bring them into Japan up to a limit determined by the MOF. The access of domestic and foreign banks to impact loans not only broke the monopoly of foreign banks in this area but it also permitted smaller banks, in particular the regional banks, to secure foreign currency funds to satisfy the needs of their clients. The change in the approach of the MOF in this area illustrates the changing character of Japanese financial regulations.

There were legitimate reasons why the government should maintain a framework of protection against short-term capital movements. In the world of the 1970s, capital flows were enormous in size and often very volatile. The expectations of investors and speculators could be upset by the breakdown of Middle East oil supplies, a major earthquake, or other less dramatic events such as continuing relatively poor (or good) economic performances of a leading economic power. These events could lead to rapid shifts in dollar flows in the first instance, or in the last case, slow, more persistent new trends emerging. To this end, the new law gave the MOF very adequate methods for neutralising foreign flows. At the centre of their arsenal were the emergency regulatory measures provided for in the new legislation under Article 21 (2) when conditions were such that

(1)   It [capital flows] might make the maintenance of the equilibrium on our country's balance of international payments difficult;

(2)   It might result in drastic fluctuation of our currency's foreign exchange rates; or

(3)   It might result in transfers of funds between Japan and foreign countries in a large volume, and thereby adversely affect our money or capital market.[55]

The first meeting of the Council on Foreign Exchange and Other Transactions on 16 December 1980 set out in rather vague terms when the emergency regulations should be activated.

The emergency regulatory measures shall be activated in appropriate harmony and combination with (1) economic policies for adjusting the basic conditions of the Japanese national economy; (2) a foreign exchange policy intended to stabilise the foreign exchange rate; and (3) the prohibition of interest payment on non-resident yen accounts and other indirect regulation.[56]

Later the Council added that the regulations should be used 'only to the minimum extent necessary . . .', giving due attention to 'the stability of external transactions such as the execution of existing contracts.'[57] By means of a ministerial ordinance, the MOF was in a situation where it could use these regulations at short notice, by issuing a notification. The MOF, in effect, remained the sole judge of what constituted sufficient reason. At the time of writing the emergency regulations had not been used.

The legal framework of the FEFTCL consisted of several levels. The law itself stood at the apex, and established the general principles of the law. The more detailed identification of responsibilities and procedures was achieved through cabinet orders and ministerial ordinances. Cabinet orders detailed the method of operation of the law at a general level, and were the outcome of negotiations between the MOF and MITI. Conflict between the two ministries was on the same points as in the law itself. The MOF and MITI had approximately the same view on how the law should be administered. They both believed that each should be able to control their own jurisdictions with the minimum of outside interference. This was done by relegating much of the detail to ministerial ordinances, a procedure which gave the ministries responsible a considerable amount of discretion in implementing and altering the full impact of the law.

Unlike cabinet orders which required the approval of cabinet, ministerial ordinances could be altered at the discretion of the ministry. Ordinances were supplemented by issuing a ministerial notification which was binding on the participants within the market.

Up to the end of 1982 the MOF had not used the above-mentioned Article 21 (2), but nevertheless some comment can be made on how the MOF (and in some areas MITI and others) could exercise its discretionary power. According to the director-general of the IFB, Katō Takashi, the policy would not differ greatly from what has gone before. The MOF viewed the reform of the law not as representing any great structural changes but more as the simplification of procedures at the ministerial ordinance level.[58] The new law did not represent a discontinuity with what had gone on in the past: the boundaries of what was covered by cabinet orders, ministerial ordinances and notifications did change marginally, and although the outlook of the law embodied in Article 1 was dramatically altered, the immediate change in substance was small. Immediate changes represented a more accurate codification of actual practices in the legal framework. These practices had been managed by administrative guidance.

Within the MOF, the role of the IFB gradually increased, as Japan became more centrally involved in the international financial system. The internationalist position of permitting freer capital flows between countries was one based upon Japan's own interests in the 1970s and early 1980s. It will continue to develop and the MOF will continue to monitor the activities of Japanese banks in the international arena. For example, in early 1983 the IFB announced a package of measures designed to reduce the risks involved in the continued growth of international financial activities of Japanese banks. The MOF showed that it still felt that it had a role to play in designing, implementing and enforcing prudential controls. The underlying principle that it, the MOF, rather than individual banks, should determine these questions remained, although it is true that the banks were being given more freedom than they had experienced at any other time in the postwar period.[59]

Over the decade of the 1980s administration of the new law will change, as it did during the 1970s. There is little to suggest, however, that the legislative revision did much to change the power of the MOF and MITI on foreign exchange and trade matters respectively. By retaining discretionary options, the MOF kept control over the rate at which Japan will integrate into the international financial system. Much changed during the 1970s and this was primarily a reflection of the needs of the Japanese economy and the benefits to be had from increased interaction with international markets. The trend towards increased interaction between Japan and other international financial markets will continue. Over time, one could expect changes in the way in which Japan administers the control system which regulates and oversees two-way capital flows, in line with changes in national interest and constraints imposed through participation in the international system.

There was no doubt that foreign interest in Tokyo as an international capital market, and in the yen as both a reserve currency and a trading currency, increased during the 1970s and early 1980s. Furthermore, the level of regulatory control was reduced considerably and the volume of capital which flowed into and out of Japan grew rapidly. On examination, however, very little of the substance of this change could be directly attributed to pressure exerted by foreign governments. There were exceptions, in the early 1970s, when the world's major industrial countries shifted from fixed to flexible exchange rates, but otherwise Japanese policymakers adjusted, in their own time, the character of regulations to suit the prevailing needs of Japan. The way in which Japan develops its policies in the 1980s will reflect more than ever a range of international considerations, but nonetheless the crux of policy will be determined by the shift in its own national interests.

The substance of the revision of the FEFTCL was in reflecting how far the actual administration of the law had changed during the 1970s. The new FEFTCL simplified and reworded the existing regulations and ensured that the government retained adequate control over capital flows while endorsing the developments that had occurred in the previous decade. The MOF and MITI were not overly enthusiastic with the political initiative, and the subsequent bargaining process showed how they could partially subvert it. Nevertheless policy is not restricted to law and during the two years since the implementation of the new law the IFB in particular has shown itself to be generally supportive of internationalisation of capital flows into and out of Japan. How policy develops during the 1980s will reflect the performance of the Japanese economy in comparison with the United States and West Germany in particular, the concerns of the BOJ towards integrating Japan further into the international financial arena and the general stability of international financial markets. The minimal interest of politicians before and after legislative reform underlines the importance of the public service. In management of capital flows the MOF plays the key role and holds most of the overt authority (although the BOJ also has some important interests). Conflict was generally contained because of the high level of concentration of control resting in the IFB.

7   The yen bond market 1970–82
Foreign influences in policymaking

The policy of the Japanese government towards the flotation of yen bonds by foreign governments, international financial institutions and corporations offers an interesting and important forum in which to explore the more general developments that have affected policymakers in Japan over the last decade. Despite forming only a relatively minor section of the domestic bond market and a small part of Japan's policy towards capital flows, the market was the testing ground and reflector of broader policy shifts. This chapter highlights the differences between implementing regulatory change through administrative and legal means. Further, the yen bond market provides a useful forum for examining in detail the proposition that Japan was by and large insensitive to the demands of international actors, but pursued policies reflecting its own interests. Over the decade of the 1970s, the stance of the MOF in the yen bond market changed on several important issues. The reasons for these changes are explored below, with careful attention paid to the roles of domestic and foreign actors in the evolution of the yen bond market. Finally, while providing evidence which supports the conclusions in other parts of the book on intra-ministry regulatory policymaking, this chapter shows briefly how domestic traditions can be challenged by the need to maintain consistency within the broader financial markets, despite mechanisms which minimise these influences.

DOMESTIC CONSTRAINTS IN REGULATORY DEVELOPMENT

The establishment of the yen bond market

When the governor of the Asian Development Bank (ADB), Watanabe Takeshi, went to Tokyo to discuss the possibility of a publicly floated ADB yen bond issue in Japan, in March 1970, no publicly floated yen bonds had been issued in Japan by foreign legal entities. The World Bank and the American Development Bank had issued bonds by private placement, but that was all.[1] In the late 1960s Japan's balance of payments had improved so much that Watanabe believed he could engineer the first issue, but in order to succeed he required at least support from the MOF.

Watanabe was himself a former officer of the MOF and had strong contacts throughout the finance industry. After the first round of discussions with the MOF, the BOJ, securities companies and the banks, it became clear that several problems existed. One related to Article 65 of the Securities and Exchange Law (SEL) which barred banks from an underwriting position in public issues. Banks were able to handle private placements freely, but public issues, such as those in the domestic corporate bond market, were the preserve of the securities companies. If banks were allowed to underwrite, argued the Securities Bureau, the essence of the functional division between banks and securities companies would be threatened. Confrontation was avoided by the securities companies returning a substantial proportion of the underwriter's fee to the banks. Another problem relating to collateral arose but was circumvented by treating the ADB as a sovereign borrower, and thus exempting it from the established collateral tradition.[2]

Strong support for the ADB issue came from the upper echelons of the MOF. Fukuda Takeo, the Minister of Finance, and Sumita Satoshi, the administrative vice-minister, were in favour of moves to establish Tokyo as an international finance centre and the ADB issue in particular.[3] Following the March visit, Watanabe returned to Tokyo in July and August to lobby for the issue, meeting both Fukuda and the governor of the BOJ, Sasaki Tadashi.[4] Lobbying concentrated on presenting the issue as an expression of support for international cooperation and the ADB, rather than as a move to promote Tokyo as a new international financial centre, as Watanabe saw this as best serving the interests of the ADB.[5] He was successful and the first yen bond issue was made in December 1970.

The timing of the change in stance of the MOF towards a yen bond market had much to do with the negotiating done by Watanabe, but in several ways the ADB issue was fortuitous. Watanabe was an 'insider' as he was a former MOF officer and still well regarded by senior officials. Further, Japan was one of the sponsoring developed countries of the ADB, and thus felt some obligations to the development bank, which was seeking a further expansion of its loans base.[6] These factors made it easier to sort out the problems, although the fact that it was approved so quickly indicated both a receptive public service and industry interests which were able to compromise on points of difference.

The first test of the government's policy came when several foreign governments including Australia, Brazil and the Soviet Union began to examine the possibility of floating bonds on the Tokyo market. Expanding the market created several technical and legal problems involving disclosure and collateral.[7] In early 1972, the Securities Bureau clarified guidelines on issuing bonds in the fledgling market.[8] The Brazilian request was refused on the grounds that the market in its early stages required borrowers of international standing. The proposed Australian issue met all criteria, and was also seen as a method for cementing the economic relationship between the two countries. In the context of the Australian issue, the main problem was determining how business that sprang from the yen bond market would be divided between securities companies and banks. Since 1947, underwriting of bonds (with the exception of national, local and government guaranteed bonds) had been handled by securities companies. Banks were restricted to the role of managing collateral, called the 'commissioned banks' role, and this role would have disappeared if collateral requirements were waived. The problem was discussed in a range of fora before a workable solution emerged. The solution incorporated no innovations, but was one where the commissioned bank handled the affairs of the issuer (advertising, preparation of contract documents etc.) without handling the mortgage element.[9]

The process which resulted in the establishment of the yen bond market was similar in broad terms to that which led to the formation of the government bond market. In the case of the government bond market, political leaders decided on a path of budget deficits which in a sense forced participating bureaus to bury their differences. In the case of the yen bond market, the minister and administrative vice-minister had both indicated their strong support for the formation of an international capital market, which served to back up the case of the IFB. Japan's balance of payments surplus meant that the Securities Bureau had no adequate grounds to prevent the market being established. This fits into our dominant mode of policymaking. The agreement was not typified by consensus but reflected the imposition of the will of the dominant domestic group on the subordinate.

Establishing the criteria for issuing reflected much more a consensus mode of policymaking. Although unable to prevent the market being established and expanded to include sovereign issuers, the Securities Bureau was still able to influence selection of issuing criteria and division of work responsibilities between banks and securities companies.[10]

In the process of establishing the yen bond market foreign interests—the issuing foreign governments—played a role in so far as their expression of interest created a demand, but their expression of interest was not the key factor in determining the outcome. Instead, the key factors were the state of the current account on the balance of payments and the gradual change in thinking in Japan concerning the links between Japan and the international economy. Foreign confidence in Japan expressed through the desire of foreign governments to issue bonds there gave reason for a change in policy, but the role of foreign interests was more catalytic and supportive than fundamental and dominating. The size of the market indicated how tentatively Japan moved away from its isolationist position.

Foreign corporations and the yen bond market

One of the peculiarities of the yen bond market during the 1970s was the almost total exclusion of corporate borrowers. In all major international capital markets corporate borrowing played an important role.[11] The explanation for their exclusion in Japan was to be found in the character of the financial system.

Japanese corporations themselves had only very limited access to the domestic bond market. In 1980 the domestic bond market provided about 3 per cent of external corporate funds, with the dominant source of external funds being borrowings from banks. In the period 1978–80, for example, Japanese corporations raised more finance on overseas bond markets than they did on the domestic corporate bond market.[12] The role of the major commissioned banks was the key to understanding this low level of bond issue and how it related to foreign corporations issuing bonds on the Tokyo market.

As stated previously, all domestic bond issues in postwar Japan were guaranteed by collateral. Abandonment of the collateral system, if combined with a more liberal attitude to flotation of bonds, would not only have meant lost collateral management commissions but also have posed a real threat to the main line of business of long-term credit banks like the IBJ. The absence of guarantees would mean that the commissioned banks would no longer set the flotation limits, and hence one could reasonably expect a shift in capital raising away from the long-term credit banks and their long-term loans towards a more diversified range, quality and scale of bonds being issued.

In the early 1970s several domestic corporations toyed with the idea of non-guaranteed domestic issues. In 1972 Mitsui Trading Company and Komatsu, with the support of the securities companies, sought to change existing regulations.

The securities companies put forward three main reasons in support of their case. First, domestic corporations were able to issue unsecured bonds overseas, and foreign corporations would no doubt like to issue bonds in Japan. Before this could occur, change in the regulations relating to domestic corporations was necessary. Second, protection of the bondholder, often cited as a reason to maintain the existing system, could be achieved if strict and appropriate financial conditions were maintained. Third, unsecured bonds would lead to an elimination of expense flowing from trust and guarantee regulations, which would result in a reduction in the cost of borrowing.[13]

The commissioned banks opposed change completely, also giving three main reasons. First, the existing system provided support for corporations which would otherwise have limited access to the capital market. Second, it provided a means to guarantee completely the investment of the general public. Third, it maintained the existing orderly system of credit. If any change occurred, banking business would suffer.[14]

The Banking Bureau, and ultimately the MOF, supported the commissioned banks: as in the case of CDs studied by the 1970 Committee on Financial System Research, the dominant view was that the benefits to the few did not justify the conflict which would have resulted. The Banking Bureau had of course quite explicit reasons for not supporting the change. Any large-scale development of unsecured bond issues would have reduced its status by downgrading its role in collection and distribution of funds. The failure of the banks and securities companies to find a common position and the lack of any overriding jurisdictional power in the Securities Bureau, which supported the position of the securities companies, meant that a stalemate resulted. The status quo was protected not by a consensus of views, but by the lack of authority of the bureau supporting change.

As with the CDs case, the issue did not disappear, but re-emerged in the late 1970s. In October 1977, the Basic Problems Research Group of the Securities Exchange Council (SEC) issued a report calling for the introduction of a system of unsecured bond issues.[15]

In April 1978 Sears Roebuck, an American retailer with close ties with the Japanese retailer Seibu, announced its intention to seek approval to issue unsecured yen bonds. In June 1978 Itō Yokadō, a Japanese retailer, issued unsecured bonds on the New York market. In December Matsushita Electric announced its intention to seek approval for an unsecured domestic bond issue in Japan. Backed by Yamaichi Securities and Nomura Securities respectively, the Sears Roebuck and Matsushita Electric cases became the subject of wide debate.[16]

The Itō Yōkadō issue in New York put timely pressure on the MOF. It enabled Sears Roebuck to argue that it would be discriminatory for Tokyo to remained closed to top-ranking foreign issuers when Japanese corporations were able to tap New York readily.[17]

Within the MOF opinions were mixed, but there was recognition of the 'discrimination' problem bound up in the issue. The IBJ was asked to examine the problem, and came up with a set of conditions under which unsecured bonds would be approved.[18] The proposal meant that about 40 overseas corporations and two domestic ones, Toyota and Matsushita Electric, would be permitted to issue unsecured bonds in Japan.[19] In March 1979 Sears Roebuck made the first corporate issue on the yen bond market, and shortly after, in April 1979, Matsushita Electric made the first unsecured bond issue by a Japanese corporation in Japan since World War II.

At the time there were two contrasting opinions on the significance of the change, strongly reflecting the fundamental attitude of the two groups towards change. The IBJ, which was strongly opposed to the wholesale abandonment of the collateral provisions in the industrial bond market, remained highly sceptical about the development, regarding it as marginal and believing that the collateral principle remained for practical purposes intact.[20] On the other hand Nomura Securities, which was at the forefront of testing the extremes of existing regulations in the bond markets at home and abroad, and was a strong supporter of unsecured bonds, believed that a new principle had been established and that it would merely take time to erode the existing framework more fully.[21] Important developments which took place in 1981 and 1982 tend to support Nomura's view.

Repercussions on the domestic industrial bond market

In 1982 Dow Chemical was given permission to issue non-guaranteed bonds in Tokyo. It was an important decision in that Dow Chemical did not meet all the financial conditions set out initially for the Sears Roebuck issue. The issue was held up for over three months on this ground but finally approved in the face of considerable foreign pressure from the United States, which was critical of the rules which barred most US corporations from procuring funds in Tokyo.[22] There was predictable resistance from the commissioned banks but the MOF, and in particular the IFB, favoured the continuation of the process of gradual change. At the end of 1982 only three foreign corporations—Sears Roebuck, Dow Chemical and NCR—had issued in Japan but this was sufficient to establish the need to re-examine the conditions for Japanese corporations issuing in the domestic market.

Under the rules introduced before the issue by Sears Roebuck, few companies were able to meet the conditions. Companies such as Hitachi, Sony and Fuji Photo Film could not satisfy the conditions. Hitachi was rated a AAA company in the United States, higher than both Dow Chemical and NCR.[23] This anomaly put the securities companies in a strong position in calling for further change. The banks offered a plan which called for the relaxation of several minor conditions, which would permit thirteen domestic corporations to issue unguaranteed bonds in Japan. The securities companies wanted a much more substantial change. They wanted the minimum asset level reduced from ¥110 billion to ¥55 billion, which would enable approximately 50 companies to issue unguaranteed bonds. A compromise solution reached by the MOF and BOJ in March 1983 effectively increased the numbers of domestic corporations permitted to issue unsecured bonds domestically from eleven to 25.[24] The more relaxed attitude to this problem was a reflection of the gradual shift towards a less regulated market. It showed that at some point the differences between what corporations could do overseas and domestically needed to be adjusted realistically, although the speed of change was considerably slower than on issues which did not affect domestic traditions.

An effective contrast can be made between the resistances to change of the elements of the yen bond market closely connected with the structure of the domestic financial system represented by the 'collateral' issue, and change in other areas. In 1970, when the yen bond market was opened, international financial institutions were the sole issuers. Gradually the range of issuers expanded. In 1972 foreign national and regional governments received authority to float bonds; in 1976 and 1977 the same authority was given to international institutions in which Japan did not participate and foreign government institutions respectively. None of these developments created domestic problems. Among foreign governments also, Japan relaxed conditions to include ASEAN issuers after 1976. All these changes were managed by the IFB and required little by way of negotiations with other parts of the MOF, and were predicated on the view of the International Finance Bureau at the time. During the 1970s it moved successively to widen the types of government and semi-government issuers permitted to float bonds on the Tokyo market; this development had little effect on domestic traditions.

This was very different from the collateral question which directly affected domestic traditions and involved considerably different opinions within the financial sector on the one hand, and the public service on the other.

On this whole question of deregulation of the broader bond market and the yen bond market in particular, the speed of policy change was largely dictated by the interaction of domestic interests. Certainly foreign corporations were an important force in 1981–82 in using the difficult international economic climate to challenge regulations which prevented their access to the Japanese financial market. Underlying this force, however, was the continuing agitation of a growing number of Japanese companies not wanting to affect adversely their international borrowing status by issuing secured bonds, and aggressive securities companies eager to break down further the influence of commissioned banks. Party politics played little part in the development of the regulatory framework, although clearly the tense international economic environment and the ever-deepening and widening range of Japanese interests internationally meant that the strength of the 'no change' case was being eaten away gradually. Continuing intra-ministry negotiations and negotiations including the BOJ were being conducted to broaden the domestic bond markets. Within the yen bond market itself the established set of rules was under constant challenge.

NON-MARKET INFLUENCES IN THE MANAGEMENT OF THE YEN BOND ISSUES

After a chequered early history, the yen bond market developed in the later part of the 1970s into a capital market of some stature in international terms. In the period 1976–80, 10.9 per cent of 'foreign bond issues' were issued in Tokyo.[25]

In the first half of the 1970s a small number of issues was made by a very narrow clientele. Of the thirteen issues between December 1970 and December 1973, nine were made by international financial institutions (the ADB and the World Bank), three by foreign governments (Australia, Mexico and Brazil), and one by the provincial government of Quebec, Canada. In international terms the quantity of yen issues was insignificant.

The early years of the market's operations illustrate to some extent the role played by the MOF and the central concerns of the MOF in the management of the market. The initial ADB issue in 1970 was the first evidence of a softening in the MOF's longstanding policy of banning the flotation of bonds in Japan by foreign entities. Although foreign aid and foreign economic policy reasoning played a large part in the MOF's decision, its willingness to consider a change in policy was premised on the existence of a strong current account on the balance of payments.[26]

It reflected the low priority accorded the market in general capital outflow policy. Policymakers were more concerned with promoting direct investment abroad than with the use of the Japanese market for borrowing by foreign institutions. Further, there was continuing domestic uncertainty towards the concept of unsecured bonds, resulting in a reluctance on the part of the groups which managed the existing domestic collateral system to open up the new yen bond market lest it adversely affect the established bond market.[27] The MOF was unwilling to challenge seriously existing domestic arrangements.

Table 7.1   Yen bond market issues and the balance of payments, 1975–82

Year	Quarter	Volume (billion yen)	No.	Current balance (US$m)	Overall balance (US$m)
1975	1	–	0	−925[a]	−690
	2	–	0	−300	−1085
	3	10	1	−23	−315
	4	10	1	566	−586
1976	1	15	1	−109	214
	2	10	1	941	808
	3	10	1	983	1256
	4	30	3	1865	646
1977	1	12	1	893	542
	2	10	1	2183	1448
	3	92	5	3261	1740
	4	182	8	4581	4013
1978	1	170	8	3971	4944
	2	237	12	4579	692
	3	165	4	5146	1645
	4	150	5	2838	−1331
1979	1	83	4	−711	−3303
	2	20	2	−1126	−4099
	3	125	5	−3229	−3721
	4	56	3	−3688	−5539
1980	1	60	3	−5810	−5592
	2	80	4	−4533	−5623
	3	65	4	−1011	2147
	4	75	4	608	672
1981	1	55	3	−2076	2424
	2	135	7	1455	−4569
	3	130	7	3531	1374
	4	155	9	1860	−1373
1982	1	173	11	−912	−3291
	2	170	9	2582	−3380
	3	195	11	2924	−73
	4	105	6	2302	1773

Note: a means current balance or overall balance deficit

Source: Derived from Zaisei kin'yū tōkei geppō, various issues

During the first five years of its operation, balance of payments considerations dominated the policy of MOF towards the yen bond market. Other factors were relatively unimportant in the actual operation of the market, although domestic factors slowed down development of the market. The period 1975–82 is much more instructive in assessing the influences on the operation of the market.

Table 7.1 lists flotations in the yen bond market from 1975 to 1982 quarter by quarter. Following the twenty-month closure of the market during 1973–75 in response to the large balance of payments deficits resulting from the 1973 oil crisis, the market experienced four sustained breaks. After 1976, the longest period when no issue was made was four months. Management policy reflected the interaction of several factors including domestic market conditions, international capital flow considerations, foreign economic policy considerations and pressure from foreign issuers.

Issue levels responding to market conditions

Despite very strong foreign interest in floating bonds in Japan in 1975 and most of 1976, the MOF pursued a policy of permitting only one issue per quarter.[28] In late 1976 it expanded the flotation framework for reasons of balance of payments[29] but despite this more relaxed attitude the level of issues fell in early 1977. The main reason was that foreign interest rates had fallen relative to the Japanese rates, making issue in Japan relatively expensive. Several planned issues were postponed.[30] It was not until the fall of the long-term government bond rate and the other long-term bond rates in May 1977 that the interest of foreign issuers was rekindled. This instance was perhaps the most clear-cut case where high domestic interest rates, without the interference of government, reduced foreign interest in the yen bond market.

A second case was when bond prices slumped and bond yields rose dramatically in June 1979. Long-term government bond yields rose substantially and this had effect on all other bond rates. Of the countries scheduled to issue at that time only Thailand went ahead, with the others delaying their issues until market stability returned.[31] Both these cases illustrated the market operating in a normal way, in response to market pressures. In many other cases government policy played a more important role.

The constraint of the balance of payments

The policy reaction of the IFB to the first oil shock was immediate and drastic when, in December 1973, it closed the yen bond market. The second oil shock was treated somewhat differently. In early 1979 there were two main views held by groups within the MOF. One group argued for policies to control capital flows, including the closure of the yen bond market. Opposed to this position was a group more conscious of Japan's growing role in international affairs, and the need to be sensitive to the requirements of foreign borrowers.[32] Negotiations between these two groups produced a compromise plan to limit monthly flotations to approximately 50 billion yen per month in the first instance. In comparison with 1974–75, the internationalist position had much more support. Policymakers were more aware of the importance of maintaining continuity in the issue market and, for this purpose, appeared to establish a floor on the reduction of issues which was supported into 1981 when the balance on current account improved appreciably. Although the level of issue during 1979 and 1980 was at a relatively high rate historically, the involvement of the MOF indicated its continued interest in the daily management of the market and of capital controls more generally. The fact that the level of direct foreign investment abroad was not subject to regulatory control, no matter how temporary, showed the discriminatory character of the regulations which were applied to the yen bond market (see chapter 6).

The constraint of the domestic bond markets

Until the late 1970s, there was little conflict between the operation of the yen bond market and other domestic bond markets. During the early years of its operation the yen bond market was relatively small, and up to 1975, government was not issuing large volumes of its own bonds.

In July and August 1978 the first indications appeared that the level of issue of government bonds was affecting the yields in the secondary market. A gap of about 0.59 percentage points appeared between the yield on new government bonds and bonds being traded within the secondary market for government bonds.[33] As a result, the securities companies and the Securities Bureau, which were both anxious about the state of the government bond market, sought to reduce the level of issues in other bond markets. They began by requesting a reduction in the level of flotation in the yen bond market. Issuers in the market and the IFB, which was still worried about the growing current account surplus, favoured a continuation of previous policy. Following a record second quarter flotation of 237 billion yen, however, only 165 billion was issued in the third quarter, of which 135 billion was issued in July alone. Concern over the stability of the government bond market was a major factor in reducing the level of issue. Securities companies claimed that the reduced level of issue reflected the 'softness of the market' and high interest rates. It was true that some foreign issuers had asked the MOF why they should be required to float their bonds at the going secondary market rate, when other domestic issuers issued at controlled rates. Although MOF replied that 'conditions for the flotation of yen bonds are decided in accordance with actual market rates, rises and falls in interest rates are large, and hence it is inevitable that the volume of flotation should also rise and fall in the same manner', several countries which wanted to issue were refused permission.[34] Between August and November there were no issues. Had issues been permitted during this period they would have placed pressure on the issue rate in the government bond market and this was considered unacceptable. When the government bond market settled down again towards the end of 1978, issuing returned to its previous high level.

The most graphic example of the impact on the yen bond market of the MOF's concern for the stability of the government bond market, occurred in late 1980 and early 1981. In an attempt to influence market expectations on the future trend of long-term interest rates, the MOF asked the securities companies to set the interest rate levels on planned issues in the yen bond market at below the market rate. The securities companies took the position that if the bonds were not authorised at market rates they would not underwrite them.[35]

As a result, the issue market remained closed during December 1980 and January 1981. On the earlier occasions of Danish and Austrian issues of April 1979, when the MOF told the securities companies to attach interest rates below the market rate they did so under duress, but retaliated by reducing the size of the respective issues.[36] These cases showed that the MOF used its market interest rate argument when it suited, and not as an inviolable principle of action. One interviewee suggested that in the late 1970s about 30 per cent of issues were made at non-market rates.[37]

Expansion as an element of balance of payments policy

Concern over the growing balance of payments surplus in 1977 was the dominant reason behind the aggressive promotion of the yen bond issues by the IFB. The announcement of a policy of one issue per month in mid-1977 represented a massive expansion in the issue policy of MOF. The quantity of bonds issued in the second half of 1977 was greater than the entire volume issued in the previous seven years. The rapid expansion was predicated on favourable market conditions.[38] That is to say, without the strong demand the level of issue could not have been achieved, but at the same time the ceiling on issues was determined by the MOF and its consideration of the balance of payments, and not by the availability of issuers. Later, in the second half of 1978, conditions in the domestic bond markets deteriorated to an extent which again constrained the level of issue.

Foreign economic policy considerations

From the time of the ADB issue in 1970, foreign economic policy considerations were one element in deciding policy towards the yen bond market. Although the IFB stated that it wanted the development of the market to be based on market forces, it had a parallel concern with assisting access to funds for international financial institutions and later certain developing countries. During 1976–80 this facilitation of access appeared to be the main foreign economic policy element of yen bond market policy.[39]

In 1976, after the Bali Conference, Japan's attitude to ASEAN began to change gradually. One manifestation of this change was the move by the Minister of Finance, Ōhira Masayoshi, to increase the access of developing countries to the yen bond market.[40] The MOF's policy towards access to the yen bond market for developing countries contained five elements:

1   the creditworthiness of the borrower;
2   whether the floater and market could agree on conditions;
3   the extent that the Japanese investors were familiar with the issuer;
4   the importance of direct foreign aid going to the country;
5   a preference for South East Asian countries.[41]

Table 7.2   Public bond issues by developing countries on the yen bond market, 1976–82

Country	No.	Volume (billion yen)
Americas	19	376
Argentina	3	55
Brazil[a]	9	176
Venezuela	4	105
Mexico	3	40
East Asia	17	210
South Korea[b]	3	30
Malaysia	3	45
Philippines	4	60
Singapore	2	25
Thailand	3	30
Indonesia	2	10
Financial institutions		
ADB	9	131
IDB	5	80

Notes: a   Seven issues by the Brazilian government and two by government-guaranteed institutes
         b   All by the Korean Development Bank, guaranteed by the Korean government

Source: Derived from Nomura Securities *Japanese Capital Market* April 1981 and *Zaisei kin'yū tōkei geppō* No. 371, March 1983

This policy became operative in late 1976 when the first South East Asian issue was floated in Tokyo. Between 1976 and 1981 ten developing countries were given access to the Tokyo market, and their borrowing record is set out in Table 7.2. Although creditworthiness of these countries varied considerably, they had several important similarities.[42] First, they were clustered geographically in the Americas and South East Asia, and second, all had either strong investment or trade links with Japan. The trade and investment links were nurtured by giving these developing countries access to Japanese capital. It was no coincidence either that African and communist countries were barred from the yen bond market.[43] While the former were refused on the grounds of both lack of creditworthiness and the lack of substantial links with Japan, the latter could not meet technical disclosure requirements. Even if they were able to meet those requirements in the future, permission to borrow would probably be based upon the political climate at the time.[44] In summary, foreign policy considerations appear to have had some impact on the composition of the market in terms of which countries were permitted to borrow and which countries were refused access to the market.

The level of issue in the yen bond market was, on occasions, also linked with the political and often rhetorical stances taken on internationalisation of the yen.

Both as Minister of Finance in 1976 and later as Prime Minister in 1978, Ōhira Masayoshi advocated a greater international role for the yen.[45] In 1976 Ōhira expressed interest in assisting 'suitable' countries with deficit problems. The MOF made it clear that the United Kingdom and France were suitable but Italy was not. In 1978, although Ōhira expressed a new readiness to have the yen used in a support currency role along with the deutsch-mark, the MOF retreated from this position with the advent of the second oil crisis in early 1979. Both these incidents reflected the gradual evoluton of a new position of Japan in the international community.

One criterion which was used to form a priority schedule of issuers was geographic region. This made it unlikely that two countries within the same geographic area, or two different public bodies within a single country, would be given permission to float bonds at the same time. This was in a sense the aid element in the market: it permitted those countries with an inferior borrowing potential to borrow more frequently than would otherwise have been possible had the market operated on creditworthiness alone. The aid element was, however, highly concentrated because few developing countries could borrow in Japan, and in terms of those countries, aggregate overseas borrowings were quite small.

Whereas the operation of the yen bond market was influenced by market forces as well as by policy factors, the operation of the private placement market was almost entirely structured by policy considerations.

The private placement market

In addition to bonds being floated through public subscription, bonds were also issued by private placement. In the 1970s the operation of the private placement market was almost entirely structured by policy considerations. The market was closed for long periods (December 1973–June 1977; October 1979–February 1981). In the two years since reopening in February 1981, the market has taken on a different complexion. Of the 46 issues, 36 were made by institutions of the developed world and ten by institutions of developing countries in Latin America and Asia. In comparison to the 1970s, the quality of the issuers has improved considerably, perhaps reflecting the greater care in selection given the growing number of defaulters among developing and East European countries.

The heightened awareness of country risk within Japan was also a central factor in the establishment of the Japan Center for International Finance in March 1983 by a group of 47 of the largest financial institutions in Japan, drawn from banks, securities companies and insurance companies.

Pressure by foreign issuers

Many groups of foreign countries had little success in advocating their plans to issue bonds in Tokyo. Communist bloc countries, African countries and the countries of the 'fourth world' were refused access. The decision to open the market to ASEAN countries reflected not only economic considerations (which were very strong) but also political ones. Japan paid considerable attention to ASEAN politically during the late 1970s. No non-ASEAN Asian country except South Korea has issued bonds in Tokyo.

There is strong evidence to suggest that the yen bond market was manipulated by government for domestic policy reasons. In the first half of the 1970s, the level of issue was largely determined by the state of the balance of payments. Later, in the second half of the 1970s, problems in the government bond market directly affected the issue rate in the yen bond market. The current account surplus on the balance of payments of 1977–79 had a major impact on the rate of issue but after that, policy was determined by considering both the balance of payments and the state of the domestic bond markets.

The larger number of issues and the greater consistency of issuing after 1978 indicated some change in government policy. From the third quarter of 1978 to the fourth quarter of 1980, with one exception, between three and five issues were made each quarter. Despite the growing domestic bond market problems and the balance of payments deficit of 1979–80, the MOF kept the market functioning, albeit at a modest level. In 1974–76 the market was either closed or only accommodated a single issue per quarter, whereas in 1979–80 an average of between three and four issues were accommodated. One explanation of the increased stability and higher level of issue was the more relaxed attitude to yen being held as an asset by foreigners. In the case of the yen bond market this was manifested in the regulations governing the volume of a yen bond issue that overseas investors could purchase. The higher the share purchased by foreign investors, the smaller was the impact on the balance of payments in the short term, although the greater the volume of yen held by foreigners the more vulnerable Japan was to speculation against the yen.

It is arguable that the increased stability of issues resulted from the increased capital inflow into Japan, and not from foreign pressure. Interviews with officers of the MOF indicated concern at foreign criticism but made it clear that the concern was for the lack of international understanding of Japan's policy and was not grounds for new policy. One officer was 'privately' critical of the MOF's policy but said domestic constraints in the state of the government bond market and accompanying more general interest rate problems were the factors governing the rate of change.[46]

In 1975, when it initially examined the possibility of reopening the market, the MOF said it was the responsibility of the stronger economies to assist international recovery. If Japan felt any responsibility it shrank back from accepting it. International criticism of Japan grew, and by October 1975 there were more than 30 borrowers waiting to issue bonds in Tokyo.[47] The market was reopened but there were only six issues in 1976. The pressure of foreign issuers existed but it was rather ineffective. The MOF closed the market in late 1980 and early 1981 but reopened it again out of concern that the reputation of the market would be damaged, and out of concern for the adverse publicity which would arise. Japan was the recipient of large amounts of short-term oil money, and was itself a major borrower on international capital markets.[48] In this case another form of foreign pressure can be identified; it can be called the pressure of the international environment. To the extent that Japanese policymakers reacted to the possibility of adverse international publicity in 1980–81, one can argue that the international environment became a factor in policy formulation. The 1980–81 episode can best be understood in terms of the argument that, as the level of interdependence between national and international financial markets grows, there will be benefits but also a new range of constraints on policymakers.[49] The actions of Japanese policymakers were designed to protect Japan's international image and national interests. The high level of yen bonds issued in 1981 and 1982 showed that the MOF had come to see the Tokyo market in an international perspective, which in the long term would reduce the ability of policymakers to adjust the level of issue according to the pressures from the domestic market, or in response to short-term movements in the current account.

The yen bond market's character did appear to change in the early 1980s. After being primarily a tool of balance of payments policy, and subject to the constraints of the domestic bond market, it was becoming an international financial market of some significance. Several factors were at the centre of this development. First, Japan was engaged in acrimonious negotiations with both Europe and the United States over trade problems and it could ill afford to let finance also become a point of controversy. Thus, despite the weak yen, to which the capital policy (but mainly United States' deficits) contributed, policymakers allowed the yen bond market to grow because of the high international demand to issue in Tokyo.

Second, a gradual shift in policy towards the financial markets did take place during the 1970s. Although the revision of the FEFTCL (1980) did not result in any major changes in the operation of the financial markets, the change in philosophy from 'controlled in principle' to 'free in principle' did capture the essence of the underlying movement throughout the 1970s. Policymakers were not about to give up the tools of control which could be required in an emergency but they were more ready to consider Tokyo as a fully fledged international financial market in the 1980s. The resolve of the MOF was put to the test in 1982 when the yen depreciated rapidly from US$1 = 225 yen to US$1 = 265 yen. The MOF did not intervene to close the market and reduce the level of capital outflow as it would have done in the early 1970s. One reason was that it was loath to give foreign governments ammunition to support the allegation that Tokyo was a 'closed' financial market. Indeed its 'openness' was one factor contributing to the weak yen.[50] Even if the issue activity did not equate with the demand to issue, it was nonetheless very high in both historical and international terms. The second reason was that it no longer suited its interests.

Within the MOF there was support for traditional interventionist methods as well as the internationalist, minimal regulation alternative. It was still the case that the authorities were intervening in the financial markets, as seen in the instances of prohibiting the purchase of 'zero coupon' bonds in 1982, and regulating the level of funds that life companies could invest in overseas securities.[51] In the background material prepared for the so-called 'Nagaoka' mission to Europe and the United States in May 1982, the controls on the yen bond market were explained: 'Yen bond issues are agreed on by discussion between securities companies and syndicate loans by planning between banks. This is an area over which the private sector controls the level of issue and not an area where administrative guidance is being practised'.[52]

While the above argument raised the question of why Japanese financiers would want to control what was to their advantage, the statement did indicate that the market would only be closed in extreme circumstances, and the meaning of 'extreme' in 1982 was very different from what it was in 1973 when the market was first closed because of a market disturbance. In 1982 the yen was being used more than ever before as a trade settlement currency (with 32 per cent of Japan's exports and 2 per cent of its imports being denominated in yen, a major increase on a decade before), and it was being held as a reserve currency to an increasing extent (the yen share of official reserves held by IMF countries rose from 0.6 per cent in 1975 to 3.7 per cent in 1980). Capital flows into and out of Japan had also increased greatly. The stability and underlying strength of the Japanese economy had built the necessary level of confidence to transform Tokyo into an international financial market. Assuming the continuation of this stability the main factor in determining the pace of change was the attitude of the government authorities. Many changes which took place in the late 1970s at the short end of the financial markets provided a basis for the formation of an international financial market, but many further regulatory changes were still necessary. Internationally, Japanese banks and corporations had made a substantial impact on financial markets.[53] In the United States, the Japanese presence was far greater than that of any other group of foreign banks.[54] It was in this context that Japanese financial authorities had to view the yen bond market. In the two years since the brief closure of the market between late 1980 and early 1981, the pressures on Japan grew considerably, along with the realisation in Japan that a carefully controlled but nevertheless more relaxed stance to issues in the yen bond market was in its best interests. Japan's interests in 1983 were quite different from those a decade earlier when the market was established.

LOCATION OF AUTHORITY IN REGULATORY AND ROUTINE POLICYMAKING

Institutional detail

The normal operating functions of the yen bond market were managed by the Capital Market Division of the Securities Bureau and the First Capital Division of the IFB. The former's concerns included stability of the domestic bond market and the protection of investors, whereas the latter was concerned with foreign exchange and foreign economic policy problems.

Three or four months before an intended issue, the prospective borrower would open negotiations with an underwriter. All underwriting business was handled by the four big securities companies (Nomura, Yamaichi, Nikko and Daiwa Securities). The issue was considered, and if found acceptable at the initial stage, it was placed on a register of prospective issues. Each securities company ranked its clients from the most preferred to the least preferred, based upon its own and the MOF's criteria for issuing. Arriving at a final ranking might include discussing particular prospective issues with the deputy director responsible for yen bond market affairs in the First Capital Division or the Capital Market Division, depending on the nature of the problem. When the MOF (either the IFB or the Securities Bureau) opposed an issue that was the end of the matter, and the issue would not proceed. Although the securities company might seek clarification from senior personnel, the outcome was unaffected. With each list in order, the securities companies met to amalgamate the four lists into one for the coming quarter.[55]

Each company naturally attempted to maximise its share of the business, but there were several general points upon which negotiations were based. One criterion the MOF insisted upon was an appropriate geographical distribution of issuers. The MOF endeavoured to distribute issues evenly between regions if at all possible, although international financial institutions were sometimes given preference. Although not a key criterion, a basic level of creditworthiness was required. In the case of developing countries, important factors were the character of ties between Japan and the borrowing entity and the acceptability of the issues to Japanese investors. Finally, the securities companies considered whether particular issues should be postponed given the climate in the issuing market at the time.

If securities companies could not reach complete agreement, the problem was taken to the MOF for arbitration. The involvement of the MOF was more noticeable when only a small number of issues were permitted and there was a backlog of demand. The view of the IFB was central to the ranking process, and the view of the Securities Bureau was important in assessing the ability of an issuer to meet disclosure regulations. Determination of the level of issue was a joint decision of the IFB and the Securities Bureau, despite comment by the MOF that the securities companies determined the level of issues. At times there was conflict between bureaus of the MOF, and between the MOF and securities companies which reflected their different interests. Most of the making and implementation of policy at the routine level was about degree and not principle. While the four modes of policymaking were present, the consensus mode prevailed in most cases, reflecting broad level of agreement on most issues.

Public service dominance in the determination of national interest

The main conflict between the two MOF bureaus in routine policymaking was in deciding the priorities among competing objectives. Balance of payments and foreign economic policy considerations might dictate an expansion in the level of issuing, but the instability of the domestic bond markets might suggest that reduction was a more appropriate policy stance. One example of this type of conflict occurred in 1976. The IFB strongly supported an increased rate of issue, whereas the Securities Bureau wanted it cut back. By encouraging the Minister of Finance to make a statement supporting its position, the director-general of the IFB was able to gain the increases he desired. When differences of opinion occurred, the intensity of each problem was considered, and a solution sought. In the above case no compromise was sought but instead one bureau, the IFB, successfully had its policy position implemented. Throughout the 1970s the Securities Bureau was a restraining force on the market's growth whereas the position of the IFB depended much upon the balance of payments. In the early 1980s both the role of Tokyo as an international financial market, and foreign economic policy considerations became more important. These parameters helped to shape the operation of the market.

In interviews with public servants and members of the finance industry, three opinions were offered on who made routine decisions in the yen bond market. A member of the Securities Bureau said that the Securities Bureau offered advice but left it up to the securities companies to make the final decisions.[56]

A member of the IFB outlined a contrasting perspective.[57] He said that negotiated settlements were the basis of most decisions. Administrative guidance was used but this did not mean the MOF made all the decisions. Rather, decisions were reached by frank discussions between the securities companies which operated the market and the MOF; and within the MOF itself there were often conflicting objectives which also had to be accommodated.

In the opinion of the securities companies, the market was controlled by the MOF, but in a way which often gave them considerable freedom. When the rate of issue was cut back, they always had the prior approval of the MOF. On other occasions they claimed to have been held back from issuing what they believed the market could handle.[58] It is difficult to say whether the apparent propensity of the securities companies to do what they were told was an actual reflection of the circumstances. Not wanting to antagonise the issuer, they found that it was sometimes a convenient argument to use. For example, when market conditions deteriorated suddenly the underwriter could be left with unwanted bonds: on these occasions the real view of the securities companies and the Securities Bureau would coincide. Hiding behind the cloak of administrative guidance could be a useful way of protecting one's interest as a whole.

It seems clear that, in general terms, when the MOF had determined its overall attitude to the problem, the operation of the market proceeded according to plan. Mutual accommodation took place because without it daily relationships would be unworkable. The IFB quite accurately emphasised the multiplicity of objectives and the informal rather than the strictly legal definition of jurisdiction, responsibility and guidance powers. Nevertheless, this amounted to MOF control when it was important. The level of concentration of control was the all-important factor: even if the level of agreement was low, the MOF was able to control the nature of market operations.

In comparison to this mode of policymaking, the attempts to alter the regulatory framework were based much more on uncompromising conflict, where parties which wanted the preservation of the existing regulatory framework were able in the 1970s to resist most pressures to change. The case of corporate bonds being issued by foreign entities illustrates this argument. Although some change did occur in regulations, the domestic tradition which favoured secured bond issues could not be easily altered. In this case, the view of the established domestic interests prevailed. Domestic interests generally dominated foreign interests on points of conflict, and for this reason the consensus mode is insufficient to understand the character of the policy process in which regulations were developed, altered and protected. Conservative incrementalism was entrenched in the policymaking process by the lack of common values between different interests, and the MOF's emphasis on maintaining market stability and balancing the demands of participants and potential participants. The difference between problems at the regulatory level and the routine level was that the parties within the MOF and the industry held sufficiently homogeneous views on the operation of the latter but not of the former. The former was bargaining over jurisdictions and rules, whereas the latter was argument over interpretation and implementation of existing rules. There were circumstances when the gap between the two narrowed, but it was more often than not present. In terms of our policymaking model, differences in both level of agreement and level of concentration of control in policymaking meant that the dominant mode of policymaking was different. In routine policymaking, modes (II) and (III) dominated whereas in regulatory policymaking, (II) and (IV) were of central importance.

One feature of the yen bond market, in both the regulatory and routine phases of policymaking, was the virtual absence of political direction. This was a technical area and as such of little interest to the LDP. One implication concerned the relative predictability of policymaking: the variables were small in number and the interest groups well known, with the major dynamic feature being the changing role that Japan was prepared to play in international economic and financial affairs. Domestic interest groups and a conservative stream in the MOF committed to maintaining the regulated interest rate system were dominant in the 1970s, producing major downturns in the rate of issue when domestic interests were impinged. However, the 1970s also saw the gradual strengthening of the IFB. The Bureau's concern for the broader issues of participation in the international economic system and the change in Japan's international interests began to have an impact on domestic interest groups seeking to maintain the status quo. It could be expected that the growth of the market will gradually affect the remaining financial traditions which are peculiarly Japanese in character.

During the 1970s, in both the development of the regulatory framework and the routine management of the yen bond market, foreign interests had little influence on policymaking. It would be wrong to dismiss their role totally because from time to time they did provide the impetus to have a matter of policy considered. Without foreign demand for yen loan funds there would not have been a market. In ordering the causal priorities, however, the roles of the public service and domestic industry interest groups and factors such as the state of the balance of payments and the government bond market dominated the development of new policy initiatives and the management of policy.

Within the MOF, the IFB's increasingly 'international' outlook allowed the market to operate with greater stability. Its reorientation may have been shaped partly by the prevailing international environment but was primarily related to the improved balance of payments position resulting from a strong current account, greater inflow of capital from Arab and other sources, and realisation of the benefits accruing from greater financial links with major trading partners. It was these factors which had, by the early 1980s, begun to figure more prominently in policymaking. The national interests of Japan were not static, and the benefits to be had from internationalising the financial markets were being increasingly appreciated. This factor, rather than foreign influence, was at the centre of the movement towards internationalisation and the gradually declining level of regulation.

8 The MOF

The influence of career and retirement patterns on policymaking

The influence of the MOF as a government ministry and economic policymaker has been long recognised. Even if administrative and policymaking power within the public service was more evenly distributed in 1980 than one or two generations previously, the MOF remained one of Japan's elite public institutions. Chapters 2 to 7 examined the role the MOF played in the development and management of a range of financial regulations and policy. Each case study explored facets of the policymaking process, leading to more general observations about the role of interest groups, the public service and the LDP in policymaking in the finance industry. This chapter involves a quite different but complementary analysis. Its aim is to explore the administrative structure and career patterns of officers of the MOF and determine the impact of these patterns on the policymaking process. The proposition is examined that career and retirement patterns and the individual character of different bureaus slow down the rate of policy development. At the outset a cautionary note is appropriate. This chapter is the most speculative in the book. It suggests that certain mechanisms operate which influence significantly the formation and implementation of policy. The paths of influence often involve the murkier elements of financial politics about which remarkably little is understood, save that they exist and are important for political survival.

CAREER PATTERNS

There were few changes in the administrative structure of the MOF in the generation to 1980. Over the decade 1969–78, the MOF recruited between twenty and 25 people each year for its career employment stream. Career employment means that the officer first completed the senior public service examination (which had a 2 to 3 per cent success rate) and then was selected for employment by one of the government ministries. Competition between applicants to enter the MOF, like the MITI and the MFA, was particularly fierce, not because it offered any short-term remunerative benefits or rapid promotion prospects—it did not—but because the responsibilities of the MOF covered many of the key functions of government, because employment in the

MOF offered considerable social status and because it opened the way for future political careers.[1]

The elite character of the MOF, rather like the British Treasury and the French Inspection des Finances, derived in part from the selection of the intake.[2] An estimate compiled from a fairly complete listing of career officers who entered the MOF between 1942 and 1972 gives the following breakdown:[3]

Tokyo University	78 per cent
Law Faculty	65 per cent
Other faculties	13 per cent
Other national universities	14 per cent
Private universities and others	8 per cent

Besides Tokyo University, other universities which have figured prominently include Hitotsubashi University, Kyoto University, Kyushu University and Tohoku University. But their prominence was relative when contrasted with the 78 per cent from Tokyo University and the 65 per cent from its Law Faculty alone. The strong representation of law suggested the administrative nature of a career in the MOF. For a department with such a heavy emphasis on financial, fiscal and tax matters, one might have expected a greater proportion from economics faculties of Japanese universities, but for historical reasons, and given the continuing importance of the administrative functions of career officers, this was not the case.[4]

The dominance of officers with legal–administrative backgrounds did not mean that there were large numbers of economic illiterates within the MOF.[5] An economics background was not a prerequisite for a career within the MOF, but once employed there every officer was given considerable formal economics training before he was promoted to a responsible position. During their third year in the MOF about one-quarter of the intake spent one or two years abroad studying for advanced degrees. The remainder were relieved of all their usual responsibilities to participate in a one-year intensive in-house training program in economics. The training in economics made few officers fully fledged economists, but at least it gave each one a basic grounding, and was indispensable in enabling them to fulfil their administrative function adequately.[6] Rather than producing economists, the first six or seven years within the MOF aimed at producing officers who were able to withstand the heavy demands placed upon them later in their careers in the areas of negotiation, presentation of argument and policy management.[7] Historically speaking, Tokyo University produced the bulk of central government public servants, and the fact that this pattern held throughout the 1970s attested to continued recognition that it was the most prestigious university in the country. In the same way that Ecole Nationale D'Administration and Ecole Polytechnique provided the bulk of the elite French public service, Tokyo University was very much the nursery for the elite career stream of public servants in Japan.[8]

For all career officers, the first six or seven years in the MOF followed an almost identical pattern.[9] The first two years were what could be called a socialisation process. The officer had little responsibility, and was kept busy, particularly when the Diet was in session, compiling statistics for the minister or the officer's superiors. This period was followed by paid 'study leave' after which he experienced his first taste of administration as a section head. After another two years he was sent to head a small tax office in the country. Although younger than most of his support staff, this job was designed to blood the officer in management of people, and exercise of leadership. Despite the fact that groundwork on policy matters as section head was an introduction to the policymaking process, it was not until appointment as assistant director of a division, on return to head office, that the officer graduated to the lowest rung of what might be called the broad policymaking process.

At the level of assistant director the administrative character of job routines began to assert itself and the officer participated in debate on policy matters within his own bureau, and between the bureau and the public sector. For example, an assistant director of the Small Banks Division of the Banking Bureau might hold discussions with personnel of general manager rank in mutual banks and credit associations; assume responsibility for keeping the LDP's Finance Subcommittee abreast of relevant policy issues, as well as keeping himself abreast of policy matters within the bureau more generally. In addition to developing new policy when required, the assistant director's other main function was to implement existing policy. This involved discussions with all groups within the finance industry, interaction with other bureaus also involved in administering the policy and, sometimes, contacts with other ministries.

Regulatory change and policy reform were both first considered, as a matter of course, at the level of assistant director. Controversial initiatives rarely originated at this level, but came from the head of the division, the director, or the head of the bureau, the director-general; and then were generally in response to industry pressure for change. On rare occasions, such as in the case of the FEFTCL, the initiative came directly from the Prime Minister.

Ordinarily the policy position of a bureau was drafted by an assistant director. The case of CDs was one example. However, there were many exceptions, such as the role played by Councillor Fukui Hiroo and Director Seki Kaname in the case of the FEFTCL. Assistant directors frequently discussed policy matters at regular meetings with their colleagues. The involvement of the director of a division in the formation of policy depended much upon the political sensitivity of the policy. Normally the director might comment informally on the draft during its preparation, reducing the likelihood of later involvement. While the role of the assistant director is important, it is inconceivable that he would attempt to develop policy outside the parameters defined by the general stance of the bureau and the division. When in doubt he would consult with his senior colleagues. In highly sensitive political matters, the decision might be taken at the level of director or director-general.

One of the most demanding tests which faced the assistant director was the presentation of draft proposals to meetings of senior bureau officers (called *kyokugi*), normally attended by the director-general and director of the responsible bureau and division, senior officers from other bureaus concerned, and the assistant director responsible for the draft. Providing the assistant director could defend adequately his draft, the document became the policy position of the bureau. These meetings and the discussion before them ensured that policy developments were in strict conformity with the policy position of the bureau as a whole.[10]

Unless they retired early, all career officers could expect to reach the level of director of a division.[11] At this level the officer was expected to manage a defined policy area and attend to the problems which arose in it.

A rotation system operated whereby directors changed their jobs every two years, in the same way as assistant directors, and relocation to another bureau was quite common. It was said by one director that understanding a policy area took two to three months, and that an individual was expected to be fully in command within six months.[12] Statements of this kind obscure the fact that this procedure had a considerable influence on the policymaking process. The mobility of career officers increased the importance of administrative procedures and the negotiating role of the MOF, but at the same time slowed down the development of policy. Even where a director wanted to activate policy reform, he could do very little as an individual. More often than not he would be relocated before the project was finished. From a research and planning viewpoint, the lack of continuity of staff reduced the likelihood of controversial recommendations being made. Further, it meant that policy review was conducted as an ad hoc project rather than side by side with the management of the existing policymaking framework.

Support for controversial projects required that they were manageable within a short-term framework or have considerable support throughout the bureau. Some policies, such as the introduction of CDs, had the support of the director-general of the responsible bureau but his short-term tenure of office was a serious constraint. As the leadership changed, the controversial elements of policy were often expunged leaving the bureau to conduct its business with the minimum of trouble.

Paradoxically, this rotation system did not always minimise conflict within the MOF as a whole. Starting with the preliminary discussions at the level of assistant director through to meetings between the senior officers of a bureau, the MOF worked as a collection of functional bureaus rather than as one ministry, and as was seen in the cases of government bonds, CDs, trading in government bonds and yen bonds, conflict between bureaus was common. Causes of conflict included jurisdictional disputes, the protection of interest groups falling within the orbit of the concerned bureau, the defence of policy options on efficiency grounds, and the perceived need to stabilise one sector despite the fact that the adoption of new policy measures had side effects on other areas. The MOF did operate as a unit in terms of elite consciousness and the transfer system ensured that personal animosity between bureaus was minimal but, for policymaking purposes, the bureau was the key unit.[13]

In a survey sampling central government public servants, respondents were asked to indicate the most important role of administrators in society, as gauged by the time they spent fulfilling that role.[14] The results are listed below:

1	the role of adjusting social costs and benefits and opposed opinions	37.1 per cent
2	the role of analysing and researching major issues, and the preparation of foundations for political decisions	36.3 per cent
3	the role of changing the social system and organisation in a desired direction	14.7 per cent
4	the role of preparing policy to reflect the opinions of political parties and the Diet	10.0 per cent
5	Other	2.0 per cent
	Total	100.0 per cent

(Number of respondents = 251)

These roles were consistent with the administrative structure of the public service ministry, and more specifically were consistent with the observed roles of officers of the MOF. The important distinction between 1, 2 and 3 indicated public servants of an incrementalist and perhaps 'Weberian' model. As one commentator rightly stated the two extremes of 'administrative' and 'political' public servants were more caricatures of reality than reality itself.[15] The Japanese case was different from Great Britain and West Germany in that political stability over a very long period produced very close contacts between the LDP and the MOF to the extent that most senior officers in the MOF had views compatible with the LDP.[16] In both Britain and West Germany, periodic changes of government ensured that 'opposition' political parties had better contacts within the public service than was the case in Japan. As a result of shared values, the LDP was able to leave policymaking in areas outside its immediate electoral interests to the MOF. Important as regulations in the finance industry were, the political leadership had little explicit involvement on many issues although, as has been argued, the shared values which linked the LDP and the MOF ensured that many policy options were rejected outright because they would have been opposed by the LDP.

Despite the existence of shared values, the MOF and the LDP did have differences on policy, or to be more precise, individual bureaus and the LDP had differences. These arose because the bureaus concerned saw a need to adjust the balance of existing regulations, or to protect existing jurisdictions. The postal savings case (chapter 5) provides a good example. These cases were few but when they did occur it was the position of the LDP that generally became policy.

Even the career head of the MOF, the administrative vice-minister, had only one or two years in that position before retiring to pursue a career in politics, banking or business, and hence opportunity for establishing 'dynasties' within the MOF was almost non-existent. This did not give the Minister of Finance any particular advantage either, as tenure of that position was also very short.[17]

In the absence of long periods of management of any policy area by a single individual, policies were generally managed in an uncontroversial routine

manner. Proposals to change existing regulations evolved within an individual
bureau and, at this level, 'consensus' images of policymaking had much value.
When proposals developed within an individual bureau were given a wider
airing, or when they required wider consent, problems often arose reflecting
competing jurisdictions, different policy objectives and different perspectives
on what was appropriate policy for the MOF, or the finance industry as a whole.
At this level, explicit recognition of conflict or of dominant modes of policymaking was necessary before the policymaking mechanism could be understood
adequately. This book has emphasised two variables, the level of agreement
between participants and the level of concentration of control over the
policymaking process, as a means to explicate the character of the policymaking
process.

THE RETIREMENT SYSTEM[18]

The impact of the administrative structure was not confined to the operating
methods within the MOF. It is necessary to examine the impact of the structure
of the retirement system as a mechanism which could influence the rate of policy
development or change. The re-employment of public servants after a fairly
early retirement has hitherto been examined as a means of dealing with
personnel problems within the public service.[19] Criticism by labor unions in
Japan has also been directed at this aspect.[20] This analysis is concerned less with
the labor relations aspects than with the impact of post-retirement work on the
adaptability and content of policy.

Most career officers in the MOF and in the public service as a whole retire in
their late forties or early fifties. A long-established custom was that when one
officer of an intake became administrative vice-minister all other members of
that intake resigned. By this time some would already have resigned, as business
or political opportunities arose. The system of early retirement was not
widespread in prewar Japan but emerged in the early postwar years as a method
of ensuring a smooth promotion ladder, and a means by which the elite of
Japan's university system could be attracted to the public service.[21] Retirement
to other semi-government, political or private enterprise jobs was accompanied
by significant salary increases.[22]

Former MOF officers in the LDP

In 1980, 52 members of the LDP (10 per cent of the 511 members of the House
of Representatives) were former members of the public service of the central
government. This compared with only eleven opposition members with similar
backgrounds.[23] In the House of Councillors the picture was the same, with only
two out of 39 members with public service backgrounds belonging to the
opposition political parties, and 37 (14.7 per cent of the 251 members)
belonging to the LDP.

Throughout their careers, the main political contacts of career public servants were with the LDP Diet members. After reaching the level of assistant director, officers were required to explain current policy initiatives and often proposed policy changes at PARC subcommittee meetings, at research group discussions and individually with members interested in the policy or legislation. Contact with opposition parties did exist. In the area of finance, two well-known opposition spokesmen, Hori Masao of the JSP and Takemoto Magoichi of the DSP, had frequent discussions with MOF officers.[24] These were better looked on as ad hoc arrangements than information mechanisms important to the policymaking or regulatory process. The establishment of a close and exclusive relationship between the MOF and the LDP could be directly attributed to more than three decades of continuous hold over government by the LDP and its conservative forerunners. LDP approval of policy proposals, whether explicit or implicit, was vital before implementation could proceed. A second reason for the close link was that the LDP, not the opposition parties, constituted the route to political power and ministerial office. In contrast, the opposition parties had developed alternative 'channels' through which members were selected. Both the JSP and the DSP fielded strong contingents of union officials and the JCP membership was dominated by party officials.

The 'representation' of each ministry in the LDP's membership in the House of Councillors and House of Representatives is set out in Table 8.1 and reveals important differences. In 1980, the MAFF had the strongest representation in the House of Councillors with eleven members (29 per cent). The MOF and the Ministry of Construction (MOC) each accounted for six members (16 per cent respectively) and former members of the Ministry of Local Government (MLG), the Ministry of Transport (MOT) and the Ministry of Labor (MOL) made up most of the remainder. A quite different pattern held in the House of Representatives. Some 21 (42 per cent) of former central government public servants in the LDP came from the MOF. The Ministry of Labor, Ministry of Local Government and MITI each had five members (10 per cent respectively). Several partial explanations can be offered for the differences of representation between the House of Councillors and the House of Representatives.

The MAFF's dominance of representation in the House of Councillors stems from its massive interest group support at the national and regional level. Similarly, other ministries with defined domestic interest group backing were able to ensure the election of members to the House of Councillors. Although the MOF's jurisdiction tended to be more general than the MAFF's, it had strong support from tobacco-related groups (regulated by the MOF) and banking and securities companies. But its relatively strong representation was more attributable to factors which were dominant in the House of Representatives.[25]

Many former MOF officers have held senior political positions. Between 1960 and 1980, three out of eight prime ministers (Ikeda, Fukuda and Ōhira) and six out of eleven finance ministers (Fukuda, Ueki, Aichi, Ōhira, Murayama and Kaneko) began their careers as officers of the MOF. Although Miyazawa Kiichi was the only member of the first Suzuki Cabinet with a MOF background, as of

Table 8.1   Central government public servants in the LDP in 1980

Ministry	House of Representatives		House of Councillors	
	Number[a]	per cent	Number[a]	per cent
MOF	21	42	6	16
MAFF	2	4	11	29
MOC	2	4	6	16
MOL	5	10	3	8
MITI	5	10	1	3
MLG	5	10	4	11
MOT	2	4	3	8
MPT	1	2	2	5
Other	7	14	2	5
Total	50	100	37	101[b]
Proportion of total LDP membership		17.5		27.9

Notes: a The exact numbers are difficult to calculate. Here we have relied on *Seiji handobukku's* description of initial occupation and checked the difficult cases with *Jinji kōshinroku.* This may understate the actual numbers but it should have a random influence on proportions

b Error due to rounding

Source: *Seiji handobukku* Shōwa 55 nen 9 gatsu and *Jinji kōshinroku* Jinji kōshinjo, Dai 30 pan

August 1980, 25 members of the House of Representatives were former officers of the MOF. Of these, 21 were members of the LDP (seven with ministerial experience), one belonged to the JSP, one to the New Liberal Club (NLC), one to the JCP and one to *Kōmeito.* Details are set out in Table 8.2.

There appeared to be two types of MOF officers who became members of the LDP in the House of Representatives. One group made the transition by marrying into 'political' families. In the 1970s arranged marriages were still widespread in Japan, and young career officers of the MOF were in 'high demand'.[26] Although the MOF officers came from varied backgrounds they often married into conservative families. Quite a number of MOF officers began their political careers as a result of their links through marriage with LDP politicians holding safe seats. Having married into a political family, the MOF officer normally continued his career in the MOF until the death or retirement of his father-in-law. The case of Morita Hajime is fairly typical.

Morita entered the MOF in 1957 and later married the daughter of former Prime Minister Ōhira. He was seconded from the MOF to serve as Ōhira's private secretary when Ōhira was Minister for Foreign Affairs in 1972–74. From 1974 to 1977 he performed the same job when Ōhira was Minister of Finance. In 1977 he returned to active duty in the MOF as an officer with the rank of director. Upon the sudden death of Ōhira in 1980, Morita resigned from the MOF and was subsequently elected to Ōhira's former constituency.

Table 8.2   Members of the Diet who began their careers in the MOF, August 1980

Name[a]	Group	Party	No. of times elected	Age
1 House of Representatives				
Fukuda Takeo	A	LDP	12	75
Maeo Shigesaburō	A	LDP	12	79
Kaneko Ippei	A (s)	LDP	8	67
Shōji Keijirō	A	LDP	8	69
Murayama Tatsuo	A (s)	LDP	7	65
Miyazawa Kiichi	B (s)	LDP	6[b]	60
Yamashita Ganri	A	LDP	6	59
Kino Haruo	A (s)	LDP	6	60
Tanaka Shōji	B	KMT	6	53
Shiozaki Jun	A (s)	LDP	5	63
Matsumoto Jūrō	A	LDP	4	62
Ochi Michio	A	LDP	4	51
Noda Takeshi	B	LDP	4	38
Fukushima Shōji	A	LDP	3	53
Ikeda Yukihiko	B (s)	LDP	3	43
Aizawa Hideyuki	A	LDP	3	60
Tsushima Yūji	B (s)	LDP	3	50
Ōhara Ichizō	A	LDP	2	55
Ōshima Hiromu	A	JSP	2	58
Miyashita Sōhei	A	LDP	2	52
Watanabe Mitsugu	B	JCP	2	52
Kakizawa Kōji	B	NLC	1[b]	46
Hamada Takujirō	B (s)	LDP	1	38
Morita Hajime	B (s)	LDP	1	46
Yanagizawa Hakuo	B	LDP	1	44
2 House of Councillors				
Shimazaki Hitoshi		LDP	3	57
Isurugi Michiyuki		LDP	3	66
Hatoyama Ichirō[c]		LDP	2	61
Fujii Hirohisa[c]		LDP	1	48
Shimojō Shin'ichirō		LDP	1	60
Tanigawa Kanzō		LDP	1	59

Notes: a   The first seven have had ministerial experience
          b   Indicates House of Councillors membership before entering the House of Representatives.
          c   Both members of the National Constituency
          A   became a member of parliament towards the end of, or at the end of, expected career in MOF.
          B   left the MOF in mid-career to fill a position where family relationship was in most cases important.
          (s) member of the Suzuki faction (previously Ōhira faction)

Source: For 1, *Seiji handobukku* 1980 nen 9 gatsu hen, and *Jinji kōshinroku dai* 30 pan, 1979. For 2, *Kokkai binran* 61 pan, August 1980, Nihon seikei shinbunsha hakkō; *Ōkurashō kenkyū* shohan, March 1979, Kanchō nyūsuha

Ikeda Yukihiko, Tsushima Yūji and Hamada Takujiro were other examples of the same pattern. At the end of 1980 nine serving MOF officers were married to the daughters of LDP politicians. A group of journalists has called these men the 'reserve force' of the LDP.[27]

An alternative way of interpreting this first group was to argue that the existence of the route from a junior officer of the MOF to political marriage and a political career was the reason for entry into the MOF. The MOF was chosen because it allowed the budding politician to form family and political connections necessary to enter the LDP with a safe seat.

Whatever the case, young MOF officers had opportunities which clearly did not exist to the same extent in other ministries. The LDP saw the MOF in terms of an elite which could provide reliable conservative candidates.

A second group entered the LDP after reaching the normal retirement age. This group from the MOF was also far bigger than that from any other ministry. All these officers had one thing in common: they held prominent posts in the areas of budgetmaking and tax. Former Prime Minister Fukuda Takeo was, for example, director-general of the Budget Bureau and, more recently, Aizawa Hideo filled the same post before being promoted to administrative vice-minister. Aizawa was elected to the House of Representatives in 1976. The concentration of backgrounds indicated the importance the LDP attached to these areas, and the importance of having members within the party with expertise in this area. In areas such as agriculture, construction, education, defence and welfare the LDP's interest was strong, and involvement in the policymaking process was intimate, but it was not reflected in the pattern of public service recruitment for the House of Representatives. The strong MOF representation in the LDP in the House of Representatives was then not simply attributable to the opportunities for ministerial and prime ministerial offices in that House, but to LDP patronage of the MOF. Belonging to the House of Representatives certainly increased the chance of higher office, but that presupposed that the opportunity existed. LDP patronage reflected the strong 'elite' character of the MOF, the respect for it within the conservative community and the very specific skills senior officers of the MOF could provide.

The consistent movement of officers of the MOF to the LDP showed, in broad political terms, the shared values of the MOF and LDP. As public servants, officers would have agreed with specific elements of the policy programs of the MOF and disagreed with others, but in general would have agreed with the overall approach and content of policymaking. As public servants, outside their own area of responsibility, they had little time to consider even the general issues. When they became politicians, their approach to economic issues would, in many cases, change out of consideration of electoral politics. The considerations of a public servant attempting to balance a range of policy objectives were different from those of a politician who had to consider his position vis-a-vis his electorate. On many matters former MOF officers would cease caring about financial policy at all, preferring to leave it to the

Banking Bureau, the Securities Bureau or the IFB. In areas such as the role of small and medium-sized financial institutions, 'social' interest rates (housing and savings interest rates) and occasionally the official discount rate, the LDP had a history of intense interest. The party attempted to steer clear of involvement in what could be called industry issues, such as those of CDs and the sale of government bonds by banks, but that was not always possible. When it did become involved, it was the MOF which supplied most of the information, and to which development of a final resolution was often entrusted.

Whereas the role of the LDP's policymaking bodies was institutionalised in the policymaking process, the same could not be said about policymaking bodies of opposition parties. The opposition was interested in a similar range of issues as the LDP. Financial regulation and financial policies were one area in which they showed little interest and even less capability to develop alternative policy positions.[28] They too showed little interest in involvement in disputes within the finance industry.[29]

Both public servants and politicians were constrained by existing administrative processes. The LDP, like the MOF, had a highly bureaucratic structure. Committees and subcommittees were not chaired by experts, but by men who were seeking broad experience.[30] Regular Cabinet reshuffles reinforced the strength of the public service in matters relating to politically non-sensitive areas of regulatory policy, and more general everyday policymaking. But on policies which were politically sensitive, the way that former officers of the MOF acted could not be determined solely on the basis of their former allegiances. Political considerations were also important.

The strong flow of MOF officers into the LDP did much to prevent the erosion of the power of the MOF. It established a trust, within a broad set of political values or a broad ideological framework, which enabled the MOF to go about much of its business unhindered by overt political interference. Communication channels between the MOF and LDP were strengthened by the entry of former MOF personnel, and sympathetic hearings were guaranteed. Disagreements did, of course, occur. Chapter 5 examined the issue of the postal savings system, and detailed the policy disagreement on pension funds. This and other examples showed the basic difference between politicians and public servants. Politicians operated in a broad sociopolitical theatre, whereas public servants operated in a much narrower administrative–economic theatre which resulted in a quite different set of factors being considered. The long period of conservative government did, however, institutionalise information flows and resulted in similar values in the MOF and the LDP on a wide range of issues. Indeed, it could be said to have become a mechanism serving to entrench political power in conservative hands.

The corollary to this statement was that without a change in government the existing set of relationships linking the LDP and the MOF would not be altered. Since in the medium term a government without the LDP, at least as a coalition partner, does not seem likely, the existing set of relationships and approach to policy found within the MOF are likely to remain unchanged.

Former MOF officers in semi-government financial institutions

The MOF was involved in public financial institutions for two reasons. One was that when the institution was originally established MOF approval was necessary. Some form of direct oversight was afforded by having a former MOF officer in an executive position. It also gave the other supervisory agency much better access to the MOF which would not hinder submissions for continued funds. Once established, however, the question of access to the MOF may not have great significance, as the other supervisory agency would campaign on its behalf for a budgetary allocation. Politically sensitive financial corporations such as the Peoples Finance Corporation (established June 1949), Housing Loan Corporation (established August 1953), Small Business Finance Corporation (established August 1953) and the Agriculture Forestry and Fisheries Finance Corporation (established April 1953) were all strongly supported by politically strong interest groups. At the time of its establishment each financial institution had some plausible *raison d'etre*, but over the years the original purpose was gradually fulfilled, and in many cases their clientele were more than adequately catered for by existing private sector institutions, with the main difference being that a public sector financial institution provided subsidised funds.

In 1980, 23 former career officers of the MOF filled executive positions in Japan's fourteen public sector financial institutions.[31] The relatively small number of executive positions filled by former MOF officers indicated that while MOF representation existed in nearly every institution, it was insufficient for the purposes of control. The MOF was the sole supervising agency in two cases, and a joint supervising agency in twelve others.

Even in the two cases where the MOF acted as sole supervising agency it did not have a majority of the executive positions, although it did fill the senior executive positions. In the case of the Japan Development Bank, a majority of executive positions were always filled by appointments from within the bank. The positions of governor and deputy governor were consistently filled by MOF and BOJ appointees.[32] In the case of the other organisation controlled by the MOF, the Peoples Finance Corporation, the largest group of executives, though not a majority, was appointed from within the organisation although the MOF generally controlled three of nine executive positions. In 1980 only one of ten executive positions was filled by internal promotion whereas the other nine were filled by former public servants, six of whom came from the Ministry of Construction (MOC).[33]

While the demands for funds changed dramatically in the twenty years from 1960, the structure of the public finance sector in institutional terms remained almost unchanged. The changed circumstances and potential misuse of public funds is illustrated by the case of the Japan Development Bank (JDB). During the 1950s most of its loans went into the development of power plants and sea transport (shipbuilding). By the 1960s the needs of the power industry had fallen but shipbuilding remained a key industry. Its loans to regional development increased dramatically. During the 1970s loans for pollution control, energy saving and technological development all increased greatly. The economic justification for making loan funds available at subsidised rates was unimportant in political terms in the sense that if there were political reasons to support an area then it was supported. It is certainly hard to argue that the sectors catered for by the JDB required access to subsidised loan funds. For example, it is hard to understand except in political terms why large hotel–recreation redevelopments required special financing.[34]

From the viewpoint of the supervising ministry, public sector financial institutions performed several non-economic functions. They formed a part of the institutional framework which assisted the ministry servicing client groups through providing both access to funds and subsidising the cost of funds. They also provided a means of placing both career and non-career officers in new jobs after their retirement from the central ministry. The executive positions 'held' by each ministry were just the cream of these positions. At a third level they were part of the ministry's operating jurisdiction. If the institution controlled by the ministry were to close, it would reduce the ministry's sphere of influence, its power within the public service as a whole. In terms of the theory that suggests that bureaucracies maximise their size, it is clearly not a rational alternative. The fact that none was dispensed with during the 1970s indicated that some rigidity existed in disbanding established institutions.[35]

The continued existence of these financial institutions casts further doubts over the efficiency objectives of the public service and underlines the importance of other objectives. Maintenance of jurisdictions by central government ministries, and the pressures from the LDP acting as an intermediary for specialised interest groups in budgetary negotiations were both strong plausible explanations for the continued existence of the institutions. Although the MOF did not itself have great power over the whole range of semi-government financial institutions, the other ministries provided an effective hindrance to policy change, and more than compensated for the lack of MOF power.

After falling from 16.7 per cent in 1964 to 13.4 per cent in 1973, government financial institutions in 1979 held 19.4 per cent of the financial assets of individuals. Although the proportion of funds being directed to the private sector fell gradually after 1964, in 1979 it still stood at the relatively high level of 38.3 per cent.[36] Some parts of the private sector still had much to gain from the retention of public sector finance. They shared support given by the various ministries and posed a major barrier to changing the existing framework.

Former MOF officers in private financial institutions

For the first two years after retirement a public servant was not permitted to work in a private corporation with which he or she had had work-related contact during the previous five years. The regulations governing work after retirement, administered by the National Personnel Authority, were designed not only to prevent flagrant abuse of the regulatory framework, but also to be seen to be regulating arrangements which would otherwise work to the betterment of individuals at the expense of the public purse.[37] Few applications for permission

Table 8.3 MOF officers from career and non-career streams entering private banks with Administrative Management Agency approval, 1970–80

	1970	1971	1972	1973	1974	1975	1976	1977	1978	1979	1980	1970–80
From MOF												
Local tax bureaus	13	13	14	9	14	14	12	14	13	20	17	153
Banking Bureau	1	2	1	1	3	1	2	6			1	18
Secretariat		1		2	1	1	2	2	2		2	10
Other[a]	1	2		1	2	1	2					11
Total	15	18	15	13	20	16	18	22	15	20	20	192
To Private Banks												
City banks, long-term credit banks				1		1						2
Regional banks	1	1	1	1	1	1	2	2	1			11
Mutual banks	2	5	2		2	1	4	4	1	3	4	28
Credit associations	12	12	12	11	17	13	12	16	13	17	16	151

Note: a Except for 1971, all other officers came from Bank Inspection Department

Source: MOF, mimeographed tables, 1981

to work in private enterprise were actually rejected by the National Personnel Authority but many problem cases were weeded out by prior consultation between the particular ministry and the Authority. On average, ten refusals were made each year between 1975 and 1980, whereas approvals ranged between 159 (1976) and 233 (1979). The ministries prominent in this process were MAFF, MOT, MITI, MOC, MPT and the MOF (including the National Tax Office). Table 8.3 details the numbers of MOF officers given approval by the National Personnel Authority between 1970 and 1980. The main group which obtained approval were non-career officers of the MOF who worked in the National Tax Office and joined credit associations upon retirement.

In contrast to the large direct flow of non-career officers to private financial institutions, only seventeen career officers entered financial institutions directly after retirement from the MOF.[38] Despite this fact, in May 1980, 89 former career officers of the MOF were employed in executive positions in private financial institutions. Table 8.4 sets out the details. Of these former officers, 85 per cent worked with regional banks, mutual banks and credit associations and 40 per cent were employed as president or deputy president. The fact that most of these officers did not enter the financial institutions directly indicates that either it was necessary to take a job in a government or semi-government organisation before entering the private financial institutions, or that the monetary benefits from that route were greater than direct entry. On the other

Table 8.4   Former MOF career officers holding executive positions in financial institutions, May 1981

Rank	Public financial institutions	City banks, long-term credit banks	Regional banks	Mutual banks, credit associations	Total
President, Deputy President	9	5	11	24	49
Director (riji)	13				13
Director (senmu)	1		12	4	17
Director (jōmu)		1	2	7	10
Advisor (komon)		4	1	1	6
Other		4	2	11	17
Total	23 (21%)	14 (12%)	28 (25%)	47 (42%)	112 (100%)

Source: MOF, private communication, June 1981, mimeo

hand, only a small number were employed in the city banks and long-term credit banks. The larger banks did not want the encumbrance of MOF officials in running the bank, and further the high level of resentment amongst career bank officials who felt that MOF officers would contribute very little to bank management kept the numbers down.[39]

The MOF and some parts of the financial sector argued that the re-employment of career MOF officers in private financial institutions offered several benefits. First, the strong management background of MOF officers was said to lift the quality of management of smaller financial institutions, and second, their knowledge of the regulations of the MOF and range of contacts within the MOF provided a substantial basis for improving the level of communications between the private sector and the MOF. The benefits that an officer of the MOF could bring to an institution depended upon his position at retirement and the authority he had in his new job. With many officers filling the president and deputy president positions there was obviously a significant potential for influence. Internal management techniques were amenable to improvement, as were accounting methods and loan risk assessment. All apparently offered some room for reduction in the cost structure of the small financial institution. It was not only executive personnel, all of whom were former career officers, that could have a positive impact on the management of the private organisation. Non-career officers also were well drilled in the rigorous management standards required by the MOF and in the techniques for achieving those standards. One would not have thought, however, that intro-ducing new management teams would have had effects as large as those created by mergers. The problem of many institutions was related to size.

Merger activity between financial institutions was concentrated on very small financial institutions, and was primarily the result of a CFSR report of 1967.[40] Since 1974 merger activity has declined sharply, and was almost non-existent among city banks, regional banks and long-term credit institutions. The last major mergers were the formation of Daiichi-Kangyo Bank and Taiyo-Kobe Bank, over a decade ago.[41]

The MOF supported mergers of financial institutions in the 1970s but gradually came to adopt a low-key position: that mergers between banks would proceed where all the parties were agreed. It changed its outward attitude in recognition of the limitations of its power. There was little explicit political support for merger activity, since LDP politicians were not greatly concerned with questions relating to financial efficiency. They cared about the continued existence of small financial institutions, which were important for the continued viability of many small and medium-sized business, and hence ultimately to the LDP's political base. If an aggressive policy of mergers was adopted and supported by the government, the LDP would be alienating part of its local support base.[42]

With mergers being so unpopular politically and among many of the small and medium-sized financial institutions, the way was set by default for greater MOF intervention. In the late 1970s many mutual banks, such as Taikō Mutual Bank, made the financial news because of revelations of bad management. The

Taikō Mutual case exemplified the MOF's way of reacting to the problem of bad management. Instead of forcing the closure of the bank or arranging some form of takeover of assets, it organised a financial support plan for the troubled institution, based on subsidised loan funds from other large private financial institutions.[43] The MOF stood by its policy of not allowing any financial institution to go into liquidation. It argued that the collapse of any financial institution would upset the confidence of the public and hence the financial order of the economic system.[44]

It is hard to see how financial stability or financial order benefit from this policy. Banks engaging in activities in which they should not be engaged were in effect given guarantees that the institution would not be allowed to collapse. There were two possible explanations. The first, that the MOF retreated from its stance of favouring amalgamations in the early 1970s because of political pressure, was outlined above. The LDP's sensitivity on the amalgamation issue was based on links between small financial institutions and individual conservative politicians. The empirical evidence is scant as much of this grey area of financial politics remains underresearched, but most informed observers agree that it was at the centre of the problem. The argument is that amalgamation of small and medium-sized financial institutions would centralise finance so that the needs of smaller business institutions (and politicians) would not be met adequately. There is a general consensus that the larger banks have little to do with grey financial transactions and are less amenable to local political influence. The existence of political pressure would be sufficient to cause the division responsible for implementing policy, the Banking Bureau's Small and Medium-sized Financial Institutions Division, to adopt a policy of emphasising improved management techniques rather than forcing institutions to amalgamate or letting market forces operate without interference.

A second, consistent, explanation was that the MOF had much to gain from bowing to the hesitancy of political, local business and labor groups towards amalgamation in that its policy to send MOF-led management teams into troubled banks assisted the MOF in placing retiring employees. According to *Yomiuri shinbun* research, 53 out of 71 mutual banks employed a total of 63 former career and non-career MOF officers. Of eighteen institutions with dubious financial standing, thirteen had MOF men, twelve in the positions of president.[45] Most of MOF's career officers—that is, the elite—retired between the age of 50 and 55, mainly finding employment in semi-government bodies, private financial institutions and as politicians in the LDP.

The practice of the MOF retiring its senior personnel into troubled financial institutions had the advantage of improving the quality of financial management within the existing financial system. On the other hand, it increased the immobilist character of the financial system by helping these banks to become increasingly skilled at protecting their own positions within the MOF and the LDP. In the absence of the retirement system there would have been greater incentive for the MOF to explore alternative ways to overcome political resistance towards reducing the number of small and medium-sized financial institutions.

The retirement system of the MOF meant that at any one time a large number of former MOF officers were located in the financial sector. In 1980, for every five career officers in the MOF, there was one retired officer in a financial institution. A large proportion were employed in small financial institutions, which were sensitive to any movement towards financial deregulation.

Although there was a large MOF 'clique' which entered the Diet on retirement there was no evidence that this group was more concerned with financial deregulation than the average LDP politician. There was a general feeling that this group had more sympathy with the views of the MOF than a second group of ex-MOF officers which used the MOF as a launching pad for political careers. From an early age, politics was the livelihood of this group, which meant that political survival came before more deregulation if and when the two conflicted. There were notable exceptions to this general views: Miyazawa Kiichi, who retired at 32 to enter the House of Councillors, was the leader of a small study group within the LDP which met regularly to discuss questions concerning the financial system. Kaneko Ippei, on the other hand, retired at 47 and later held the position of Minister of Finance before becoming, in 1981, one of the leading supporters of the retention of the present savings interest rate decisionmaking mechanism. In all, the level of interest of Diet members in financial matters was low except when major or important parts of their constituency were affected by government policy. Hence on the issues of postal savings, deregulation of deposits, and the small-scale finance sector, the LDP supported the interests of the status quo. To do otherwise would have jeopardised areas of political support.

The retirement system directed personnel towards what were essentially the inward-looking sectors of the financial industry: the government financial sector and the small and medium-sized banking institutions. The flow of personnel from the MOF to these areas was unlikely to promote financial deregulation for the reason that it served neither the interest of the retiring officers or the LDP, although in the long term it could be expected to improve the administration of the individual financial units. The three types of personnel flows, to the private financial institutions, public financial institutions and the LDP, all strengthened the information channels among the MOF, the financial industry and the LDP, but did so in a way which entrenched existing interests. The MOF attempted to improve and ensure the financial stability of the banking system, but every effort was subject to a range of constraints: practical financial policy meant that the improvements that did occur were incremental rather than radical in character. Incremental change may in the long term be more effective and more persevering than short sharp changes in policy but, in the context that it is used here, it is taken to mean slowing down the rate of policy change rather than the steady, progressive connotations which might also be attached.

Retirement processes linked the MOF with the political and financial world in Japan in a unique way. The MOF had stronger links with the LDP than did other ministries, illustrated most vividly by the large number of former officers of the MOF that became politicians. This process expressed the confidence of the LDP in personnel of the MOF, and contributed to a significant information flow between the two bodies. In particular, it made the MOF very aware of political constraints on policymaking. Although leaving MOF to its own devices on many purely industry matters, the LDP retained strong control over decisionmaking on politically sensitive issues. Deregulation that did occur was in the 'non-political' sector dominated by large banks and securities companies. Interest group considerations dominated the thinking of the LDP, and ultimately the MOF, on the issue of financial deregulation and the management of the existing regulatory framework.

The nexus between the MOF and the LDP was one which grew and consolidated in the 1960s and 1970s and ultimately contributed to the maintenance of the status quo in politically sensitive areas of banking. Change did occur but this was largely because it could no longer be avoided, and was not a direct response to the views advocated by some groups which wanted more deregulation to improve financial efficiency. Taken together, the factors analysed in this chapter were important structural mechanisms which contributed to slowing down the rate of change in financial policymaking.

9   Conclusions

This book has attempted to examine a set of propositions within the limited framework of the Japanese financial markets in order to explain the way in which regulatory policymaking is formulated and to a lesser extent the way in which it is implemented. The detailed case studies throw up some interesting conclusions which warrant further examination in later research. Our purpose here has been to demystify the operation of the MOF and provide a base on which understanding of contemporary financial policy can be built.

There can be little argument with the statement that the character of the Japanese financial system began to change slowly during the 1970s, and that the speed of change accelerated during the early 1980s. The extent of reform was, however, far from uniform and this fact reflected not only the different demands for change but also how each demand was handled within the policymaking framework. Certainly, the detailed case studies provide little support for arguments based exclusively on efficiency or contentions that the movement towards a completely deregulated set of financial markets was inevitable.

The overall role of the LDP manifested itself in two ways. On the one hand its impact was crucial in areas in which it took a direct interest, but these were confined to a small section of the financial system; on the other hand its broad approach to business set the framework in which the public service operated.

No matter how strong the MOF was as a ministry, and it was one of the most powerful, it was shown to be relatively helpless in the face of effective political alliances built within the LDP. These alliances arose from matters which had important electoral implications such as postal savings, where its view prevailed. The interest of the LDP in matters such as personal savings, which the MOF tended to downgrade, meant that the interests of the personal savings sector were better represented in policymaking than might at first be apparent. The gradual decline in political support from the late 1950s to the late 1970s made the LDP more aware of the need to maintain the backing of existing support groups.

The areas in which the LDP expressed an interest had a significant impact on the overall shape of the financial system. Political resistance to policies aimed at improving the economic efficiency of small and medium-sized financial institutions through promoting merger activity slowed down the rate of change in the

212

structure of the banking sector. Political and public service support for semi-government financial institutions caused their function as financial intermediaries to expand when one would have expected it to contract as the financial markets became more flexible and mature.

The LDP also had a more subtle influence on the overall approach of the MOF. There is little doubt that the MOF was for the most part the policymaking authority in the development of financial regulations. Indeed, few politicians within the LDP saw any need for themselves to become involved explicitly in matters concerning financial regulations. But, and this is an important caveat, they were aware, as the MOF was also aware, of the implicit political restrictions on the development of new policy. There were few disputes between the LDP and the MOF because over the years selection of senior personnel ensured the maintenance of the parameters established by the LDP. As these changed, so did the development and management of new policy. Rarely did the system produce mavericks. Officers who made it to the top had gained the confidence of both their contemporaries and the elite of the LDP.

In the majority of cases examined in this study the LDP had little or no direct involvement. In the development of the government bond market, the CDs market, the development of the new FEFTCL and the yen bond market, the MOF was the crucial arena in policymaking. In order to examine these cases in particular (but other cases as well) a two-parameter, four-mode model of policymaking was introduced. The case studies sought to examine differences in the level of concentration of control and level of agreement in regulatory policymaking by distinguishing between:

1 policy outcomes that were controlled by a single bureau;
2 policy outcomes that were the result of negotiations between two or more bureaus within the MOF;
3 policy outcomes that were the result of negotiations between two or more ministries.

In 1, the bureau controlling the policymaking process was by and large able to impose its view. Controlling the process conveyed a large say in the policy content. The pervasiveness of the dominance mode was related to the nature of the policy change envisaged. In the CDs case, the environment in the broader financial system prevented change at an earlier date. In other areas also external constraints could be expected to prevent the independent determination of policy. There was a chance of differences of opinion being present within the bureau controlling the policymaking process, but a compromise was generally possible because of the highly developed administrative interactions at this level.

In 2 and 3, unity, consensus and dominance modes were supplemented by a conflict mode. Here the objection to a policy proposal by one party was sufficient to prevent any initiative being undertaken and ensured that the essence of the status quo was maintained unless, of course, political intervention occurred on the side of the groups or group campaigning for reform of the existing regulations. This was itself an unlikely, though not unheard of, occurrence.

The conflict mode of policymaking was fundamentally different from the consensus mode used by some writers to describe policymaking in the 1960s and 1970s in areas such as budgeting and agriculture, where compromise operated within a relatively fixed process based on shared values. In regulatory policymaking in the financial system those shared values appeared to decline in importance in the public service and industry in the 1970s and early 1980s.

Important differences in approach to policy within the MOF were documented in case studies on CDs, trading in government bonds, the development of policy towards interest rates and relating to the regulatory framework of the yen bond market. These differences reflected the existence of competing jurisdictions between the bureaus within the MOF, the representation of different interest groups within the finance industry by different bureaus, and at times fundamentally different objectives and opinions towards regulation of the financial system.

It was, therefore, both inappropriate and incorrect to assume that agreement could always be reached between bureaus such as the IFB, the Banking Bureau and the Securities Bureau on matters of regulatory or, for that matter, general financial policymaking. The bureau rather than ministry was the prime unit of policymaking when it came to solving disputes within the MOF resulting from jurisdictional issues rather than efficiency considerations. In the cases of CDs and the sale of government bonds by banks, conflict was strong, and despite the potential contribution of each instrument to solve specific financial problems, jurisdictional issues and interest group infighting delayed the reform of the existing regulatory framework and had an impact on the character of the instruments when they were introduced finally. The point which needs to be emphasised here, however, was the character of the jurisdiction—efficiency dichotomy. The MOF as an institution showed that it was capable in the long term of responding to the pressures of the market and of overcoming jurisdictional differences between bureaus. By the early 1980s it could also be argued that the Minister's Secretariat, hitherto relatively unimportant, was beginning to play a more central and effective role in resolving differences between bureaus. It remains to be seen whether this role will develop.

Despite the dominant role of the public service in single ministry disputes (that is, the MOF), the lack of political interest in many issues, the overlapping of jurisdictions and the differences in approach based on the bureau as the principal unit of policymaking, made the notion of conflict a better characterisation of the policymaking process than consensus in many instances. A fall in the basic level of agreement between groups within the finance industry and the need to give due emphasis to the possibility of low concentration of control within the MOF were factors which supported this conclusion. In turn, this had implications for the speed and shape of policy change.

In disputes between ministries, conflict was of considerable importance and was a significant factor immobilising policy development. Jurisdictions, objectives and interest group bases differed sharply. The early attempts to change the

FEFTCL, in the 1950s and 1960s, were scuttled by the divergent positions of the MOF and MITI, and the extent of change in the 1978–80 revision was also greatly reduced by inter-ministry conflict. Ministries presented their cases in terms of national interest, but often this was little more than a smokescreen for the protection or advancement of jurisdictional or sectional interests. When the LDP was itself not a participant in the regulatory policymaking process, inter-ministry conflict was a potent barrier to regulatory change. In contrast, in areas of more routine character, ministries kept out of each other's way and administered their own fields of influences. Here conflict was of less importance.

In summary, the notion of consensus is inadequate to describe regulatory financial policymaking. The case studies illustrated each mode of policymaking and showed that the consensus mode was most often present in the area of policy implementation. In the area of regulatory policymaking, the extent of conflict differed according to the level of concentration of control and the level of agreement. The dominance and conflict modes of policymaking were of considerable importance.

The suggestion that conflict within the public service in Japan was a predominantly immobilist force in regulatory policymaking represents a departure from existing policymaking literature. There are two possible explanations for this. One is that little work has previously been done on regulatory policymaking in Japan. A second and consistent explanation is that the 1970s produced a series of factors which underlined the different interests of groups within the financial system. These factors included:

1   the maturation of branch banking in Japan in the late 1960s which increased the pressures for change as the larger banks looked for new markets;
2   the spread of corporate activities abroad which necessitated more sophisticated financial management and led to demands for a wider range of improved domestic financial services;
3   the expansion of banking and securities activity abroad which provided not only a release for pent-up desires to expand domestically but also a place for gaining experience in a wide range of financial activities controlled exclusively in Japan by competing financial institutions, giving them a basis for providing those same services should domestic regulations change;
4   the fundamental change which occurred in the flow of funds in Japan, leading to increased pressure for deregulation of interest rates;
5   the different macroeconomic conditions which led to a shift in the emphasis of monetary policy to the control of the rate of inflation, and hence greater interest in the BOJ in freely operating money markets.

It was also argued that immobilism in policymaking could be attributed to the administrative structure, and to career and retirement patterns in the MOF. The evidence presented in chapter 8 (and there is need for further research in this area) indicated that the emphasis on administration, the system of job rotation and the lack of systematic long-term planning hindered the development of new policy initiatives, and at least reinforced immobilist patterns found in the detailed case studies. The retirement system, which linked the LDP, the MOF and the small and medium-sized financial institutions, was an important factor in ensuring that change which adversely affected the long-term future of small and medium-sized financial institutions would be minimised. A cautionary note must be added. For the past decade efficiency concerns have been at, or just below, the surface in this area. Continuing computerisation and diffusion of electronic banking will increase the pressure for cost-cutting amalgamation and could result in the acceptance of reduced numbers of smaller financial institutions.

The 1970s was not only a decade when some change did occur, but also when the seeds for further change were sown. Changes in financial demands of private enterprise, government and the household sector led to a diversification of services being offered. The demands of the central government for funds from the financial sector had perhaps the most profound effect on the whole financial system. The constraints of the existing system led to the destabilisation of the government bond market, and to some extent the very foundations of the financial system.

The response of the MOF was both cautious and unwilling, at least in the first instance, to deviate radically from its well-established regime of 'the MOF knows best' and 'rule by regulation'. The evidence presented in this volume shows that the MOF maintained its policies unless there was concerted pressure on it to act. The MOF did not lead the way in suggesting that certain regulatory changes would produce increased efficiency within the financial system. In general, the MOF acted in response to a complex set of factors relating to jurisdictional matters, financial soundness, efficiency criteria and political constraints. Its role was to keep the system functioning smoothly and effectively within the confines of the social fabric in which it operated.

It is extremely difficult to arrange these factors in order of importance. Politics was important in some areas, jurisdictional considerations and efficiency factors in others. From the late 1970s, however, market forces led parts of the MOF to address more forthrightly questions of the future shape of the system. This point will be addressed shortly.

The MOF was by no means the only group that had an immobilist impact on the development of new regulatory policy. Industry groups supporting the preservation of the status quo did so because they felt that their identity and *raison d'etre* would be lost if any fundamental structural change occurred. The range of new domestic and international financial demands outlined above made it clear that some change was needed. These groups (the small and medium-sized banks and the long-term financial institutions) were able to protect their fundamental position because of their significance politically, and the support they received from the public service. The shelving of proposals for change generally did little to help their immediate position but meant that it would not deteriorate rapidly in response to growing competition.

As a result, in a period when the underlying financial needs of the Japanese economy were changing rapidly, the institutional framework was immobilised partly by domestic factors. Opposition to change was effective in particular areas because of the interest of the LDP in maintaining the viability of the small and medium-sized financial sector and indirectly because of the effective set of links between the LDP, the MOF and those financial institutions.

One important source of dynamism was the activities of larger banks and securities companies within the finance industry. In the changing economic environment, institutions such as city banks, which favoured regulatory change, became increasingly dissatisfied with the existing regulatory framework. As the decade of the 1970s progressed the possibilities for domestic expansion dwindled, and it became more difficult to maintain traditional market shares. International expansion was one available option and they pursued it vigorously. International expansion required only international competitiveness and experience, both of which were quickly acquired, whereas breaking down domestic barriers required overcoming political and public service alliance against change.

A more direct and crucial dynamic element was the role of market pressures. Political pressures which resulted in tax levels being held down helped to create a budget deficit of significant proportions and with it a rapid rise in government bond issues. The development of the secondary market for government bonds has placed the MOF under great pressure to adjust the full range of its financial policies to recreate a sense of stability within the industry. It could be argued that this 'stability', in the sense of a relatively stable financial framework, is a thing of the past, and the early 1980s produced some evidence that policymakers were adjusting to the new realities.

The MOF initiated more relaxed policies towards the regulation of banking and the range of instruments that could be used within Japan. In the 1970s Japan also fully consolidated its position as the world's third largest economy. Since then the MOF inevitably has had to consider its positions and policies more carefully than before with respect to the international environment. Interaction between the Japanese financial system and the international capital and money markets increased greatly in the early 1980s, as did interest in Japanese stocks and the use of yen as a reserve currency. The response of policymakers was cautious and for the most part reflected a reconsideration of Japanese interests in the changing international and domestic economy. On occasions foreign financial institutions were active in pushing for particular policy changes, but they were not a major force in determining the rate or content of policy change.

Clearly policymakers had to use the international economic and financial system as a reference point, and it was far from stagnant. From time to time there were calls by foreign governments and foreign corporations and financiers for a less regulated Japanese market. Over the decade of the 1970s the operations of the FEFTCL changed, as did the regulations applying to financial operations by foreigners in the Japanese money markets and bond markets. All these changes took place with reference to domestic participants and the structure, organisation and operation of the total domestic financial system. Domestic institutional and political constraints weighed heavily in all discussions on regulatory change. But it should also be noted that both the MOF and the BOJ support in principle the idea of internationalising the Japanese financial system. What this means in practical terms is beginning to emerge: it is clear that policies which evolve will not be a straightforward reflection of economic demands but will reflect also jurisdictional issues, domestic political concerns and Japan's changing international interests. Some of the financial system will remain relatively untouched by these developments but the rise in international financial interdependence and Japan's obviously important position in the world economy should see the deregulation of the late 1970s and early 1980s continue to go ahead.

Finally, this analysis has made no attempt to cover exhaustively all the inputs into the policymaking process, nor does it identify all the features of that process. For example, it makes no explicit mention of the role of the Diet, or of opposition political parties. The Diet was an arena in which some important political dramas were acted out but was relatively unimportant in the area of finance. The long period of continuous LDP government resulted in a solidification and bureaucratisation of flows of information. The LDP and the public service developed a very close understanding, with the main issues being decided before debate in the Diet, and the opposition political parties being almost shut out of the consultation process. The period 1976–80 certainly gave the opposition parties, and hence the Diet, a greater function when the former gained control of many Diet committees, but the imbalance remained. The roles of the Diet and the opposition political parties were limited, at least in the area of most financial regulations.

This book suggests a series of more general conclusions relevant to the broader process of policy development, notwithstanding the fact that it has only explored the narrow area of the financial market. These conclusions are that:

1 the LDP's role in policymaking varies greatly. Sometimes it plays no direct role but when it does it has effective veto power. On other occasions its position is implicit in the policy adopted by the responsible ministry. Hence its influence on the development or protection of regulatory policy is often more than what is casually apparent. This conclusion suggests the need to reassess the literature which claims a progressive growth in the power of the public service in the policymaking field;

2 the key role of the public service is to operate the existing regulatory system and policies. Administrative processes and career patterns, both before and after retirement, encourage the maintenance of the existing structure of industry. Since this conclusion flies in the face of, for example, some commonly accepted images of the operation of MITI, there is a need to re-examine carefully the range of activities of public servants to see whether differences exist between the operation of ministries;

3 the fact that proposals must be articulated through the public service means that, without shared values within the finance industry, the case for change must be able to demonstrate the benefits of change to the whole industry or the unbearable costs involved in the maintenance of the existing regulatory

framework. Shared values might exist at the very general level of questions relative to growth or political preferences. Beyond that, however, it is inappropriate to assume that shared values exist. Without this assumption the nature of the political backing of the different groups within the industry or, alternatively, the level of agreement between participants, and the level of concentration of control of the authorities should help in determining how the industry might be expected to change. As in any other modern industrial economy, the stance of the party with political power has important regulatory and therefore allocative implications;

4   the role of the public service is complex and cannot be matched up with any particular model explaining government behaviour. It juggles the roles of pursuing the national interest, ensuring the maintenance of its own jurisdiction and working with industry groups. Although it plays a prominent role in the regulatory process, it does not always dominate. Regulatory change occurs when there are shared values in industry and the supervisory body (or bodies) approves; when the supervisory body (or bodies) believes change is justified and has sufficient control of the policymaking process to ensure change; or when a high degree of market instability forces conflicting parties to compromise. The lack of any of these elements could prevent change from occurring in different policy areas;

5   irreconcilable conflict between ministries and within ministries, based on differences in jurisdictions, aims and vested interests, can immobilise the development of policy (particularly the case where the LDP has no direct interest in the policy area). This proposition suggests the need to define more carefully the role of 'consensus' policymaking. This book offers a workable model with which to examine the policymaking process. This model explicitly recognises the existence of dominance and conflict modes. The analysis shows that there is significant variation in policymaking processes both at one point in time and over time, and that this point is important in order to understand the policymaking processes;

6   the dominance of domestic participants in the policymaking process, and the role of private groups in actively seeking change to make the regulatory framework more appropriate to the contemporary environment, suggest that change will not necessarily produce a homogeneous international society. Internationalisation is valuable only in so far as it assists in promoting the goals and ambitions of those that are participants within the policymaking process.

This book on regulatory policymaking in the Japanese financial markets has detailed the character of developments in regulatory policy and the nature of the regulatory process. The case studies illustrate vividly the richness and complexity of the regulatory policymaking framework and, in particular, the importance of conflict and dominance modes of policymaking, in addition to the more commonly cited consensus mode. The book documents the barriers to change and the character of problems involved in forging stronger links between the Japanese and international financial markets. Despite idiosyncracies which stem from the Japanese institutional and political framework, it is likely that there is much in the process of regulatory policymaking in Japan's financial markets which policymakers and participants in other countries will recognise.

APPENDIXES

1 Major measures influencing the flow of capital

Period I, February 1971–November 1973

Short-term flows

Framework for individual use of foreign currency expanded (2.1971).
Non-residents banned from purchasing short-term government securities (3.1971).
Further expansion of individuals' rights to use foreign currency (6.1971).
* Controls placed on prepayment of exports (8.1971).
* Controls on balance of free yen deposits (8.1971).
* Regulations tightened concerning holding yen bond funds in yen (8.1971).
* Strengthening of yen conversion system (9.1971).
* [These regulations were temporarily eased between December 1971 and January 1972. This policy switch reflected concern about the impact of the yen revaluation.]
Reintroduction of controls on prepayment of exports (2.1972).
Controls on prepayment of exports strengthened (6.1972).
Reserve deposit of 25 per cent of increase of free yen account introduced (6.1972).
Reserve deposit raised to 50 per cent of increase of free yen account (7.1972).
Limit on free remittance lifted (11.1972).
Other measures related to first, second and third yen defence plans had a similar impact.

Long-term flows

Floating bonds overseas for domestic use stopped in principle (2.1971).
Acquisition by non-residents of non-listed public company bonds prohibited (5.1971).
Quantity restrictions liberalised on outward direct investment and in real estate investment (7.1971).
Ban lifted on acquisition of non-listed public bonds with maturity exceeding one year. However, acquisition of new stocks and bonds in net terms must equal zero.

Period II, November 1973–June 1976: Encouragement of Inflow, Restraint on Outflow

Short-term flows

Restrictions on prepayment for export eased (11.1973).
Eased further (1.1974).
Limit on free remittance reduced (7.1974).

223

Use by individuals of foreign currency restricted (12.1973).
Both categories restricted further (4.1974).
Foreign currency held by residents and corporations restricted (1.1974).
Reserve deposit rate on free yen account reduced from 50 per cent to 10 per cent (12.1973).
Reserve deposit system suspended (9.1974).
Holding of short-term foreign government securities banned (1.1974).
Regulations controlling purchase of short-term government securities abolished (8.1974).

Long-term flows

Japanese banks prohibited from making medium- and long-term loans abroad. Restrictions on non-resident investors' acquisition of stocks abolished (11.1973) and similarly on securities (12.1973).
Corporations permitted to float bonds externally for external use (12.1973).
Yen bond market closed (12.1973).
Corporations permitted to float bonds externally for domestic use (11.1974).
[The yen bond market was reopened in 7.1975 largely for political purposes, although it was the first indication of a more general policy change]

Period III, June 1976–June 1977: Encouragement of Inflow, Relaxation of Restrictions on Outflow

Short-term flows

Easing of restrictions on outward remittance (6.1976). Liberalised further (6.1977).
Expenditure framework on individual trips abroad expanded (6.1976). Liberalised (6.1977)
Remittance from sales of bonds held for more than six months liberalised (6.1977).

Long-term flows

[Yen bond market reopened (7.1975).]
Liberalised purchase of listed securities by non-residents (6.1976).
Framework on yen bond market expanded greatly during 1977–78 such as explicit statement in government 'Foreign Economic Policy Statement of 3.8.77.'
Foreign non-quoted stock become permitted purchases for individuals (6.1976).
Japanese banks permitted to lend abroad on maturities greater than one year (level regulated). Also permitted to become involved again in Euromarket borrowing (11.1976).

Period IV, June 1977–January 1979: Restrictions on Short-term Inflows, Policy on Outflows Unchanged

Short-term flows

Introduction of reserve deposit of 25 per cent on non-resident free yen account outstanding balance (6.1977).
Introduction of reserve deposit on increase in balance of free yen account of 50 per cent (11.1977). Increased further (3.1978).

Floating short-term government bonds suspended. A non-discriminatory measure, but directed at speculative non-resident inflows (11.1977).

Ease in regulations on purchase of overseas short-term securities which had been prohibited (6.1977).

Big expansion of framework of approved trade-related expenses (8.1977).

Loans by Japanese banks abroad, for less than one year, which had been prohibited, permitted (6.1977).

Long-term flows

Introduction of ceilings on impact loans; Japanese corporations 'asked' to delay overseas borrowings (7.1977).

Relaxation of overseas property purchase restrictions (6.1977).

Relaxation of regulations controlling overseas portfolio investment by pension funds (6.1977).

Relaxation in framework of loans abroad by Japanese banks (6.1977).

Acquisition of bonds by non-residents, with maturities of less than five years and one month, prohibited (3.1978).

Period V, January 1979–: Relaxation on Inflows

Short-term flows

Reduction from 100 per cent to 50 per cent of reserve deposit on increase in free yen account (1.1979).

Short-term impact loan reduced to zero (2.1979). Regulations terminated (5.1979).

Non-residents permitted to operate in *gensaki* market (5.1979).

Speed of conversion of yen bonds funds into foreign currency regulations relaxed (5.1979).

Import usance period extended from 140 to 180 days (5.1979).

Step-up inflow of impact loans (11.1979).

Long-term flows

Long-term impact loan regulations relaxed (5.1979).

Notes: Over the 1970s many regulations were simplified, thus encouraging transaction flows up to a point. Regulations such as those relating to foreign exchange positions have limited the flexibility of foreign exchange banks and corporations adjusting their stance according to their own estimates of the market. Regulations relating to import usance (not documented in full) have also had some bearing on the timing of flows, but since Japanese are unable to speculate in the same way with inflows (export prepayments), one would not expect this to be significant.

    Finally, we have made no attempt to indicate the extent of administrative guidance, except for some brief comments with reference to yen bonds. The government set frameworks such as those for impact loans (short and long) and the extent that corporations used overseas markets, which also contributed to the extent of capital flows. It could be said that formal regulations controlled short-term flows, while informal regulations applied to long-term flows.

2   Report of the proceedings of the advisory committee

The following full report of the meeting was released in English by the MOF:

Proceedings of the Advisory Committee on Legal System of Foreign Exchange and Foreign Trade (April 23, 1979)

This Committee was organised in August 1978, with a purpose of discussing the basic direction for establishing new legislation system under the principle of freedom of external transactions, in reflection of our country's basic stance of achieving open economy.

Up till now the Committee held 6 sessions in total, and the below given are its proceedings:-

1. Basic idea

(1) A part of the members advanced a view that the Cabinet Orders and Ministerial Ordinances should at first be amended for further liberalisation in substance, because the amendment of the Law itself tends to take much time. However, prevailing opinions urged to amend the Law itself as soon as possible for incorporation therein of the principle of freedom as well as for further liberalisation in substance, because (i) the current legal system of prohibition in principle is causing unnecessary criticism and misunderstanding among various foreign countries, and (ii) it is necessary to clarify our country's stance for the open economy in consideration of such international environments as the Tokyo summit conference scheduled in June.

(2) While it is unanimously agreed to introduce basic principle of freedom of external transactions, under the current international economic situation of rapid changes, no objection is raised against the necessity for retaining a legal mechanism which can effectively cope with such anomalies as the turbulent upvaluation of Yen exchange experienced in 1977 and the last autumn.

(3) Opinions were also advanced which admitted that the existence of certain non-liberalised sectors were unavoidable, due to the reason that a time is necessary to adjust our system, such as financial system etc., with those of other countries, among which differences still exist as a matter of fact, up till the time when those differences come to be adjusted.

2. Opinions on each type of transaction

(1) Current transactions

(a) Foreign trade

The prevailing opinions were that no basic amendment in this field is necessary, because after several steps of liberalisation, the current regulations on export and import of goods contain only minimum list of restricted goods, and expression of the relevant provisions already conform to the principle of freedom, but taking this opportunity administrative procedures such as export certification should be broadly simplified.

(b) Current invisible transactions

Opinions were unanimous that although the current degree of liberalisation is already on fairly advanced stage, service transactions should be liberalised substantially towards the almost full liberalisation on this occasion.

However, the majority members admitted unavoidability of certain restrictions on service transactions involving such sensitive items as weaponry technology, natural resources, energy, etc.

(c) Settlement method

A part of members advocated that the regulations on the settlement method should be extensively liberalised in consideration of our recent foreign exchange position.

But, the majority opinions contested that if certain types of settlement method were allowed without restrictions, they might cause excessive leads and lags, adversely affect established international trade practice, and make the proper overview of our external transactions difficult. They therefore concluded that certain restrictions should be retained on such special settlement methods as open account system, deferred trade payments, etc., after having expanded the scope of freedom as far as practicable.

Opinions were also advanced that in view of facilitating and stabilising transactions of small-scale exporters of such goods as textile, general merchandise, etc., the current principle of export L/C requirement should be retained.

(2) Capital transactions

(a) It was unanimously agreed that although capital transactions should also be liberalised in principle, a legal mechanism should be retained which can effectively cope with abnormal situations, because by their nature capital transactions can, unlike current transactions accompanying movement of goods or services, be done relatively easily and in a large amount.

(b) The majority opinions agreed that the instances that require activation of regulatory measures on capital transactions should include not only such quantitative ones as turbulent fluctuations of our currency's foreign exchange rates by massive movements of speculative funds, difficulty in maintaining equilibrium of our international balance of payments, or damages to our money and capital markets, but also such qualitative ones as extraordinary or abnormal dealings that adversely affect domestic and foreign money markets, or derogate from our international credence, but when applying latter regulations, judgement should be done after taking various aspect of the matter into consideration synthetically.

(c) The committee majority also agreed that in order to make it possible to have a constant overview of the actualities of foreign exchange transactions, the current system of authorised foreign exchange bank should be retained, and the necessary measures should be taken so as to enable the authorities to timely and effectively cope with the above-mentioned eventualities.

(d) As to the actual ways and means of such regulations, two opinions were advanced; one advocating indirect measures which utilise the market mechanism as far as practicable, another arguing that such indirect measures are indecisive and ineffectual in certain instances, and therefore both direct and indirect measures should be made applicable, for the free choice of the one best suited for the given situation.

(3) Direct domestic investment and introduction of foreign technology

No objection was raised against the advisability of abrogation of the Foreign Investment Law and amalgamation thereof into the Foreign Exchange Law for the convenience of those concerned, many of whom are at present often at a loss to know whether a given case comes under the Foreign Investment Law or the Foreign Exchange Law.

As to the inflow of direct foreign investment and technology, opinions prevailed that they should also be placed under the principle of freedom, but at the same time a legal mechanism should be retained which can prevent exceptional adverse effects from taking place to those sensitive fields as the four hardcore sectors including agriculture, forestry, fishery and also to our national industry, economy, or security.

3. Conclusion

By presenting the above-mentioned proceedings, which set forth basic guide lines for the revision of the relevant laws, the Committee concludes that its duties have been accomplished.

The Committee wants to take this opportunity to express its wishes that since the revision of this time is keenly watched by those interested both inside and outside of our country, all efforts should be exercised for the soonest possible presentation of the relevant bill to the Diet on the basis of these proceedings, and its smooth passage therethrough. The above given Committee's opinions should also be taken into consideration for the future enactment and amendment of the relevant Cabinet Orders and Ministerial Ordinances.

Source: Advisory Committee on Legal System of Foreign Exchange and Foreign Trade, 'Proceedings', mimeo, c. 1980.

3 The structure and function of bureaus within the MOF

Minister's Secretariat

Organisation:

The Minister's Secretariat consists of the Secretarial Division, the Overall Coordination Division, the Accounts Division, the Division Controlling Local Finance Bureau, the Research and Planning Division, the Special Officer for Health and Welfare, the Chief Inspector of the Local Finance Bureau, the Comptroller of the Japan Tobacco and Salt Public Corporation, the counsellors and the councillors.

Functions:

The Minister's Secretariat is in charge of assisting the Minister and the Parliamentary and Administrative Vice-Minister in all administration of the Ministry of Finance and adjusting differences of opinion among the Bureaus to enable the Ministry to operate smoothly as an organisation; investigating, planning and drafting of important matters outside administration of each Bureau; matters concerning secrecy, personnel changes, discipline; coordination and adjustment of the competent administration; inspection, report and taking charge of laws, ordinances and official notes; investigation and drafting of the organisation and the full number of regular personnel; matters concerning public information and the National Diet; matters concerning accounts of the Ministry of Finance; general supervision over management of the competent administration under the jurisdiction of Local Finance bureaus; investigation and formulation of statistics of domestic and foreign finance and economy; investigation, planning and drafting of the monopoly system and supervision over the Japan Tobacco and Salt Public Corporation.

Securities Bureau

Organisation:

The Securities Bureau consists of the Coordination Division, the Capital Market Division, the Corporation Finance Division, the Secondary Market Division, the Securities Companies Division and the Inspection Division.

Functions:

The Securities Bureau is in charge of investigation and planning of systems concerning trading of securities, issuing and trading markets of stocks, bonds and other securities, registration of public offering sale or tender offer of securities, certified public accountants, and securities companies and investment trusts; licensing and supervision of securities exchanges, securities finance companies, securities companies and investment trust companies; registration and supervision of the Securities Dealers Association of Japan; review of registration statement of public offering, sale or tender offer of securities and periodical reports; other matters relating to public and corporate accounting.

Banking Bureau

Organisation:

The Banking Bureau consists of the Coordination Division, the Commercial Banks Division, the Special Banks Division, the Small Banks Division, the Research Division, the Special Officer for Savings Promotion, the Insurance Department, which consists of the First Insurance Division and the Second Insurance Division, and the Banking Inspection Department, which consists of the Control Division and the Examination Division.

Functions:

The Banking Bureau is in charge of planning and formulation of the policies on financial institutions; supervision over the Bank of Japan; control over the interest rates of financial institutions; supervision over the Deposit Insurance Organisation; licensing of a person to carry on a commercial banking business and supervision over the licensee; licensing of a person to carry on business as a mutual loan and savings bank or a credit association or other financial institutions for small business, and supervision over the licensee; supervision over the Export–Import Bank of Japan, the Japan Development Bank and other government financial institutions; research, planning and formulation of the banking system; formulation of the annual savings promotion plan and encouragement of savings; other matters relating to insurance.

Financial Bureau

Organisation:

The Financial Bureau consists of the Coordination Division, the Treasury Division, the Government Debt Division, the First Fund Planning and Operation Division, the Second Fund Planning and Operation Division, the Local Fund Operation Division, the Fund Management Division, and six other divisions relating to the management of National Property.

Functions:

The Financial Bureau is in charge of coordination and adjustment of the Treasury, coordination of public finance and monetary system, general coordination of domestic finance, and coordination of domestic and international finance; research, planning and drafting of Treasury system, government debt system; adjustment of the receipts and payments of Treasury Bills; issue, redemption and interest payment of government bonds (including treasury bills); control and operation of the Trust Fund and control of the Industrial Investment Special Account; compilation of the Fiscal Investment and Loan Program; matters concerning loans to local governments.

International Finance Bureau

Organisation:

The International Finance Bureau consists of the Coordination Division, the Legal Division, the International Organisations Division, the Research Division, the Short-term Capital Division, the Foreign Capital Division, the Overseas Investment Division, the Oveseas Public Investment Division and the Overseas Private Investment Division.

Functions:

The International Finance Bureau is in charge of research and planning of international finance and the foreign exchange system; matters concerning adjustment of balance of payments; management of the Foreign Exchange Fund and matters concerning the Foreign Exchange Special Account; matters concerning foreign exchange rates; control of foreign exchange transactions under the jurisdiction of the Ministry; authorisation, supervision and inspection of foreign exchange banks and money changers; matters concerning OECD, IMF, IBRD, IFC, IDA, ADB and AFDF; matters concerning foreign aid; matters concerning overseas private investment; matters concerning inflow of foreign capital; making statistics of foreign exchange and balance of payments.

Other bureaus include the *Budget Bureau*, the *Tax Bureau*, the *Customs and Tariffs Bureau* and the *National Tax Administration Agency*.

Source: Extract from Institute of Administrative Management *Organisation of the Government of Japan* Tokyo, September 1980, pp. 54–57. See also Sugiyama Keiichi *Ōkurashō kenkyū* Tokyo: Kanchō nyūsusha, 1979.

4 Official groups related to the issue of government bonds

Conference on Government Bond Issuance

Attendance:

Minister of Finance: governor of BOJ; chairman of Financing System Council; president of Federation of Bankers' Associations; president, Association of Securities Companies; chairman of Committee on Financial System Research; chairman of Securities and Exchange Council; representative of Syndicate Underwriting Government Guaranteed Bonds; an academic representative; deputy-governor of the BOJ; administrative vice-minister of the MOF.

Object:

To exchange opinions on the flotation volume of national bonds and other bond categories, particularly government-guaranteed bonds.

Held:

Once a year towards the end of the Calendar Year.

Bond Flotation Council

Attendance:

From the MOF: administrative vice-minister*; director and deputy-director-general of the Financial Bureau; Parliamentary counsellors (*Shingikan*); directors of General Affairs Division and the Government Debt Division in Financial Bureau; and Councillors (*Kanbōkikakukan*) of Planning.

From the BOJ: deputy governor*; directors of the Government Bond Department, the Business Department and the Coordination and Planning Department.

From the Underwriters' side (eleven members): three presidents of city banks, and a representative from regional banks, trust banks, mutual banks, credit associations, agricultural financial distributors, life insurance associations, non-life insurance companies and the securities companies (from the four biggest, in three-month rotation).

Object:

At the president/chairman level, questions relating to the underwriting volume and the introduction of new products are discussed. At the director-level meetings, such things as changes of flotation conditions and quantity for the following month are discussed.

Held:

The president level meets once a year while the director–general/manager classes normally meet regularly each month.
*These individuals only attend president-level meetings.

Source: Mimeographed material received in interview with city bank official, November 1980.

NOTES

Introduction

1 Book-length contributions in English include T.J. Pempel *Policy and Politics in Japan* Philadelphia: Temple University Press, 1982; Chalmers Johnson *MITI and the Japanese Miracle: The Growth of Industrial Policy 1925–1975* Stanford: Stanford University Press, 1982; T.J. Pempel *Patterns of Japanese Policymaking: Experiences from Higher Education* Boulder: Westview Press, 1978; Alan G. Rix *Japan's Economic Aid* London: Croom Helm, 1980; John Creighton Campbell *Contemporary Japanese Budget Politics* Berkeley: University of California Press, 1977; Haruhiro Fukui *Party in Power* Canberra: Australian National University Press, 1970; Chitoshi Yanaga *Big Business in Japanese Politics* New Haven: Yale University Press, 1971

2 One feature of the Japanese policymaking literature is its emphasis first on understanding Japan, a tendency which has led to less emphasis being placed on the comparative aspects of policymaking. Pempel, *Policy and Politics in Japan*, makes a useful attempt to address this issue and underscores the difficulties in comparative work. The analysis of this book largely ignores the Marxist approach despite the interest of Marxian analysts in the issues addressed here. See C. Crouch (ed.) *State and Economy in Contemporary Capitalism* London: Croom Helm, 1979, especially articles by Colin Crouch and Frank Longstreth. A good survey of the literature up to the mid-1970s is Haruhiro Fukui 'Studies in Policymaking: A Review of the Literature' in T.J. Pempel (ed.) *Policymaking in Contemporary Japan* Ithaca: Cornell University Press, 1977, pp. 22–59

3 *Australian Financial System: Final Report of the Committee of Inquiry* Canberra: Australian Government Publishing Service, September 1981, pp. 2–8

4 The literature is outlined briefly in notes to the introduction and later chapters

5 See Charles E. Lindblom 'The Science of Muddling Through' *Public Administration Review* 19, 1959, pp. 77–88; and 'Still Muddling, Not Yet Through' *Public Administration Review* November–December 1979, pp. 517–25; Theodore J. Lowi 'American Business and Public Policy, Case Studies and Political Theory' *World Politics* July 1964; Theodore J. Lowi 'Four Systems of Policy Politics and Choice' *Public Administration Review* July–August 1972

6 See B. Guy Peters 'Bureaucracy, Politics and Public Policy' *Comparative Politics* 2, 3, 1979, pp. 339–58

7 For general references see Fukui *Party in Power* pp. 83–89. Also see Murakawa Ichirō *Seisaku kettei katei* Gyōseikikō shirîzu No. 121, Tokyo: Kyōikusha, 1979; Campbell *Coutemporary Japanese Budget Politics* pp. 121–34; Michael W. Donnelly 'Setting the Price of Rice: A Study in Political Decisionmaking' in Pempel *Policymaking in Contemporary Japan*

234

8   Hugh Heclo and Aaron Wildavsky *The Private Government of Public Money* London: Macmillan, 1974, p. 6

9   Ministerial ordinances (*shōrei*) are regulations which are drafted by individual ministries on the basis of existing legislation and can be implemented without the authority of the Diet. Notifications (*tsūtatsu*) are one form of administrative guidance without a legal basis except that the ministry's role is to oversee activity within a particular jurisdiction. They are usually adhered to by participants in the market for fear that the ministry will impose other forms of restrictions. There have been many cases where individual corporations have objected to particular forms of guidance. See also Pempel *Policymaking in Contemporary Japan* pp. 143–200

10   See Johnson *MITI and the Japanese Miracle* pp. 25, 249–50, 272–73

11   According to one interview, the Prime Minister meets once a week with the LDP's Secretary General, the Chairman of PARC and the General Affairs Committee, the Minister of Finance and Cabinet Secretary to review the state of economic policy. This serves to let the Prime Minister and the Minister of Finance know in detail the feelings of senior party officials and vice versa. Interview with an officer of PARC, February 1981

12   T.J. Pempel 'The Bureaucratization of Policymaking in Post-war Japan' *American Journal of Political Science* 18, 4, 1974

13   A useful survey article is Richard A. Posner 'Theories of Economic Regulation' *Bell Journal of Economics and Management Science* 5, Autumn 1974, pp. 335–58. For an interesting treatment of the problem of industry influence on regulatory policy see Paul J. Quirk *Industry Influence in Federal Regulatory Agencies* Princeton: Princeton University Press, 1981, pp. 3–21

14   See Posner 'Theories of Economic Regulation'. See also Peter L. Swan 'The Campbell Report and Deregulation' Australian Graduate School of Management Working Paper, Series 82–019, November 1982

15   One could suggest this is what happened to some extent to agricultural policy in Japan in the 1960s and early 1970s

16   G.J. Stigler 'Theory of Economic Regulation' *Bell Journal of Economics and Management Science* 2, 1, 1971, pp. 2–21

17   See Quirk *Industry Influence* p23 and chapter 3; Swan 'The Campbell Report'; and William A. Niskanen *Bureaucracy and Representative Government* Chicago: Aldine Press, 1971. Lombra puts the problem from an economist's perspective: 'The main problem is not that we are unable to understand analytically what is happening but rather that institutional changes in the discretionary policies that are necessary for economic policy are difficult to implement . . . Policy will be dominated by special interests—public and private—as long as the political power structure is dominated by such interests.' Here Lombra is suggesting that public and private interests do not necessarily equate with the best economic policy mixes. The literature on the economics of the bureaucracy represented by Niskanen and the work of Olson also support these general conclusions. The quote is from Raymond E. Lombra 'Policy Advice and Policymaking: Economic, Political and Social Issues' in Michael R. Herbert, M. Kaufman and Raymond E. Lombra (eds) *The Political Economy of Policymaking* Beverley Hills: Sage Publications, 1979, p. 29

18   Edward R. Tufte *Political Control of the Economy* Princeton: Princeton University Press, 1978. This book is probably the best starting point in the political cycle literature. See also D.A. Hibbs and H. Fassbender (eds) *Contemporary Political Economy* Amsterdam, North Holland: 1981. For an application to Japan see Takashi Inoguchi 'Explaining and Predicting Japanese General Elections 1960–1980' *Journal of Japanese Studies* 7, Summer 1981, pp. 285–318

19   Graham T. Allison *Essence of Decision* Boston: Little, Brown and Co., 1971, p. 68

20   Rix *Japan's Economic Aid*

21 Allison *Essence of Decision* p. 71
22 Lindblom 'Still Muddling'
23 Allison *Essence of Decision* p. 144ff.
24 Robert A. Katzman *Regulatory Bureaucracy: The Federal Trade Commission and Anti Trust Policy* Cambridge, Mass.: MIT Press, 1980
25 See Chalmers Johnson *Japan's Public Policy Companies* New York: A.E.I., 1978, pp. 101–14; and Chalmers Johnson 'The Reemployment of Retired Government Bureaucrats in Japanese Big Business' *Asian Survey* 4, 11, 1974, pp. 953–56. See also Kent Calder 'Yowai kigyō hodo kanryō o arigatageru' *Asahi jānaru* 30 November 1979, pp. 18–26
26 Lowi, 'Four Systems of Policy'; James Q. Wilson (ed.) *The Politics of Regulation* New York: Basic Books, 1980
27 I am grateful to T. Mathews for a comment which has stimulated me to reconsider this issue and for comments by J.A.A. Stockwin which have done much to improve the quality of the final presentation
28 Aurelia D. George, The Comparative Study of Interest Groups in Japan: An Institutional Framework, paper presented at the Australian National University, 29 March 1982
29 The debate on policymaking processes has been clouded by an inappropriate focus on the degree of informal discussions and the existence of a process of decision-making in corporations which highlights 'a bottom-up, group oriented and consensus seeking process'. M.Y. Yoshino 'Emerging Japanese Multinational Enterprises' in Ezra F. Vogel (ed.) *Modern Japanese Organisation and Decisionmaking* Tokyo: Charles E. Tuttle and Co., 1980, p. 158. The terms *nemawashi* and *ringi* are frequently used to describe respectively the informal negotiations and the internal decisionmaking process within corporations
30 Sugimoto and Mouer have drawn attention to the problems of the consensus-based literature in general terms. Yoshio Sugimoto and Ross Mouer 'Japanese Society: Stereotypes and Realities' *Papers of the Japanese Studies Centre No 1*, Melbourne, June 1981
31 For example, see the surveys on Japan in *The Economist* 27 May and 3 June 1967 and 31 March 1973. Also see Ezra F. Vogel 'The Social Base of Japan's Postwar Economic Growth' in *United States International Economic Policy in an Interdependent World*, vol. 2, 1971. This view may have been appropriate for the early 1950s. For example see H. Fukui 'Economic Planning in Post-war Japan: A Case Study in Policymaking' *Asian Survey* 12, April 1972. For an economist's view of Japan's economic performances up to the early 1970s see Andrea Boltho *Japan: An Economic Survey 1953–1973* Oxford: Oxford University Press, 1975, pp. 57–72
32 P.H. Trezise and Yukio Suzuki 'Politics, Government and Economic Growth in Japan' in Hugh Patrick and Henry Rosovsky (eds) *Asia's New Giant: How the Japanese Economy Works* Washington, D.C.: The Brookings Institution, 1976, esp. p. 808, and Brian Ike 'The Japanese Textile Industry: Structural Adjustment and Government Policy' *Asian Survey* 20, 5, 1980, p. 536
33 Aurelia D. George 'The Japanese Farm Lobby and Agricultural Policy-Making' *Pacific Affairs* 54, 3, Fall 1981, pp. 409–30
34 Campbell *Contemporary Japanese Budget Politics* p. 111
35 See Gerald L. Curtis 'Big Business and Political Influence' in Ezra F. Vogel (ed.) *Modern Japanese Organisation* pp. 36–51; Ehud Harari 'Japanese Politics of Advice in Comparative Perspective' *Public Policy* 22, Fall 1974; Yung Ho Park 'The Governmental Advisory Commission System in Japan' *Journal of Comparative Administration* February 1972, pp. 435–67 (and bibliography therein); Muramatsu Michio *Sengo nihon no kanryōsei* Tokyo: Tōyō keizai shinpōsha, 1981, chapter 7

36   Hawker, Smith and Weller identify six different strands of studies examining public
     policy. They are studies of structure and administrative process studies, studies
     examining the cost-effectiveness of output, applications of economic theory to the
     study of political and bureaucratic behaviour and hortatory studies. See the section
     on 'Public Policy and Policy Processes' in Geoffrey Hawker, R.F.I. Smith and
     Patrick Weller (eds) *Politics and Policy in Australia* Brisbane: University of
     Queensland Press, 1979, pp. 6–21

1   An institutional overview

1   Gotō Shin'ichi 'Ginkōhō kaisei zen'ya—gyōsei shidō no kenkyū' *Kin'yū to ginkō* 1
     June 1978, pp. 62–67; Hugh Patrick, The Evolution of Japan's Financial System in
     the Interwar Period, seminar paper given at the Australian National University, 27
     November 1979, mimeo. For perhpas the best annotated bibliography on Japanese
     financial history see Nihon ginkō chōsakyoku, Kin'yūshi kenkyū no dōkō, July
     1976, mimeo
2   For an interesting perspective see Hugh Patrick 'Japanese Development in Historic-
     al Perspective, 1868–1980' Center Discussion Paper No. 398, Economic Growth
     Center, Yale University, March 1982
3   The financial sector was not as much affected as other parts of the economy in terms
     of the direct impact of policies on private or public institutions. The formation of the
     Policy Board in the BOJ was one move designed to increase the independence of the
     BOJ from the MOF. The insertion of a clause in the Securities and Exchange Law
     which prohibits the direct underwriting of government bonds by the BOJ had a
     similar purpose. See Eleanor M. Hadley *Anti-trust in Japan* Princeton: Princeton
     University Press, 1970, pp. 157–65
4   See Ōkurashō hyakunenshi henshūshitsu *Ōkurashō hyakunenshi* (gekan) Tokyo:
     Ōkura zaimukyōkai, 1969
5   See Ginkōkyoku kin'yū nenpō bessatsu *Ginkōkyoku genkō tsūtatsushū—shōwa 54
     nenban* Tokyo, 1980. We are not suggesting that these are unique to the MOF in
     Japan. They are also a familiar feature of many other financial systems
6   See Ōkurashō shōkenkyoku hen *Ōkurashō shōkenkyoku nenpō* (annual)
7   This is not to say the impact of each regulation was maintained throughout the
     period. Whereas the regulation controlling the growth of branching networks was
     important during the 1960s, by the end of the 1970s most banks had completed their
     branch networks. The emphasis then shifted to the control over the rate at which
     mechanised branches and sub-branches could be opened and the swapping and
     relocation of branches
8   Hadley *Anti-trust in Japan* pp. 403–407; Chalmers Johnson *Japan's Public Policy
     Companies* Washington: A.E.I.—Hoover Policy Studies, 1978, pp. 87–99; Kōzō
     Yamamura *Economic Policy in Post War Japan* Berkeley: University of California
     Press, 1967, pp. 27–28
9   See Yoshio Suzuki *Money and Banking in Contemporary Japan* New Haven: Yale
     University Press, 1980, pp. 3–13, 62–63; Kure Bunji *Kin'yū seisaku—nihon ginkō no
     seisaku un'ei* Tokyo: Tōyō keizai shinpōsha, 1973, pp. 58–62
10   In 1961 a government body of enquiry, the Committee of Financial Systems
     Research, held a series of hearings to examine the overloan phenomenon. In its
     report of 1963, it concluded that while there were clearly some very positive side
     effects of the development in the short term, it was something that ought not to be
     institutionalised. The report recommended the normalisation of the relationship
     between the BOJ and the city banks as soon as was practicable. See Kin'yū seido
     kenkyūkai hen *Futsū ginkō no arikata to ginkō seido no kaisei* Tokyo: Kin'yū zaisei jijō
     kenkyūkai, 1979, pp. 428–52

11 Suzuki *Money and Banking* pp. 13–14, 64: Kure *Kin'yū seisaku* pp. 30–31
12 Saitō Kazusane and Tamura Tetsuo (ed.) *Nihon ginkō* Tokyo: Zaikei shōhōsha, 1981, pp. 152–67
13 The accepted wisdom is that BOJ policy was largely controlled by the MOF, and this appears to hold for the 1960s and early 1970s. Since the rapid inflation of 1973–74 the BOJ exercised considerably more control over monetary policy, and, on occasions, this has led to substantial differences of opinion with the MOF. For an example of the earlier view see Gardner Ackerly and Hiromitsu Ishi 'Fiscal, Monetary and Related Policies' in Hugh Patrick and Henry Rosovsky (eds) *Asia's New Giant* Washington D.C.: The Brookings Institution, 1976
14 See Hugh Patrick 'Finance, Capital Markets and Economic Growth in Japan' in Arnold W. Samatz (ed.) *Financial Development and Economic Growth* New York: New York University Press, 1972, pp. 114–16, 121; Suzuki *Money and Banking* pp. 26–29, 64
15 An English version of the plan was published by the Economic Planning Agency *New Economic Plan of Japan (1961–70)—Double National Income Plan* Tokyo: Japan Times, 1961
16 *Nihon keizai shinbun* 6 February 1967
17 Kin'yū seido kenkyūkai hen *Futsū ginkō no arikata to ginkō seido no kaisei* pp. 472–87; Tokuda Hiromi 'Kin'yū seido chōsakai tōshin o megutte' *Fainansu* 6, 5, pp. 3–9; also see the interview between Tokuda and Nakamura of the Federation of Bankers' Associations in *Kin'yū* August 1970, pp. 8–18
18 For detailed institutional treatments see The Bank of Japan *The Japanese Financial System* 1978; Federation of Bankers' Associations of Japan *Banking System in Japan* 1979; see also the volumes in Kyōikusha's 'Sangyōkai shirīzu', Nos. 101–11 (all are individual titles published during 1979–80). These volumes cover all sectors of the finance industry and are useful primers
19 This was markedly different from both the UK and the US where conditions of entry were not substantially different from other industries. In the US, foreign entry into domestic banking grew sharply during the 1970s. See Lawrence G. Goldberg and Anthony Saunders 'The Growth of Organisational Forms of Foreign Banks in the US' *Journal of Money, Credit and Banking* 13, 3, 1981, pp. 365–74. See also Peter S. Rose 'Entry into US Banking Markets—Dimensions and Implications of the Charter Process' *The Anti-trust Bulletin* Spring 1980
20 On a deposits basis, five Japanese banks rank between ten and nineteen on a world scale, eleven in the top 50 and 24 in the top 100. *Kin'yū zaisei jijō* 24 August 1981, pp. 42–45
21 The 'funds base' is defined to include all deposits, bonds, CDs etc., that is, the current liabilities of the bank. The figures on fund size throughout the section on banks are effective at the end of March 1981. See *Kin'yū zaisei jijō* 14 September 1981
22 See Makimura Shirō and Tamaru Tsutomu *Chihō ginkō* Tokyo: Kyōikusha, 1979, pp. 156–65
23 These regulations have changed over the years. See Chūshō kigyō kin'yū senmon kikan nado no arikata to seido no kaisei ni tsuite—fusoku shiryō, 1980, mimeo, pp. 116–20
24 IBI Inc. *The Japanese Financial System—The Function of Foreign Banks* 25 December 1978, p. 18
25 *Kin'yū zaisei jijō* 3 August 1981, p. 89. In comparison, foreign banks in the UK in December 1980 accounted for 19 per cent of sterling advances and 72 per cent of foreign currency advances. See 'Foreign Banks in London—Annual Review' *The Banker* November 1981, pp. 101–53. Also see pp. 125–33 for comments on the growth of foreign banking in the UK

26 Alfred Brittain 'Proposal for Creation of Tokyo Offshore Banking Centre', English text of an article which appeared in *Kin'yū zaisei jijō* 3 November 1980, mimeo, p. 2

27 See Eric W. Hayden 'Internationalizing Japan's Financial System' *An Occasional paper on the Northeast Asia–United States Forum on International Policy* Stanford University, December 1980, pp. 24–28; Hosomi Takashi 'Tokyo IBF sōsetsu ni tsuite no Hosomi shian' *Kin'yū zaisei jijō* 24 January 1983; Ofushoa-bankingu chōsadan hōkoku *Kokusai Kin'yū sentā no genjō to tenbō* Tokyo: Kin'yū zaisei jijō kenkyūkai, 1982

28 For an introductory review of the securities industry at large see Japan Securities Research Institute *Securities Market in Japan 1977* Tokyo, 1977

29 Patrick *Finance and Economic Growth* pp. 120–21; See Tokushū: 'Atarashii tanki kin'yū shijō' *Nihon kōshasai jōhō* 8 May 1979, pp. 17–18, 33–42. In English, see Mark Borsuk 'How the *gensaki* market works' *Euromoney* May 1979, pp. 86–94. (Despite some arithmetic problems, Borsuk's article outlines the important features of the *gensaki* market)

30 See Chino Yoshitoki 'Kagi nigiru tanki kin'yū shijō no hatten' *Nihon keizai kenkyū sentā* 15 December 1982

31 The organisational structure and functional responsibilities of the bureaus within the MOF of interest in this book are set out in Appendix 3

32 One example of this was the role of city banks and long-term credit banks acting as managing underwriters for bond issues. In earlier issues in the Eurobond markets, joint participation with the securities companies was more normal. In another case, a city bank managed its own Eurobond issue. Both these activities would have been prohibited in Japan's domestic markets. See Stephen Bronte 'Japan and the Euromarkets—How the Japanese Banks Muscled in on the Security Houses' *Euromoney* November 1979, pp. 74–89; Hayden 'Internationalizing Japan's Financial System' pp. 12–13. One interesting method of following the shifts in policy is through the explanations in the yearbooks of the individual bureaus of the MOF. For example, see Ōkurashō kokusai kin'yūkyoku hen *Ōkurashō kokusai kin'yūkyoku nenpō* (annual since 1977)

33 Before 1964 the IFB's functions were incorporated in the Exchange Bureau

34 Suzuki *Money and Banking* pp. 219–20

35 Yoshio Suzuki, Monetary Control and Anti Inflation Policy, paper presented at the International Conference held on 5 and 6 August, 1981, Tokyo, p. 1

36 This was a view expressed by many interviewees in the MOF, BOJ and the banking sector. See also *Asahi shinbun* 8 October 1980 (evening edition)

37 The term 'compensatory deposit' refers to the practice where banks required a percentage of a loan to be redeposited with the bank, hence resulting in a higher effective interest rate. The practice was frowned on by the MOF

38 There have been a range of studies outlining the characteristics of the Japanese financial system. These include in English: Suzuki *Money and Banking*; OECD *Monetary Policy in Japan* Paris, December 1972; Ackerly and Ishi 'Fiscal, Monetary and Related Policies'; the special issue on the Japanese Financial System in *Japanese Economic Studies* Winter 1977–78. The most recent and controversial piece is Eisuke Sakakibara, Yūzō Harada and Robert Feldman, The Japanese Financial System in Comparative Perspective, A Study Prepared for the Use of the Joint Economic Committee, Congress of the US, 12 March 1982. Recent works in Japanese include Nihon keizai shinbunsha (ed.) *Kin'yū shisutemu* (Ronshū: Gendai no kin'yū mondai 4) Tokyo: Nihon keizai shinbunsha, 1980; Horiuchi Akiyoshi *Nihon no kin'yū seisaku* Tokyo: Tōyō keizai shinpōsha, 1980; Okumura Hirohiko et al. *50 nendai ni okeru wa ga kuni kin'yū shisutemu no tenbō* Tokyo: Nomura sōgō kenkyūjo, September 1980; and Yokoyama Akio *Gendai no kin'yū kōzō—Atarashii kin'yū riron o motomete* Tokyo: Nihon keizai shinbunsha, 1977

39 The same type of market arrangements existed a decade earlier. See Hugh T.
    Patrick 'Japan's Interest Rates and the "Grey" Financial Market' *Pacific Affairs* 38,
    3–4, pp. 326–44
40 Saitō and Tamura (eds) *Nihon ginkō* p. 127
41 Yūbin chokin ni kansuru chōsa kenkyūkai *Yūbin chokin ni kansuru chōsa kenkyūkai
    hōkokusho* Tokyo, 1980, pp. 135–41
42 The new deficit was confined to intermediate goods industries such as petroleum and
    electrical power. The processing and assembling industries remained in financial
    surplus. Plant and equipment investment levels in the latter were consistently below
    the level of retained funds. Reliance on external finance was low. The reverse was
    true in the intermediate goods industries. Whereas the ratio of interest-bearing
    liabilities to total liabilities fell steadily throughout the 1970s in the processing and
    assembly industries, the same was not true in the intermediate goods industries and
    the non-manufacturing industries. See BOJ Economic Research Department 'Re-
    cent Developments in Corporate Financing' *Special Paper No. 85* February 1980
43 For the duration of the 1970s and up to March 1981, the short-term price rate was
    the official discount rate plus 0.5 per cent. From March 1977 there has been no
    explicit obligation to follow the BOJ lead, but little actually changed. See Matsuza-
    wa Takuji 'Kin'yū rūru ni terashi seizen to jiyūka o suishin seyo' *Kin'yū zaisei jijō* 23
    August 1982. This article sets out the basic issues and represents the viewpoint of
    big city bankers. See also Kure Bunji 'Sengo no nihon sōsai (ge)' *Kin'yū to ginkō* 12
    December 1980, p. 101
44 The groups of financial institutions classed as 'banks' (city banks, regional banks,
    trust banks and long-term credit banks) had much higher diffusion rates than the
    mutual banks and credit associations during periods of both increasing and falling
    official discount rates. This could indicate the different types of borrowers that form
    the main clientele of these institutions and the associated level of competition.
45 Interviews with MOF, BOJ and banking officials during 1980–81
46 Interview with a senior BOJ official, June 1980
47 As clarification, the interest rate in the bond issue market was set by the MOF but
    this was not the case in the secondary bond market
48 See *Ginkōkyoku kin'yū nenpō* shōwa 56 nendo pp. 14ff; Saijō Nobuhiro 'shinginkōhō
    to ginkō no shōkengyōmu' *Shōken keizai gakkai nenpō* pp. 64–73; Nagata Shun'ichi
    'Shinginkōhō no shikō to ginkō gyōsei no jiyūka danryokuka' *Zaisei kin'yū tōkei
    geppō* 12.1982, No. 368, pp. 1–8

2 Government bond market

1 For two interesting and authoritative historical accounts see Gotō Shin'ichi 'Ginkōhō kaisei zen'ya'; Kōshasai hikiuke kyōkai *Nihon kōshasai shijōshi* Tokyo, 1980,
   pp. 37–125; and Nakajima Masataka *Nihon no kokusai kanri seisaku* Tokyo: Tōyō
   keizai shinpōsha, 1977, pp. 38–120. The figure for outstanding bonds includes
   domestic government bonds, local government bonds, public corporation bonds,
   bank debentures and industrial bonds
2 See for example Johnson *MITI and the Japanese Miracle*
3 In 1958 the LDP won 61.5 per cent of the seats, in 1960 it won 63.4 per cent and in
   1963 it won 60.7 per cent. The nature of economic growth was such that the
   government was not required to use deficit financing as an anticyclic fiscal tool.
   During this period the growth of income was rapid, and, by corollary, so was the
   growth of government revenue. The key constraint on economic development was
   the supply of foreign exchange. Economic downturns were induced by the
   tightening of monetary policy, particularly using the discount rate and window

guidance on the growth of loans from commercial banks to industry. The level of investment activity would quickly reaccelerate on the first indication by government that the foreign exchange bottleneck had been overcome. The underlying strength of the economy was highlighted by growth performance of over 6 per cent in real terms during the recessions of 1957–58 and 1961–62. For detailed analyses of this period, or part of it, see Hugh Patrick *Monetary Policy and Central Banking in Japan* Bombay: Bombay University Press, 1962; Ackerly and Ishi 'Fiscal, Monetary and Related Policies' and OECD *Monetary Policy in Japan*

4   At the time there were several competing positions. See M. Bronfenbrenner 'Four Positions on Japanese Finance' *Journal of Political Economy* 58, 4, 1950, pp. 281–88

5   Abe Yasuji *Ginkō-Shōken kakine ronsō oboegaki* Tokyo: Nihon keizai shinbunsha, 1980, p. 89

6   The decision to go ahead, announced formally on 27 July 1965, was important politically and economically. From a political standpoint, it was a clear statement of the Prime Minister, Satō Eisaku, that the government was continuing its support of high growth, while from an economic viewpoint, it was necessary to boost flagging confidence. In the four months after the announcement, the Stock Exchange index rose 40 per cent, indicating clearly how the market received the fiscal package.

7   For a chronology of events from May 1965 to January 1966, see Rizaikyoku kokusaika, Kokusai hakkō sankō shiryō IV, mimeo, 1966, pp. 1–57. Also see articles in the *Nihon keizai shinbun* 18 May 1965, 6 June 1965, 14–17 June 1965, 21 July 1965

8   The following analysis draws heavily on interviews with members of each managing underwriter group from 1976–80, on interviews with one long-term credit bank and officials from MOF's Financial Bureau

9   See the reports of the Committee on Financial System Research, the Fiscal System Council and the Securities and Exchange Council in Kokusai hakkō sankō shiryō IV pp. 119–53

10   ibid. p. 9

11   Kitamura Kyōji (ed.) *Kokusai* Tokyo: Kin'yū zaisei jijō kenkyūkai, 1979, p. 70. For a brief summary of other legal questions, see pp. 46–52

12   For example, *Nihon keizai shinbun* 30 July 1965. This had also been mentioned in the Committee on Financial System Research; see Kokusai hakkō sankō shiryō IV, p. 121. See also the interim report of the Fiscal System Council of 11 November 1965 in ibid. pp. 137–39

13   The position of the securities companies is set out in two documents 'Kokusai hakkō ni tsuite no iken' (11 August 1965) and 'Naikokusai hakkō ni tsuite' (27 October 1965). The position of the Federation of Bankers' Associations is set out in 'Kokusai hakkō ni kansuru iken' (2 November 1965). See Kokusai hakkō sankō shiryō IV, pp. 169–79

14   This system was really only established in the early postwar years. See Abe *Ginkō-Shōken kakine ronsō oboegaki* pp. 93–94

15   The Banking Bureau's position was reflected in the report of the CFSR, which was released on 8 November 1965. The report of the CFSR stated that it strongly favoured public underwriting in preference to underwriting by the BOJ. It argued that bonds issued by the BOJ would have an impact on effective demand which might result in unmanageable inflation, not to mention the impact that it could have on the ability of the BOJ to implement monetary policy effectively. Flotation by public underwriting would affect the availability of funds to private institutions but, as long as the government's demand for funds was kept in manageable proportions, it did not envisage this creating problems. Although the CFSR was made up mainly of businessmen, bankers, academics and usually several retired public servants, its reports were generally a close reflection of the views of the Banking Bureau.

On 11 November 1965, the SEC, also an official committee of the MOF but in this case linked closely to the Securities Bureau, issued a report on the government bonds question. It came to similar conclusions to those of the CFSR report, fully supporting the underwriting syndicate option, and arguing for the market to be operated in much the same way as existing bond markets. On the same day, a report by the Fiscal System Council (which was closely tied to the Budget Bureau) stated a similar position. It stated that the main problems with BOJ underwriting would be its impact on the confidence of the population and the damaging effect on international confidence in Japan. See Kin'yū seido chōsakai, ' "Kokusai hakkō ni tomonau kin'yū seido no arikata" ' ni kansuru tōshin' in Kokusai hakkō sankō shiryō IV, pp. 120–21; Shōken torihiki shingikai 'Kōshasai shijō no arikata kara mita kokusai hakkō no shomondai ni tsuite' in ibid. pp. 151–52; and 'Zaisei seido shingikai chūkan hōkoku' (1 November 1965) in ibid. p. 139

16 The membership of the syndicate was one issue which created considerable controversy. See ibid. pp. 94–96

17 For summaries of the yearly and monthly meetings between the floater and underwriter, 1965–70, see the Kokusai hakkō sankō shiryō, various issues (I have looked at vols. 4–14)

18 See for example Kokusai hakkō sankō shiryō 14, sono 1, pp. 37–39

19 There are several official groups related to the issue of government bonds. See Appendix 4

20 Interview with an officer of the Financial Bureau, October 1980

21 Kokusai hakkō sankō shiryō IV, p. 152

22 For example see Nakajima *Nihon no kokusai kanri seisaku* pp. 167, 173

23 At the end of fiscal 1974, the financial institutions held government bonds with a face value of 1.9 trillion yen, or 19.7 per cent of outstanding government bonds. The BOJ held 2.9 trillion yen or 30 per cent. The TFB operated in a similarly supportive way, making use of surplus funds which it derived from access to post office savings deposits. Its holding fluctuated widely, according to demand for funds through the FILP and supply of funds. At the end of fiscal 1974 it held government bonds valued at 4.1 trillion yen, or 42.7 per cent of outstanding holdings.

24 In 1972 there were some concessions made by the MOF on the secondary market development. In announcing a proposed higher volume of flotation in fiscal 1972, the MOF made slight adjustments to the underwriting shares which resulted in slightly increased shares for the mutual banks, credit associations, the Norin Chukin Bank, the life insurance and non-life insurance companies. In return, these institutions were permitted to resell their holdings (after one year) in the secondary market. Up to that time, administrative guidance by the MOF had prevented any sale in the secondary market. Concession though it was, the remainder of the financial institutions—the city banks, regional banks and long-term credit banks—which underwrote 72 per cent of bonds floated, were still not permitted to sell their holdings of government bonds on the open market, and as a result even after these concessions there was little development of the secondary market. *Kin'yū zaisei jijō* 3 April 1972, pp. 14–15

25 Interviews with two city bank officials, October 1980. See also Kitamura Kyōji 'Kokusai no tairyō hakkō to kokusai kanri seisaku' *Fainansu* August 1980, p. 36

26 Interest rates began falling in late 1975 and there was a general expectation that long-term interest rates would return to their quite stable, low levels of the 1960s. When interest rates are falling, or at least not expected to rise appreciably in the long-term, the perceived risk of holding bonds in the bond market is small. Interviews with members of the financial community indicated that expectations regarding interest rates was one reason why bankers were not so concerned over volume and the direct link between primary markets and secondary markets interest

yields. There was acute embarrassment when I asked 'Why didn't you pressure the government earlier? The answer seems to be simply that the need was not perceived

27 The reason that it was not exact was that bonds could not be traded for a period of one year in the initial period after the relaxation. The rate for a bond with nine years to maturity compared with ten years to maturity was theoretically different, although in practice it was of little relevance

28 See Kitamura 'Kokusai no tairyō hakkō to kokusai kanri seisaku' pp. 43–45

29 Kōshasai hikiuke kyōkai *Nihon kōshasai shijōshi* pp. 218ff.

30 Kitamura 'Kokusai no tairyō hakkō to kokusai kanri seisaku' pp. 28–30; Kōshasai hikiuke kyōkai *Nihon kōshasai shijōshi* pp. 351–72

31 Based on Pechman's figures in K. Kaizuka and J.E. Pechman, 'Taxation', in *Asia's New Giant* pp. 323–25. For a comparative treatment of the impact of elections on economic policy see Tufte *Political Control of the Economy*

32 With the benefit of hindsight we may well doubt the efficacy of this policy action taken by the MOF in 1974 and 1975. The oil price rises had undermined the confidence of investors. The tax reduction did little to boost confidence or promote new rounds of private expenditure (either in investment or consumption). Evidence indicates a rise in savings, and little commensurate rise in expenditures. The tax cuts may then have increased the severity of the downturn rather than alleviating it

33 William V. Rapp and Robert A. Feldman 'Japan's Economic Strategy and Prospects' in William J. Barnds (ed.) *Japan and the United States* New York: New York University Press, 1979, p. 116

34 See Campbell *Contemporary Japanese Budget Politics* pp. 111–14 for broad conclusions on budgeting in the 1960s and early 1970s

35 Kitamura (ed.), *Kokusai* pp. 47, 56–57

36 Between the House of Representatives elections in December 1976 and June 1980, the LDP did not have a working majority in the HRBC. It held 25 of the 50 positions which, after allowing for selection of chairman, was an effective minority. In the HRFC, it held the barest of majorities, holding for the most part 21 out of 40 positions. At one stage in 1979 this dropped to twenty, which after allowing for the chairman was an effective minority. See *Kokkai binran*, various issues

37 Most debate on government bonds occurred in the HRFC. For debate between 1975–79 see Kokkai shūgiin *Dai 76 kai kokkai shūgiin ōkuraiinkai giroku* (dai 3 gō, 12 November 1975; dai 4 gō, 19 November 1975; dai 5 gō, 3 December 1975); *Dai 80 kai kokkai shūgiin ōkuraiinkai giroku* (dai 17 gō, 5 April 1977; dai 18 gō, 6 April 1977, dai 19 gō, 12 April 1977; dai 20 gō, 13 April 1977; dai 21 gō, 19 April 1977); *Dai 84 kai kokkai shūgiin ōkuraiinkai giroku* (dai 24 gō, 12 April 1978; dai 25 gō, 18 April 1978; dai 26 gō, 19 April 1978); *Dai 87 kai kokkai shūgiin ōkuraiinkai giroku* (dai 12 gō, 14 March 1979; dai 13 gō, 16 March 1979; dai 14 gō, 20 March 1979)

38 *Dai 75 kai kokkai shūgiin ōkuraiinkai giroku* dai 5 gō, 3 December 1975, pp. 2–14. See esp. pp. 2–5, 13–14

39 Interview with a DSP parliamentarian, December 1980

40 *Asahi shinbun* 1 and 30 October 1982

41 A detailed assessment of the role of Minister's Secretariat needs further study. Its growing importance was alluded to in private communications with a senior Securities Bureau officer, March 1983

42 Interviews with officials of the Financial Bureau, August and October, 1980

43 Calculated as a simple mean of ratios for each issue. Based on MOF data mimeo. One case (April 1980) showed relatively little interest on the part of the underwriters. Their bids totalled about 80 per cent of the offered quantity, of which about 70 per cent was accepted by the MOF

44 The initial flotation plan called for raising 2.7 trillion yen by tender, but the revised plan reduced this level to 1.2 trillion yen. The main reduction was in three-year

issues which were cut back from a planned 1.7 trillion yen to 0.68 trillion yen

45 See *Ekonomisuto* 21 June 1983, pp. 24–38

46 See *Asahi shinbun* 19 November 1980. For summaries of the main issues, see *Nihon keizai shinbun* 17 November 1980; *Asahi shinbun* 27 October 1980, 15, 19 and 25 November 1980

47 Interview with a city bank official, October 1980

48 Views within the MOF were far from unified. One Financial Bureau source suggested that, a priori, one could not say the TFB always acted as a pro-Banking Bureau agent. It entered the market when two conditions were fulfilled together: 1 It had surplus funds (which did not always coincide with troubles in the secondary market); 2 yields were high. This statement underlines the conflict in the MOF with respect to access to funds which flow into the TFB. Interview with a Financial Bureau official, October 1980

49 See *Nihon keizai shinbun* 10 April 1979 and *Nihon kōshasai shijō* 16 April 1979, p. 8

50 *Asahi shinbun* 7 and 10 April 1979; *Nihon keizai shinbun* 8 April 1979

51 Interview with Financial Bureau official, October 1980

52 Interview with city bank official, October 1980. See also *Nihon keizai shinbun* 18 April 1980 and *Nihon kōshasai shijō* 23 April 1979, p. 5

53 Interview with a city bank official, October 1980

54 Interview with city bank official, November and December 1980. For a series on the April negotiations see *Asahi shinbun* 10, 11, 12 April 1980

55 Representing the Federation of Japanese Bankers' Associations were Seki Masahiko of Mitsui Bank and Murata Munetada of Nomura Securities Co. Ltd. See *Nihon keizai shinbun* 8 April 1980

56 Even when the government bond market went into its 'crisis phase' in the second half of 1981, the MOF maintained its hierarchy of interest rates, although the gaps between different rates fell sharply. See *Kin'yū* September 1981, p. 61

57 See Kitamura (ed.), *Kokusai* pp. 3–9, 43, 46

58 The role of the Financial Bureau also grew in the process of budget formation. This also reflected the high level of government bond issues. From the Budget summer review session within the MOF (July–September 1979), the problem of government bond issues became so acute that they began to be treated as an *independent* variable in the budgetary process.

During at least the first twelve years of bond issuing, the level of national bonds was a *dependent* variable in budget negotiations. Preliminary estimates for the budget were made by the Tax and Budget Bureaus respectively, and by the time of the presentation of firmer estimates, these two bureaus had come to some agreement on the estimate for the following year's bond flotation program. The program was subsequently entrusted to the Financial Bureau for fulfilment. In short, budgetary conditions (including the impact of the rather frequent downward adjustment in tax) determined the quantity of bonds that were issued. Throughout this period there was a predisposition within the government to minimise the debt burden, and in this it was by and large successful. The job of the Financial Bureau was a relatively straightforward one: it simply ensured that the required quantity was issued. Compared with its role in recent years, the function of the Financial Bureau, and in particular of its Government Debt Division, was relatively passive. Its role as sole negotiator with the underwriting group was, at it remains today, its home territory. Outside this narrow precinct, its function was more that of an 'implementor' than a decisionmaker. In the period before the 1973 oil crisis, long-term interest rates were very stable. Long-term government bond rates fluctuated between 6.717 per cent and 7.189 per cent—a mere 0.472 percentage points. The picture was similar to all other government-controlled areas.

The advent of the oil crisis and the period of adjustment to new economic realities left a large savings–investment gap, which the government attempted to fill with a public works program. National bonds were used to finance that program. For reasons outlined earlier, the volume of national bonds issued grew sharply from 1975. This sharp growth seems to have had a major impact on the process of deciding the volume of bonds to be issued in a given year. This new trend can be thought of as the movement of national bonds from the position of a *dependent* variable to that of an *independent* variable in the budgetary process. There have been two factors behind this development.

First, the Government Debt Division itself adopted a more positive stance towards its role in the determination of annual flotation volumes. From 1979, the Government Debt Division formulated estimates of expected market capacity for the following fiscal year. These estimates were then fed into budget negotiations. Although the accuracy of these estimates (which are prepared with the assistance of the BOJ) were subject to wide margins of error, they were at least an attempt to consider the ability of the market to raise the funds required to fulfil expenditure plans.

Second, the market itself has begun exerting an independent influence on the estimation of yearly volume. In a free market we could argue that the floater has reached its limit when the yields demanded by the market begin to lose their 'normal' relationships with other interest rates, and require consistently higher yields to satisfy a given demand. The volume itself may vary considerably according to availability of funds, the extent of competing demands (such as the level of private demand for funds) and some assessment of expected future prospects. The fact that the market reached this limit caused an increase in the instability in the government bond market and the growing realisation that all other markets would be likewise affected. This change from dependent variable status to independent variable status was a manifestation of the degree of alarm caused by the government bond problem

59   The securities companies' shares in the government bond underwriting syndicate were: 6.8 per cent (fiscal 1975), 15.8 per cent (fiscal 1976), 24.1 per cent (fiscal 1977), 19.4 per cent (fiscal 1978), 11.4 per cent (fiscal 1979) and 25.2 per cent (fiscal 1980). Source: *Kin'yū* January 1982, p. 72

60   Interview with a city bank official, October 1980

3   Establishment of the CDs market

1   Matsushita Takashi 'Jōtosei yokin (CD) wa doko made ureru ka' *Nikkei kōshasai shijō* 8 May 1979, p. 10. Figures differ between sources. See also 'CD dōnyū-go no tanki kin'yū shijō' *Sumitomo ginkō keizai geppō* September and October 1979, p. 12; M. Craig *The Sterling Money Markets* London: Gower Press, 1976

2   *Nihon keizai shinbun* 6 February 1967

3   'Chūshō kigyō kin'yū seido no arikata ni tsuite' in Kin'yū seido kenkyūkai hen *Futsū ginkō no arikata to ginkō seido no kaisei* pp. 462–71

4   See 'Ippan minkan kin'yū kikan no arikata nado ni tsuite' in ibid. pp. 472–87. See also Kin'yū seido kenkyūkai hen (Ōkurashō ginkōkyokunai) *Kin'yū seido chōsakai shiryō* (vol. 4)—*Futsū ginkō seido—Bōeki kin'yū* Tokyo, 1970

5   Kin'yū seido kenkyūkai hen *Futsū ginkō no arikata to ginkō seido no kaisei* p. 480

6   Kin'yū seido kenkyūkai hen *Kin'yū seido chōsakai shiryō* pp. 342–43, 348

7   *Nihon keizai shinbun* 1 July 1968; *Asahi shinbun* 2 September 1968

8   Total deposits are defined as deposits of 'All Banks' (city banks + regional banks + long-term credit banks + trust banks) + mutual banks + credit associations + postal savings system

9   Tokuda Hiromi 'Kin'yū seido chōsakai tōshin o megutte' *Fainansu* 6, 5, 1970, pp. 3–4

10   Interview with a former Banking Bureau official, July 1980

11   While most interviewees used the word 'premature' (*shōsō*), one said that the problem was not prematurity but that CDs represented too much of a challenge to the system, since at that time discussions centred around US- and UK-type CDs. This is consistent with the explanation offered here. Items such as long-term fixed deposits which did not upset the balance of the financial system were introduced with the minimum of fuss. Interview with a banker, June 1980

12   'Kaigai ni okeru hōgin no CD hakkō' in *Ōkurashō ginkōkyoku kin'yū nenpō* 48 nenban, pp. 32–33

13   'Tokushū: Kaigai de jitsugen shita CD hakkō' *Kin'yū zaisei jijō* 4 September 1972, pp. 30–36

14   'Hōgin rondon shiten no CD hakkō o jiyūka' *Kin'yū zaisei jijō* 13 November 1972, p. 10; *Nihon keizai shinbun* 20 November 1972, 6 December 1972

15   'Sumitomo, togin ga gaika date CD hakkō o shinsei' *Kin'yū zaisei jijō* 5 June 1972, pp. 11–12. See also *Nihon keizai shinbun* 29 May 1972, 25 August 1972

16   *Nihon keizai shinbun* 12 May 1975

17   Ken'ichi Ishigaki and Masahiro Fujita 'The Development of International Business by Japanese Banks' *Australia–Japan Research Centre Research Paper No. 86* August 1981

18   Kin'yū seido kenkyūkai hen *Futsū ginkō no arikata to ginkō seido no kaisei* p. 1

19   It was to examine the relationship between the financial sector and the economy; to look at the role of banks in this relationship; to look at the role of banks in distributing capital; to examine the principles of bank management; to investigate the problems with the range of services offered by banks; to examine the need for developing the scope of banking business and to reassess the supervision requirements for banks. ibid. pp. 1–2. The main body of the 1979 report appears on pp. 1–219

20   As its first task, the FPRG was asked by Tokuda to examine three themes: the future of the financial institutions given the changes in the underlying economic environment; the social and public responsibility of banks; and the potential areas into which banking might expand. The third theme occupied the FPRG for six sessions (sessions nine to fourteen, from December 1977 to April 1978). During this period, issues relating to disclosure, the future of banking business abroad, the sale of government bonds at bank windows and the introduction of new deposit types were discussed. The CDs question was included in this last category, and attention here is confined to this narrow issue. See Kin'yū kenkyūkai hen *Kongo ni okeru wa ga kuni no kin'yū kikan no arikata—kin'yū mondai kenkyūkai no hōkoku naiyō* Tokyo, 1978

21   Non-official committees like the FPRG had existed in other bureaus for some time, so the Banking Bureau was not breaking new ground. See 'Ginkōkyoku ni mo "Kin'yū seisaku kenkyūkai"' *Kin'yū zaisei jijō* 16 May 1977, pp. 10–11. For impressions of the first set of meetings of the FPRG by its chairman, Itō Mitsuharu of Chiba University see 'Kakine o sagete "tokusei" ni yoru tokka o sokushin' *Kin'yū zaisei jijō* 5 June 1978, p. 17

22   Kin'yū kenkyūkai hen *Kongo ni okeru wa ga kuni no kin'yū kikan no arikata* pp. 260–69

23   See Tachi Ryūichirō 'Keizai gakusha no sekinin' *Kin'yū zaisei jijō* 3 July 1978. This comment by Tachi might have included a touch of sour grapes. Tachi was a member of the CFSR and later the subcommittee and CDs Discussion Group. For another view, see Kure Bunji 'Kin'yū mondai kenkyūkai hōkokusho o yonde' *Kin'yū zaisei jijō* 19 June 1978

24   Attitudes of some of the participants in the FPRG are included in a series of articles

on the group's first report. The articles include comments by the head of the group, Professor Itō Mitsuharu, of Chiba University, by a representative of the group, Professor Kaizuka Keimei, of Tokyo University, by the director-general of the Banking Bureau, Tokuda Hiromi, and finally by a member of the Banking Bureau, Noda Minoru. See 'Tokushū: Kin'yū mondai kenkyūkai hōkoku' *Kin'yū zaisei jijō* 5 June 1978

25 A brief summary of each meeting can be found in *Kin'yū zaisei jijō* 1 May 1978, pp. 20–22; 22 May 1978, pp. 14–16; 12 June 1978, pp. 12–14; 19 June 1978, pp. 14–16; 3 July 1978, p. 21; 17 July 1978, p. 41; 24 July 1978, p. 27; and 31 July 1978, pp. 12–13

26 Kin'yū kenkyūkai hen, *Kongo ni okeru wa ga kuni no kin'yū kikan no arikata* pp. 63–64, 260–61

27 ibid. pp. 95–97

28 ibid. pp. 75–76, 261–62

29 For example, see Wakatsuki Haruhiko 'CD dōnyu wa "kyōsha no ronri" no sen'ō de wa nai no ka' *Kin'yū zaisei jijō* 17 July 1978, pp. 28–33

30 This type of statement was made on several occasions by regional bankers in interviews in May and November 1980

31 Kin'yū seido kenkyūkai hen *Futsū ginkō no arikata to ginkō seido no kaisei* pp. 201–3

32 Kōshasai hikiuke kyōkai, CD mondai ni hansuru shōkenkai no iken (an), 20 July 1978, mimeo 10 pages

33 ibid. pp. 6, 9–10

34 In a press conference on 6 September 1978, the governor of the BOJ, Morinaga Teiichirō, stressed the importance of deregulated interest rates. See *Nihon keizai shinbun* 7 September 1978

35 Kin'yū seido kenkyūkai hen *Futsū ginkō no arikata to ginko seido no kaisei* pp. 203–8

36 The fear that introduction of CDs would lead to increased interest rates was also expressed by other opponents at the FPRG, including the representative of the trust banks and Kurozumi Takashi from *Eiken Kagaku*, representing small and medium-sized industry. See Kin'yū seido kenkyūkai hen *Futsū ginkō no arikata to ginkō seido no kaisei* pp. 94, 206–7

37 *Kin'yū zaisei jijō* 2 October 1978, p. 10

38 'CD dōnyū no engun? Ec kurofune raishū no gaiatsu? *Kin'yū zaisei jijō* 22 May 1978; *Nihon keizai shinbun* 10 May 1978; *Oriental Economist* July 1978, pp. 6–10

39 Rarely was the role of foreign banks mentioned in interviews, unless promoted. One key participant dismissed their role as 'amari nakatta' ('not much at all'). Interview with a former Banking Bureau officer, July 1980

40 These are not necessarily accurate reflections of overall profitability, but nevertheless represent a large proportion of bank business. Taken from BOJ calculations in its *Economic Statistic Annual*, various editions, from table entitled 'Income & Expenses of Ordinary Banks' e.g. pp. 150–1 of 1980 edn

41 The distinction between publicly stated reasons (tatemae) and actual reasons (honne) was first brought to my attention by an early interview with an officer of the BOJ. In subsequent interviews with MOF officers who participated in the actual decisionmaking process this idea was reinforced. Interviews began with the expression of published reasons before moving sometimes (not always) to actual reasons

42 *Kin'yū zaisei jijō* 31 July 1978, p. 13

43 *Kin'yū zaisei jijō* 18 September 1978, pp. 12–13

44 'Shiji sareta shin-kin'yū koritsuka no hōkō', interview with Tokuda Hiromi, *Kin'yū zaisei jijō* 5 June 1978, pp. 24–25

45 Interview with an officer of the Banking Bureau, June 1980

46 Interviews with two officers of the Banking Bureau, May and June 1980

47 'CD kondankai de no kentō mo hakkō e no tetsuzuki' *Kin'yū zaisei jijō* 2 October 1978, pp. 10–11
48 Interview with a former Banking Bureau official, January 1981
49 Interviews with a member of the CFSR, January 1981; and three officials of the BOJ, June 1980
50 Interview with a member of the CFSR, January 1981; interview with a former Banking Bureau official, January 1981
51 'CD kondankai de no kentō mo hakkō e no tetsuzuki'
52 Interview with a member of the CFSR, January 1981
53 These differences were more of law than of use. See Matsushita 'Jōtosei yokin(CD) wa doko made ureru ka'; and 'CD dōnyū-go no tanki kin'yū shijō' p. 12
54 *Nihon keizai shinbun* 1 and 9 December 1978
55 Interview with an official of the BOJ, June 1980
56 *Nihon keizai shinbun* 7 September 1978, 8 December 1978; and 'CD hakkō de kyōsō honban ni hairu kin'yūkai' *Kin'yū zaisei jijō* 15 January 1979. In the final report of the Committee on Financial System Research of 27 December 1978, four reasons were given for the introduction of CDs:

1 to promote the liberalisation of interest rates and hence improve the efficiency of monetary policy;
2 to deepen and develop the short-term capital markets;
3 to widen the limit of banking business and extend the level of participation of foreign banks in the Japanese financial system as a means of promoting internationalisation;
4 to respond to widening asset selection demands of business.

See Kin'yū seido kenkyūkai hen *Futsū ginkō no arikata to ginkō seido no kaisei* pp. 28–29
After the issuing of this statement it was up to the MOF to finalise details. The concrete plan itself was finalised in the CDs Discussion Group. The trading procedures were developed by the Fuji Bank, which in 1978 was the secretariat bank for the Federation of Bankers' Associations. On 15 March 1979, MOF requested the Policy Board of the BOJ to exempt CDs from Temporary Interest Rate Law Legislation. On 16 March 1979, this was considered by the Temporary Interest Rate Council. A notification was issued by the Banking Bureau on 30 March setting out formally the details for CDs. On the same day cabinet orders and other legislative amendments were carried out. Interview with a Banking Bureau officer, June 1980. Even at the December CFSR meeting and after it dissent from the outcome was expressed, even though such dissent was ineffectual. The city banks were not satisfied in all their demands, even though they had a few real grounds for complaint
57 It became operational again when Miyamoto became director-general
58 Ryutaro Komiya and Kozo Yamamoto, The Officer in Charge of Economic Affairs in the Japanese Government, revised mimeo, August 1979, pp. 16–19. In this article the role of consensus is stressed with little attention being paid to conflict. More will be said of this in chapter 7
59 See Fujiwara Sakuya 'Shin-ginkō kyokuchō—Yonesato Hiroshi' *Kin'yū to ginkō* 1 August 1979, pp. 74–77; 'Yonesato ginkō gyōsei o hihan suru' *Kin'yū to ginkō* 18 April 1980, pp. 32–35. See also Abe *Ginkō shōken kakine ronsō oboegaki*; and Kakuma Takashi *Ōkurashō ginkōkyoku* Kyoto: PHP kenkyūjo, 1979
60 Interviews with officials of the Banking Bureau and city bankers
61 Fujiwara 'Shin-ginkō kyokuchō'; and 'Yonesato ginkō gyōsei o hihan suru'; also interviews with one JSP and one DSP politician

4 The issue of trading in government bonds

1 The terms *dīringu* and *madoguchi hanbai* are often applied to these areas respectively. In short, the problem is called the *madohan* ('window sales') problem, despite the fact that the most important aspect is bank dealing

2 *Kin'yū zaisei jijō* 12 April 1982

3 Abe *Ginkō-Shōken kakine ronsō oboegaki* pp. 51–62

4 Rizaikyoku sōmuka, Rizaikyoku chōsa kikaku shiryō 2, mimeo, July 1966, pp. 207–8; Rizaikyoku kokusaika, Kokusai hakkō sankō shiryō 4, mimeo, 1966, p. 85. A feeling for the environment in 1965 was obtained in several interviews

5 Abe *Ginkō-Shōken kakine ronsō oboegaki*, pp. 107-9. The range of laws applying and the contradictions are briefly explained. See Kōshasai hikiuke kyōkai *Nihon kōshasai shijōshi*; and Rizaikyoku sōmuka, Rizaikyoku chōsa kikaku shiryō 2, for different examinations of the period

6 In a meeting of the City Banks Discussion Group in July 1972, the four largest city banks favoured a change in the existing regulations, but the smaller the banks were, the more negative the comments. A comment by a middle-sized city bank was typical: 'wouldn't it be best to see how the post office went first' or in other words the small banks wanted the public sector to test the market and profitability. If the market's viability was proven the banks were prepared to become involved. The initiative of the larger banks quickly fizzled out. 'Kokusai madoguchi hanbai o meguru ginkō, shōken naibu jijō' *Kin'yū zaisei jijō* 17 July 1972 in Kin'yū zaisei jijō kenkyūkai *Sengo kin'yū zaisei uramenshi* Tokyo: Kin'yū zaisei, 1980, pp. 502–7. See also Zenkoku ginkō kyōkai rengōkai *Ginkō kyōkai 30 nenshi* Tokyo, 1979, pp. 89–90

7 Interviews with a former Banking Bureau official, January 1981

8 ibid. See also 'Fukaku shizuka ni senkō suru ginkō no kokusai madohan sakusen' *Kin'yū zaisei jijō* 19 December 1977; *Nihon keizai shinbun* 30 August 1976, 15 and 29 September 1976, 2 October 1976, evening edns

9 The biggest banks, the city banks, did not have a formal association although they did have an informal discussion group called the City Banks Discussion Group. In the late 1970s it became more active, although there was little recorded publicly about its functions. Its main aim was to promote free exchanges of views. The different interests which were present within even this group limited its effectiveness. Interview with two city bankers, May 1980 and June 1980

10 For a general introduction see Sei Hiizu *Shōkengyōkai* (Sangyōkai shirīzu No. 112) Tokyo: Kyōikusha, 1979

11 Toshi ginkō konwakai ikensho, Kokusai no madoguchi hanbai ni tsuite no kangaekata, mimeo, 21 December 1977

12 Nakajima Masataka *Nihon no kokusai kanri seisaku* Tokyo: Tōyō keizai shinpōsha, 1977, pp. 3–4, 175, 188–93

13 'Fukaku shizuka ni senkō suru ginkō no kokusai madohan sakusen'. Also see *Nihon keizai shinbun* 3, 4, 6 and 7 December 1977

14 *Nihon keizai shinbun*, 6 and 26 December 1977, 15 January 1978. Interview with former Banking Bureau official, January 1981

15 Kin'yū seido kenkyūkai *Futsū ginkō no arikata to ginkō seido no kaisei* Tokyo: Kin'yū zaisei, 1979, pp. 7–10

16 'Shōken seido kara no mittsu no mondaiten' *Ginkō to kin'yū* 1 August 1979, pp. 16–18

17 For example see the comment made by one committee member that the reports had been completed before they came to the committees for final assent. 'Shingikai no arikataron no sozai to naru "kokusai madohan" ' *Kin'yū zaisei jijō* 9 July 1979, pp. 10–11

18 Yamauchi shōkengyō kyōkai kaichō and Kikui kōshasai hikiuke kyōkai kaichō,

Yōbōsho, to Minister of Finance, summary, mimeo, 20 November 1979

19 Togin konwakai, Yōbōsho, to director-general, Banking Bureau, mimeo, 14 December 1979

20 Interview with official of a securities company, October 1980. See also *Nihon keizai shinbun* 16 January 1981

21 'Jikangire chikazuku ginkōkyoku vs togin rengō kessen' *Kin'yū zaisei jijō* 16 February 1981, p. 11

22 Nihon shōkengyō kyōkai, Ginkō ni yoru kokusai nado no madoguchi hanbai oyobi dīringu ni tsuite, October 1970, mimeo, 9 pages

23 Comparisons made in ibid. p. 2

24 To be sure the outcome is problematic. It really depends on the extent that the securities companies attempted to ensure price stability on the one hand and to exercise their oligopolistic market power on the other hand

25 In an interview with a research officer of a large securities company, the comment was made that the general feeling in the research group was that the economic argument was weak, and not likely to succeed. The research group, it should be noted, was more inclined to push positively for change and not to defend the status quo. The arguments promoted in the government bond case, he believed, were for the consumption of politicians and not solid economic arguments. Interview with an official of a large securities company, July 1980

26 The securities companies were known for their skill in laundering money and for passing on inside information on shares to politicians. The phrase 'laundering' is not mine but that used by an official of a long-term credit bank who suggested corruption in the links between securities companies and politicians was a topic worth serious research. Interview with an official of a long-term credit bank, August 1980. Similar comments were also made by two politicians

27 These relationships were almost accepted truths, although it is embarrassingly difficult to give quantitative evidence. Contributions of small banks to individual political candidates is one form of fund movement, whereas in large banks the funds tend to move to public funds of political organisations. In 1979 the thirteen city banks contributed 727 million yen to the LDP, compared with 378 million yen from the 63 regional banks and 267 million yen from the securities companies. The city banks' contribution was about 5 per cent of the public funds declared by the LDP. In contrast, the flow of non-public funds and services received from small regional and mutual banks was of considerable importance

28 This was the impression gained from interviews. At least, it was very apparent that Mitsubishi felt the discussions had been inadequate

29 *Kin'yū zaisei jijō* 27 April 1981, pp. 10–11

30 *Asahi shinbun* 20 November 1980 and 6 December 1980; see also 'Ginkōhō no zenmen kaisei ni tsuite (jō)' *Kin'yū* June 1981, p. 15

31 *Asahi shinbun* 13 December 1980; *Nihon keizai shinbun* 18 December 1980

32 The financial sector (including city and regional banks, securities companies and insurance companies) supplied approximately 19 per cent of contributions from political organisations in the LDP in 1979. Contributions from political organisations made up about 70 per cent of the LDP's income. See Hirose Michisada *Hojokin to seikentō* Tokyo: Asahi shinbunsha, 1981, p. 239 and *Jijō no ugoki* Tokyo, October 1980, p. 5

33 *Nihon keizai shinbun* 18 December 1980

34 *Asahi shinbun* 25 December 1980; *Nihon keizai shinbun* 31 December 1980

35 *Nihon keizai shinbun* 11 and 14 January 1981

36 The banks were represented by Yamada Hajime (president of Mitsubishi Bank), Yoshikuni Jirō (president of Yokohama Bank) and Ikeura Kisaburō (president of the Industrial Bank of Japan). *Nihon keizai shinbun* 21 February 1981

37 *Nihon keizai shinbun* 17 February 1981, evening edn
38 *Nihon keizai shinbun* 10 March 1981, 8, 15 and 21 April 1981
39 Interview with PARC research officer, February 1981
40 *Kin'yū zaisei jijō* 27 April 1981
41 The three LDP parliamentarians, including one former banker, interviewed during the proceedings of the Joint Committee stated that support was small. According to one interviewee, despite the linkage at the general level, LDP politicians were sceptical of the bona fides of city banks. This view was echoed in many discussions with bankers who saw the relationship between city banks and the LDP as quite distant, although workable, and the relationship between smaller banks and the LDP much closer. This issue is taken up in chapter 8
42 For example, underwriting of government bonds by securities companies dropped from 24.8 per cent in fiscal 1978 (2.6 trillion yen) to 13.2 per cent (1.8 trillion yen) in fiscal 1979
43 This was the unanimous view of those politicians and research workers in political parties who were interviewed in late 1980 to early 1981
44 'Ginkōhō no zenmen kaisei ni tsuite (chū)' *Kin'yū* July 1981, p. 27–28
45 For example 'Jikangire chikazuku ginkōkyoku vs togin rengō kessen'

5 Postal savings system

1 The FILP was often called the Second Budget because of its size. It was used as a method of financing public works expenditures, particularly industry-oriented expenditures in the 1950s and 1960s, which did not require the consent of the Diet. Throughout the period 1960–80, welfare items grew in importance. Whereas in fiscal 1960 housing accounted for 12.8 per cent of funds allocated, by fiscal 1980 it was planned to spend 25.6 per cent of funds in this area. Over these two decades the size of the fund grew 30-fold. See Noguchi Yukio *Zaisei kiki no kōzō* Tokyo: Tōyō keizai shinpōsha, 1980. If there is a weakness in Campbell's *Contemporary Japanese Budget Politics*, it is his failure to examine adequately the FILP
2 The MPT was responsible for a wide range of activities beyond the postal savings system. See Kyōikusha hen *Yūseishō Gyōsei kikō shirīzu* No. 110, Tokyo: Kyōikusha, 1979
3 See Yūbin chokin ni kansuru chōsa kenkyūkai *Yūbin chokin ni kansuru chōsa kenkyūkai hōkokusho* Tokyo, 1980, pp. 294–96 for the key clauses
4 ibid. p. 295, Article 12
5 Article 12.2 of the Postal Savings Law reads: 'when altering the postal savings interest rates the Minister of Posts and Telecommunications should take into account that the postal savings system was designed as a simple means of safeguarding the savings of the small depositer, should pay attention to promoting saving in the public interest, and should also consider the interest rates of other financial institutions.' ibid. p. 295. See also Heiwa keizai keikaku kaigi *Yūbin chokin jigyō no mondaiten to tenbō* Tokyo, 1980, pp. 20–22
6 The gap between the growth in household income and the growth in CPI fell from 3.8 per cent in the 1960s to 1.8 per cent in 1970s. Calculation using 'Worker Households' in BOJ *Economic Statistics Annual*, various issues
7 For example between 1960 and 1970 the postal savings rate (using the interest rate for fixed quantity deposits) was altered on one occasion whereas the official discount rate was altered sixteen times
8 When interest rates on bank deposits were increased, postal savings interest rates also rose. In the decade between April 1970 and September 1980, deposit interest rates were increased on eleven occasions. On ten occasions they were altered

simultaneously throughout the financial system, and on the eleventh, in July 1973, the postal savings rate was increased first

9   Interview with an officer of the Postal Savings Bureau, MPT, March 1981

10 See *Nihon keizai shinbun* 31 August 1969; 9, 10 and 28 October 1970; 7, 8, 14 and 20 January 1971; 7, 8 and 9 April 1971; *Kin'yū zaisei jijō* 8 January 1971, 18 January 1971, 19 July 1971, 26 July 1971

11 The official discount rate fell from 6.25 per cent in October 1970 to 4.75 in December 1971. The average city bank lending rate fell from 7.545 in the second half of fiscal 1970 to 7.154 in the second half of fiscal 1971 or only 26 per cent of the fall in the official discount rate. Banks were reluctant to let their profit margins decline. One of the problems of further falls in the official discount rate without a fall in the savings rate, emphasised by the governor of the BOJ, was the impact on the profitability and management of small financial institutions. See *Kin'yū zaisei jijō* 27 September 1971 and 11 October 1971

12 *Asahi shinbun* 4 December 1971; *Nihon keizai shinbun* 20 and 24 December 1971, 21 December 1971, evening edn; Takiya Yuki (ed.) *Rekidai yūsei daijin kaikoroku* vol. 5. Tokyo: Kyōdō tsūshinsha, 1974, pp. 140–41

13 ibid. pp. 141–42

14 On the day before the fall in the official discount rate, Mizuta and Hirose discussed the matter on the telephone. At a high-level MPT conference (*Shōgi*) on the same day, it was decided not to change the postal savings rate. *Asahi shinbun* 23 December 1971. See also *Nihon keizai shinbun* 14 April 1972

15 Takiya (ed.) *Rekidai yūsei daijin kaikoroku* vol. 5, pp. 142–43

16 When the initial plan was announced on 8 February 1972, it was met by strong bureaucratic opposition from the MOF and the MAFF. Both ministries argued that the widening of the postal savings system into lending functions would adversely affect the operations of established banking and agricultural institutions under their respective managements. Despite this opposition from two of the most powerful ministries within the public service, the scheme was introduced with the support of LDP and opposition parliamentarians. Within the LDP alone, 290 Diet members belonged to a group established specifically to support the measure. Privately, even the Minister of Agriculture, Fisheries and Forestry, Akagi Munenori, supported the measure. ibid. pp. 143–49

17 According to one interviewee, in the BOJ and in outside academic circles there was some discussion favouring an early tightening of monetary policy. Interview with a BOJ official, June 1980

18 *Nihon keizai shinbun* 11 and 26 May 1972. Also see comments on the leadership of Governor Sasaki during the incident, in Kure Bunji 'Sengo no nichigin sōsai' *Kin'yū to ginkō* 12 December 1980, pp. 91–95

19 *Kin'yū zaisei jijō* 17 January 1977, pp. 10–11

20 *Nihon keizai shinbun* 9 January 1977, 6 January 1977, evening edn

21 *Asahi shinbun* 14 January 1977; *Nihon keizai shinbun*, 19 January 1977

22 During the tenure of the Fukuda Cabinet, the LDP held 25 of the 50 positions on the House of Representatives Budget Committee. Under the system of selection of committees, the government requires considerably more than half of the elected members to achieve majorities in all the committees. For an explanation of this point see J.A.A. Stockwin, *Divided Politics in a Growth Economy*, 2nd edn, London: Wiedenfeld and Nicolson, 1982, p. 95

23 As it was, the budget was amended against the government's wishes. Taxes were reduced by 300 billion yen.

24 *Nihon keizai shinbun*, 14 January 1977, evening edn, 10 February 1977, evening edn; *Asahi shinbun* 13 and 25 February, 1977

25 The concern showed the importance attached to the short-term economic outlook

figures. The release of the figures on 4 March 1977 was followed a week later, on 11 March 1977, by the formal decision to reduce the official discount rate. For a good summary of the main events from January to March 1977 see 'Seisaku kidōsei ubatta sanken bunritsu' *Kin'yū to ginkō* 28 April 1977, pp. 6–11

26   *Nihon keizai shinbun* 14 April 1977, evening edn, 16 April 1977; *Asahi shinbun* 14 and 15 April 1977

27   Although the decision to lower the postal savings rate went off without incident, a minority of members of PTAC did draw attention to the high level of inflation and added several conditions to the final decision. See *Asahi shinbun* 11 May 1977

28   Following the July 1977 elections, the LDP representation in the House of Councillors fell from 126 out of 249 to 124 out of 251. With the addition of independents it retained a slender majority

29   Interview with an official of the Postal Savings Bureau, MPT, January 1981

30   *Nihon keizai shinbun* 17 and 25 May 1972, 19 May 1972, evening edn. See also *Nihon keizai shinbun* 26 September 1975

31   Gurūpu Q. 'Ōkura vs yūsei—jinginaki yūcho sensō' *Gendai* June 1981, pp. 273–74. The entire article provides an interesting account of the conflict between the MOF and the MPT

32   See speech by the director-general of the Banking Bureau in the House of Councillors Finance Committee debate on 26 May 1981, in *Kin'yū* July 1981, pp. 49–50

33   Suzuki *Money and Banking* p. 177

34   Interview with a senior BOJ official, April 1981

35   See Suzuki 'Monetary Control'

36   See *Kin'yū* June 1981, p. 79

37   *Kin'yū to ginkō* 28 April 1977, pp. 7, 10

38   *Kin'yū* June 1981, p. 69

39   At the end of fiscal 1979, approximately 96 trillion yen was held in tax-free accounts of banks while 52 trillion yen (the total of outstanding deposits) was held in the postal savings system. Since 1971 there was also an increasing proportion of individual savings held in the non-tax framework. See *Kin'yū zaisei jijō*, 29 September 1980, pp. 18–19

40   There are four main trade union organisations in Japan, with the General Council of Japanese Trade Unions (membership 4.55 million) being the largest by far. In 1980, 68 per cent of its supporters were public servants. Other organisations include: Japan Confederation of Labor (*Dōmei*) with strong links with the DSP, and predominantly private enterprise (93 per cent) membership of 2.16 million; Metal Workers Federation (*Kinzoku rōkyō*); Federation of Independent Unions (*Chūritsu rōren*) and National Federation of Industrial Unions (*Shinsanbetsu*). Total union membership in 1980 was 12.37 million. Kokumin seiji nenkan henshūiinkai hen *Kokumin seiji nenkan 1981* Nihon shakaitō chūō honbu kikanshikyoku, pp. 935–36. See also Yamaguchi, A. and Sugimori, K. *Rōkumi giin ga shakaitō o sashita* Tokyo: Nisshin hōdō, 1980

41   Gerald L. Curtis *Election Campaigning Japanese Style* New York: Columbia University Press, 1971, pp. 179–210

42   Herbert Passin 'The House of Councillors: Promise and Achievement' in Michael K. Blaker (ed.) *Japan at the Polls* Washington: American Enterprise Institute, 1976, pp. 32–3

43   Aurelia D. George, The Strategies of Influence: Japan's Agricultural Co-operatives (Nōkyo) as a Pressure Group, unpublished PhD thesis, Australian National University, Canberra, 1980, pp. 230–34

44   Interview with LDP parliamentarian, April 1981

45   George, The Strategies of Influence, p. 403. See also Aurelia D. George 'The

Japanese Farm Lobby and Agricultural Policy-Making' *Pacific Affairs* 54, 3, Fall 1981, pp. 409–430. The problem of defining what constitutes a support group member makes effective comparison difficult. However, one could logically expect the agriculturally based support groups to have a more limited upper membership than groups supporting the post office. In the case of agriculture, there are many Diet members from urban constituencies who oppose increased agricultural protection. In the case of the post office, the group opposing the MPT is predominantly that group which began their careers in the MOF—a group of 30–40 Diet members. It was only in 1980 that the banking associations began attempting to establish a political presence as groups of electoral significance, rather than as groups within the financial community.

46   See note 16

47   See Itō Daiichi *Gendai nihon kanryōsei no bunseki* Tokyo: Tokyo daigaku shup-pankai, 1980, pp. 272ff.

48   Interview with an officer of the Financial Bureau, January 1981

49   Interview with a research officer of PARC, February 1981

50   Interview with LDP parliamentarian, February 1981; interview with an officer of the MPT, January 1981. Although termed a neutral committee by the MOF, examination of the membership shows that the type of report that could have been expected was largely defined by the membership. The five-man committee included former Professor of Economics at Tokyo University, Arisawa Hiromi; well-known free marketeer and president of *Nihon keizai shinbunsha*, Enjōji Jirō; the head of the Japan Economic Research Centre, Ōkita Saburō; a well-known economic analyst and chairman of *Sōgō seisaku kenkyūkai*, Tsuchiya Kiyoshi; and Yoshikuni Ichirō, the president of the Regional Promotion and Facilities Corporation. Tokushū: 'Yūchokon "Tōshin" zenbun' *Kin'yū zaisei jijō* 31 August 1981, pp. 25–35. For commentary on the report see *Kin'yū zaisei jijō* 14 September 1981

51   Tokushū: 'Yūchokon "Tōshin" zenbun' p. 27

52   It covered itself in a sense with the argument that the depositors were part of the economy and what was good for the economy must be good for them. The argument might have had substance in the 1960s when high real rates of income growth were being achieved, but it had little in the late 1970s and early 1980s when real income growth was non-existent. ibid. p. 28

53   A group within PARC's Subcommittee on Communications examining Basic Problems of the Postal Savings System suggested that the argument of 'equal footing' should not only refer to instances where the private sector financial institutions were disadvantaged but also to cases where the range of services offered by the postal savings system was restricted. For example, the inability of the MPT to secure a market rate of return on postal savings deprives the postal savings system of revenue amounting to 200 billion yen per year. If this inequity were corrected the apparent deficits in the accounts of the postal savings system would become surplus. See Jiyūminshutō seimu chōsakai tsūshin bukai yūbin chokin kihon mondai shōiinkai 'Kokumin no tachiba kara kangaeta kore kara no yūbin chokin' *Kin'yū* June 1981, pp. 82–3

54   Tokushū: 'Yūchokon "Tōshin" zenbun' p. 33

55   'Seiiki kara seiiki e yūchokon tōshin no yukue wa ...' *Kin'yū zaisei jijō* 31 August 1981, pp. 10–11. See also *Kin'yū zaisei jijō* 7 September 1981, p. 6

56   The proceedings of the Diet debates were reproduced by the Federation of Bankers' Associations in Zenkoku ginkō kyōkai rengōkai, Gurīn kādo seido ni kansuru kokkai rongi, mimeo, September 1980. This booklet contains debates that appeared in *Kin'yū* between May and September 1980

57   Kin'yū mondai kenkyūkai hen *Yūcho tai ginkō sensō* Tokyo: Yell Books, 1977, p. 78. (This is not connected with the FPRG of the Banking Bureau.) Yūbin chokin ni

kansuru chōsa kenkyūkai *Yūbin chokin ni kansuru chōsa kenkyūkai hōkokusho* Tokyo, 1980, p. 257

58 While there were no denials of this, few actually stated it positively, but rather put the 'Abe line' (explained in the text below). Also see *Asahi shinbun* 17 February 1981, 14 March 1981; and *Nihon keizai shinbun* 17 April 1981

59 Yūseishō, 'Gurīn kādo seido to yūbin chokin ni tsuite kin'yū dantai no shuchō ni taisuru yūseishō no kangaekata (August 1980)', *Kin'yū zaisei jijō*, 8 September 1980, pp. 27–33; *Asahi shinbun*, 26 September 1980

60 *Asahi shinbun*, 14 March 1981

61 Debate included the dual savings interest rate system, the green card system, the impact of the shift of funds to the post office, and the impact on monetary policy. See *Kin'yū*, January, February, May, June and July 1981 (No. 406, 407, 410–12)

62 See Gurūpu Q. 'Ōkura vs yūsei—jinginaki yūcho sensō' pp. 292–94

63 Zenkoku ginkō kyōkai rengōkai et al. 'Yūbin chokin ni kansuru gutaiteki yōbō' *Kin'yū* June 1981, p. 81; *Nihon keizai shinbun* 30 March 1980

64 *Nihon keizai shinbun* 30 March 1980

65 In September 1981 it was estimated that the MPT position had 320 supporters and the MOF position 180. *Asahi shinbun* 2 September 1981. In February of the same year an LDP politician supporting the MPT case put the figures at 350 and 20–30 respectively. Support for the MPT was relatively static, but support for the MOF had grown substantially reflecting the bank campaign of 1981

6 New foreign exchange law

1 *Nihon keizai shinbun* 12 January 1978

2 For three interesting versions of events in the early 1970s, see Robert Solomon *The International Monetary System, 1945–76: An Insider's View* New York: Harper Row, 1976; John Williamson *The Failure of World Monetary Reform 1971–74* Sunbury on Thames, Middlesex: Nelson, 1977; and Michael J. Brenner *The Politics of International Monetary Reform: The Exchange Issue* Cambridge, Mass.: Ballinger Publishing Co., 1977

3 For a general account of Japan's role in the international economy from 1945 to the early 1970s, see Lawrence B. Krause and Sueo Sekiguchi 'Japan and the World Economy' in Patrick and Rosovsky (eds) *Asia's New Giant* pp. 383–458
For an introduction to foreign exchange regulations in some OECD countries, see OECD *Regulations Affecting International Banking Operations of Banks and Non-Banks in France, Germany, The Netherlands, Switzerland and the United Kingdom* Paris, 1978

4 Impact loans are untied foreign currency loans made by predominantly foreign banks operating in Japan. Until 1980 Japanese banks were not allowed to make impact loans. In the late 1970s and early 1980s they provided an important marginal source of funds for Japanese corporations. See IBI Inc., The Japanese Financial System in the Function and Performance of Foreign Banks, December 1978, mimeo, pp. 18–19

5 Ōhashi Muneo (ed.) *Kokusai kin'yū* fiscal 1980 edn, Zaikei shōhōsha, p. 117. For an examination of measures on the development of inward capital flow policy in the 1960s, see Robert S. Ozaki *The Control of Imports and Foreign Capital in Japan* New York: Praeger, 1972

6 Sakai Kenzō (ed.) *Kokusai kin'yū* fiscal 1978 edn, Zaikei shōhōsha, p. 133

7 Ōkurashō kokusai kin'yūkyoku hen *Ōkurashō kokusai kin'yūkyoku nenpō dai I kai* 1977, pp. 175, 177

8 Sakai (ed.) *Kokusai kin'yū* fiscal 1978 edn, pp. 136–37

9 See Kunio Yoshihara *Japanese Investment in Southeast Asia* Honolulu: University Press of Hawaii, 1978; and Terutomo Ozawa *Multinationalism, Japanese Style; The Political Economy of Outward Dependency* Princeton: Princeton University Press, 1979

10 The flow of investment into real estate fell from US$120 million in fiscal 1973 to US$18 million in fiscal 1974

11 Perhaps the most detailed study of foreign economic involvement in Japan is Dan Fenno Henderson *Foreign Enterprise in Japan: Laws and Policies* Tokyo: Charles E Tuttle and Co., 1975

12 Calculated by subtracting direct investment from total capital outflow

13 *Ōkurashō kokusai kin'yūkyoku nenpō dai I kai* pp. 180–82

14 See Ōkurashō kokusai kiny'ūkyoku hen *Ōkurashō kokusai kin'yūkyoku nenpō dai 5 kai* 1981, pp. 108–9 for an outline of the institutional framework

15 Interviews with officers of the IFB, May 1980 and former officer for the MOF, July 1980

16 Indeed, with the new FEFTCL being introduced in December 1980, the volume of funds entering Japan increased greatly. See *Asahi shinbun* 25 December 1980

17 *Kokusai kin'yū*, fiscal 1978 edn, pp. 174–75

18 See for example Fujioka Masao 'Kokusai kyōryoku o susumeru tsūka seisaku' *Kin'yū zaisei jijō* 25 April 1977, pp. 20–25

19 Fujioka Masao 'Kawase kanri no ōhaba kansoka to kongo no tenbō *Kin'yū zaisei jijō* 18 July 1977, pp. 14–20; Kishida Shunsuke 'Gaika saimu junbiritsu no hatsudō to kawase kin'yū seisaku no shintenkai' *Kin'yū zaisei jijō* 13 July 1977, pp. 16–20

20 Interview with former official of MOF, July 1980

21 This is not to say that some criticism did not take place. The British Chancellor of the Exchequer, Dennis Healey, was strongly critical of Japan's 'neomercantilism'. *Nihon keizai shinbun* 2 October 1977

22 Morinaga Teiichirō 'Watakushi no nai-gai keizai, kin'yūkan' *Tōyō keizai* 28 January 1978, pp. 28–33. Takano and Ōkawa suggest that on several occasions in autumn 1978, Fukuda met with a small group of advisors such as Kashiwagi (Bank of Tokyo and Former Ministry of Finance *Zaimukan*), Hosomi (advisor to the Industrial Bank of Japan and former *Zaimukan*) and Suzuki (advisor to Nomura Securities and former representative to the IMF) to discuss what dollar defence measures the US should be asked to consider. See Takano Yasushi and Ōkawa Kentarō 'Ōkurashō no hasan' *Bungei shunjū* December 1978, p. 181

23 *Mainichi shinbun* 15 October 1977

24 *Mainichi shinbun* 27 October 1977

25 *Kin'yū zaisei jijō* 13 March 1978

26 *Nihon keizai shinbun* 23 December 1977

27 *Nihon keizai shinbun* 12 January 1978

28 In March 1978 the MOF announced several further simplifications to regulations on capital flows. For details, see *Kin'yū zaisei jijō* 13 March 1978

29 My analysis cannot be regarded as complete, as the influences on Prime Minister Fukuda have been hard to evaluate fully. A definitive answer must await further research

30 Hiroo Fukui *Commentary on the amendment of the Foreign Exchange and Foreign Trade Control Law* Ministry of Finance, Japan, March 1980, p. 3

31 In total, two senior officers from the MOF and the three most involved officers from MITI were interviewed for this study

32 Interview with an officer of MOF, May 1980

33 Trade flows were controlled through chapter 6 of the old FEFTCL, entitled Foreign Trade

34 Interview with an officer of MITI, May 1980

35 Interview with an officer of MITI, April 1981
36 Interview with an officer of MOF, July 1980
37 At the end of 1980, 186 banks held foreign exchanges licences including all city, long-term, trust and foreign banks; 58 out of 63 regional banks, 38 out of 71 mutual banks and three out of four semi-government banks
38 *Nihon keizai shinbun* 5 March 1979
39 *Kin'yū zaisei jijō* 21 May 1979
40 See for example *Ōkuraiinkai giroku dai 22 gō* shōwa 54 nen 5 gatsu 23 nichi, p. 18
41 There were exceptions to these principles. Foreign banks were allowed to oversell dollars because of their weak deposit base. Domestic banks were prohibited from overselling, and were subject to stringent overbuying restrictions. The figures are not published but, according to an interviewee, the Bank of Tokyo, because of its status as a specialist foreign exchange bank, had the largest quota. Interview with city banker, October 1980
42 Interview with a senior officer of a trading company, September 1980
43 'Tamegin no 'ken'eki' o obiyakasu kawase kanrihō no kaisei' *Kin'yū zaisei jijō* 12 March 1979, pp. 10–11; 'Zento tanan no gaitame shinpō no jisshi' *Kawase shijō* No. 356, p. 19; *Nihon keizai shinbun* 5 March 1979. Interview with an officer of the MOF, July 1980
44 See Stephen Krasner *Defending the National Interest: Raw Materials Investment and US Foreign Policy* Princeton: Princeton University Press, 1978
45 There are no adequate public summaries of the debates. Short articles of little substance appeared in the newspapers and *Kokusai kin'yū*, various issues
46 Interview with an officer of the MOF, July 1980
47 Proceedings of the Advisory Committee on Legal Systems of Foreign Exchange and Foreign Trade, 23 April 1979, mimeo, p. 3
48 Interview with an officer of MOF, July 1980
49 Quote from George, The Comparative Study of Interest Groups in Japan
50 *Asahi shinbun* 17 September 1978
51 *Kin'yū zaisei jijō* 12 March 1979; *Kin'yū zaisei jijō* 21 May 1979; and 'Zento tanan no gaitame shinpō no jisshi' pp. 18–20
52 For a brief look at the implications of the law see Hiroo Fukui 'The Outline of the New Foreign Exchange and Foreign Trade Control Law and Other Regulations' *Tokyo Money* 5, 1, 1981, pp. 2–17
53 The fact that the drafting of the revised law had been completed by the time of the final meeting further reinforces this interpretation. See articles in *Asahi shinbun* 27–29 November 1980 and 30–31 January 1981
54 We are not implying that discrimination exists in this case, but simply that international speculators are the most likely group to engage in this activity
55 Ministry of Finance *Foreign Exchange and Foreign Trade Control Law* (as amended by Law No. 65 dated 18 December 1979) Tokyo, March 1980, pp. 12–13. This document is an unofficial translation of the new FEFTCL
56 Ministry of Finance, Main features of the Amended Foreign Exchange and Foreign Trade Control Law, February 1981, mimeo, p. 1
57 ibid.
58 *Look Japan* 10 June 1981, p. 9
59 *Kin'yū zaisei jijō* 30 May 1983, pp. 37–38

7 Yen bond market 1970–82

1 Watanabe Takeshi *Ajia kaigin sōsai nikki* Tokyo: Nihon keizai shinbunsha, 1973,

p. 98. For details of government loans to foreign governments see Rix *Japanese Economic Aid* London: Croom Helm, 1980, pp. 224–25

2   Interview with an officer of a long-term credit bank, June 1980

3   'Hakkō jōken de nanzan shita ajia kaiginsai no hakkō' *Kin'yū zaisei jijō* 7 December 1970

4   Watanabe *Ajia kaigin sōsai nikki* p. 103

5   Interview with a former ADB official, May 1981

6   Interview with a former ADB official, May 1981

7   Documents received in interviews

8   *Nihon keizai shinbun* 24 February 1972

9   Interview with long-term credit bank (also a commissioned bank), July 1980. Long-term credit banks, city banks and trust banks mainly undertook the role of commissioned banks

10   'Endate gaisai ni kakeru kokusai shihon shijō e no kitai' *Kin'yū zaisei jijō* 6 March 1972

11   Along with the absence of corporate borrowing, the clustering of interest rates in the issue market stamped the yen bond market as different from other bond markets. The table below provides the data base to examine this issue. Between 1975 and 1980 the market appeared to make a small allowance for the quality of issuers. When blocs of countries are ranked by their relationship with the NTT secondary market rate and the government bond rate, a fairly consistent picture emerges. International financial institutions and industrialised countries were treated more favourably than South American countries and members of ASEAN. The variation between the blocs of countries was, however, very small. For the period up to December 1980 the difference between industrialised countries and ASEAN countries was about 0.4 percentage points, and industrialised countries and South American countries 0.2 percentage points. Variations on the Euromarkets were between 1–2 percentage points. If the market were responsive to market conditions, one would expect to find much larger variations between these average issues rates, and the fact that these did not occur supports the view that non-market factors still play an important part in setting yen bond market issue rates.

Relationship between the yen bond market issue rates and other rates: July 1975–December 1980

	(a)	(b)
International financial institutions[a]	−0.21	−0.12
Industrialised countries[b]	−0.15	+0.03
South America[c]	+0.06	+0.23
ASEAN[d]	+0.31	+0.38

Notes: (a) Yen bond issue yield—NTT secondary market yield
           (b) Yen bond issue yield—Government bond secondary market yield
           a   International financial institutions were ADB, IBRD and European Investment Bank
           b   Industrialised countries were Denmark, Sweden, and Australia
           c   South American countries were Argentina, Brazil, Mexico and Venezuela
           d   ASEAN countries were Malaysia, Philippines, Singapore and Thailand

The relationship between the yen bond market issue yield and either the NTT market or the government bond market was not consistent during the 1970s. Up to early 1977, flotation yields were less than NTT yields. Between May 1977 and May 1978, this relationship disappeared with a more random relationship appearing. From May 1978 to May 1980, the broad essence of the earlier relationship returned. After May 1980 it again disappeared. The relationship with the government bond market also showed some inconsistency. Up to February 1979, yen bond issue yields were consistently above the yield on government bonds in the secondary market. This period corresponds to the period when the government bond market was relatively stable. During the year from March 1979 to April 1980, the relationship reversed completely, and the yield on government bonds became higher than the issue yield on yen bonds.

Interaction between market influences and policy influences determined the level of yen bond issue yields. On some occasions market factors played an important role but even in 1980 policy factors were of overriding importance. If we rank government bonds, NTT bonds and yen bonds from lowest yielding to highest yielding, yen bonds fall between the other two. The influence of overissuing in the government bond market disturbed the traditional relationship between government bonds and NTT bonds, with secondary market yields of government bonds sometimes exceeding NTT bonds. These inversions were not reflected in the issue market. To the extent that the inversions were reflected in the yen bond issue market, it was more responsive to market conditions. One must be equivocal in calling this a market rate as on occasions the 'market rate' in the government bond market was not representative of the market conditions in the long-term bond markets more generally. The government and the securities companies often used the unstable government bond rate as a means for cutting back the issue levels in the yen bond market

12 In the period 1978–80, Japanese corporate borrowing abroad stood at 115 per cent of the level of corporate borrowing in Japan. The figure was calculated using an exchange rate in 1978 of 208, in 1979 of 222 and in 1980 of 226. It includes convertibles, straight bonds and depository receipts

13 Komatsu Masao 'Matsushita denki mutanposai hakkō no imi suru mono' *Kin'yū zaisei jijō* 6 August 1979, pp. 44–45

14 ibid. p. 45

15 Shōken torihiki shingikai kihon mondai iinkai 'Nozomashii kōshasai shijō no arikata ni kansuru hōkokusho' 18 October 1977, reproduced in Nihon keizai shinbunsha hen *Ronshū: Gendai no kin'yū mondai—1*, pp. 288–92. See also 'Mutanpo shasai no hakkō ni tsuite (sono ichi)' August 1972, in ibid. pp. 306–9

16 Komatsu 'Matsushita denki mutanposai hakkō no imi suru mono' pp. 45–48; 'Mutanposai ga hi o tsuketa ginkō shōken no atsui arasoi' *Kin'yū zaisei jijō* 5 February 1979

17 'Mutanposai ga hi o tsuketa ginkō shōken no atsui arasoi'

18 Interview with an officer of a long-term credit bank, July 1980

19 'Mutanposai' *Nihon kōshasai shijō* 26 February 1979, pp. 2–8

20 Interview with an officer of a long-term credit bank, July 1980

21 Interview with an officer of a securities company, July 1980

22 *Nihon keizai shinbun* evening edn, 10 March 1982

23 In February 1982 Standard and Poors rated both as A+ companies

24 Asano Junji 'Honkaku teichaku e oikaze fuku saiken "kakuzuke"' *Ginkō to kin'yū* 12 August 1982; *Kin'yū* 3, 1983, p. 63

25 OECD *Financial Market Trends*, various issues

26 Interview with two former ADB officers, May 1981. See also 'Endate gaisai no hakkō ni shin-rūru' *Kin'yū zaisei jijō* 21 August 1972, p. 13; *Asahi shinbun* 17 November 1972

27 See Suzuki Yasuyuki 'Mutanposai dōnyū o dō kangaeru ka' *Kin'yū zaisei jijō* 24 April 1972, pp. 42–45

28 *Nihon keizai shinbun* 20 October 1975; *Asahi shinbun* 5 April 1976. At this point the MOF proposed that issues be expanded to one every two months. The balance of

payments did not improve as rapidly as expected so the rate of expansion was not as rapid as planned

29 *Nihon keizai shinbun* 13 August 1976
30 The ADB issue was cancelled, and the American Development Bank and Austrian government issues were postponed. *Nihon keizai shinbun*, 19 January 1977, and evening edn of the same day
31 *Nihon keizai shinbun* 16 June 1979. On this occasion a Finnish issue was postponed. Securities companies would not accept the price requirements of prospective floaters because of the unstable price in the government bond market
32 The former director-general of the IFB, Fujioka Masao, advised that the MOF should speak to banks and securities companies to ask for a slowdown in issue but to keep the market alive. Interview with a former MOF official, July 1980
33 Although this gap was small when compared with the gaps which emerged between 1979 and 1982, at that stage, and in international terms, it was highly significant
34 Quote from *Nihon keizai shinbun* 4 November 1978, evening edn. See also *Nihon keizai shinbun* 17 October 1978
35 *Nihon keizai shinbun* 23 January 1981. In this case the high interest rate were the factor which affected the level of issue. The MOF's attempt to influence the market was quite explicit. One problem was apparently a shortfall of funds with institutional investors, such as Norin Chukin Bank. Institutional investors dominated the market. Interview with an official of a long-term credit bank, July 1980
36 The Danish issue was cut from 30 billion to 15 billion yen and the Austrian issue from 20 billion to 18 billion yen. *Nihon keizai shinbun* 30 March 1979
37 Interview with an IBJ official, July 1980
38 At the time, long-term interest rates were very low relative to international interest rates, and also low in absolute terms
39 Apart from the public statements suggesting this, the pattern of borrowing provides substantive evidence to support this view
40 *Nihon keizai shinbun* 13 August 1976. It was not until Fukuda became Prime Minister that relations with the ASEAN countries improved significantly. See 'Japan's relations with South East Asia after a year of initiatives' *Australian Foreign Affairs Record* January 1978, pp. 4–8. See also *Nihon keizai shinbun* 17 and 20 July 1977
41 *Nihon keizai shinbun* 21 March 1976
42 By the end of 1981 the variance in ASEAN credit worthiness was relatively small when compared with South American countries. For loans issued by public and private groups, their average spread above LIBOR was: Malaysia 0.39 per cent, South Korea 0.64 per cent, Thailand 0.59 per cent, Philippines 0.89 per cent, Brazil 2.05 per cent, Argentina 0.80 per cent, Mexico 0.62 per cent, Peru 1.05 per cent and Venezuela 0.57 per cent. *Euromoney* February 1982, pp. 47–51
43 According to a securities company source, three applied but were refused on the basis of credit worthiness. Interview with a securities company official, July 1980
44 In the initial stages, securities companies could refuse to underwrite an issuer. At a later stage the MOF could also refuse permission. One East European case was taken to the MOF by the securities companies but was rejected. ibid.
45 *Nihon keizai shinbun* 13 August 1978; *Nihon keizai shinbun* 16 December 1978
46 Interview with an officer of the MOF, April 1981. The general problem of deregulating interest rates was outlined in the introduction
47 *Nihon keizai shinbun* 20 February 1975
48 To put the matter into a global picture, the German market had also closed, and the Swiss market was quite limited. *Nihon keizai shinbun* 31 March 1981
49 Richard N. Cooper *The Economics of Interdependence: Economic Policy in the Atlantic Community* New York: McGraw-Hill, 1968, pp. 148–59

50 For a view which I find difficult to support, see C. Fred Bergsten 'What to do about the US–Japan economic conflict?' *Foreign Affairs* 60, 5, 1982 pp. 1059–75. Bergsten suggests a number of temporary measures designed to strengthen the yen. One is the sharp limitation of greater use by the Japanese government of international capital sources to raise long-term funds to cover the budget deficit. This recommendation is most surprising. The current policy towards capital outflows was developed gradually during the 1970s in line with developing Japanese interests and with the encouragement of the international borrowing and investing community. Curtailing the quantity of investment outflow would not only invite external criticism that Japan was withholding access to its financial markets but also would be against the interests of the many countries that benefit from the existing policy, such as Australia, which has benefited from the heavy inflow into Australian government securities. As in the case of beef, United States pressure for favoured treatment would result in an adverse impact in third country markets.

There is little doubt that if the Japanese government began issuing its long-term securities on the long-term markets at the same time as closing its own capital market to outside borrowers, it would come under intense criticism from third countries, even if the United States approved of the measure. But what of Japan's own interests? The cost would not be limited to international criticism. Any limitation on capital outflows without good reason would seriously damage Japan's bid to establish Tokyo as a capital market of international stature, and, while it could be undertaken within the framework of the new foreign exchange legislation, a stop–go policy towards capital movements would do nothing to promote confidence of international investors in the yen. For the first time, the Ministry of Finance is beginning to take a more relaxed attitude towards foreign governments holding yen as a reserve currency. It should not be discouraged from pursuing this line of thinking even for the sake of something as important as the US–Japan relationship, particularly when the cure suggested involves so many evils and may not even then get to the core of the problem.

51 ' "Jiyū" ka "kisei" ka ōkurashō kokusai kin'yūkyoku no tatemae to honne' *Ginkō to kin'yū* 17 June 1982. See also *Asahi shinbun* 4 and 18 September 1982

52 ' "Jiyū" ka "kisei" ka ōkurashō kokusai kin'yūkyoku no tatemae to honne'

53 In 1981 private companies made 143 issues on international markets valued at US$5.01 billion or, if government institutions were included, 156 issues totalling US$5.68 billion

54 Stephen Bronte 'The Japanese Attack on Corporate America' *Euromoney* September 1982

55 Interview with two officers of the Securities Bureau, July 1980; interview with an officer of the IFB, July 1980; interview with an officer of a securities company, July 1980

56 Interview with an officer of the Securities Bureau, July 1980

57 Interview with an officer of the IFB, July 1980

58 Interview with an officer of a securities company, July 1980

8 The Ministry of Finance

1 There is a range of articles which describes the MOF and the officers it attracts. See for example Stephen Bronte 'Inside the Tokyo Ministry of Finance' *Euromoney* June 1979, pp. 24–39; Ōkurashō aramashi, Shōwa 55 nendo, mimeo; Kusayanagi Daizō 'Kanryō ōkoku ron' *Bungei shunjū* June 1974, pp. 162–78; Kakuma Takashi *Dokyumento ōkurashō ginkōkyoku* Kyoto: PHP Kenkyūjo, 1979; Yamamura Yoshi-haru *Ōkura kanryō no fukushū* Tokyo: Kō shobō, 1979; Kakizawa Kōji *Kasumigaseki*

ni-chōme no ōkurashō kanryō wa megane o kaketa dobunezumi to iwareru zasetsukan ni nayamu sugoi erītotachi kara Tokyo: Gakuyō Shobō, 1977

2   For an excellent treatment of elites in French society see Ezra N. Suleiman *Elites in French Society* Princeton: Princeton University Press, 1978. The seminal work on the British Treasury is H. Heclo and A. Wildavsky *The Private Government of Public Money: Community and Policy inside British Politics* Berkeley: University of California Press, 1974

3   Sugiyama Keiichi (ed.) *Ōkurashō kenkyū* Tokyo: Kanchō nyūsusha, 1979, pp. 294–421. The list does not include people who left the MOF, or died, in the early stage of their careers. The assumption was that this proportion was randomly scattered. Data of the MOF showed that during the period 1960–70 the entries in *Ōkurashō kenkyū* total 90 per cent of the actual intake. The total size of the list used for the calculation was 870. An analysis done by Hata Ikuhiko in 'Senzenki kanryōsei yowa' *Fainansu* 18, 4, 1982 shows very similar results. His figures are for 1949–82 (sample size 870) during which Tokyo University provided 83 per cent of the intake. Between 1970 and 1982 Tokyo University provided 78.8 per cent, Kyoto University 10.4 per cent, Hitotsubashi 7.6 per cent, and the rest 3.2 per cent

4   Komiya Ryūtarō and Yamamoto Kōzō, The Officer in Charge on Economic Affairs in the Japanese Government, mimeo, 1979, pp. 7–8

5   It should be noted that a Law School degree means that two years are spent in obtaining a general education and only two further years on specialist subjects. See Kubota Akira *Higher Civil Servants in Post War Japan* Princeton: Princeton University Press, 1969

6   Interview with an officer of the Minister's Secretariat, MOF, October 1980. Also see Komiya and Yamamoto 'The Officer in Charge on Economic Affairs' pp. 14–15

7   A very personal account of those demands is Kakizawa *Kasumigaseki ni-chōme no okurashō kanryō*

8   Suleiman *Elites in French Society* pp. 95–108

9   The account that follows draws on Komiya and Yamamoto 'The Officer in Charge on Economic Affairs' pp. 8–19 and on discussions with many MOF officers, from first year recruits through to directors-general

10 Acceptance of the policy by the MOF as a whole depended upon the involvement of other bureaus in the policy areas and their attitude towards the new policy. Where conflict did occur it was sometimes resolved, with a ministry position emerging, but on other occasions, as in the case of trading in bonds by banks, bureaus failed to resolve their differences, and thus talk of a 'ministry position' was impossible. For an example in the Tokyo University manuscript collection, see Ōkurashō ginkō-kyoku, Yokin kinri kisei no kanwa (gokuhi), Shōwa 45 nen 3 gatsu, mimeo

11 According to a survey by Muramatsu the average age at which career officers attain the rank of director is 43.8 years. Muramatsu Michio *Sengo nihon no kanryōsei* Tokyo: Tōyō keizai shinpōsha, 1981, p. 71. The assistant directorship was an important part of an officer's career. During his eight to ten years at this level he would be given four or five assignments, often in different bureaus, on which his future career would largely depend. Although there was little discernible difference in the rate of progress of different officers up to the level of director, the nature of assignments was an effective indicator of 'seniority', and ultimately of the ability to progress through to the level of director-general or even the position of administrative vice-minister. Within each bureau one division, called the Coordination Division, functioned as the major liaison window with other ministries and bureaus, and was also responsible for coordinating policy within the bureau. The director of the Coordination Division was effectively a senior among equals

12 Interview with an officer of the MOF, April 1981

13 One potential interviewee refused to be interviewed at the last minute when he learned that he had been transferred to another bureau with which he had had sharp conflict during an earlier appointment

14 Muramatsu *Sengo nihon no kanryōsei* p. 104

15 Robert D. Putnam 'The Political Attitudes of Senior Civil Servants in Britain, Germany and Italy' in Mattei Dogan (ed.) *The Mandarins of Western Europe* New York: John Wiley & Sons, 1975, pp. 89–91

16 Interview with officer of the MOF, October 1980; interview with former officer of the MOF, January 1981. The view of these officers, both of whom had considerable experience in personnel matters, was generally representative of wider opinion on this matter

17 For a list of recent administrative vice-ministers and ministers see Kyōikusha *Ōkurashō* Tokyo, 1979, pp. 241–44, 252–53

18 The Japanese often use the phrase *amakudari*, which literally means 'descent from heaven'. I have avoided use of the word in line with this book's aim of producing an analysis understandable to the non-Japanese specialist but also because the word is often used with pejorative connotations. Here the aim is to understand the system and draw attention to its weak points

19 See Kent Calder 'Yowai kigyō hodo kanryō o arigatagaru' *Asahi jānaru* 30 November 1979, pp. 18–26; Chalmers Johnson 'The Reemployment of Retired Government Bureaucrats in Japanese Big Business' *Asian Survey* 4, 11, 1974, pp. 953–65

20 For a yearly analysis of Japanese public servants retiring to public sector positions see Seirōkyō *Amakudari hakusho* Tokyo: Seifu kankei tokushu hōjin rōdō kumiai kyōgikai, (dai 1 kai–dai 12 kai)

21 Johnson 'The Reemployment of Retired Government Bureaucrats' p. 965

22 In 1981 the basic monthly salary of an officer who had entered the Ministry 30 years earlier was 708 000 yen. This is approximately the time it takes to reach the position of vice-minister. The president of the Peoples Finance Corporation who retired as vice-minister in 1979 was earning a monthly salary of 1 005 000 yen per month in October 1980 plus very substantial pension benefits. Retirement pension for executive positions of public enterprise are very lucrative, and calculated (in 1980) on a basis of monthly salary at retirement × (no. of months worked before 31 March 1978 × 45/100 + no. of months worked after 31 March 78 × 36/100). Thus for any officer beginning work after April 1978, his pension equates to 36 per cent of his final monthly salary × no. of months worked, a lucrative retirement benefit. Retirement benefits are far less for normal salary workers in these public corporations (which make up over 99 per cent of employees). The above salary estimates do not include fringe benefits and other allowances nor do they include the public service pension. See Seirōkyō *Amakudari hakusho* pp. 176–79. Johnson *Japan's Public Policy Companies* pp. 101–14 also examines comparative salaries of government officials before and after retirement

23 Komiya and Yamamoto 'The Officer in Charge on Economic Affairs' p. 26, cite considerably higher figures for 1978. They were House of Representatives: LDP 69, other 20; House of Councillors: LDP 47, other 20. The difference could reflect changes in the period, but also probably include definitional differences. I have followed *Seiji handobukku* quite closely although all former ministerial secretaries were checked to see whether they actually had a bureaucratic background. Most did not and these were excluded. These differences would not have a major bearing on the conclusions drawn in the text

24 Interviews with opposition members of Parliament, December 1980 and April 1981

25 For a short analysis of support bases of bureaucratic candidates in the 1974 House of Councillors election see Herbert Passin 'The House of Councillors' pp. 20–22

26 Translation of *Gendai*'s October 1980 article 'Probing into New Family and Marriage connection of Diet Members' (United States Information Service translation service)

27 ibid. p. 29

28 Whereas the opposition parties sought and achieved some impact on fiscal policy, evidenced by the successful tax cut in 1977, they showed little desire to contribute to debate on the shape of the financial system. For example, the Policy Committee support staff of the JSP had five people working on economic questions—one related to overseas matters, two to industrial matters and two to fiscal and monetary matters. *Kōmeitō* had approximately the same number, and the DSP two people. Interviews with party secretariats, December 1980, February and March 1981. The DSP put some effort into defining its economic policies. In 1978 the DSP produced a 470-page document: Minshatō seisaku shingikai *Nihon keizai no atarashii sentaku* Minshatō kyōsenkyoku 1978. In this report the financial system barely received a mention. The government bond problem was about as close as the analysis gets to the problem, see pp. 89–98. Contacts between the MOF and the opposition parties strengthened during the period 1976–80 when the LDP lost its majorities in many of the committees of the House of Representatives and was manifested concretely in the formation of a new position with a rank just below director-general (called daijin kanbō tantō shingikan). See *Nihon keizai shinbun* 15 June 1977

29 In all my discussions with opposition members, no one would commit himself to supporting change on the trading in government bonds issue. Apart from the recognised financial experts, the interest of other Diet members was only tangentially related to finance

30 Within the LDP's official party structure there were over 400 positions with titles of chairman or deputy chairman. Many politicians 'belonged' to various groups because it was the done thing to be seen to belong. Attendance at committee meetings might be as little as five members—the office holders. It was not uncommon for politicians to become party chairmen of policy areas in which they had no interest. Interviews with an officer of the PARC secretariat and LDP politicians

31 The institutions are Hokkaido and Tohoku Development Corp., Okinawa Development Finance Corp., Peoples Finance Corp., Medical Care Facilities Financing Corp., Environmental Sanitation Business Financing Corp., Agriculture, Forestry and Fisheries Finance Corp., Small Business Finance Corp., Small Credit Insurance Corp., Housing Loan Corp., Finance Corp. of Local Public Enterprise, Japan Development Bank, Export–Import Bank of Japan, Central Cooperative for Agriculture and Forestry and Central Bank for Commercial and Industrial Cooperatives. The figure does not include the large number of non-career public servants that end their working lives in public corporations. Seirōkyo *Amakudari hakusho* gives the fullest coverage on this issue

32 For the period 1965–1981. Data supplied by the JDB

33 Four of the executive histories of government finance corporations are tabulated opposite:

34 See the series 'Zaitō—Chōhiman taishitsu' in *Asahi shinbun* 30 September 1980; 1, 2, 3, 4 October 1980

35 The work of the Second Administrative Reform Commission is not considered in this book, but in the long term it may have an impact on the matters under discussion

36 Kaizuka Keimei 'Seifu kin'yū ni tsuite' *Kin'yū* No. 413, August 1981, p. 27

37 Details are set out in the National Public Law, Article 103, and National Personnel Authority Regulation 14–4 (last revised 21 December 1968) 'Employment in Private Corporations', see *Kokka kōmuinhō dai 103 jō* and *Jinjiin kisei 14–4* (Eirikigyō e no

Sources of executives for four government financial institutions

	A		B		C		D	
	1980	1967–80	1980	1967–80	1980	1967–80	1980	1967–80[a]
Number of executives	9	8–10	8	8–10	9	7–9	10	10–11
Distribution (per cent)								
Internal	44	48	38	27	44	16	10	15
Private sector	0	0	0	11	0	0	0	1
Government ('amakudari')	56	49	62	58	56	80	90	84
Not clear	0	3	0	4	0	4	0	0
	100	100	100	100	100	100	100	100

Notes: A Peoples Finance Corporation
B Small Business Finance Corporation
C Agriculture Forestry and Fisheries Finance Corporation
D Housing Loan Corporation
a In the case of the Housing Loan Corporation, the statistics do not cover 1968, 1970 and 1971

Source: Seirōkyō *Amakudari hakusho* 1978 nendo, 1979 nendo, 1981 nen.

shūshoku). A brief summary of the regulations is found in the introduction to the yearly list of approvals. See Jinjiin *Eirikigyō e no shūshoku no shōnin ni kansuru nenjihōkokusho* shōwa 55 nen. There are no legal regulations relating to movements into public authorities, although in recent years there has been some attempt to control abuses of the system. See Tokushu hōjin no yakuin no senkyo ni tsuite (kakugi kettei, shōwa 52.12.23), mimeo and Tokushu hōjin no yakuin ni tsuite (kakugi ryōkai, shōwa 54.12.18), mimeo

38   Of the seventeen, only two were employed directly in a city or long-term credit bank. This analysis looks only at the movement from the MOF to private financial institutions; the flow from the BOJ is also large. See 'Nichigin no rakujitsu— ōkurashō no shiretsu naru posuto sōdatsusen' *Kin'yū to ginkō* 15 November 1978, pp. 50–55

39   Despite this, in 1980, there were several MOF officers holding senior positions in major banks, including Ishino Shin'ichi, president of Taiyo-Kobe Bank; Kashiwagi Yūsuke, president of Bank of Tokyo; Yoshikuni Jirō, president of Yokohama Bank; Yasukawa Shichirō, president of Long-Term Credit Bank of Japan

40   See Kin'yū seido kenkyūkai hen *Futsū ginkō no arikata to ginkō seido no kaisei* pp. 462–71

41   See 'Kōbe ginkō no gappei' *Kin'yū zaisei jijō* 19 February 1973

42   There is also the question of contribution to finances of the LDP by small and medium-sized financial institutions. We are unable to throw any meaningful empirical light on to this question

43   Memo from officer of the Banking Bureau, received June 1981. Mutual banks faced a number of problems which were beyond the control of individual managers. The attempted merger between Sumitomo Bank and Kansai Mutual Bank illustrated

some of the problems involved with mergers. The Kansai Mutual Bank was an average-sized mutual bank, but was tiny when compared with Sumitomo Bank, one of the largest city banks in Japan. Although there was some support within Kansai Mutual Bank for the merger, strong opposition came from two sources. One was the bank's branch managers, who saw their future careers being adversely affected if Kansai Mutual were absorbed into Sumitomo. The other source of opposition was the clients of Kansai Mutual who argued that the merger would reduce their access to funds and financial services. Whether the criticisms were valid or not, the merger was successfully thwarted. If employees objected to a proposed merger there was little chance that it would go ahead, and further, the Kansai Mutual–Sumitomo case suggested that mergers between units of greatly contrasting size were unlikely to succeed because this agreement would not be forthcoming. Mergers could be induced if the small bank were on the verge of financial collapse, but then the incentive for the large bank would be far less. Mergers between medium-sized mutual banks, or even between the small and medium-sized mutual banks, seemed to offer the prospect of cost reduction and the possibility of more adequate competition with the larger regional banks and city banks, but for the reasons cited above even these mergers were unlikely. This is one area which requires much more research. Comments are based on discussions with politicians, public servants and research staff of politicians. For comments on the Taiko Mutual Bank case see *Kin'yū zaisei jijō* 28 May 1979, 4 June 1979; *Asahi shinbun* 20 May 1979 (editorial). For comments on another troubled mutual bank, Tokuyo Mutual Bank, see *Kin'yū zaisei jijō* 17 September 1979; *Nihon keizai shinbun* 9 February 1981; and *Asahi shinbun* 10 February 1979

44 Interviews with two senior BOJ officers, April and May 1981. The BOJ clearly did not agree with MOF policy, as it refused to supply funds to Taiko Mutual or the other troubled banks. Privately, senior BOJ officers expressed puzzlement at the MOF's position, although they were willing to concede that the explanation was probably political. Interviewees throughout the financial sector backed up this opinion. The logic of the economic argument was almost non-existent. The Taiko Mutual Bank's assets amounted to barely 1 per cent of the assets of all mutual banks. In terms of the banking sector, the proportion was 0.1 per cent. A government guarantee on the existing bad debts of the institution or use of the Savings Deposit Insurance Scheme could have permitted the institution to close without any long-term effect on financial order. The existing branch activities and clients could have been sold by tender to another financial institution

45 *Yomiuri shinbun* 18 June 1979

Index

Abe, Shintarō, 108–9, 139
administrative guidance, 15, 98, 109, 137, 149–50, 153, 164–8, 170, 188, 190; Banking Law, 109, 112
Advisory Committee on the Legal System of Foreign Exchange and Foreign Trade (Advisory Committee), 156, 160–62; proceedings, 226–8
Aichi, Kiichi, 199
Aizawa, Hideo, 202
Allison, Graham T., 17, 18
Arase, Kōichirō, 131
Association of South East Asian Nations (ASEAN), 148, 178, 183, 186–7

balance of payments policy, 144–6, 151, 153, 173, 175, 192; yen bond market, 180–83
banks, dispute with Banking Bureau, 108, 176; loan market, 38–9; mergers, 208–10; mismanagement, 208–9; participation in government bond market, 99–108; relations with MOF, 107, 158–9; see also city banks, long-term credit banks, mutual banks, regional banks, trust banks
bank amalgamation, 26–7, 137, 208–10, 216
bank loan market, 38–9
Bank of Japan (BOJ), 32–4, 48, 53–6, 218; CDs debate, 86, 93–5; deregulation of short-term money markets, 39–43, 86; foreign exchange law, 144; government bonds, 48–54; links with city banks, 27–8; Policy Board, 41, 128; postal savings issue, 123, 125; relations with MOF, 33, 34, 86, 178; savings

interest rate, 122–5, 129–30; support for interest rate deregulation, 38–43
Banking Bureau, 32, 44, 62–5, 67, 76–7, 79–81, 91–7, 101–5, 107–11, 116–17, 124, 137, 176, 203, 209, 214, 230
Banking Law, 25, 26, 45, 102, 105, 107–12, 117
bills market, 38–41
Bō, Hideo, 129
Bond Flotation Council, 51, 232–3
bond issues, unsecured, 176–9
Bond Underwriters' Association, 59, 85, 103
Budget Bureau, 50–51, 60, 65
bureau-level policymaking, 74–5, 79, 90–95, 112–14, 213–14
Burns, Arthur, 154

Cabinet, 121, 126, 137, 141, 156, 162, 203
call market, 28–9, 34, 38–43
Campbell, J.C., 21
capital flows, 142, 145–53, 165–7; regulatory policy, 223–5
capital market, 43–5, 179; notion of risk, 44
case studies, 13, 23–4
certificates of deposit (CDs), 29, 36–8, 74–97, 106, 118, 135, 195, 214; contrast with trading in government bonds case, 112–17; debate on introduction, 81–90; discussion fora, 79–81, 87; floating abroad, 77–9; history, 74–5; industry position, 81–7; MOF position, 77, 87–90, 94–5; negotiability, 91, 94–5; see also BOJ, corporations, regional banks
CDs Discussion Group, 93–6